CONTEMPORARY TOPICS IN COGNITIVE NEUROSCIENCE SERIES

Series Editors:
Stanislas Dehaene, Collège de France, Paris
Alvaro Pascual-Leone, Harvard Medical School, USA
Jamie Ward, University of Sussex, UK

Reflecting contemporary and controversial issues in the study of cognitive neuroscience, the series aims to present a multi-disciplinary forum for cutting edge debate that will help shape this burgeoning discipline. It offers leading figures in the field and the best new researchers the opportunity to showcase their own work and theories, placing them in the wider context of the field.

Titles in the series may be authored or edited; each book must aim to make a contribution to a specific topic by reviewing and synthesizing the existing research literature, by advancing theory in the area, or by some combination of these missions.

Published titles in the series

Neuroscience of Decision Making
Edited by Oshin Vartanian & David R. Mandel

Forthcoming
Neural Bases of Human Belief Systems
Edited by Frank Kruger & Jordan Grafman

Language and Action in Cognitive Neuroscience
Edited by Yann Coello and Angela Bartolo

For more information about the series, please visit **www.psypress.com/ctcn**

NEUROSCIENCE OF DECISION MAI

The intersection between the fields of behavioral decisioi
neuroscience has proved to be fertile ground for interdiscipl
Whereas the former is rich in formalized models of choice,
with techniques for testing behavioral models at the bra
result, there has been the rapid emergence of progressively
cated biological models of choice, geared toward the devel
more complete mechanistic models of behavior.

This volume provides a coherent framework for distilli
key themes that have emerged as a function of this researc
highlights what we have learned about judgment and decisi
result. Although topics that are theoretically relevant to
decision-making researchers are addressed, the book also
what beyond the traditional boundaries of this area to tac
will be of interest to a greater community of scholars.

Neuroscience of Decision Making provides contempora
reading for researchers and students of cognitive psych(
ence, philosophy, and economics.

Oshin Vartanian obtained his PhD in experimental psychc
versity of Maine, followed by postdoctoral fellowships in
science at York University and DRDC Toronto, where l
Defence Scientist. He is the recipient of the Daniel E. Berl
the American Psychological Association's Division 10
research by a junior researcher, and holds an Adjunct As
position in the Department of Psychology at the Univers
Scarborough.

David R. Mandel is an adjunct professor of psychology :
of Toronto and a senior defence scientist at DRDC Tc
heads the Thinking, Risk, and Intelligence Group. His :
interest include thinking and reasoning, judgment and (
and the application of behavioral science to issues in the
and security. He is the lead editor of *The Psychology (*
Thinking, published by Routledge/Taylor & Francis.

Neuroscience of Decision Making

Edited by Oshin Vartanian & David R. Mandel

Psychology Press
Taylor & Francis Group

NEW YORK AND HOVE

First Published in 2011
by Psychology Press
711 Third Avenuc,
New York, NY 10017
www.psypress.com

Published in Great Britain
by Psychology Press
27 Church Road
Hove, East Sussex BN3 2FA

Psychology Press is an imprint of the Taylor & Francis Group, an Informa business

Copyright © 2011 Psychology Press

Typeset in Times by RefineCatch Limited, Bungay, Suffolk, UK
Printed and bound in the USA by Sheridan Books, Inc., Ann Arbor, MI, on
acid-free paper
Cover design by Andrew Ward

Library of Congress Cataloging in Publication Data
A catalog record for this book is available from the Library of Congress

ISBN: 978–1–84169–489–4

Contents

List of contributors

Editors

Oshin Vartanian Department of Psychology, University of Toronto Scarborough, 1265 Military Trail, Toronto, ON, Canada, M1C 1A4

David R. Mandel Department of Psychology, University of Toronto, 100 St. George Street, Toronto, ON, Canada, M5S 3G3

Chapter contributors

Antoine Bechara CRC Chair in Decision Neuroscience, Department of Psychiatry, McGill University, Canada and Department of Psychology, University of Southern California, USA

Ryan Bogdan Department of Psychology, Harvard University, 1220 William James Hall, 33 Kirkland Street, Cambridge, MA 02138, USA

Kalina Christoff Department of Psychology, University of British Columbia, 2136 West Mall, Vancouver, BC, Canada, V6T 1Z4

Wim De Neys Laboratoire CLLE (CNRS, Université de Toulouse), Maison de la Recherche, 5 allcé A. Machado, 31058 Toulouse Cedex 9, France

Stanislas Dehaene Laboratoire de Sciences Cognitives et Psycholinguistique, CNRS/ENS/EHESS, Paris, France

Mauricio R. Delgado Department of Psychology, Rutgers University, 101 Warren Street, Newark, NJ 07102, USA

Daniel G. Dillon Department of Psychology, Harvard University, 1220 William James Hall, 33 Kirkland Street, Cambridge, MA 02138, USA

Vinod Goel Department of Psychology, York University, Toronto, ON, Canada, M3J 1P3

Alan Gordon Department of Psychology, University of British Columbia, 2136 West Mall, Vancouver, BC, Canada, V6T 1Z4

Jordan Grafman Traumatic Brain Injury Research Laboratory, Kessler Foundation, West Orange, NJ 07052, USA

Avram J. Holmes Department of Psychology, Harvard University, 1220 William James Hall, 33 Kirkland Street, Cambridge, MA 02138, USA

Daniel Houser Interdisciplinary Center for Economic Science, George Mason University, 4400 University Drive, MSN 1B2, Fairfax, VA 22030, USA

Robert Kurzban Department of Psychology, University of Pennsylvania, 3720 Walnut St., Philadelphia, PA 19104, USA

David R. Mandel DRDC Toronto, 1133 Sheppard Avenue West, P.O. Box 2000, Toronto, ON, Canada, M3M 3B9

Jorge Moll Cognitive and Behavioral Neuroscience Unit, LABS-D'Or Hospital Network, Rio de Janeiro, RJ 22281-080, Brazil

John P. O'Doherty Trinity College Institute of Neuroscience and School of Psychology, Trinity College Dublin, Dublin, Ireland

Diego A. Pizzagalli Department of Psychology, Harvard University, 1220 William James Hall, 33 Kirkland Street, Cambridge, MA 02138, USA

James K. Rilling Department of Anthropology, Emory University, 114 Anthropology Building, 1557 Dickey Drive, Atlanta, GA 30322, USA

Alan G. Sanfey Department of Psychology, University of Arizona, 1503 E University Blvd, Tucson, AZ 85704, USA

Mariano Sigman Integrative Neuroscience Laboratory, Physics Department, University of Buenos Aires, Buenos Aires, Argentina

Rachelle Smith Department of Psychology, University of British Columbia, 2136 West Mall, Vancouver, BC, Canada, V6T 1Z4

Elizabeth Tricomi Division of the Humanities and Social Sciences, California Institute of Technology, MC 228-77, Pasadena, CA 91125, USA

Oshin Vartanian DRDC Toronto, 1133 Sheppard Avenue West, P.O. Box 2000, Toronto, ON, Canada, M3M 3B9

Erte Xiao Department of Social and Decision Science, Carnegie Mellon University, 208 Porter Hall, Pittsburgh, PA 15213, USA

Angela J. Yu Computational & Cognitive Neuroscience Lab, Department of Cognitive Science MC 0515, University of California, San Diego, 9500 Gilman Dr, La Jolla, CA 92093, USA

List of figures and tables

Figures

Tables

Introduction

Oshin Vartanian and David R. Mandel

BACKGROUND AND RATIONALE

The intersection between the fields of behavioral decision research and neuroscience would appear to be fertile ground for interdisciplinary research. Whereas the former is rich in formalized models of choice, the latter is rife with techniques for testing behavioral models at the brain level. Nevertheless, it is only recently that an integrative approach has been embraced leading to the emergence of a full-fledged neuroscience of decision making. For example, in their introduction to *Neurobiology of Decision-making*, Damasio and colleagues argued that neuroscience had overlooked decision making as much as it had overlooked emotion (Damasio, Damasio, & Christen, 1996). Although this was an accurate description of the state of affairs in the mid-1990s, it is no longer true today. The intervening years have witnessed a steady narrowing of the gap between the two fields as neuroscientific approaches have been employed ever more frequently to tackle key theoretical and applied issues in judgment and decision making. There is a growing sense that biological data can inform judgment and decision-making research by shedding light on its component cognitive and emotional processes (Sanfey, 2007). Our aim with this book has been to provide a coherent framework for distilling some of the key themes that have emerged as a function of this research program, and to highlight what we have learned about judgment and decision making as a result of this process.

Our selection of topics for this book has been determined by three factors. First, we have opted to focus on topics that are theoretically relevant to judgment and decision-making researchers, and about which a critical mass of knowledge in the neurosciences has emerged. These topics include reward and loss, risk and uncertainty, and cooperation and trust, representing the core sections in the current volume. Given the complexity of the problems in these topical areas, it is our belief that a triangulation of approaches is necessary for testing key hypotheses involving brain–behavior correspondences. This is reflected in the diversity of approaches used by our contributors to address these problems, including behavioral experiments, brain imaging, neuropsychology, electrophysiology, computational modeling, and investigations of neurotransmitter systems. Where appropriate, our contributors have also borrowed insights from the animal literature to shed light on human behavior. This multifaceted approach by which decision neuroscientists have studied these topics has already borne fruit by contributing to the development of increasingly sophisticated models for processes that are of interest to behavioral decision theorists. Perhaps chief among those processes are the neural systems underlying the computation of subjective value (O'Doherty & Bossaerts, 2008) and probability (Knutson, Taylor, Kaufman, Peterson, & Glover, 2005), topics of continued and intense study in this area.

Second, our choices have been influenced by some of the larger theoretical ideas that have had marked impact on thinking not just among behavioral decision researchers, but also among the greater community of scholars in philosophy, psychology, and economics. Chief among those are ideas involving the existence of multiple systems for judgment and decision making (Evans, 2008), and the significance of emotion for understanding human behavior (Loewenstein, Weber, Hsee, & Welch, 2001). Essentially, the upshot of these developments is widespread agreement among researchers that there is no unitary "module" in the brain for judgment and decision making, but rather multiple parallel processes—including emotional processes—that operate to determine choice behavior (Bechara, this volume; Christoff, Gordon, & Smith, this volume; De Neys & Goel, this volume; Sanfey & Rilling, this volume). Given that evidence from the neurosciences has contributed extensively to the development of these ideas in the greater research community (Damasio, 1994; Frank, Cohen, & Sanfey, 2009), a number of our chapters address these influential currents in thinking, in the process evaluating their empirical contributions to understanding judgment and decision-making processes, more specifically.

Third, we have ventured somewhat beyond the traditional boundaries of judgment and decision-making research and included chapters that discuss the role of judgment and decision-making processes in selective higher-order cognitive activities such as planning, creative problem solving, and spontaneous thought. There is much evidence to suggest that higher-order cognitive activities are componential in nature, and that the ability to make optimal judgments and decisions represents one of the critical components for success in such activities. Although traditionally the literatures on planning, creative problem solving, and spontaneous thought have not made explicit contact with work in judgment and decision making, we were motivated to reduce the gap between these areas by highlighting the integral role that judgment and decision-making processes play in those mental activities. This approach was made possible because recent evidence from the neurosciences suggests that higher-order mental activities such as reasoning, planning, and problem solving are built on shared neural systems, and that when analyzed in terms of component processes mental activities that appear different at the macro level in fact share commonalities at the micro, neural level (De Neys & Goel, this volume; Vartanian, this volume). In this regard, we are already witnessing how the neurosciences are redefining concepts and categories invoked in the study of higher-order cognition, as well as their inter-relations.

ORGANIZATION OF THE VOLUME

We begin the book with the section entitled "Theoretical models", which includes two chapters that address issues of general theoretical interest to our readership. Mariano Sigman and Stanislas Dehaene analyze the cognitive and neural architectures of simple decisions. They present behavioral and neural evidence to support their argument that three key puzzles in decision making—decision duration, decision variability, and slow processing—arise from the brain architecture within which decision making occurs. By grounding behavioral features of simple decisions onto basic biology, this chapter sets the stage for interpreting the brain–behavior correspondences discussed in the book. We (Mandel and Vartanian) follow in the next chapter with a discussion of context effects on judgment and decision making, a topic of key concern in the neuroscience of choice (Doya, 2008). Our chapter combines a critical review of the behavioral and neuroscientific literatures on context effects with the presentation of novel experimental data to test hypotheses about their neural and psychological origins. We endeavor to show that current behavioral and neural evidence supports the assertion that the field has entered a stage in which context-dependence of choice must be seen as central to decision theory, and as something that cannot be ignored without incurring a severe loss of explanatory completeness (Goldstein & Weber, 1997).

The next section, entitled "Risk and uncertainty", includes three chapters that address problems in this key topical area for judgment and decision-making researchers. Antoine Bechara offers an historical synopsis that traces the intellectual trajectory of thinking about the role of emotion on decision making from Phineas Gage to the influential somatic marker hypothesis. He embraces modern thinking by outlining specific conditions under which emotions can be useful and disruptive to decision making, and describes the multiple cortical systems that comprise the emotional circuitry of the brain, each of which mediates specific aspects of choice under uncertainty. In the chapter that follows, Angcla Yu distinguishes among various types of uncertainty as a function of their sources. Her approach rests on the assumption that if one were able to offer formal computational descriptions of varieties of uncertainty, then one would be in a better position to understand the brain systems that implement each variant. She offers evidence showing that the neuromodulator acetylcholine plays a critical role in coping with uncertainty in sensory processing and attentional control, embedding her findings in the greater role that acetylcholine plays in expected uncertainty (Yu & Dayan, 2005). Finally, Wim De Neys and Vinod Goel employ a classic problem in the judgment under uncertainty literature—the so-called "Lawyer-Engineer" problem—to show that belief-mediated and normative responses activate dissociable neural systems in the brain. In addition, using neural evidence, they show that when beliefs and norms clash the inability to respond normatively is not a function of lack of awareness regarding that conflict, but rather due to an inability to overcome belief-based responding. Not only does their chapter speak to the engagement of multiple systems of decision making in the brain, but it also demonstrates that the systems that are engaged for heuristic and analytic responding in the context of this decision-making task are the same ones that are engaged for similar purposes in the context of deductive-reasoning tasks (Goel, 2007). This points to the importance of studying component processes across different tasks that can in turn highlight similarities in neural structure among different mental activities.

Our third section, entitled "Reward and loss", includes three chapters that describe the contributions of neural systems that underlie the computation of reward and loss to judgment and decision making. Mauricio Delgado and Elizabeth Tricomi argue that to successfully steer decision making, not only does the brain need to register the hedonic aspects of reward or punishment, but it must also exhibit the ability to learn from experience involving reward and punishment, bypass time-consuming and energy-demanding computations, and ignore spurious associations between events and outcomes. They invoke a wealth of experimental findings in making the case that the striatum may be able to process reward-related information in such a way so that it can meet these difficult demands. In the process they offer a rich description of the functional specialization of the various regions of the striatum. Next, John O'Doherty reviews the current state of knowledge about the neural mechanisms that underlie learning about rewards and punishments, differentiating between different types of value signals that are used by humans as a function of task demands. Furthermore, he describes the putative computational mechanisms by which predictive valuation signals might be learned through experience, and reviews evidence for the operation of such mechanisms in the brain. Ending this section, Diego Pizzagalli, Daniel Dillon, Ryan Bogdan, and Avram Holmes review the basic research on the neural correlates of reward and punishment, distinguishing between the functions of the ventral striatum, amygdala, the orbitofrontal cortex, and the anterior cingulate cortex in relation to outcome anticipation and action representation. They then extend this knowledge to a characterization of depression as abnormal incentive processing. Their chapter shows how knowledge gained about the reward circuitry of the brain can be used to understand underlying mechanisms of psychopathology, and how knowledge learned from studying healthy and disordered populations can be exchanged fruitfully to expand understanding of valuation processes in both populations.

The fourth section of the book, entitled "Cooperation and trust", deals with aspects of choice that are influenced by interpersonal and social norms governing behavior. Alan Sanfey and James Rilling start the section by focusing their chapter on research in the neurosciences that investigates social decision making involving dyadic interactions. They review research on game theory involving several central tasks such as Prisoner's Dilemma games, the Trust Game, and the Ultimatum Game. Their review sheds light on various factors that determine choices in the context of these tasks, including affiliation and trust, competition, and adherence and violation of social norms. This chapter also serves an important auxiliary purpose by highlighting the link between decision neuroscience and the emerging field of neuroeconomics, which more focally deals with the understanding and prediction of decisions about rewards (Clithero, Tankersley, & Huettel, 2008; see also Glimcher, Camerer, Poldrack, & Fehr, 2009). Next, Daniel Houser, Robert Kurzban, and Erte Xiao discuss social and biological empirical evidence on motives for punishment. They focus on the effects of punishment on cooperation, delineating conditions under which punishment is likely to be effective and ineffective in fostering cooperation. They then focus on various motives for punishment, including norm expression, egalitarianism (fairness), and emotion expression. Their chapter makes a strong case for the role of punishment in interpersonal exchange, and supports it further by bringing biological data to bear on this issue. In combination, the two chapters in this section present convincing evidence that dyadic and multi-person interactions are strongly influenced by the interaction of multiple systems in the brain, and that understanding choices is also contingent on understanding the social norms that govern action selection.

The fifth and final section of this volume, entitled "Goal-directed decision making", deals with the contributions of planned and spontaneous cognitive processes to judgment and decision making. As noted earlier, the inclusion of this section was motivated by our desire to highlight the role of judgment and decision-making processes in selective higher-order mental activities. In the first chapter, Kalina Christoff, Alan Gordon, and Rachelle Smith argue that although 30% of thoughts that people have can be classified as mind wandering, the contribution of this form of mental activity to cognition has been neglected compared with the contributions of goal-directed mental activity. They examine the neural and cognitive mechanisms that underlie spontaneous thinking, and argue that this form of thought contributes to judgment and decision making by consolidating new memories and the adaptive re-consolidation of old memories in relation to current tasks and emotions. Next, Jorge Moll and Jordan Grafman review the cognitive and computational perspectives on planning, and provide a description of the cognitive components of plan decision making that can be mapped onto the brain. They argue that the crucial components of plan-specific decision making are primarily stored in the prefrontal cortex (PFC) as a component of the plan itself, with plan execution assisted by motor and other processes carried out by the basal ganglia, motor cortex, and other cortical regions such as the parietal lobes. The accumulated imaging and neuropsychological evidence strongly suggests that the major representation of plan-level knowledge in the human brain—including plan-specific decisions—occurs in the PFC, and that specific features of the plans are encoded and stored in subregions within PFC. The book closes with a chapter by Oshin Vartanian on creativity. He argues that the tendency of creativity researchers to study only those processes that are unique to creativity has led to a dearth of attention paid to judgment and decision-making processes in creative cognition, a problem that is rectified when creativity is viewed as one of many avenues for solving everyday problems. He presents behavioral and neural evidence to support the important role decision making plays in creativity, especially in relation to selecting solution paths.

SUMMARY

Over the last decade we have witnessed the emergence of progressively more sophisticated biological models of choice. Gaps in knowledge remain. For example, currently we know much less about the neural systems that underlie computation of probability than those that underlie computation of reward (Sanfey, 2007). Nevertheless, the field is moving toward ever more complete mechanistic models of human decision making (O'Doherty & Bossaerts, 2008). In the process, this work is able to offer new and incisive tests of hypotheses derived from behavioral theories of judgment and decision making. It is our hope that this book provides a framework for thinking about some of the key issues in this area, as well as capturing the aspirations of this research program.

REFERENCES

Clithero, J. A., Tankersley, D., & Huettel, S. A. (2008). Foundations of neuro-economics: From philosophy to practice. *PLOS Biology*, *8*, 2348–2353.

Damasio, A. R. (1994). *Descartes' error: Emotion, reason, and the human brain.* New York: Grosset/Putnam.

Damasio, A. R., Damasio, H., & Christen, Y. (Eds.). (1996). *Neurobiology of decision-making.* Berlin: Springer-Verlag.

Doya, K. (2008). Modulators of decision making. *Nature Neuroscience*, *11*, 410–416.

Evans, J. St. B. T. (2008). Dual processing accounts of reasoning, judgment, and social cognition. *Annual Review of Psychology*, *59*, 255–278.

Frank, M. J., Cohen, M. X., & Sanfey, A. G. (2009). Multiple systems in decision making: A neurocomputational perspective. *Current Directions in Psychological Science*, *18*, 73–77.

Glimcher, P., Camerer, C., Poldrack, R., & Fehr, E. (Eds.). (2009). *Neuroeconomics: Decision making and the brain.* London: Academic Press.

Goel, V. (2007). Anatomy of deductive reasoning. *Trends in Cognitive Sciences*, *11*, 435–441.

Goldstein, W. M., & Weber, E. U. (1997). Content and discontent: Indications and implications of domain specificity in preferential decision making. In W. M. Goldstein & R. M. Hogarth (Eds.), *Research on judgment and decision making* (pp. 566–617). Cambridge: Cambridge University Press.

Knutson, B., Taylor, J., Kaufman, M., Peterson, R., & Glover, G. (2005). Distributed neural representation of expected value. *Journal of Neuroscience*, *25*, 4806–4812.

Loewenstein, G. F., Weber, E. U., Hsee, C. K., & Welch, N. (2001). Risk as feelings. *Psychological Bulletin*, *127*, 267–286.

O'Doherty, J. P., & Bossaerts, P. (2008). Toward a mechanistic understanding of human decision making. *Current Directions in Psychological Science*, *17*, 119–123.

Sanfey, A. G. (2007). Decision neuroscience: New directions in studies of judgment and decision making. *Current Directions in Psychological Science*, *16*, 151–155.

Yu, A. J., & Dayan, P. (2005). Uncertainty, neuromodulation, and attention. *Neuron*, *46*, 681–692.

Section I
Theoretical models

Why does it take time to make a decision? The role of a global workspace in simple decision making

Mariano Sigman and Stanislas Dehaene

INTRODUCTION

The research that we report in this chapter was motivated by three surprisingly simple questions that turn out to have deep consequences for cognitive brain architecture:

- Why does it take so much time to take a decision?
- Why is decision time so variable?
- Why can we take only one decision at a time?

Why does it take so much time to take a decision?

Like any other form of computation, brain computing takes time. Thus, it may seem obvious that each of our decisions should take some minimal duration, ultimately linked to axonal, synaptic, and dendritic propagation delays. Yet the intriguing question is: Why does it take *so* much time to take a decision? We do not necessarily refer here to the arbitrary long durations of certain choices (although this too plays its part). It can take hours, days, or months to choose where and for how long to go on vacation, and with whom, and how, and so on and so on. Decision difficulty is illustrated by the metaphor of Buridan's ass (honoring the 14th-century French philosopher Jean Buridan), who supposedly died when placed in between a stack of hay and a pail of water, unable to decide whether to eat or drink first. But far from the limits of starving or pathological decision making, simply deciding which of two numbers is larger, or which of two tones is of a higher pitch, takes between 500 and 1500 ms—a surprisingly long time, when considering synaptic delay and the timing of selective responses to sensory stimuli.

Responses to sensory stimulation in the primary visual cortex can be recorded as early as 50 ms, and the brainstem knows about the presence of a stimulus 20 ms after its presentation. Even after many relays of information and a few synapses, in about 180 ms information about a sensory stimulus is accessible to virtually all visual brain areas (Thorpe, Fize, & Marlot, 1996). The brain knows whether an object is a face, or a tree, at about 100 ms (monkey) or 170 ms (human), yet acting on this information to make a choice—a remarkably easy problem—takes 5, or 10, or 15 times more. Propagation of information and delay lines are thus simply not a good answer to explain why deciding takes so much time.

Why is decision time so variable?

Decision variability, in turn, may also seem to be a consequence of basic biology. Fluctuations in membrane voltage potential, in synaptic connectivity and efficiency—among other sources of biological noise—make the brain a highly stochastic machine. As a result, brain computations are unreliable, which explains why we sometimes make mistakes and why decisions are sometimes faster and other times slower.

Once again this simple intuition turns out to be wrong. While certainly biological components are noisy, they can combine into extremely precise machines assuring, among others, extremely reliable DNA replication or spiking devices (neurons) with remarkable precision. There are countless demonstrations of this fact. Bryant and Segundo (1976) first noticed that spike timing accuracy could be extremely precise and that reliability depends on the particulars of the input driving the neuron. More recently, this intriguing property received renewed attention and has been demonstrated in pyramidal neuron circuits (Mainen & Sejnowski, 1995), in vivo recordings of the H1 neuron in the visual system of the fly *Calliphora vicina* (de Ruyter van Steveninck, Lewen, Strong, Koberle, & Bialek, 1997), and other subcortical (Butts et al., 2007) and cortical structures in the mammalian brain (Cecchi, Sigman, Alonso, Martinez, & Chialvo, 2000; Gur, Beylin, & Snodderly, 1997; Kara, Reinagel, & Reid, 2000). Beyond the biophysical and anatomical details and their implications for the nature of the neural code, a remarkable corollary of these studies is that the brain can perform certain computations with exquisite precision. Thus, the question of why decisions (as well as other noisy neuronal computations) are so variable requires a better explanation than simply biological noise.

Why can we take only one decision at a time?

A ubiquitous aspect of brain function is its quasi-modular and massively parallel organization, with a large number of processors (neurons, columns, or entire areas) operating simultaneously (Hubel & Wiesel, 1959, 1968). For example, in the visual modality, a yet undefined number of visual areas perform different feature analysis (Felleman & Van Essen, 1991; Van Essen, Anderson, & Felleman, 1992) and within each visual area, a parallel ensemble of cortical columns samples simultaneously the visual scene (Hubel & Wiesel, 1965). Multiple copies of retinotopic maps allow a fast coverage of the environment at a vast field of view. This vast parallel machine can perform, with seemingly no effort and extreme rapidity, tasks that, until recently, were judged virtually impossible for contemporary artificial machines, such as invariant object recognition.

The paradox, however, is that this extraordinary parallel machine is incapable of doing various mental calculations in parallel or, even to perform a single large arithmetic calculation that requires multiple steps. How come it is so easy to recognize moving objects, but so difficult to multiply 357 times 289? And why, if we can simultaneously coordinate walking, group contours, segment surfaces, talk, and listen to noisy speech, can we only make one decision at a time?

The proposal that we make is that an answer to all three puzzles—decision duration, decision variability, and slow seriality—arises from the brain architecture for decision making. In accordance with other investigators (Bundesen, 1990; Logan & Gordon, 2001; Sternberg, 1969, 2004), we contend that any simple decision task can be decomposed into separate processing stages (sensory, decision, and motor) and that the decision stage has specific properties of pooling information, attaining a threshold and broadcasting the result, which confer to mental decisions their peculiar properties.

CONTRIBUTIONS OF DIFFERENT STAGES TO RESPONSE-TIME MEAN AND VARIABILITY

Factor analysis: Changing the mean without changing the variance

The results discussed in this chapter emerge from an exhaustive analysis of a very simple decision task. This task is number comparison, which involves deciding whether a digit presented on the screen is larger or smaller than a fixed reference.

Different manipulations of the task can render it more difficult (Figure 1.1a) including: *notation* (target number presented in Arabic digits or in spelled words), *distance* (numerical distance between the target number

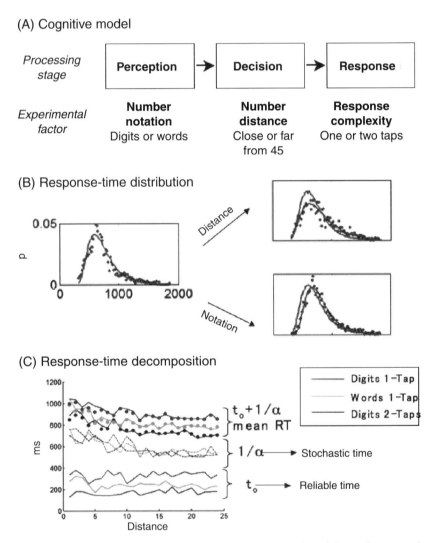

Figure 1.1 Features of the number comparison task. (a) Illustration of the number comparison task and the notation, distance, and response complexity factors. (b) A change in notation resulted in a rigid shift of the RT distribution; a change in numerical distance resulted in a wider distribution. (c) Decision (stochastic time) was only affected by numerical distance. Response and notation manipulations affected only the non-decision time. See color plate.

and the reference), and *response complexity* (whether subjects were asked to tap once or twice to indicate their choice). These manipulations change the difficulty of the task—the mean response time slows down when numerical distance decreases and when numbers are presented in spelled words (Dehaene, 1996; Moyer & Landauer, 1967; Sigman & Dehaene, 2005). These effects are additive—that is, the mean increase due to the distance factor is independent of the effect of notation (Dehaene, 1996; Pinel, Dehaene, Riviere, & LeBihan, 2001), thus establishing a first indication that they involve independent processing stages and can be factored from the entirety of the task (Sternberg, 1969, 2004).

A surprising observation resulted from an analysis of the effects of these factors on response-time variability. Although the precise dependence of the mean and variance may vary (Wagenmakers & Scott, 2007), a simultaneous increase in the dispersion and in the mean is expected from any stochastic (noisy) process. Indeed, the distance manipulation, as expected, resulted in a significant increase of the dispersion, which paralleled the increase in the mean. Strikingly, however, the notation and response complexity, while inflicting an important change in the mean, did not affect the dispersion of the RT distribution (Figure 1.1b).

Modeling decision making: The contribution of processing stages to RT mean and variance

The decision-making process has been modeled as a noisy integrator that accumulates evidence provided by the sensory system (Gold & Shadlen, 2001; Link & Heath, 1975; Luce, 1986; Ratcliff, 1988; Schall, 2000; Schwarz, 2001; Shadlen & Newsome, 1996; Usher & McClelland, 2001; Vickers, 1970). Although many variants have been proposed, the basic idea is that perceptual evidence in favor of each of the available response alternatives is stochastically accumulated in time. A decision is taken whenever evidence in favor of one response exceeds a predetermined threshold. Decision thus results from a random walk of an internal abstract variable up to a fixed bound. In the simplest scheme, all the variance in response time is attributed to this integration process.

This analysis establishes a possible parsing of our task into components: A fixed component to transform the sensory information into an abstract internal variable (here broadly called the perceptual or P component), another fixed component to execute the response (motor or M component), and the accumulation of evidence itself (central or C component)—the latter being the only variable process.

This decomposition model was tested by analyzing how the shape of the response-time distributions varied with the experimental manipulations (Figure 1.1c). The histograms of response times were fitted to a simple model based on a fixed onset delay (t_o, the sum of the P and M component) plus a forced random walk with slope (α) and diffusion constant (σ) until it reaches a fixed threshold (T). T can be set to 1 without loss of generality and, for simplicity, we assumed that s was the same for all six experimental conditions, while a and t_o could vary (none of the results depended qualitatively on the particular choice of σ). $1/\alpha$ characterizes the integration time (which explains all the variance), while t_o captures fixed components that do not contribute to the variance. Our approach was to remain with the simplest possible model, whose sole purpose was to separate stochastic and invariant contributions to reaction times.

The results showed that the shapes of the distributions changed in two qualitatively different manners. A change in notation resulted in a rigid shift of the distribution; a change in numerical distance resulted in a widening of the RT distribution (Figure 1.1b). A parametric dependence with the distance (Figure 1.1c) revealed that t_o changed with notation and response manipulations but was unaffected by distance. On the contrary, the decision time changed exclusively with distance, independently of the notation and response modality.

Furthermore, these results indicate that a cognitive task can be parsed in stages that provide a reliable contribution to response time, and other stages that provide a highly stochastic contribution to response time. Is this decomposition related in any manner with the serial and parallel nature of these computations? In the next section we show that indeed such a parallel decomposition can be demonstrated experimentally.

PARSING A COGNITIVE TASK INTO SERIAL AND PARALLEL PROCESSING STATES

When two tasks are presented simultaneously (or sequentially at a short interval), a delay in the execution of the second task is systematically observed (Kahneman, 1973; Pashler & Johnston, 1989; Smith, 1967; Telford, 1931). This interference effect is referred to as the Psychological Refractory Period (PRP). It has also been explained by a model that involves three stages of processing: (1) a perceptual component (P); (2) a central component (C); and (3) a motor component (M), where only the central component establishes a bottleneck (Pashler, 1994; Pashler & Johnston, 1989; Ruthruff, Pashler, & Klaassen, 2001; Schweickert, 1980; Schweickert & Townsend, 1989; Sternberg, 1969). PRP experiments have associated the central component to "response selection", the mapping between sensory information and motor action (Pashler & Johnston, 1998). Other processes have also been implicated in the central bottleneck—not just response selection, such as mental rotation (Shepard & Metzler, 1971; Van Selst & Jolicoeur, 1994).

Interference analysis constitutes a very powerful experimental technique to understand the internal structure of a task. The logic of these experiments resembles the classic scattering methodology in physics, where the internal structure of an element (e.g., particle, molecule, etc.) is understood by colliding it with an experimental probe. In our experimental setup, the task under study (the number comparison task) was performed simultaneously or quasi-simultaneously with a probe task (the tone task). The tasks were chosen to involve entirely distinct sensory modalities (auditory versus visual) and responses (left versus right hand). The delay in the onset of the two task targets (number and tone), here called "stimulus onset asynchrony" or SOA, was controlled experimentally. To achieve a full separation of the three components, we presented the two tasks in both possible orders (Sigman & Dehaene, 2005): number followed by tone, or tone followed by number.

Under the assumptions of the PRP model, the P and M components can be carried out in parallel with another task, but the central stage is the only one that provides a bottleneck, in the sense that the central component of each task (C1 and C2) cannot be carried out simultaneously. These simple premises lead to a large number of concrete predictions on the family of curves for response time to the first and second tasks (here called RT1 and RT2) as a function of delay, and how these values change with a manipulation of the P, C, and M components of either task. The sets of predictions are summarized in Figure 1.2, and the logic leading to these predictions can be found in Sigman and Dehaene (2005). Here we summarize the main aspects.

When the number task (perturbed by different experimental manipulations) is performed first, all the manipulated variables should have a main effect on RT1, but only some of those effects (those that affect P and C components of the first task) should propagate to the response time of the second task. Furthermore, they should do so only at short inter-stimulus delays, within what we may call the "interference regime" (Figure 1.2a). In addition, SOA should not affect RT1 and should inflict no increase in RT2 for short SOA values and a linear increase with a slope of 1 for large SOA values. This assumes—as we do throughout this chapter—that RT2 is measured from the onset of the trial. In the convention in which RT2 is measured from the presentation of the second stimulus, the model predicts that RT2 decreases with a slope of −1 for short SOA durations and is constant for large SOA values.

When the number task came in second, the model predicts that there should be no effect of the manipulated variables on the first tone task. The response time to the second task should exhibit a constant increase (independent of delay) when the change affects the M and C components and should change only for large delays when the change affects the P

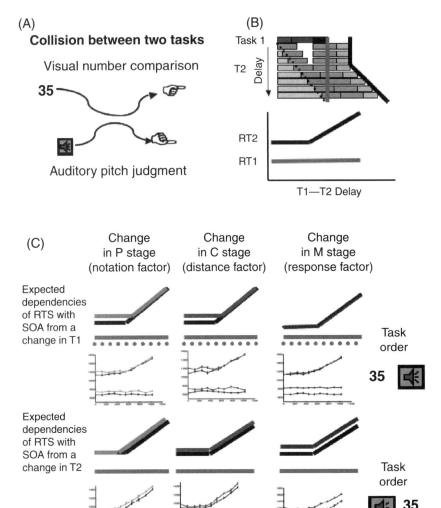

Figure 1.2 Sketch of basic task predictions. (a) Sketch of the dual-task. (b) Scheme of the main PRP effect. The vertical axis shows response time. The column on the left indicates the first task, and each color box within the column represents a different stage of processing: Perceptual component (P) (green), central component (C) (red) and motor component (M) (blue). The series of columns on the right indicate the processing time for task 2 at different delays (Δ), labeled in the x-axis. Response to the first task is independent of Δ. The response time to task 2 represented by the black line is unchanged for small Δ, while at sufficiently large Δ (non-interference regime) it increases linearly with a slope of 1, with Δ. (c) In the top panel the number task is performed first, in the bottom panel, second. In both cases, the number task is manipulated by the three factors of notation, distance, and response complexity. In all panels the code is identical: RT1 is colored grey, while RT2 is colored black. The "easy" condition is represented by a solid line and the "difficult" condition by a dotted line. All the data can be explained in terms of the PRP model: Notation (top row) affects the P component, distance (middle row) affects C, and response complexity (bottom row) affects M. See color plate.

component (Figure 1.2b). This is one of the critical predictions of the model since it implies that certain computations required for T2 perception can be performed during T1 queuing and thus argues for a coexistence of serial and parallel processing within the same task.

Every single prediction of the model was verified experimentally (Figure 1.2c). For example, in the response manipulation—when number was presented first and subjects were asked to tap the response button once or twice—we observed a large response cost (175 ms) on the first task, but none of that effect was propagated to the second task, typical of a post-bottleneck manipulation (a M1 component that operates in parallel with the C2 component). Similarly, the effect of notation was no longer observed for short SOA values when the number task was presented second, indicating a pre-bottleneck parallel stage (a P2 stage operating in parallel with P1 and C1 stages).

All the results taken together provide strong evidence that our three experimental factors (notation, distance, response complexity) mapped onto distinct stages of the PRP model. Notation manipulation affects a stage of processing prior to the bottleneck, the response manipulation to a parallel stage of processing occurring after the bottleneck, and the distance manipulation was the only factor to affect a serial stage of processing. It is striking, of course, that the task decomposition offered by the PRP and the response variability methods converged so tightly.

BRIDGING DYNAMICS AND ARCHITECTURE: A SYNTHETIC MODEL OF TASK ORGANIZATION

Taken together, the analyses of response variability and of interference suggest that the integration of evidence in time to reach a decision constitutes the only central process in a simple cognitive task that links perceptions to actions and thus that *there is a consistent parsing of a cognitive task based on variance or interference analysis.* This led us to develop a theoretical framework providing a synthesis of three basic aspects of cognitive architecture: (1) its chronometric organization; (2) its parallel and serial nature; and (3) its temporal reliability or stochasticity. We postulated that only the integration process establishes a serial bottleneck, while all other stages can proceed in parallel with stages of another task (Figure 1.3a).

While extremely simple, the model makes powerful mathematical predictions in experiments in which the order of the presentation of the two tasks and their relative offset in presentations are varied as described in the previous two sections. Moreover, it establishes a subtle, yet very critical prediction: The precise distribution of response times for the second task should be determined, according to the model, from the distributions of

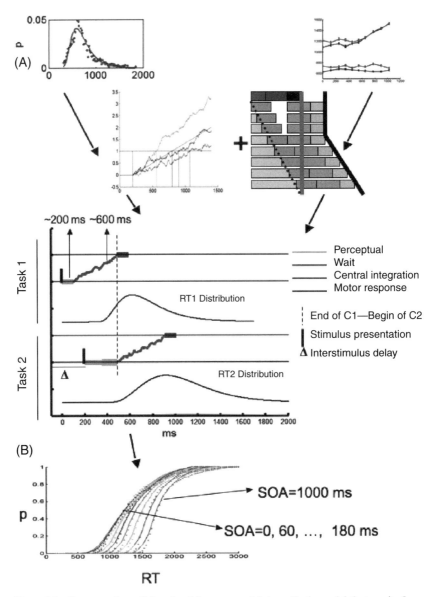

Figure 1.3 Features of parallel and serial processes. (a) A synthetic model that results from a consistent parsing based on stochastic and reliable components (left) and from interference experiments of the PRP. Perceptual and motor stages are reliable in time and can be carried out in parallel with stages of another task, while the central stage consists of a noisy integration (a random walk) until a decision threshold is reached. The central stage of task 2 cannot start until the central stage of task 1 is finished. Thus, this establishes a bottleneck and characterizes a serial process. (b) The distribution of reaction times to the second task is wider than that to the first task because it combines the intrinsic variance of task 2 (the time to reach threshold) and the variance in onset of the central stage of task 2, which is set by the end of the central stage of task 1. This distribution can be predicted correctly by the model. See color plate.

both tasks when performed in isolation or as a first task in a dual-task procedure.

If both tasks were performed in a completely sequential manner, the resulting response-time distribution would be the convolution of the two original distributions. If both tasks were performed in parallel, the response-time distribution of the compound task would be identical to the distribution when the task is performed in isolation. However, the PRP model states that only the central processing stage is sequential and thus that some operations can be done in parallel. The precise RT2 distribution can still be calculated (see Sigman & Dehaene [2005] for the details) and, crucially, this calculation is parametric, since it depends on the duration of the M1 and P2 components. Confronting the distributions of the first and second tasks thus provides access to the durations of parallel processing stages, which are not directly accessible to measurement.

We found a very good fit of the ensemble of RT distributions for varying SOAs. The fit required an additional parameter—a rigid shift of 125 ms in time for all distributions of RT1 (see below for the rationale of this parameter). The durations of the parallel processing stages obtained from the interference experiment were essentially identical to the ones based on the shape of the RT distributions to the first task, and which yielded estimates of $1/\alpha$ (the time of integration), and t_o (a fixed delay).

More recently, we explored a further prediction of this model. If the effect of interference is simply to reschedule processing stages within a task, varying the timing but not the characteristics (duration, precision, variability, etc.) of each processing stage, the quality of the decision is unaffected by a concurrent task. We thus studied the functional dependencies of response times and error rates in a dual-task experiment where each task involved a non-symbolic (analogic) decision. In this situation, as in most decision comparison tasks with a scalar measure of the evidence, the extent to which two stimuli can be discriminated is determined by their ratio, referred to as the Weber fraction. Consistent with the predictions, we observed that: (1) Response times replicated the main features observed in prior dual-task studies, showing a strong delay in the execution of the second task, which decreases as SOA increases, and no effect on the first responded task. (2) On the contrary, we did not observe any significant effect on the total number of errors or on the distribution of errors as a function of the numerical distance between the target and the reference, suggesting that the decision process itself is delayed but its workings are unaffected by task interference (Kamienkowski & Sigman, 2008).

In summary, our simple model was essentially capable of predicting the precise shape of a large family of distributions, corresponding to different SOA values, task orders, and experimental manipulations of the number task. We found, however, a consistent departure from this simple model: A systematic and constant increase on RT1 that became evident from direct exploration and from the necessity of including a rigid shift in time on RT1 to account for a correct convolution of both tasks in a model of dual-task performance. In the last section, we return to this subtle but important departure from the simple sequential model, which will be the gate to a new series of experiments.

SERIAL AND PARALLEL PROCESSING IN THE HUMAN BRAIN: DYNAMICS, ARCHITECTURE, AND NETWORKS

Methodological developments to understand dynamics and architecture in the human brain

What is the neurophysiological basis of the postulated processing, and particularly of the central decision stage? The purely passive model of the PRP interference predicts that task interference results exclusively from a change in the dynamics of the processing stages within each task, without any additional engagement of other brain areas. This constitutes a challenge for neurophysiology since it implies observing shifts in time without any change in total amount of activity during dual-task interference. This challenge explains why most previous studies have relied on Event Related Potential (ERPs). These experiments have systematically showed delayed (and on occasions also reduced) components, such as the N2PC, P3, and lateralized readiness potentials (Arnell & Duncan, 2002; Arnell, Helion, Hurdelbrink, & Pasieka, 2004; Brisson & Jolicoeur, 2007a, 2007b; Brisson, Robitaille, & Jolicoeur, 2007; Dell'acqua, Jolicoeur, Vespignani, & Toffanin, 2005; Luck, 1998; Osman & Moore, 1993; Sessa, Luria, Verleger, & Dell'Acqua, 2007). Using time-resolved fMRI (Formisano & Goebel, 2003; Kim, Richter, & Ugurbil, 1997; Menon, Luknowsky, & Gati, 1998), Dux and collaborators showed delayed activity in prefrontal cortex in a PRP paradigm (Dux, Ivanoff, Asplund, & Marois, 2006), suggesting that a frontal network was one of the fundamental nodes responsible for the central bottleneck of information processing. None of those studies, however, provided a complete analysis of the neurocognitive task architecture at the whole-brain level.

We sought to achieve such a full decomposition of each task into processing stages, in order to understand their parallel or serial nature as we did in the previous series of behavioral experiments. This ambitious goal required an important methodological advance: We needed to estimate timing information invariantly across different brain regions, to distinguish changes in onset latency and in duration (Bellgowan, Saad, & Bandettini, 2003), and then to cluster the timing information into distinct stages based on a precise model of task sequencing.

We first demonstrated that fMRI could be used to recover the precise timing of all the stages in a complex composite task, reconstructing the controlled stream of brain activations in a sequence of cognitive operations (sensory, motor, verbal) (Sigman, Jobert, Lebihan, & Dehaene, 2007). Our Fourier-based methodology—described thoroughly in Sigman et al. (2007)—showed that single-event fMRI can evaluate changes in activation timing with a rather good precision of 100–200 ms. We then used this methodology in a simplified version of the PRP experiment described in the previous section. Only four SOA (two short and two long) values were used, the number task was presented second, and numbers were presented only in Arabic digits and with a single response modality.

We performed independent identical experiments with time-resolved fMRI and with high-density ERP recordings (Sigman & Dehaene, 2008). The timing information from both imaging techniques was clustered into components, guided by the psychological model of the task sequence described in the previous section. This allowed us to parse the execution of the two tasks into a series of processing stages with different timing properties, to understand which nodes were involved in one or both tasks or in coordinating dual-task execution, and which stages proceeded in parallel with each other or imposed a serial bottleneck.

Factorizing a physiological stream into response components and investigating their temporal superposition

To understand the dynamics of different brain processes involved in the dual-task condition, we first decomposed the ERP data using scalp templates identified from the ERP recorded at the largest SOA in which the execution of both tasks does not overlap in time. We simply identified the main topographies at each local maximum of the total voltage power recorded over all electrodes (Figure 1.4a). These components could easily be identified as the N1 and P3 components corresponding to each task. While more components could potentially have been identified by a more sophisticated analysis, our aim was not to identify all the independent processes within a task, but rather to understand the dynamics and architecture of these basic response components within the interference regime.

To do so, we decomposed each ERP, at each SOA and each time point, into a linear combination of the four scalp templates—this is referred to simply as the "time course of the ERP components". We observed that the time course of the components (Figure 1.4b) fitted with predictions derived from our sequential model, if one supposes that the N1 components map onto perceptual processes and the P3 components onto central processes (Del Cul, Baillet, & Dehaene, 2007; Sergent, Baillet, &

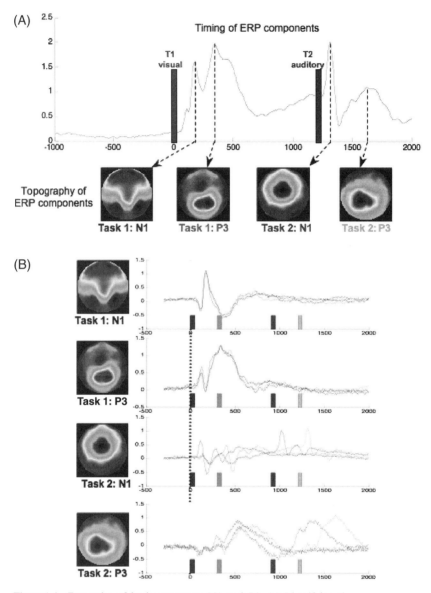

Figure 1.4   Dynamics of brain processes: N1 and P3. (a) Identifying the response components (N1 and P3), when the two tasks are performed without interference. (b) Dynamics of each component: Components of task 1 (first two panels) are unaffected by SOA. N1 component of T2 (third panel) follows stimulus presentation, P3 component reflects a bottleneck for short SOAs. See color plate.

Dehaene, 2005). The time course of the N1 and P3 components of the first task (denoted as T1_N1 and T1_P3) was unaffected by changes in SOA values (first and second rows in Figure 1.4b), indicating that, as predicted by the PRP model, the first task unfolded strictly identically within and outside the interference regime. This observation also testifies to the efficiency of the decomposition procedure, which was able to identify the visual components of the T1 task even when they were superimposed with simultaneously occurring auditory components.

The time course of the components of the second task showed a very distinct pattern. The T2_N1 component was strictly time locked to T2 onset, as expected for a perceptual component of task 2. It peaked at a fixed latency after T2 presentation, both within and outside the interference regime, and thus its latency increased linearly with SOA. The time course of the T2_P3 component of task 2, on the other hand, showed little effect of SOA within the interference regime and a shift proportional to the change in SOA in the non-interference regime, as expected for a central component of task 2. This is also expected from a motor component (since these predictions are valid for all post-bottleneck stages) and, given that the locus of the P3 for each task appears to be lateralized to the right for T1 and to the left for T2 (in accordance with the lateralization of the response of each hand), it is possible that this component may be indexing a motor component. Two observations make this interpretation unlikely: First, previous results have related the P3 to central processing (Sergent et al., 2005; Del Cul et al., 2007). Second, and most importantly, if the P3s indexed motor components, they could overlap in time (i.e., the P3 of the second task could be executed in parallel with the P3 of the first task). Our observation suggests the contrary, since T2_P3 appears to be locked to the ending of T1_P3.

Altogether, the data suggest that T2 presentation immediately engages a sensory processing stage, which unfolds as a series of damped oscillations over a period of about 300 ms after T2 onset (Figure 1.3, third row), followed by a central component that starts about 250 ms after T2 onset and peaks at 380 ms, but is systematically delayed by the simultaneous performance of another central process of a concurrent task.

As with the behavioral experiments, while the passive bottleneck model was capable of explaining the bulk of the observations, some details of the ERP analysis did suggest several departures from the simple model proposed: A modulation of the amplitude of the N1 component, reflecting sensory attenuation during concurrent task processing, the ramping of the N1 component, revealing task 2 sensory expectation after task 1 completion, and the emergence of the task 2 P3 component before stimulus presentation. These important departures will be discussed in the next section.

Brain networks of serial and parallel processing in the human brain

ERPs provide high temporal resolution, but they are notoriously imprecise for localization. Here, we took advantage of the fact that the PRP phenomenon induces large delays of several hundred milliseconds, which, as discussed previously, are measurable with fMRI (Sigman et al., 2007). For the context of this chapter, it is important to know that the analysis is based on the phase of the response that provides an estimate of the "temporal center of mass" and thus:

1. For a change in the onset of neural activation, only the phase of the hemodynamic response should vary, not the amplitude. The change in the phase should be identical to the change in delay.
2. For a change in duration of activation, both phase and amplitude should increase, with the slope of the phase change reflecting half of the actual change in the duration of neuronal activation (Sigman et al., 2007).

We therefore recorded whole-brain fMRI images at a sampling time (TR) of 1.5 s and computed the phase and amplitude of the hemodynamic response on each trial, for each subject and each voxel. A large network of brain areas (Figure 1.5a) exhibited phases consistently falling within the expected response latency for a task-induced activation (a liberal interval of 2–10 s). As expected for a complex dual-task experiment with visual and auditory stimuli, these regions included: (1) bilateral visual occipito-temporal cortices; (2) bilateral superior temporal auditory cortices; (3) motor, premotor, and cerebellar cortices; and (4) a large-scale bilateral parieto-frontal network. How is this large network organized in time during dual-task performance?

As with the ERPs, we relied on the model to determine our analytic strategy in order to parse the fMRI data (Figure 1.5b). Our method allowed us to fully parse the responsive brain areas into five different networks based on their temporal profile of response. The functional neuroanatomy of these networks (Figure 1.5b) was, for the most part, in tight accordance with the theoretical predictions.

For the brain network involved exclusively in task 1, timing of the activation, and hence the phase of the fMRI response, should not change with SOA. This first network (blue, no phase variation) comprised regions in extra-striate visual cortex, left motor-cortex, and the most medial part of the posterior-parietal cortex as well as an extended subcortical network. This network is expected for a visual number comparison task with a right-hand response.

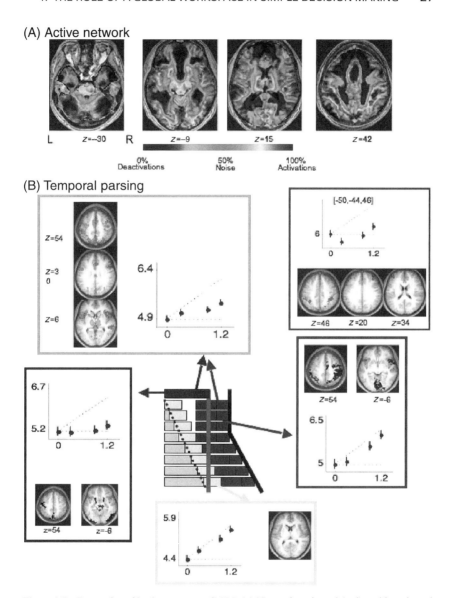

Figure 1.5 Dynamics of brain processes: fMRI. (a) Network activated (red) and inactivated (blue) during dual-task performance as identified by a phase coherence analysis. (b) Parsing the brain network in distinct dynamic processing stages, according to their phase profile. Blue: The brain network involved exclusively in task 1. Yellow: The brain network involved in the perceptual component of task 2. Red: The brain network involved in the central and motor components of task 2. Cyan: Regions involved in both tasks. Green: The brain network involved in executive coordination of both tasks. See color plate.

For the brain network involved in the perceptual component of task 2, the timing of activations, and hence the phase of the fMRI response, should increase in direct proportion with SOA. This second cluster (yellow, slope-1 linear phase response) was the smallest and involved exclusively bilateral auditory cortex, including Heschl's Gyrus and more lateral regions of temporal cortex—a plausible network for the sensory processing of the second task (auditory pitch judgment).

For the brain network involved in the central and motor components of task 2, activation should be unchanged for short SOA—due to queuing— and thus a delay should only be observed for long SOAs resulting in a non-linear phase dependence with SOA. fMRI voxels with this temporal profile were found in the right motor cortex, right Supplementary Motor Area (SMA) (remember that target T2 is responded to with the left hand), and bilateral intraparietal activation. Interestingly this cluster also included the most medial parts of the visual cortex. This unexpected finding might relate to the fact that subjects resumed attention to the fixation cross after conclusion of the two tasks.

The previous networks assume that the distinct dynamic processes of the two tasks always engage distinct brain regions, which of course is not a necessary implementation of the model—indeed it seems much more likely that some of the stages of tasks 1 and 2 engage identical brain regions. We therefore investigated one of the most interesting theoretical predictions— that the serial bottleneck may result from a broad shared network between both tasks, even when sensory and response modalities of both tasks are distinct. Regions involved in both tasks should show an increase in phase corresponding roughly to one half of these indicated by regions corresponding to task 2. We found that this profile corresponded to a massive cluster, involving an extended bilateral network that included the bilateral posterior parietal cortex, premotor cortex, SMA, anterior part of the insula, and the cerebellum. Actually, voxels involved in both tasks should increase with a slope of 0.5 in the noninterference regime, but show no increase in the interference regime, since the total duration of both tasks is unchanged (see Figure 1.2b). The resolution of our methodology was in the limit to resolve this issue and we could not distinguish reliably the slope of 0.5 from the slope of 0 in the interference regime.

For all these regions, if the effect of SOA is simply to alter the onset time of distinct processes, the amplitude of the fMRI activation should remain constant. This was indeed a very consistent experimental observation, in striking contrast with the observed broad repertoire of phase profiles. It indicates that all of the above changes corresponded to purely dynamical reorganizations of task components, without any change in activation strength.

In summary, we measured the phase of the fMRI response in the whole brain at high temporal resolution in order to parse the responsive network into distinct processing stages. Sensory areas tracked the objective time of stimulus presentation, while a bilateral parieto-prefrontal network correlated with the dual-task sequential delay. An extended bilateral network, which included the bilateral posterior parietal cortex, premotor cortex, SMA, anterior part of the insula, and the cerebellum, was shared by both tasks during the extent of dual-task performance. Consistent with the EEG findings, this provides physiological evidence of the coexistence of serial and parallel processes within a cognitive task.

BEYOND THE SIMPLE SEQUENTIAL MODEL: A HIERARCHICAL SCHEME FOR DECISION MAKING AND EXECUTIVE CONTROL

A consistent picture emerges from the previous behavioral and physiological experiments. A simple model of task architecture accounted for a large number of observations on mean and variability of response times, the precise shape of the distribution of response times of the first and second task in dual-task procedures, the effect of numerous experimental manipulations on these variables, and the precise dynamics of the different physiological components and networks identified with high resolution EEG and fMRI. However, in each instance, we observed minor but consistent and reproducible departures, which suggested that the model is necessarily incomplete.

The first marked departure came from our behavioral observations. Responses to the first task in the PRP paradigm, while independent of SOA, were found to be slower than when performing the task in isolation (Jiang, Saxe, & Kanwisher, 2004; Sigman & Dehaene, 2005). We reasoned that this may be related to an executive control stage engaged before performing the first task, in order to prepare for the instruction of performing the two tasks in a specific order. We hypothesized that in situations in which task order is unknown, this executive time should increase, reflecting a hierarchy of decision processes: First, in terms of which task to respond to and second, the specific decision involved in each task. We conducted a new series of experiments to understand the precise architecture of computations in this more ethological situation of unknown task order. Following a similar analysis of the effect of experimental factors on response-time distributions, we could conclude that in this situation of task uncertainty, executive components (engaging and disengaging in a task) had to be incorporated into our original model to account for critical behavioral observations (Sigman & Dehaene, 2006).

Evidence for the involvement of such executive components could also be derived from the human physiological data. In the ERP analysis we observed that, while the timing of the peak of the N1 component of task 2 was in strict accordance with the predictions of the passive bottleneck model, several other observations deviated from this model. First, we observed a reduced amplitude of the sensory N1 within the interference regime compared with outside the interference regime. Second, the temporal course of the N1 component ramped prior to stimulus presentation, probably reflecting task expectation and preparation (Figure 1.6a). Finally, an auditory P3 component emerged at long SOAs, even before any

(A) Introspective RT is a reliable measure

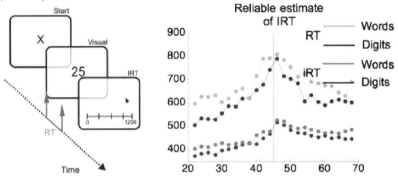

(B) The dual-task delay is inaccessible to introspection

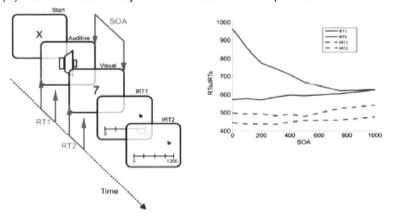

Figure 1.6 Temporal dynamics of processes. Introspection of response time and its failure during dual-task processing. (a) A number comparison task followed by an estimate of introspective response time (IRT) indicated that, although there is a consistent under-estimation (reflecting a poor calibration of absolute IRT), subjects' estimate of IRT is very tightly correlated with RT. (b) On the contrary, the 300 ms delay of the PRP was unnoticed in introspection. Subjects always thought that they were taking a constant time for task 2, regardless of SOA. See color plate

auditory stimulus was presented. This anticipatory component peaked around 500 ms, thus coinciding nicely with the end of the visual P3 evoked by task 1. This ERP sequence is compatible with the hypothesis that, as soon as subjects completed task 1, they re-oriented their attention to prepare for task 2, reflecting an executive component of task engagement (Allport, Styles, & Hsieh, 1994; De Jong, 1993, 1995; Jentzsch, Leuthold, & Ulrich, 2007; Logan & Gordon, 2001; Meiran, Chorev, & Sapir, 2000; Ruthruff et al., 2001; Sigman & Dehaene, 2006). In addition, it suggests that the absence of top-down control may explain the amplitude attenuations observed during interference (Gilbert & Sigman, 2007).

We also found an indication of executive components involved in the active coordination of task processes in the fMRI experiment, by finding a cluster of voxels that was not expected by the purely sequential model. Those voxels showed a purely non-linear component with an increase in phase at the shortest SOA (Figure 1.5b, green cluster). This cluster, which was not predicted by the passive bottleneck model, involved exclusively a bilateral fronto-parietal network, previously found to be involved in processing bottlenecks in dual-task performance (Dux et al., 2006; Marois, Chun, & Gore, 2000; Marois and Ivanoff, 2005), in effortful but not in automatic tasks (Ashbridge, Walsh, & Cowey, 1997), and ubiquitously present in a large variety of goal-directed tasks (Duncan & Owen, 2000).

Cognitive theories have debated about the exact nature of the processes causing the PRP bottleneck. It has been suggested that it involves only a passive queuing of response-selection processes (Pashler, 1984) or, on the contrary, that it might involve a more extended set of processes that may vary with the exact nature of each experimental design, including executive components of task engaging and disengaging (Allport et al., 1994; Jentzsch et al., 2007; Logan & Gordon, 2001; Meiran et al., 2000; Ruthruff et al., 2001; Sigman & Dehaene, 2006, Pashler 1994) as well as delays in response initiation (De Jong, 1993, 1995; Meyer & Kieras 1997; Sigman & Dehaene, 2006). While a vast set of data can be explained simply in terms of response selection, certain aspects of the data argue clearly in favor of an "extended bottleneck" that may manifest in different manners related to executive function and consciousness, depending on context and specific paradigms. Indeed, we found it necessary to include executive components (engaging and disengaging in a task) in a more ethological situation of task uncertainty where the order of actions to achieve a complex goal is unknown. Furthermore, the extended array of areas affected by the PRP suggests that a broad array of processes causes the delay. Although this large set of areas might implement just a single cognitive stage of response selection, it seems more likely to correspond to the deployment of multiple hierarchically organized executive operations (Koechlin & Jubault, 2006; Koechlin, Ody, & Kouneiher, 2003).

We thus are led to envisage a model in which decisions occur serially at any of several possible levels of cognitive architecture. There are simple task decisions (Which key should I press for this stimulus?), but also higher-level executive decisions (Which of these two stimuli should I process first? Am I finished with the first stimulus? Can I orient attention to the second?). Importantly, our evidence so far suggests that all of these decisions involve overlapping parieto-prefrontal networks and are serially arranged in time, such that the need for a higher-level decision pushes all other lower-level decisions further back in time. This is reminiscent of Buridan's problem—sometimes our attempts to control our decisions actually delay our responses rather than improve them. However, the stochastic random-walk mechanism of decision making has one interesting property: Even when there is zero evidence favoring either alternative, the internal "Brownian motion" quickly leads to tipping over to one side or the other, in finite time only marginally slower than when actual evidence is present. Thus, we are never completely paralyzed by a decision—though we are often slowed by a serial chain of executive control operations.

A MOMENT OF THOUGHT: EVIDENCE FROM INTROSPECTION AND METACOGNITION

Our approach to understanding cognitive architecture involved a variety of methodologies. A common aspect to most of them was combining chronometry (through additive factor analysis) with other experimental tools such as interference, EEG, and time-resolved fMRI. Recently, we also investigated whether the chronometric technique could be used to address, in a precise quantitative manner, the introspective knowledge of one's own mental content. A fascinating question is whether there are limits to our own introspection (Hart, 1965; Jack & Roepstrorff, 2003, 2004; Lutz, Lachaux, Martinerie, & Varela, 2002; Nelson, 1996; Overgaard, 2006; Wundt, 1897/1999), and whether introspective access to specific processing stages presents a precise, well-determined relation to our neurocognitive architecture. Indeed, it has often been speculated that a key property of the parallel stages of a task is that they operate outside of our awareness and are therefore opaque to introspection (e.g., Posner, Snyder, & Davidson, 1980). Might the decision stage also coincide with the conscious stage in task processing?

To explore which processing stages were accessible to introspection during the PRP, we again asked participants to perform the number comparison task, either in isolation or in a PRP design with a concurrent tone-discrimination. The novel aspect was that, following each of their responses, participants also indicated their introspective estimation of response time (IRT) by clicking with the mouse on a continuous graded scale spanning 0 to 1200 ms and labeled every 300 ms.

The results we obtained were extremely clear cut (Figure 1.6). IRT turned out to be an extremely reliable and sensitive measure, tightly correlated with objective RT in a single-task context and sensitive to factors (i.e., notation) affecting response time by less than 50 ms. In a psychological refractory period task, however, the objective processing delay resulting from interference with a second concurrent task was totally absent from introspective estimates. That is, during the interference regime, the participants were totally unaware that their responses to the second task had been slowed by as much as 300 ms (Figure 1.6). Thus, awareness and accessibility to introspection seemed to be tightly linked to the availability of the central decision system—when this system was free, all stages of a cognitive task contributed to introspective response time, but when it was occupied by another task, participants were no longer aware of the duration of the perceptual and queuing stages of the PRP task.

DISCUSSION: COGNITIVE ARCHITECTURE OF THE NEVER-HALTING MACHINE

Several cognitive theories shared the hypothesis that while most mental and neural operations are modular, certain specific controlled processes require a distinct functional architecture that can establish flexible links among existing processors. This process has been called the central executive (Baddeley, 1986), the supervisory attentional system (Shallice, 1988), the anterior attention system (Posner, 1994), the capacity limited stage (Chun & Potter, 1995), the global workspace (Baars, 1989; Dehaene, Kerszberg, & Changeux, 1998), or the dynamic core (Tononi & Edelman, 1998). Yet in all of these different versions, it shares three critical aspects: (1) binding of information from many different modules; (2) uniqueness of its contents; and (3) sustained activity for a few hundred milliseconds. These aspects are also characteristic of consciousness and thus it has been proposed that engagement of the central system may be a requirement for conscious processing (Baars, 1989; Dehaene & Naccache, 2001; Tononi & Edelman, 1998). It is proposed, in a two-stage model, that an early stage permits the rapid, initial evaluation of the visual world. Only during a second, capacity-limited stage, does information become conscious when the neural population that represents it is mobilized into a brain-scale state of coherent activity that involves many neurons distributed throughout an extended network of the brain (Baars, 1989; Dehaene & Naccache, 2001; Tononi & Edelman, 1998).

Combining models from psychophysics and human physiology, we could disentangle the unfolding of processing stages during a compound cognitive task and relate this architecture of stages to their dynamic organization and stochasticity. The data converged to a model that proposes:

- an initial perceptual processing of incoming stimulus, which is performed in a modular (parallel) fashion and is very reliable in time, as indexed by the N1 latency of the event-related potential
- followed by a central process involved in the flexible coordination of information according to specific task requirements, which is intrinsically serial and involves a stochastic integration, as traditionally used to model decision making in single tasks, and as indexed by the P3 component of the ERP.

Our findings of the dynamics of T2 processing in the PRP fit well with the ERPs of other interference experiments such as the attentional-blink and masking experiments (Del Cul et al., 2007; Sergent et al., 2005). In these experiments it was found that the first ~270 ms, indexed by P1 and N1 components, were independent of conscious access and this was followed sequentially by a central distributed workspace, indexed by a P3 component, involving prefrontal and parietal network, which was engaged only in trials in which the stimulus accessed conscious processing.

These results have led to the proposal that the P3 component of the EEG may be related to access to a global coherent workspace associated with flexible coordination of information, which in turn may mediate conscious reportability (Del Cul et al., 2007; Sergent et al., 2005). According to this theory, a distributed set of neurons with long axons provides a global "broadcasting" system enabling communication between arbitrary and otherwise not directly connected brain processors (Baars, 1989; Dehaene et al., 1998; Dehaene & Naccache, 2001). Global neuronal workspace theory can explain why response selection generally imposes a dual-task bottleneck. In most psychological tasks, the relation between stimuli and responses is entirely arbitrary and thus requires the temporary mapping between otherwise independent processors. Establishing such a new arbitrary interconnection should involve central workspace mediation.

Supporting this interpretation, interference is drastically reduced for highly practiced or non-arbitrary tasks (Greenwald, 2003; Lien, McCann, Ruthruff, & Proctor, 2005; Lien, Proctor, & Allen, 2002). More evidence for the existence of a common global workspace involved in conscious processing and in the executive and flexible coordination of processing modules results from behavioral experiments that have combined the basic features of different manifestations of central processing such as the PRP (two rapid responses) or the attentional blink (extinction of a second rapidly presented stimulus). These experiments suggest that processing limitations may arise in part from a common bottleneck (Jolicoeur, 1999;

Marois & Ivanoff, 2005; Wong, 2002). Finally, our observation that the objective processing delay resulting from interference with a second concurrent task is totally absent from introspective estimates further suggests that subjective introspection of time spent on a task tightly correlates with the period of availability of global workspace activity (Corallo, Sackur, Dehaene, & Sigman, 2008).

Simply to illustrate these ideas, we provide a basic sketch of the postulated brain dynamics during the blink and the PRP (Figure 1.7). In both experimental designs, certain aspects of T2 processing—indexed by the N1 and mediated by a transient activation of sensory cortex—can proceed while T1 is engaged in a broad and coherent state of processing occupying the central workspace. While the nature of this sensory memory of T2 is not fully understood and requires theoretical and experimental investigation (Gegenfurtner & Sperling, 1993; Graziano & Sigman, 2008; Sperling, 1960), it appears to constitute a labile form of memory that can be overridden by the presence of a mask, consistent with current theories and experimental evidence of masking by object substitution (Del Cul et al., 2007; Di Lollo, Enns, & Rensink, 2000). The presence of a mask after

ATTENTIONAL BLINK
- T2 is masked, resulting in extinction.
- The second stimulus does not access consciousness.

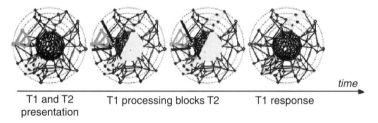

time

| T1 and T2 presentation | T1 processing blocks T2 | T1 response |

PSYCHOLOGICAL REFRACTORY PERIOD
- T2 is sustained and thus can access the workspace after a delay.
- This delay is inaccessible to introspection.

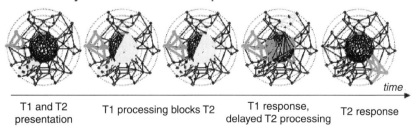

time

| T1 and T2 presentation | T1 processing blocks T2 | T1 response, delayed T2 processing | T2 response |

Figure 1.7 A simple sketch of the dynamics of modular and workspace processing during the PRP and the attentional blink. See color plate.

T2 can thus lead to the attentional blink (AB) phenomenon, whereby participants fail to detect the presence of T2 although it demonstrably caused a strong initial perceptual activation. In the absence of masking, T2 can access the workspace and T2 is therefore processed with the delay observed as the PRP phenomenon. AB and PRP are therefore envisaged as two very similar phenomena, arising from the same constraints of parallel-serial architecture.

While there are no direct correlates of these findings in single-cell awake monkey physiology (there is currently no demonstration of the PRP in non-human primates), some chronometric aspects can be related to the dynamics of neuronal activation in single task. The neurophysiological bases of simple perceptual decision making have been widely studied in tactile (Hernandez, Zainos, & Romo, 2002; Romo, Hernandez, & Zainos, 2004; Romo & Salinas, 1999) and visual discrimination tasks (Bichot, Schall, & Thompson, 1996; Britten, Newsome, Shadlen, Celebrini, & Movshon, 1996; Britten, Shadlen, Newsome, & Movshon, 1992; Hanes & Schall, 1996; Schall & Bichot, 1998; Shadlen & Newsome, 2001; Thompson, Bichot, & Schall, 1997; Thompson, Hanes, Bichot, & Schall, 1996). These studies have revealed direct physiological correlates of the accumulation process postulated in formal response-time models. Some neurons appear to code for the current perceptual state. For instance, neurons in the middle temporal visual area (MT) appear to encode the amount of evidence for motion in a certain direction (Britten et al., 1992; Shadlen & Newsome, 1996). Other neurons, distributed in multiple areas, including posterior parietal cortex, dorsolateral prefrontal cortex, and frontal eye fields, appear to integrate this sensory information and thus show stochastically increasing firing rates in the course of decision making (Kim & Shadlen, 1999; Shadlen & Newsome, 1996, 2001). In agreement with the accumulation model of decision making, the rate of increase varies with the quality of sensory evidence (Mazurek, Roitman, Ditterich, & Shadlen, 2003; Shadlen & Newsome, 1996, 2001), and the response is emitted when the firing exceeds a threshold (Hanes & Schall, 1996). Furthermore, accumulation of information about the upcoming response appears in the firing train after a latency of about 200 ms (Gold & Shadlen, 2000; Roitman & Shadlen, 2002), which is relatively fixed for a given task and might thus index the duration of the initial perceptual stage.

Further evidence of such a dynamic arrangement comes from recordings from the primary visual cortex of awake monkeys, which have shown that a visual stimulus evokes a first transient response, followed by a sustained wave of activity (Lamme & Roelfsema, 2000; Lamme, Super, Landman, Roelfsema, & Spekreijse, 2000; Lee, Yang, Romero, & Mumford, 2002; Li, Piech, & Gilbert, 2006, 2008; Luck, Chelazzi, Hillyard, & Desimone, 1997; Reynolds, Chelazzi, & Desimone, 1999;

Roelfsema, Lamme, & Spekreijse, 1998; Roelfsema, Lamme, Spekreijse, & Bosch, 2002) at a latency of about 200 ms, nicely coincident with the latency of integration in parietal and prefrontal areas and of the engagement of the P3 process. These two responses have very different functional dependencies: The first transient response is largely determined by stimulus properties and can be explained by classical bottom-up receptive field properties. On the contrary, the second response can be modulated by different cognitive and contextual factors. For instance, it is amplified if the local stimulus is salient and attended (as in figure–ground experiments) and it can virtually disappear if the stimulus is masked (which presumably precludes its access to consciousness) or by anesthetics. This specificity suggests an engagement of the central workspace system in the second wave of activity and that the same neuron may be involved in distinct processing stages within the same task. Further experiments are required to determine whether this second wave of activity shows a dual-task delay characteristic of the serial processing bottleneck.

Altogether, neurophysiological and brain-imaging studies suggest that, beyond an initial and relatively reliable perceptual delay of about 200 ms, a decision stage begins that involves a process of stochastic accumulation of evidence and the joint activation of a distributed network of areas, with partially changing topography as a function of the nature of the task, but with frequent if not systematic co-activation of parietal and premotor regions. Our results suggest that this accumulation system is slow (which might be required to flexibly combine information in different sensory, mnemonic, and motor modalities), is variable (probably due to an active, dynamic reverberating and integrating state), and is responsible for establishing the PRP bottleneck. Thus, while certain neural computations (probably mediated by hard-wired circuits confined to small portions of sensory space) can be very fast, precise, and parallel, linking such information together in a coherent workspace results in a slow, variable, and intrinsically sequential computation.

The challenge for the next few years will be to understand which precise biophysical mechanisms are involved in this coherent workspace and why they result in such dynamic and architectonically distinctive properties. At present, our results simply suggest that this bottleneck might occur because the cerebral accumulation system is broadly distributed and largely shared across tasks, and thus must be entirely "mobilized", at any given moment, by whichever task is currently performed. Considerable research has examined the neurophysiology of a single cognitive operation, but much less is known on how we chain these basic operations into complex tasks. The results described here constitute a first step toward a progressive understanding of the chaining of simple computations into complex compound tasks.

REFERENCES

Allport, D., Styles, E., & Hsieh, S. (1994). Shifting intentional set: Exploring the dynamic control of tasks. In C. Umilta & M. Moscovitch (Eds.), *Attention and performance XV* (pp. 421–452). Cambridge, MA: MIT Press.

Arnell, K. M., & Duncan, J. (2002). Separate and shared sources of dual-task cost in stimulus identification and response selection. *Cognitive Psychology*, *44*, 105–147.

Arnell, K. M., Helion, A. M., Hurdelbrink, J. A., & Pasieka, B. (2004). Dissociating sources of dual-task interference using human electrophysiology. *Psychonomic Bulletin & Review*, *11*, 77–83.

Ashbridge, E., Walsh, V., & Cowey, A. (1997). Temporal aspects of visual search studied by transcranial magnetic stimulation. *Neuropsychologia*, *35*, 1121–1131.

Baars, B. J. (1989). *A cognitive theory of consciousness*. Cambridge: Cambridge University Press.

Baddeley, A. D. (1986). *Working memory*. Oxford: Clarendon Press.

Bellgowan, P. S., Saad, Z. S., & Bandettini, P. A. (2003). Understanding neural system dynamics through task modulation and measurement of functional MRI amplitude, latency, and width. *Proceedings of the National Academy of Sciences USA*, *100*, 1415–1419.

Bichot, N. P., Schall, J. D., & Thompson, K. G. (1996). Visual feature selectivity in frontal eye fields induced by experience in mature macaques. *Nature*, *381*, 697–699.

Brisson, B., & Jolicoeur, P. (2007a). Cross-modal multitasking processing deficits prior to the central bottleneck revealed by event-related potentials. *Neuropsychologia*, *45*, 3038–3053.

Brisson, B., & Jolicoeur, P. (2007b). A psychological refractory period in access to visual short-term memory and the deployment of visual-spatial attention: Multitasking processing deficits revealed by event-related potentials. *Psychophysiology*, *44*, 323–333.

Brisson, B., Robitaille, N., & Jolicoeur, P. (2007). Stimulus intensity affects the latency but not the amplitude of the N2pc. *Neuroreport*, *18*, 1627–1630.

Britten, K. H., Newsome, W. T., Shadlen, M. N., Celebrini, S., & Movshon, J. A. (1996). A relationship between behavioral choice and the visual responses of neurons in macaque MT. *Visual Neuroscience*, *13*, 87–100.

Britten, K. H., Shadlen, M. N., Newsome, W. T., & Movshon, J. A. (1992). The analysis of visual motion: A comparison of neuronal and psychophysical performance. *Journal of Neuroscience*, *12*, 4745–4765.

Bryant, H. L., & Segundo, J. P. (1976). Spike initiation by transmembrane current: A white-noise analysis. *Journal of Physiology*, *260*, 279–314.

Bundesen, C. (1990). A theory of visual attention. *Psychological Review*, *97*, 523–547.

Butts, D. A., Weng, C., Jin, J., Yeh, C. I., Lesica, N. A., Alonso, J. M. et al. (2007). Temporal precision in the neural code and the timescales of natural vision. *Nature*, *449*, 92–95.

Cecchi, G. A., Sigman, M., Alonso, J. M., Martinez, L., & Chialvo, D. (2000). Noise in neurons is message dependent. *Proceedings of the National Academy of Sciences USA*, *97*, 5557–5561.

Chun, M. M., & Potter, M. C. (1995). A two-stage model for multiple target detection in rapid serial visual presentation. *Journal of Experimental Psychology: Human Perception and Performance, 21*, 109–127.

Corallo, G., Sackur, J., Dehaene, S., & Sigman, M. (2008). Limits on introspection: Distorted subjective time during the dual-task bottleneck. *Psychological Science, 19*, 1110–1117.

De Jong, R. (1993). Multiple bottlenecks in overlapping task performance. *Journal of Experimental Psychology: Human Perception and Performance, 19*, 965–980.

De Jong, R. (1995). The role of preparation in overlapping-task performance. *Quarterly Journal of Experimental Psychology: A, 48*, 2–25.

de Ruyter van Steveninck, R. R., Lewen, G. D., Strong, S. P., Koberle, R., & Bialek, W. (1997). Reproducibility and variability in neural spike train. *Science, 275*, 1805–1808.

Dehaene, S. (1996). The organization of brain activation in number comparison: Event-related potential and the additive-factor methods. *Journal of Cognitive Neuroscience, 8*, 47–68.

Dehaene, S., Kerszberg, M., & Changeux, J. P. (1998). A neuronal model of a global workspace in effortful cognitive tasks. *Proceedings of the National Academy of Sciences USA, 95*, 14529–14534.

Dehaene, S., & Naccache, L. (2001). Towards a cognitive neuroscience of consciousness: Basic evidence and a workspace framework. *Cognition, 79*, 1–37.

Del Cul, A., Baillet, S., & Dehaene, S. (2007). Brain dynamics underlying the nonlinear threshold for access to consciousness. *PLoS Biology, 5*, e260.

Dell'acqua, R., Jolicoeur, P., Vespignani, F., & Toffanin, P. (2005). Central processing overlap modulates P3 latency. *Experimental Brain Research, 165*, 54–68.

Di Lollo, V., Enns, J. T., & Rensink, R. A. (2000). Competition for consciousness among visual events: The psychophysics of reentrant visual processes. *Journal of Experimental Psychology: General, 129*, 481–507.

Duncan, J., & Owen, A. M. (2000). Common regions of the human frontal lobe recruited by diverse cognitive demands. *Trends in Neurosciences, 23*, 475–483.

Dux, P. E., Ivanoff, J., Asplund, C. L., & Marois, R. (2006). Isolation of a central bottleneck of information processing with time-resolved fMRI. *Neuron, 52*, 1109–1120.

Felleman, D. J., & Van Essen, D. C. (1991). Distributed hierarchical processing in the primate cerebral cortex. *Cerebral Cortex 1*, 1–47.

Formisano, E., & Goebel, R. (2003). Tracking cognitive processes with functional MRI mental chronometry. *Current Opinion in Neurobiology, 13*, 174–181.

Gegenfurtner, K. R., & Sperling, G. (1993). Information transfer in iconic memory experiments. *Journal of Experimental Psychology: Human Perception and Performance, 19*, 845–866.

Gilbert, C. D., & Sigman, M. (2007). Brain states: Top-down influences in sensory processing. *Neuron, 54*, 677–696.

Gold, J. I., & Shadlen, M. N. (2000). Representation of a perceptual decision in developing oculomotor commands. *Nature, 404*, 390–394.

Gold, J. I., & Shadlen, M. N. (2001). Neural computations that underlie decisions about sensory stimuli. *Trends in Cognitive Sciences, 5*, 10–16.

Graziano, M., & Sigman, M. (2008). The dynamics of sensory buffers: Geometric, spatial and experience dependent shaping of iconic memory. *Journal of Vision, 8*, 1–13.

Greenwald, A. G. (2003). On doing two things at once: III. Confirmation of perfect timesharing when simultaneous tasks are ideomotor compatible. *Journal of Experimental Psychology: Human Perception and Performance, 29*, 859–868.

Gur, M., Beylin, A., & Snodderly, D. M. (1997). Response variability of neurons in primary visual cortex (V1) of alert monkeys. *Journal of Neuroscience, 17*, 2914–2920.

Hanes, D. P., & Schall, J. D. (1996). Neural control of voluntary movement initiation. *Science, 274*, 427–430.

Hart, J. T. (1965). Memory and the feeling-of-knowing experience. *Journal of Educational Psychology, 56*, 208–216.

Hernandez, A., Zainos, A., & Romo, R. (2002). Temporal evolution of a decision-making process in medial premotor cortex. *Neuron, 33*, 959–972.

Hubel, D. H., & Wiesel, T. N. (1959). Receptive fields of single neurones in the cat's striate cortex. *Journal of Physiology, 148*, 574–591.

Hubel, D. H., & Wiesel, T. N. (1965). Receptive fields and functional architecture in two nonstriate visual areas (18 and 19) of the cat. *Journal of Neurophysiology, 28*, 229–289.

Hubel, D. H., & Wiesel, T. N. (1968). Receptive fields and functional architecture of monkey striate cortex. *Journal of Physiology, 148*, 574–591.

Jack, A. I., & Roepstrorff, A. (2003). Trusting the subject I. *Journal of Consciousness Studies, 9*, 9–10.

Jack, A. I., & Roepstrorff, A. (2004). Trusting the subject II. *Journal of Consciousness Studies, 11*, 7–8.

Jentzsch, I., Leuthold, H., & Ulrich, R. (2007). Decomposing sources of response slowing in the PRP paradigm. *Journal of Experimental Psychology: Human Perception and Performance, 33*, 610–626.

Jiang, Y., Saxe, R., & Kanwisher, N. (2004). Functional magnetic resonance imaging provides new constraints on theories of the psychological refractory period. *Psychological Science, 15*, 390–396.

Jolicoeur, P. (1999). Concurrent response-selection demands modulate the attentional blink. *Journal of Experimental Psychology: Human Perception and Performance, 25*, 1097–1113.

Kahneman, D. (1973). *Attention and effort.* Englewood Cliffs, NJ: Prentice-Hall.

Kamienkowski, J. E. & Sigman, M. (2008). Delays without mistakes: Response time and error distributions in dual-task. *PLoS ONE, 3*, e-3196.

Kara, P., Reinagel, P., & Reid, R. C. (2000). Low response variability in simultaneously recorded retinal, thalamic, and cortical neurons. *Neuron, 27*, 635–646.

Kim, J. N., & Shadlen, M. N. (1999). Neural correlates of a decision in the dorsolateral prefrontal cortex of the macaque. *Nature Neuroscience, 2*, 176–185.

Kim, S. G., Richter, W., & Ugurbil, K. (1997). Limitations of temporal resolution in functional MRI. *Magnetic Resonance in Medicine, 37*, 631–636.

Koechlin, E., & Jubault, T. (2006). Broca's area and the hierarchical organization of human behavior. *Neuron, 50*, 963–974.

Koechlin, E., Ody, C., & Kouneiher, F. (2003). The architecture of cognitive control in the human prefrontal cortex. *Science, 302,* 1181–1185.

Lamme, V. A., & Roelfsema, P. R. (2000). The distinct modes of vision offered by feedforward and recurrent processing. *Trends in Neurosciences, 23,* 571–579.

Lamme, V. A., Super, H., Landman, R., Roelfsema, P. R., & Spekreijse, H. (2000). The role of primary visual cortex (V1) in visual awareness. *Vision Research, 40,* 1507–1521.

Lee, T. S., Yang, C. F., Romero, R. D., & Mumford, D. (2002). Neural activity in early visual cortex reflects behavioral experience and higher-order perceptual saliency. *Nature Neuroscience, 5,* 589–597.

Li, W., Piech, V., & Gilbert, C. D. (2006). Contour saliency in primary visual cortex. *Neuron, 50,* 951–962.

Li, W., Piech, V., & Gilbert, C. D. (2008). Learning to link visual contours. *Neuron, 57,* 442–451.

Lien, M. C., McCann, R. S., Ruthruff, E., & Proctor, R. W. (2005). Dual-task performance with ideomotor-compatible tasks: Is the central processing bottleneck intact, bypassed, or shifted in locus? *Journal of Experimental Psychology: Human Perception and Performance, 31,* 122–144.

Lien, M. C., Proctor, R. W., & Allen, P. A. (2002). Ideomotor compatibility in the psychological refractory period effect: 29 years of oversimplification. *Journal of Experimental Psychology: Human Perception and Performance, 28,* 396–409.

Link, S. W., & Heath, R. A. (1975). A sequential theory of psychological discrimination. *Psychometrika, 40,* 77–111.

Logan, G. D., & Gordon, R. (2001). Executive control of visual attention in dual tasks. *Psychological Review, 108,* 393–434.

Luce, R. D. (1986). *Response times.* New York: Oxford University Press.

Luck, S. J. (1998). Sources of dual-task interference: Evidence from human electrophysiology. *Psychological Science, 9,* 223–227.

Luck, S. J., Chelazzi, L., Hillyard, S. A., & Desimone, R. (1997). Neural mechanisms of spatial selective attention in areas V1, V2 and V4 of macaque visual cortex. *Journal of Neurophysiology, 77,* 24–42.

Lutz, A., Lachaux, J. P., Martinerie, J., & Varela, F. J. (2002). Guiding the study of brain dynamics by using first-person data: Synchrony patterns correlate with ongoing conscious states during a simple visual task. *Proceedings of the National Academy of Sciences USA, 99,* 1586–1591.

Mainen, Z. F., & Sejnowski, T. J. (1995). Reliability of spike timing in neocortical neurons. *Science, 268,* 1503–1506.

Marois, R., Chun, M. M., & Gore, J. C. (2000). Neural correlates of the attentional blink. *Neuron, 28,* 299–308.

Marois, R., & Ivanoff, J. (2005). Capacity limits of information processing in the brain. *Trends in Cognitive Sciences, 9,* 296–305.

Mazurek, M. E., Roitman, J. D., Ditterich, J., & Shadlen, M. N. (2003). A role for neural integrators in perceptual decision making. *Cerebral Cortex, 13,* 1257–1269.

Meiran, N., Chorev, Z., & Sapir, A. (2000). Component processes in task switching. *Cognitive Psychology, 41,* 211–253.

Menon, R. S., Luknowsky, D. C., & Gati, J. S. (1998). Mental chronometry using latency-resolved functional MRI. *Proceedings of the National Academy of Sciences USA*, *95*, 10902–10907.

Meyer, D. E., & Kieras, D. E. (1997). A computational theory of executive cognitive processes and multiple-task performance: Part 1. Basic mechanisms. *Psychological Review*, *104*, 3–65.

Moyer, R. S., & Landauer, T. K. (1967). Time required for judgements of numerical inequalities. *Nature*, *215*, 1519–1520.

Nelson, T. O. (1996). Consciousness and metacognition. *American Psychologist*, *51*, 102–116.

Osman, A., & Moore, C. M. (1993). The locus of dual-task interference: Psychological refractory effects on movement-related brain potentials. *Journal of Experimental Psychology: Human Perception and Performance*, *19*, 1292–1312.

Overgaard, M. (2006). Introspection in science. *Consciousness and Cognition*, *15*, 629–633.

Pashler, H. (1984). Processing stages in overlapping tasks: Evidence for a central bottleneck. *Journal of Experimental Psychology: Human Perception and Performance*, *10*, 358–377.

Pashler, H. (1994). Dual-task interference in simple tasks: Data and theory. *Psychological Bulletin*, *116*, 220–244.

Pashler, H., & Johnston, J. C. (1989). Chronometric evidence for central postponement in temporally overlapping tasks. *Quarterly Journal of Experimental Psychology*, *41A*, 19–45.

Pashler, H., & Johnston, J. C. (1998). Attentional limitations in dual-task performance. In H. Pashler (Ed.), *Attention* (pp. 155–189). Hove: Psychology Press/Erlbaum.

Pinel, P., Dehaene, S., Riviere, D., & LeBihan, D. (2001). Modulation of parietal activation by semantic distance in a number comparison task. *Neuroimage*, *14*, 1013–1026.

Posner, M. I. (1994). Attention: The mechanisms of consciousness. *Proceedings of the National Academy of Sciences USA*, *91*, 7398–7403.

Posner, M. I., Snyder, C. R., & Davidson, B. J. (1980). Attention and the detection of signals. *Journal of Experimental Psychology*, *109*, 160–174.

Ratcliff, R. (1988). Continuous versus discrete information processing modeling accumulation of partial information. *Psychological Review*, *95*, 238–255.

Reynolds, J. H., Chelazzi, L., & Desimone, R. (1999). Competitve mechanisms subserve attention in macaque areas V2 and V4. *Journal of Neuroscience*, *19*, 1736–1753.

Roelfsema, P. R., Lamme, V. A. F., & Spekreijse, H. (1998). Object-based attention in the primary visual cortex of the macaque monkey. *Nature*, *395*, 376–381.

Roelfsema, P. R., Lamme, V. A., Spekreijse, H., & Bosch, H. (2002). Figure–ground segregation in a recurrent network architecture. *Journal of Cognitive Neuroscience*, *14*, 525–537.

Roitman, J. D., & Shadlen, M. N. (2002). Response of neurons in the lateral intraparietal area during a combined visual discrimination reaction time task. *Journal of Neuroscience*, *22*, 9475–9489.

Romo, R., Hernandez, A., & Zainos, A. (2004). Neuronal correlates of a perceptual decision in ventral premotor cortex. *Neuron*, *41*, 165–173.

Romo, R., & Salinas, E. (1999). Sensing and deciding in the somatosensory system. *Current Opinion in Neurobiology, 9*, 487–493.

Ruthruff, E., Pashler, H. E., & Klaassen, A. (2001). Processing bottlenecks in dual-task performance: Structural limitation or strategic postponement? *Psychonomic Bulletin and Review, 8*, 73–80.

Schall, J. D. (2000). From sensory evidence to a motor command. *Current Biology, 10*, R404–406.

Schall, J. D., & Bichot, N. P. (1998). Neural correlates of visual and motor decision processes. *Current Opinion in Neurobiology, 8*, 211–217.

Schwarz, W. (2001). The ex-Wald distribution as a descriptive model of response times. *Behavior Research Methods, Instruments & Computers, 33*, 457–469.

Schweickert, R. (1980). Critical-path scheduling of mental processes in a dual task. *Science, 209*, 704–706.

Schweickert, R., & Townsend, J. T. (1989). Trichotomy: Interactions of factors prolonging sequential and concurrent mental processes in stochastic discrete mental (PERT) networks. *Journal of Mathematical Psychology, 33*, 328–347.

Sergent, C., Baillet, S., & Dehaene, S. (2005). Timing of the brain events underlying access to consciousness during the attentional blink. *Nature Neuroscience, 8*, 1391–1400.

Sessa, P., Luria, R., Verleger, R., & Dell'Acqua, R. (2007). P3 latency shifts in the attentional blink: Further evidence for second target processing postponement. *Brain Research, 1137*, 131–139.

Shadlen, M. N., & Newsome, W. T. (1996). Motion perception: Seeing and deciding. *Proceedings of the National Academy of Sciences USA, 93*, 628–633.

Shadlen, M. N., & Newsome, W. T. (2001). Neural basis of a perceptual decision in the parietal cortex (area LIP) of the rhesus monkey. *Journal of Neurophysiology, 86*, 1916–1936.

Shallice, T. (1988). *From neuropsychology to mental structure.* Cambridge: Cambridge University Press.

Shepard, R. N., & Metzler, J. (1971). Mental rotation of three-dimensional objects. *Science, 171*, 701–703.

Sigman, M., & Dehaene, S. (2005). Parsing a cognitive task: A characterization of the mind's bottleneck. *PLoS Biology, 3*, e37.

Sigman, M., & Dehaene, S. (2006). Dynamics of the central bottleneck: Dual-task and task uncertainty. *PLoS Biology, 4*, e220.

Sigman, M., & Dehaene, S. (2008). Brain mechanisms of serial and parallel processing during dual-task performance. *Journal of Neuroscience, 28*, 7585–7598.

Sigman, M., Jobert, A., Lebihan, D., & Dehaene, S. (2007). Parsing a sequence of brain activations at psychological times using fMRI. *Neuroimage, 35*, 655–668.

Smith, M. C. (1967). Theories of the psychological refractory period. *Psychological Bulletin, 67*, 202–213.

Sperling, G. (1960). The information available in brief visual presentations. *Psychological Monographs: General and Applied, 74*, 1–29.

Sternberg, S. (1969). The discovery of processing stages: Extension of Donders' method. *Acta Psychologica, 30*, 276–315.

Sternberg, S. (2004). Separate modifiability and the search for processing modules.

In N. Kanwisher & J. Duncan (Eds.), *Attention and performance XX* (pp. 125–142). Oxford: Oxford University Press.

Telford, C. W. (1931). The refractory phase of voluntary and associative responses. *Journal of Experimental Psychology*, *14*, 1–36.

Thompson, K. G., Bichot, N. P., & Schall, J. D. (1997). Dissociation of visual discrimination from saccade programming in macaque frontal eye field. *Journal of Neurophysiology*, *77*, 1046–1050.

Thompson, K. G., Hanes, D. P., Bichot, N. P., & Schall, J. D. (1996). Perceptual and motor processing stages identified in the activity of macaque frontal eye field neurons during visual search. *Journal of Neurophysiology*, *76*, 4040–4055.

Thorpe, S., Fize, D., & Marlot, C. (1996). Speed of processing in the visual system. *Nature*, *381*, 520–522.

Tononi, G., & Edelman, G. M. (1998). Consciousness and complexity. *Science*, *282*, 1846–1851.

Usher, M., & McClelland, J. L. (2001). The time course of perceptual choice: The leaky, competing accumulator model. *Psychological Review*, *108*, 550–592.

Van Essen, D. C., Anderson, C. H., & Felleman, D. J. (1992). Information processing in the primate visual system: An integrated systems perspective. *Science*, *255*, 419–423.

Van Selst, M., & Jolicoeur, P. (1994). A solution to the effect of sample size on outlier elimination. *The Quarterly Journal of Experimental Psychology Section A: Human Experimental Psychology*, *4*, 631–650.

Vickers, D. (1970). Evidence for an accumulator model of psychophysical discrimination. *Ergonomics*, *13*, 37–58.

Wagenmakers, E., & Scott, B. (2007). On the linear relation between the mean and the standard deviation of a response time distribution. *Psychological Review*, *114*, 830–841.

Wong, K. F. E. (2002). The relationship between attentional blink and psychological refractory period. *Journal of Experimental Psychology: Human Perception and Performance*, *28*, 54–71.

Wundt, W. M. (1897/1999). *Outlines of psychology*. Bristol: Thoemmes Press.

CHAPTER TWO

Frames, brains, and content domains: Neural and behavioral effects of descriptive context on preferential choice

David R. Mandel and Oshin Vartanian

INTRODUCTION

At 7:51 am on Friday, January 12, 2007, a man wearing jeans, a long-sleeve T-shirt, and a Washington Nationals baseball cap began to play his violin at the L'Enfant Plaza metro station in Washington DC. Over the next 43 minutes, 1097 people passed him by. Among them, only seven stopped to listen for at least a minute. Twenty-seven gave him money, most without breaking their pace, for a grand total of $32 and change. Only one person, who gave the man $20—more than half of what he earned—realized that the "fiddler" was Joshua Bell, one of the world's most celebrated musicians, who had just played six timeless pieces of music on a violin handcrafted by Stradivari in 1713 and worth an estimated US$3.5 million. Two days earlier, Bell had performed at a theater in Boston where merely "pretty good" seats sold for $100. This study, organized by *The Washington Post* (Weingarten, 2007), poignantly illustrates the importance of context on subjective valuation. As Weingarten put it, "He [Bell] was, in short, art without a frame." The Bell demonstration, of course, was not designed to carefully disentangle the possible causal determinants of people's ostensible indifference toward beauty in a mundane environment, but rather to conjure in our minds the idea that, in two disparate contexts, the *same* man playing the *same* music on the *same* exquisite instrument could be valued and treated so differently.

The argument that context matters hence presupposes that there are certain fundamental similarities to the contrasted events in question that do not change and, moreover, that the attributes that do change are in some sense more superficial than the invariants—sufficiently superficial as not to invalidate the comparison. As we shall see, this notion is fundamental to decision research on the effects of framing and content on judgment and choice. Those features we regard as central and invariant form the so-called *deep structure* of an event or problem, whereas those that reflect peripheral or circumstantial features form the so-called *surface structure* (Wagenaar, Keren, & Lichtenstein, 1988). The fact that context does matter is therefore of interest precisely because, for so long, decision theorists had presupposed that it should and would not matter. In this chapter, we extend earlier discussions of this topic both from an analytic perspective and from an empirical perspective, which in the latter case we do by introducing recent behavioral and neuroscientific findings on the effect of two types of contextual factors—namely, framing and content—on judgment and decision making.

Our focus on context is closely related to earlier discussions of content effects on decision making (e.g., Goldstein & Weber, 1997; Rettinger & Hastie, 2001; Wagenaar et al., 1988), but is broader in the sense that it permits discussion of other effects, such as framing, which we do not, strictly speaking, regard as content effects (cf. Goldstein & Weber, 1997). Our focus also reflects a slightly different centering of intellectual priorities. That is, discussions of content effects in the decision-making literature arise primarily in response to the domain-independent view of decision making captured by early ideas and theories about decision making that had largely set the course for later empirical studies (e.g., Bernoulli, 1738/1954; Savage, 1954; von Neumann & Morgenstern, 1947). In the classical view, all decisions could essentially be represented by a gambling metaphor with only two pertinent variables degrees of value and degrees of belief—whose product expressed the (subjective) expected utility (or worth) of the gamble. The currency of the gamble (e.g., money earned, lives saved, territory acquired, etc.) was believed to be of no particular consequence, at least not in terms of affecting the process by which decisions were made (Goldstein & Weber, 1997). In other words, the semantic content of a decision-making problem was treated as immaterial. Theoretical discussions of the importance of content in decision-making problems have thus focused on the incompleteness of the classical view, which given its tenets could not account for more recently revealed content effects.

Our interest in context in contradistinction to content *per se* focuses largely on the discriminative judgment process required to assign certain aspects of a problem or event to its deep structure and other aspects to its surface structure. Within this discussion we treat content effects as an example of the context-dependent nature of judgment and decision making, but it is important to clearly articulate the sense in which we consider variations in content as an example of contextual change. *The New Oxford Dictionary of English* defines *context* as "the circumstances that form the setting for an event, statement, or idea, and in terms of which it can be fully understood and assessed" (2001, p. 396). According to this definition, contextual factors are circumstantial. At first blush, then, one might wonder why the content of a problem would be treated as a contextual factor since it is by no means evident that the former is merely a circumstantial factor. Indeed, the content might seem to constitute a central part of what any given problem is about. For instance, a decision about how to save 600 lives at stake might seem fundamentally (and not merely circumstantially) different from a decision about how to save $600 at risk of being lost. Indeed, one might, quite reasonably, claim that a comparison of the two problems is a classic case of comparing apples with oranges.

To understand why content variations such as these may be regarded as instances of contextual variation, we must on the one hand consider the distinction between deep and surface features and on the other hand consider the theoretical tenets of the domain-independent view of decision making articulated by the classical theorists. As noted earlier, such theorists viewed all decision problems as reducible to gambles whose currency represents a surface feature of the problem. From this theoretical perspective, content variations *are* circumstantial (i.e., contextual) precisely because they do not—indeed, could not within those theoretical frames— alter the deep-structure representation of the problem. That is, from the perspective of classical decision theory, if the abstract representation of a problem matches another, the comparison is indeed between apple and apple and not apple and orange. Thus, content effects are instances of context effects not in some absolute sense but rather in relation to a particular theoretical and representational vantage point—almost always defined by the researcher in behavioral decision research.

We shall return to a discussion of content effects on decision making later in the chapter. However, we first turn our attention to an "intermediate" type of context effect, *framing*, which refers to the manner in which options, acts, or outcomes are described. Like content effects, framing effects are precluded from playing a meaningful role in classical decision theories, but unlike content effects, they are predicted by Kahneman and Tversky's (1979) influential *prospect theory* to systematically influence decision making. The demonstration of framing effects on choice has played an important role in the debate over the rationality of human decision making, with evidence of such effects usually interpreted as indications that rational choice is quite predictably violated (Stanovich & West, 2000; Tversky & Kahneman, 1981). Although we do not dispute the claim that framing may sometimes have powerful influences on decision making, and that some of those influences may be difficult to justify as rational, we also believe that it is important to assess those claims carefully. An important part of that task brings us back to the question of how people—including theorists who study framing effects—discriminate deep versus surface structure in decision-making problems.

Finally, to orient the reader, we should note that both sections of the chapter that follow are bounded by two foci. First, we are concerned here with context effects that are descriptive in nature. The studies we review and consider involve manipulations of context that are embedded in linguistic descriptions. In some cases these descriptions pertain to the manner in which options are formulated, while in other cases they pertain to the cover story that establishes the domain in which the decision task "takes place". There are of course many other ways in which context could be manipulated, such as through changes to actual location (as in our opening example), changes to circumstantial aspects of auditory or visual stimuli, or manipulation of fortuitous "priming" stimuli that are either subliminal or supraliminal, but these topics remain beyond the scope of this chapter. Second, we are concerned here with the effect of context on decision making involving preferential choice under conditions of risk or uncertainty. Once again, there are other areas of research that could have been reviewed. For instance, there is a vast literature on the effect of content on reasoning (Evans, Newstead, & Byrne, 1993), which may alternatively be construed as decisions about the epistemic status of propositions. Our aim here, however, is to build more directly on past work on the effect of descriptive context on preferential or value-based choice (e.g., Goldstein & Weber, 1997; Rettinger & Hastie, 2001; Wagenaar et al., 1988), drawing on a discussion of recent neuroscientific research that sheds new light on the topic.

FRAMING EFFECTS AND PROSPECT THEORY: A FOOT IN THE DOOR FOR CONTEXT

Like its predecessors, prospect theory is currency neutral, making no positive predictions about potential content effects. However, unlike its predecessors, prospect theory does selectively open the door to context effects by making predictions about the effect of "decision frames" on choice. Tversky and Kahneman (1981) originally conceived of frames as being partly the result of how aspects of a decision problem are described and partly the result of how a decision maker mentally represents those aspects. For instance, optimists, by virtue of their disposition, tend to frame situations involving mixed outcomes (i.e., some good and some bad) as instances of the glass being half full, whereas pessimists would tend to see the same situations in terms of the glass being half empty. However, since dispositions are not subject to experimental manipulation, subsequent research focused on the manner in which information could alternatively be described. For instance, a food product consisting of 10% fat and 90% other non-fat ingredients could be described as "10% fat" or "90% fat-free". Although the descriptions change, the deep structure presumably does not. That is, both frames denote the same thing, and one should be able from either description to easily infer its counterpart. If you know that the food you are eating is 10% fat, you should also know that it is 90% fat free. One frame implies the other.

Rational theories of choice, which subsume the classical decision theories, do not permit surface features of problems, such as the way in which events are formulated, to influence choice. Indeed, the principle of descriptive invariance (Kahneman & Tversky, 1984) states that alternative formulations of the same events should be treated by decision makers in precisely the same manner if their decisions are to be regarded as internally consistent, coherent, or rational. While prospect theory did not challenge the normative status of the invariance principle, it did offer new predictions regarding how framing would systematically influence choices. An important basis for the prediction is the theory's assumption that the values of prospects (namely, options) are evaluated relative to subjective reference points. Positive changes from the reference point (e.g., current wealth) are coded as gains and negative ones as losses.

The theory further posits that subjective value is a concave function of currency value in the gains domain and a relatively steeper convex function of currency value in the losses domain, giving rise to the well-known S-shaped value function. An important implication of this proposed psychophysical function is that decision makers will tend toward risk-aversion in the gains domain and toward risk-seeking in the losses domain. For instance, it leads to the prediction that a $200 gain for sure should be favored more than a 1 in 3 chance of a $600 gain (people would prefer the sure thing), whereas a $200 loss would be disliked more than a 1 in 3 chance of a $600 loss. Moreover, in decision-making problems involving mixed outcomes—namely, those comprising a combination of gains and losses—the frame invoked is proposed to influence the reference point brought to mind in the decision maker.

To illustrate this prediction, consider Tversky and Kahneman's (1981) well-known Asian Disease Problem (ADP). Participants were presented with the following cover story:

> Imagine that the US is preparing for the outbreak of an unusual Asian disease, which is expected to kill 600 people. Two alternative programs to

combat the disease have been proposed. Assume that the exact scientific estimate of the consequences of the program are [sic] as follows . . .

In the gain-frame condition, participants were asked to choose between the following prospects:

If Program A is adopted, 200 people will be saved.
If Program B is adopted, there is a 1 in 3 probability 600 people will be saved, and 2 in 3 probability that no people will be saved.

In comparison, in the loss-frame condition, participants were asked to choose between the following prospects:

If Program C is adopted, 400 people will die.
If Program D is adopted, there is a 1 in 3 probability that nobody will die, and 2 in 3 probability that 600 people will die.

When the options were framed in terms of lives saved (i.e., gains), 72% chose the certain option (Program A). However, when the options were framed in terms of deaths (i.e., losses), 78% chose the risky option (Program D). Meta-analyses (Kühberger, 1998; Kühberger, Schulte-Mecklenbeck, & Perner, 1999) have indicated that Tversky and Kahneman's (1981) framing effect is greater in magnitude than the mean effect size across other ADP-type studies. Nevertheless, on average, the effect of framing is of moderate magnitude. The effect, therefore, is clearly replicable and, in that sense, "real".

According to Tversky and Kahneman, the alternative frames of the two prospects are like different visual perspectives of the same scene. In the case of the ADP, the gain frame is proposed to bring to mind a reference point of zero lives saved, from which the sure 200 is more attractive than the 1 in 3 chance of 600. In contrast, the loss frame is proposed to bring to mind a reference point of zero lives lost, from which a sure loss of 400 is more painful than a 2 in 3 chance of losing all 600.

Importantly, though, most theorists have accepted the argument that the deep structure of the problem is identical under the two framing conditions. Kahneman and Tversky (1984) in fact claimed that "it is easy to verify that options C and D in Problem 2 are undistinguishable in real terms from options A and B in Problem 1, respectively" and, hence, "the failure of invariance is both pervasive and robust" (p. 343). Although Tversky and Kahneman claimed that the descriptive equivalence of the two sets of options was easily verifiable, it is difficult to see how such verification could be offered. Indeed, no more than an appeal to the reader's intuition was ever offered. Nor does the empirical evidence indicate that people realize the extensional equivalence of the reframed options. Using an ADP isomorph, Mandel (2001) asked participants whether they agreed that the certain option implied the complementary expected outcome that Tversky and Kahneman (1981) proposed (e.g., whether 200 lives saved implied 400 lives lost). Roughly a third of the sample—36% for the certain option and 32% for the risky option—did not agree with this interpretation.

The descriptive equivalence assumption is also questionable because of an important confound in the experiment—namely, the certain option is always more ambiguous than the risky option it is paired with due to missing information (Kühberger, 1995; Mandel, 2001). With option A, there are 400 lives about which participants are told nothing; with option C, there are 200 such cases. In contrast, participants are informed of all possible outcomes and their associated probabilities in options B and D. A plausible effect of asymmetric ambiguity might be to increase the likelihood of interpreting the certain option to mean that *at least* 200 will be saved under the gain frame and *at least* 400 will die under the loss frame. Consistent with this hypothesis, Berkeley and Humphreys (1982) noted that option A seems to connote a much stronger sense of agency than option C, which would support the "at least" interpretation of the expected outcomes. Moreover, Macdonald (1986; see also Jou, Shanteau, & Harris, 1996) proposed that people tend to automatically qualify statements about numeric quantity with the modifiers "at least" or "or more".

If options A and C are interpreted as minimum values and options B and D are interpreted as precise values, then it would be utility maximizing—and quite rational by normative standards—to choose the certain option under the gain frame and the risky option under the loss frame. Two approaches have been used to examine this asymmetric-ambiguity account. First, Kühberger (1995) used an additive method in which the asymmetry in option ambiguity was eliminated by including the missing information in the certain options. Second, Mandel (2001) used a subtractive method in which the asymmetry was eliminated by deleting the second proposition from the risky options. Both investigators replicated the framing effect when the original descriptions of the options were used, but importantly both also demonstrated that the framing effect was eliminated when ambiguity across options was properly controlled.

Mandel (2009) recently conducted a more direct test in which the asymmetry in prospect ambiguity was systematically manipulated independent of gain–loss framing. Replicating Kühberger (1995), the framing effect predicted by prospect theory was found when the sure option was missing information, but eliminated when the missing information was provided (see Figure 2.1). Importantly, and contrary to the prediction of prospect theory, a reverse framing effect was found when—

contrary to the standard version of the ADP—the sure option had the missing information supplied and the risky option was missing information (see Figure 2.1). That is, in the reverse-asymmetry condition, participants in the gain-frame condition were presented with the prospects:

If Program A is adopted, 200 people will be saved and 400 people will not be saved.
If Program B is adopted, there is a 1 in 3 probability 600 people will be saved.

And, participants in the loss-frame condition were presented with the prospects:

If Program C is adopted, 400 people will die and 200 people will not die.
If Program D is adopted, there is a 2 in 3 probability that 600 people will die.

Under these conditions, participants were actually *more* risk-seeking in the gain-frame condition than in the loss-frame condition.

We propose that these findings support a conversational account of framing effects in which the missing information in the description of a prospect invites the interpretation "at least *N*" for quantities that are not set at the limit within the context of the problem. Thus, in the reversed-asymmetry condition, the risky option in the gain-frame condition may be read as "there is *at least* a 1 in 3 probability that 600 people will be saved", whereas the risky option in the loss-frame condition may be read as "there is *at least* a 2 in 3 probability that 600 people will die". We suspect that the conversational implicatures drawn represent attempts to resolve linguistic ambiguities in light of the available contextual cues and the representations they evoke, on the one hand, and knowledge of conversational norms, on the other hand.

In terms of the latter, it is normative to be brief and, of course, also to be relevant in communication (Grice, 1975). These injunctions or "maxims", as Grice called them, can sometime require tradeoffs and/or clever solutions that affect judgment and decision making (Hilton & Slugoski, 2000). For instance, if 200 lives saved implies 400 deaths too, it would be redundant to say both. The Gricean maxim of being brief would dictate truncation to one expression or the other (Reyna & Brainerd, 1991). However, given the uncertain context of the ADP (i.e., emergency response plans to deal with a forecasted epidemic), it might also add value to the communication to choose a frame that in some sense conveyed the anticipated direction or propensity of outcome as part of the subtext, and this would be in keeping with Grice's *principle of cooperation*, whereby

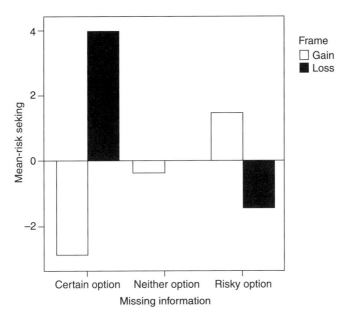

Figure 2.1   Mean risk-seeking as a function of frame and missing information. From Mandel (2009). Mean risk-seeking is calculated by coding preferences of the sure-thing option −1 and preferences of the risky option +1, and then multiplying these values by subjects' strength of preference judgments—namely, the extent to which they viewed their chosen alternative as superior to the non-chosen alternative.

interlocutors structure their utterances to be meaningful, relevant, yet concise. Choosing a gain frame might therefore subtly convey a trend toward saving lives or, as Berkeley and Humphreys (1982) put it, a greater sense of agency, while a loss frame might alternatively convey a trend toward losing lives and having little control. Thus, listeners might be inclined to treat the frame as nonarbitrary but rather chosen for its relevance, with gain framing signaling that *at least* the number specified would be saved, and with loss framing alternatively signaling that *at least* a certain number would die.

The conversational account thus acknowledges that the question of whether two descriptions are perceived as extensionally equivalent by decision makers is an empirical issue. Most research on framing has accepted the theorists' representation of the problem as valid and, moreover, has assumed that the subject's performance can be interpreted in relation to that representation as if it were his or her own. By comparison, our view is that in order to define an effect of description on judgment or choice as a strict framing effect (or what Kahneman & Tversky [1984] called *formulation effects*), it is incumbent on researchers to show that the subject regards the alternative descriptions as essentially the same. To the extent that the alternative descriptions are not regarded as such, then whatever effect may have been shown does not properly constitute an instance of framing and should not be described as such. One might still question the soundness of an individual's interpretation of the relevant statements. However, that is quite different from claiming that alternative frames can produce incoherence in judgment or choice, and the normative basis of such critiques would be considerably weaker.

The conversational account also implies that other contextual factors, such as content effects, will moderate the effect of alternative descriptions on judgment and choice because conversational implicatures will be drawn in light of such features, which serve as stimuli for constructing representations of events, acts, and contingencies under conditions of interpretational uncertainty. Consistent with Beach's (1990) image theory, we propose that these representations go beyond the mere initial editing of problem features as prospect theory proposes, and will usually trigger considerations of social norms, moral principles, and goals that are appropriate in light of these considerations. Indeed, Wagenaar et al. (1988) have shown that framing manipulations within decision-making problems having the same purported deep structure nevertheless elicit different effects that depend on a complex interaction of content, perspective, and action–inaction effects, for which prospect theory, like earlier psychophysical models based on the gambling metaphor, cannot account.

At present, there are no specific neuroscientific tests of the pragmatic account of framing that we advance here. However, there is much known about the neuroscience of language comprehension that can guide future research. For instance, considerable evidence demonstrates that the left hemisphere is sufficient for information processing when the task is symbolic and its relevant features are available for extraction. This has led Gazzaniga (1989, 2000) to propose his influential "left hemisphere interpreter" hypothesis, according to which the left hemisphere is viewed to be dominant for inference making. However, recent evidence suggests that the right hemisphere is engaged when the problem space is underdetermined, allowing for interpretational uncertainty (Goel, Stollstorff, Nakic, Knutson, & Grafman, 2009; Goel, Tierney, Sheesley, Bartolo, Vartanian, & Grafman, 2007). If the framing effect in ADP-type problems is a function of conversational implicatures, one might expect to find the right hemisphere playing an important role in this task. Specifically, on the basis of the research just cited, we would predict that deliberation in the ADP-type problems would result in more right hemisphere activation when the prospects were worded using Mandel's (2001) subtractive method in which there was missing information than using Kühberger's (1995) additive method in which the missing information was filled in for both prospects.

Moreover, we would predict that "framing effects" in ADP-type problems would be attenuated in persons with right hemispheric lesions that impede their ability to draw conversational implicatures.

An alternative hypothesis is suggested by Pylkkanen and McElree's (2007) magnetoencephalography (MEG) study, which found that coercing a meaning out of ambiguous sentences such as "The journalist *began* the article before his coffee break" activates the ventromedial prefrontal cortex (VMPFC), whereas doing so for less ambiguous sentences such as "The journalist *wrote* the article before his coffee break" does not activate this region. The VMPFC has been implicated in social cognition (Damasio & Van Hoesen, 1983; Gallagher & Frith, 2003), and Pylkkanen and McElree's (2007) findings suggest that resolution of ambiguity involving human agents activates this region. Thus, we might expect a similar pattern of activation in ADP-type problems where the prospects that imply some form of human agency are relatively ambiguous.

Although such neuroscientific hypothesis tests await future research, there has been one neuroscientific study that has directly examined the framing effect. De Martino, Kumaran, Seymour, and Dolan (2006) investigated the neural underpinnings of the framing effect using functional Magnetic Resonance Imaging (fMRI). In each task trial, subjects were shown a message indicating the amount of money that they would initially receive (e.g., "You receive £50"). Subjects then had to choose between a sure option and a risky option. In gain-frame trials, the sure option was formulated as the amount of money kept from the initial amount (e.g., keep £20), whereas in loss-frame trials, the sure option was formulated as the amount lost from the initial amount (e.g., lose £30). The risky option was always represented as a pie chart depicting a 40% chance of keeping the full amount and a 60% chance of losing the full amount.

Analysis of the behavioral results revealed that subjects were risk-averse in the gain frame and risk-seeking in the loss frame, as predicted by prospect theory. At the neural level, bilateral amygdala activation was significantly greater in trials where subjects made frame-congruent choices (i.e., choosing the sure option in the gain frame and the risky option in the loss frame) than in trials where they made frame-incongruent choices (i.e., choosing the risky option in the gain frame and the sure option in the loss frame). By contrast, frame-incongruent choices produced significantly greater activation in the anterior cingulate cortex (ACC). Finally, significant negative correlations were found between the degree to which subjects were susceptible to the framing effect and activation in the right orbitofrontal cortex (R-OFC) ($r = -0.8$) and also the VMPFC ($r = -0.75$).

Whereas the amygdala is involved in emotional processing and reward-related learning (LeDoux, 1996; see also O'Doherty, this volume; Pizzagalli, Dillon, Bogdan, & Holmes, this volume), the ACC is involved in cognitive conflict and error monitoring (Van Veen & Carter, 2006). As De Martino et al. (2006) propose (see also Kahneman & Frederick, 2007), the greater activation of the amygdala in frame-congruent choices and of the ACC in frame-incongruent choices indicates opponency between two neural systems. Specifically, their findings suggest that ACC activation on frame-incongruent choices reflects the detection of conflict between response tendencies based on an emotional system and an analytic system. The observed correlations between susceptibility to the framing effect and regions of the orbital and medial prefrontal cortex (OMPFC), but not the amygdala *per se*, further suggest that susceptibility to framing is not merely due to a more emotional response, but rather to how emotional cues provided by the amygdala are integrated into a mental representation of the alternatives. Furthermore, the OMPFC and amygdala are known to have strong reciprocal connections, with the former playing a key role in the representation of emotional stimuli necessary for the predictive value of outcomes to be properly assessed (Dolan, 2007). The notion that violations of normative principles such as descriptive invariance are attributable to activation of neural regions that play a role in the representation of value may lend support to recent cognitive accounts that emphasize the role of outcome representations in the manifestation of such biases (Mandel, 2008).

Of course, in light of our earlier discussion of the role of conversational implicature in the manifestation of framing effects, it is fair to ask whether the alternative frames in De Martino et al.'s (2006) study share the same deep structure. That is, did subjects understand the sure prospect in the gain frame to mean *precisely* £20 of the initial £50 would be kept and, conversely, did they understand that prospect in the loss frame to mean *precisely* £30 of the initial £50 would be lost? Notwithstanding the findings of past research that cast doubt on the equivalence of frames in ADP-type problems (e.g., Kühberger, 1995; Mandel, 2001, 2009), we suspected that in the context of De Martino et al.'s study the majority of subjects would regard these frames as equal in meaning. That is, they would interpret the quantities as exact values rather than minimum values (e.g., "*at least* £20 would be kept"). Unlike the ADP, the game-show-like context used in De Martino et al.'s study is consistent with drawing an implicature that the values are precise and under the full control of whoever is responsible for establishing the "game".

We put this hypothesis to the test, asking 21 subjects to choose an option in the gain frame and in the loss frame (with the order of frames counterbalanced across subjects). After each choice, we also asked subjects to indicate whether they thought the sure option (i.e., "Keep £20" or "Lose £30") meant (a) "keep/lose at least N", "keep/lose precisely N", or "keep/lose at most N". The two versions of the problem were presented on separate pages. As predicted, we found that 17 (81%) indicated "precisely" in both frames. We also found that 16 of these 17 subjects (94%) showed no framing effect. Specifically, 50% chose the sure option in both conditions and the other 50% chose the risky option in both conditions. These findings are consistent with the earlier conversational account we proposed and the findings of Mandel (2009), in particular. Of course, it is unclear why our findings and De Martino et al.'s differ. It is possible that the difference in the effect of framing across these two studies is owing to differences in characteristics of the samples. About half of our subjects had a graduate degree in the sciences, though none claimed to recognize the aim of the task.

Thus, it remains a lingering question whether De Martino et al.'s (2006) subjects who demonstrated a framing effect tended to interpret the values presented in the sure option as precise values or lower bounds. Answering this question is important in order to clarify the descriptive and prescriptive implications of their findings. For instance, if their subjects who exhibited a framing effect tended to interpret the value expressed in the sure option as a lower bound, then the activation of the amygdala would not be in response to merely descriptive attributes of mixed outcomes that are fundamentally the same but rather to the coding of distinct outcomes that do indeed vary in reward value (i.e., losing at least £30 is objectively worse than keeping at least £20). Moreover, "inconsistent" preferences under such circumstances would be quite rational—arguably more rational than ostensibly consistent choices would be. An intriguing hypothesis is that activation of OMPFC would not only predict susceptibility to framing, but also a tendency to interpret the values presented as precise values rather than upper or lower bounds. This hypothesis is consistent with our current understanding of OMPFC's role in representing value-laden stimuli. It is also consistent with Pylkkanen and McElree's (2007) findings that the VMPFC is activated in problems requiring the interpretation of ambiguous agentic actions.

As the title of this section suggests, prospect theory offered a foot in the door for context to influence decision making. However, the manner in which framing was proposed to influence decision making was highly constrained, following mainly from purported psychophysical properties of valuation (and, though not discussed here, also psychophysical properties of decision weighting). Recent behavioral findings indicate a much broader role of context, and also call into question some of the most fundamental assumptions underlying the literature on framing. These findings suggest that alternative descriptions thought to share the same deep structure may be perceived as having different deep structures by a significant proportion of individuals. In instances where such is the case, one might wonder whether it is even appropriate to call the variations in description "contextual" factors, since they apparently do change something fundamental about the target of evaluation, and not merely its circumstantial features.

Yet, the conversational account proposed here also suggests that contextual information in conjunction with pragmatic conversational inferences plays a key role in the resolution of ambiguity, and that it is precisely this process of resolving ambiguity that leads to the perceived differences in deep structure, which in turn shape the nature of choices. That contextual information appears to draw heavily on the *content* of decision problems, from which inferences that help shape representations of acts, outcomes, and contingencies may be drawn. Accordingly, we now turn our attention directly to the effect of content on decision-making processes.

CONTENT EFFECTS ON DECISION PROCESSES: CONTEXT MOVES CENTER STAGE

Given its longstanding commitment to psychophysical models of choice that assumed context independence, behavioral decision theory has been slow to appreciate the significance of content effects on decision processes. As Goldstein and Weber (1997) describe, the field can be characterized as having gone through a series of stages whereby, with each transition, its awareness of the significance of content has been progressively broadened. In the first stage, behavior was thought to be content-independent. In the second stage, it was occasionally acknowledged that behavior was content-dependent, but the reasons for such effects were thought to be of little or no theoretical interest. In the third stage, behavior was thought to be content-dependent for reasons that are somewhat interesting but still not a core part of theory. And, finally, in the fourth stage, context-dependence is seen as central to theory and as something that cannot be ignored without incurring a severe loss of explanatory completeness.

An important insight prompting the shift to the last stage was that content effects not only affected decision outcomes, they also had predictable effects on the selection of decision strategies (e.g., Goldstein & Weber, 1997). For example, Rettinger and Hastie (2001) found that among decision problems that had the same formal characteristics but different content, not only did risk attitudes vary, but the type of strategy invoked in order to arrive at a choice also varied by content. For instance, subjects' process reports revealed that a decision problem set in a legal context was much more likely to rely on narrative strategies than a decision problem set in a monetary gambling context. Notably, these differences in risk tolerance and decision strategy emerged even though content did not have an effect on the subjective values of the option being considered. Thus, the effect of content on decision strategy could not be attributed to changes in valuation.

Variations in content can also affect decisions by changing people's perspectives on what their decisions are fundamentally about. For instance, Mandel (2006) showed that, whereas the endowment effect (i.e., the tendency to sell a commodity in one's possession for more than one would be willing to pay to purchase it; e.g., see Kahneman, Knetsch, & Thaler, 1990) was evident in a case described in a purely economic context (namely, between you and a second-hand CD dealer), when the context was changed such that the other person was described as an acquaintance the endowment effect was eliminated, and when the other individual was described as a friend the endowment effect was actually reversed, contrary to the prediction of prospect theory. Mandel (2006) proposed that the relational context of the exchange changed the social norms that subjects judged as applicable under the circumstances. With acquaintances, reciprocity or fairness is likely to be perceived as normative, leading to pressures for equality in buying and selling offers. With friends, by comparison, generosity is more likely to be viewed as normative, especially for sellers, leading to selling offers that are lower than buying offers (i.e., a reversal of the endowment effect).

In a recent fMRI study, we (Vartanian, Mandel, & Duncan, in press) examined how changes in descriptive content influenced preferential choice in a case of decision making under conditions of uncertainty. In particular, we sought to examine whether a decision task involving saving human lives produced a different pattern of neural activation than a comparable task involving saving money. We reasoned that the life problem would invoke moral considerations that would be absent in the cash problem, and that such considerations would not only affect risk tolerance, they would also manifest in different neural activation patterns. For example, Mandel and Vartanian (2008) recently showed that moral dilemmas that involved choices where humans would have been harmed regardless of the action taken—an example of what Tetlock, Kristel, Elson, Green, and Lerner (2000) have referred to as *tragic tradeoffs*—generated a stronger sense of moral conflict and a reduced sense of confidence in subjects than moral dilemmas that involved choices where harm to humans could have been avoided by diverting the danger to a priceless commodity, even though in both conditions subjects exhibited similar choices.

Specifically, we reasoned that human-life problems may make subjects more sensitive to the prospect of failure to save lives. We predicted that choices to save lives would consequently be characterized by greater risk-aversion than choices to earn cash. Neurologically, we predicted that the dorsal striatum, by virtue of its sensitivity to motivational context and goal-directed action to increase reward (Delgado, Stenger, & Fiez, 2004;

O'Doherty, Dayan, Schultz, Deichmann, Friston, & Dolan, 2004), would be activated more in life decisions, consistent with a view of the decision maker as "motivated actor". In contrast, we predicted that the insula, given its role in risk prediction and probability signaling (Carlsson, Andersson, Petrovic, Petersson, Ohman, & Ingvar, 2006; Clark, Bechara, Damasio, Aitken, Sahakian, & Robbins, 2008), would be activated more in decisions about cash, consistent with a view of the decision maker in this domain as "financial risk analyst".

Subjects in our experiment were instructed to complete a series of gambles between two options (decks) of identical expected utility, where one option was paired with a certain outcome in each trial (e.g., saving $400 out of $1200 at risk of loss or saving 4 lives out of 12 at risk of death) and the other option was paired with a variable, uncertain outcome (e.g., saving either $0 or $1200 in the cash problem and saving either 0 or 12 lives in the life problem) (see Figure 2.2). Content was manipulated within subjects across blocks. After each trial, subjects received feedback on the outcome of their chosen deck as well as the other deck, following which they were presented with a fixation stimulus before moving on to the next trial.

Consistent with previous results involving decisions with outcome feedback (Barron & Erev, 2003), overall, participants were risk-averse, choosing the sure option in 59% of trials. However, as predicted, subjects were more risk-averse and more sensitive to loss in the life than cash domain. When choices from the uncertain deck were followed by negative feedback (i.e., selecting from the certain deck would have yielded a better outcome), they exhibited a tendency to switch to the certain deck in the subsequent trial, but only in the life domain. Stated differently, subjects were more likely to employ a *win–stay–lose–shift strategy* (e.g., Messick, 1967; Nowak & Sigmund, 1993) in the life domain than in the cash domain, staying with the risky option if it yielded a positive result in the previous trial and shifting to the sure option if it did not. Moreover, when choices of the uncertain deck were followed by negative feedback, response latencies were longer in the subsequent trial in the life domain, but shorter in the cash domain. In combination, the behavioral data strongly suggest that decision making in the life domain was mired with more conflict than decision making in the cash domain.

Regarding the neural findings, as predicted, a direct contrast at the time point when choices were made (Figure 2.2) revealed relatively higher activation in the anterior caudate nucleus in the life domain than in the cash domain (see Figure 2.3), consistent with the responsiveness of this region to motivational context and goal-directed action to increase reward. In contrast, there was relatively higher activation in the posterior insula in the cash domain than in the life domain (see Figure 2.3), consistent with its

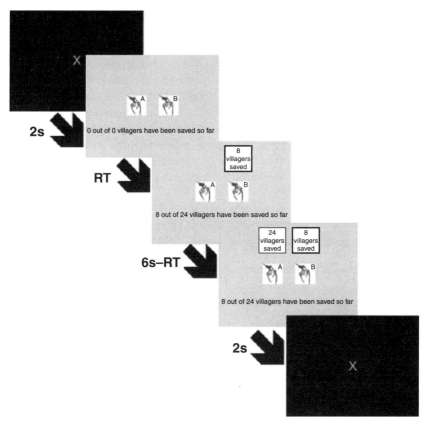

Figure 2.2   Trial structure. From Vartanian et al. (in press). Each session (life, cash) involved two blocks of 24 trials of identical structure. The figure represents the first trial from a life block involving selection from the certain deck followed by feedback. The length of each trial was 10 seconds. Following the termination of all 24 trials a slide was presented for 2 seconds, indicating the total savings/earnings from that block.

role in assessing the predictability of stimuli and probability signaling, a critical component of risk prediction. We also found distinct neural patterns of activation in response to negative feedback as a function of content. Specifically, there was relatively higher activation in the subgenual anterior cingulate when participants received negative feedback in the life domain than when they received negative feedback in the cash domain (see Figure 2.4). This is consistent with this region's sensitivity to negative feedback that occurs specifically in contexts involving humans (see van den Bos, McClure, Harris, Fiske, & Cohen, 2007). Furthermore, choosing the uncertain deck in trial n following negative feedback in the uncertain deck in trial $n - 1$ was associated with relatively higher activation in the dorsal hippocampus (bordering on posterior amygdala) in the life domain than in the cash domain (see Figure 2.5), consistent with the role of the hippocampus in context-driven memory in relation to cognitive representations of potential dangers (Hasler, Fromm, Alvarez, Luckenbaugh, Drevets, & Grillon, 2007).

Taken together, our results suggest that whether the content of a gamble includes the presence or absence of lives can function as a strong contextual variable, influencing choice (i.e., greater risk-aversion), decision strategy (i.e., greater reliance on a win–stay–lose–switch strategy), response latency (i.e., longer response times following negative feedback on risky choices), and their neural correlates as just mentioned. Let us now

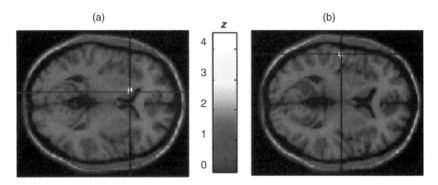

Figure 2.3   Neural activation for choice as a function of context. From Vartanian et al. (in press). The anterior caudate nucleus was activated more when subjects made choices in life problems (a). The posterior insula was activated more when subjects made choices in cash problems (b). See color plate.

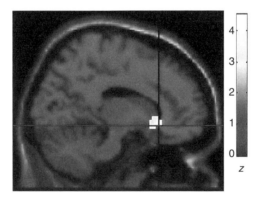

Figure 2.4   Neural activation as a function of negative feedback and context. From Vartainian et al. (in press). The subgenual anterior cingulate was activated more when subjects received negative feedback in life domain than when they received negative feedback in the cash domain. See color plate.

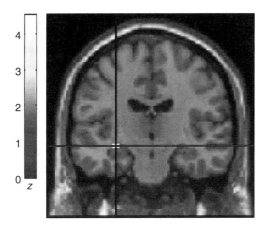

Figure 2.5   Neural activation as a function of negative feedback, subsequent choice, and context. From Vartanian et al. (in press). The dorsal hippocampus (bordering on posterior amygdala) was activated more in the life than cash domain when subjects opted to return to the uncertain deck on trial n following negative feedback on trial $n - 1$. See color plate.

consider the latter in greater detail, beginning with the observed activation in the anterior caudate nucleus when subjects made choices in the life domain. We interpret this finding in terms of O'Doherty's (2004; O'Doherty et al., 2004) "actor-critic" model, which dissociates between the functions of the ventral and dorsal striatum. According to the model, whereas the ventral striatum ("the critic") is involved in the formation of predictions about expected future rewards (see also Delgado & Tricomi, this volume), the dorsal striatum ("the actor") acts on those learned predictions to maximize long-term reward by selecting better options more frequently. This model is supported by data showing that the dorsal striatum is sensitive to variations in contextual cues, given that such cues provide signals to the dorsal striatum for action selection (Delgado et al., 2004). The greater activation of the anterior caudate nucleus (located within the dorsal striatum) in the life domain than in the cash domain indicates that the problems involving saving lives (even hypothetical lives!) engage neural regions associated with selection of actions to maximize long-term reward. These findings would seem to suggest, then, that context can influence the subject's motivations and, potentially, the subject's subsequent decision.

Whereas the activation in the anterior caudate nucleus was related to the time point when choices were made, context also affected the neural signal when the outcomes of subjects' choices were revealed. Specifically, the subgenual anterior cingulate was activated more when subjects received negative feedback in the life domain than when they received negative feedback in the cash domain (Figure 2.4). As mentioned earlier, our findings are consistent with those of van den Bos et al. (2007), who have shown that this region is sensitive to receiving negative feedback that occurs in a "social" context—namely, one involving interactions between two humans rather than a human and a computer. In fact, our results extend earlier findings by demonstrating that the mental representations of humans may be sufficient for activating the subgenual anterior cingulate in the face of negative feedback. In part, the involvement of the subgenual anterior cingulate in receiving negative feedback in the life domain may be due to the role that this region plays in the experience of emotion more generally.

There are two lines of clinical evidence that support this interpretation. First, lesions to the subgenual cingulate cause an inability to experience emotion in relation to concepts that normally evoke emotion (Damasio, Tranel, & Damasio, 1990). Second, regional cerebral blood flow is reduced in the subgenual cingulate in depressed patients (Drevets et al., 1997), consistent with the generally reduced emotional responsiveness observed in this population. The results suggest that the context in which negative feedback occurs can modulate the activation of regions that respond to emotion, thus extending the neural signatures of context effects to responses to outcomes as well as choice.

Finally, having demonstrated that context affects the neural signatures of choice and outcome processing, our results also suggest that it may affect the interplay between those two processes. Specifically, we investigated the neural response when subjects made choices in trial n as a function of type of choice and outcome in trial $n - 1$. Our results showed that when risk-seeking choices received negative feedback, opting to return to the risky option was associated with relatively higher activation in the dorsal hippocampus in the life domain than in the cash domain (Figure 2.5). Reinforcement learning paradigms have shown that there is functional dissociation between the amygdala and hippocampus in fear conditioning. The amygdala is activated in encoding stimulus–response contingencies as a function of outcome. This is consistent with data showing that in fear-conditioning paradigms the amygdala is activated more in the early phase of conditioning as it encodes stimulus-outcome contingencies, after which it disengages and other regions take over to direct action as a function of encoded associations (Marschner, Kalisch, Vervliet, Vansteenwegen, & Büchel, 2008).

In contrast, rather than encoding contingencies early on, the hippocampus is involved in the formation of context-dependent memories about stimulus-outcome associations (Hasler et al., 2007). In fact, in fear conditioning and extinction paradigms activation in the hippocampus has been shown to be correlated positively with the magnitude of extinction memory, $r = 0.71$ (Milad, Wright, Orr, Pitman, Quirk, & Rauch, 2007). The results of our experiment suggest that context affects the link between decision outcomes and subsequent decisions, as risk-seeking choices following negative outcomes in the life domain are associated with relatively higher activation in the hippocampal system. Stated differently, it appears that the human brain is poised to remember instances of risk-taking involving human life that led to failure, and to activate those memory representations in subsequent decisions.

The multiple effects of content on centers of neural activation are especially remarkable if we consider that the manipulations undertaken here were merely descriptive and that the "decision-making context" was in fact purely hypothetical. That is, these differences emerged simply in response to *imagining* being in a situation where one had to save lives or money at risk of loss and to *imagining* the described consequences of their choices. We can only expect that the effects of content on both behavioral and neural measures would be even more pronounced if the decision-making problems and their consequences had been real, although we do not assume a straightforward extrapolation of our findings to the real world. If the literature on context effects has taught us anything, it is not to take changes in circumstance for granted. Obviously, a shift from decision making in hypothetical situations to decision making in real situations would constitute more than a "mere" circumstantial modification.

CONCLUDING REMARKS

Our examination of the effect of descriptive context on preferential choice has highlighted the importance of taking into consideration the decision maker's representation of aspects of the decision problem. In this regard, our argument might be seen as falling into what Jungermann (2000) labeled the optimist's camp, focusing in particular on what he termed "the structure argument" (e.g., see Berkeley & Humphreys, 1982; Hogarth, 1981; Phillips, 1983). That is, we have raised concerns about the assumptions that theorists have made regarding the parsing of deep and surface structure in decision problems; concerns that, in turn, call into question whether decisions are really as incoherent as they have been portrayed by the pessimists' camp.

These questions, we believe, strike at the heart of any reasoned discussion of context because in the absence of sound criteria for deciding what manipulations are fundamental (i.e., not "merely" context) or circumstantial (i.e., "merely" context) there is no principled basis to proceed. Our view on this issue is that the structure argument *per se* neither reflects optimism nor pessimism regarding human performance. Acknowledging the importance of taking the decision maker's representation of a problem into account does not make an *a priori* case for the quality of their decision in light of their representations. There is certainly still the opportunity for incoherence to present itself even when choices are assessed in relation to the decision maker's understanding. Indeed, it is possible that seemingly coherent choices might be found to be incoherent upon such analysis. That is an empirical question, the answer to which should not be presupposed or biased by para-theoretical camp allegiances.

We would say, though, that our objection over "theorist-centricity" points mainly to the analytical and theoretical inadequacies of relying solely on the theorists' interpretation, and the logical difficulties that the approach presents for drawing sound inferences about the coherence of people's decisions. Although taking steps to measure decision makers' representations surely adds a level of complexity to the design of behavioral research, we believe it is well worth the effort—especially in an area so often characterized by evaluative conclusions regarding human performance.

The meta-theoretical orientation we thus advocate is similar to Dennett's (1991) *heterophenomenology*—namely, phenomenology of another, not oneself. Dennett regards heterophenomenology as an attempt to overcome what he called "lone-wolf autophenomenology"—the traditional (Cartesian) phenomenological view that accepts the individual's self-reports as being authoritative. In general, behavioral decision theorists have had little difficulty rejecting that perspective, being well aware that subjects often are willing to "tell more than they can know" (Nisbett & Wilson, 1977). But behavioral decision theorists have been more susceptible to a similarly Cartesian view in which the subjects' representation is ignored, denied, or treated as irrelevant, while the theorist's representation is elevated to the status of reality or proof. Our focus on the triad of the subjects' representation or phenomenology, the subjects' behavior (e.g., choices, response times, and reactions to feedback), and the subjects' neural behavior is thus part of a meta-theoretical orientation that seeks to triangulate the totality of the subjects' responses in order to formulate a more accurate view of human performance in light of human experience and the biological underpinnings of both performance and experience.

This approach, we believe, is particularly important at this juncture since the neuroscience of judgment and decision making offers many new lines of evidence that could be brought to bear on theory generation and theory testing. We have endeavored to show how manipulations of content not only affect behavioral measures such as risk attitude, response time, and decision strategies following outcome feedback, but also how such manipulations affect the neural signatures accompanying those behavioral responses. It is difficult to dismiss the effects of context on decision making when the effects manifest themselves not only in terms of choices and decision strategies but also in terms of the regions of the brain that are differentially activated.

The findings we presented in the section on content effects foreshadow theoretical developments in which contextual stimuli are understood to influence decision making, at least in part, through their activation of specific neural regions that in turn increase the probabilities of certain decision strategies, response tendencies, and experiences while decreasing the probabilities of alternative strategies, response tendencies, and experiences. We have little doubt that the emerging body of neuroscientific studies on judgment and decision making, which is still in its infancy, will play an important role not only in buttressing acceptance of what Goldstein and Weber (1997) described as the "fourth stage" in which context dependence is regarded as fundamental to decision theory, but also in shaping and constraining the theories that develop within that meta-theoretical perspective through entirely new lines of evidence. More generally, it is difficult to imagine how neuroscience's newfound abilities to peer into the brain will not have a significant transformative effect on our fundamental understanding of how people make judgments and decisions.

REFERENCES

Barron, G., & Erev, I. (2003). Small feedback-based decisions and their limited correspondence to description-based decisions. *Journal of Behavioral Decision Making*, *15*, 215–233.

Beach, L. R. (1990). *Image theory: Decision making in personal and organizational contexts*. Chichester: John Wiley & Sons.

Berkeley, D., & Humphreys, P. (1982). Structuring decision problems and the "bias heuristic". *Acta Psychologica*, *50*, 201–252.

Bernoulli, D. (1738/1954). Exposition of a new theory on the measurement of risk. *Econometrica*, *22*, 23–36.

Carlsson, K., Andersson, J., Petrovic, P., Petersson, K. M., Ohman, A., & Ingvar, M. (2006). Predictability modulates the affective and sensory-discriminative neural processing of pain. *Neuroimage*, *32*, 1804–1814.

Clark, L., Bechara, A., Damasio, H., Aitken, M. R. F., Sahakian, B. J., & Robbins, T. W. (2008). Differential effects of insular and ventromedial prefrontal cortex lesions on risky decision-making. *Brain*, *131*, 1311–1322.

Damasio, A. R., Tranel, D., & Damasio, H. (1990). Individuals with sociopathic behavior caused by frontal damage fail to respond autonomically to social stimuli. *Behavioural Brain Research*, *41*, 81–94.

Damasio, A. R., & Van Hoesen, G. W. (1983). Emotional disorders associated with focal lesions of the limbic frontal lobe. In K. M. Heilman & P. Satz (Eds.), *Neuropsychology of human emotion* (pp. 85–110). New York: Guilford Press.

De Martino, B., Kumaran, D., Seymour, B., & Dolan, R. J. (2006). Frames, biases, and rational decision-making in the human brain. *Science*, *313*, 684–687.

Delgado, M. R., Stenger, V. A., & Fiez, J. A. (2004). Motivation-dependent responses in the human caudate nucleus. *Cerebral Cortex, 14*, 1022–1030.

Dennett, D. (1991). *Consciousness explained*. New York: Penguin Press.

Dolan, R. J. (2007). The human amygdala and orbital prefrontal cortex in behavioural regulation. *Philosophical Transactions of the Royal Society London B: Biological Sciences, 362*, 787–799.

Drevets, W. C., Price, J. L., Simpson, J. R. Jr., Todd, R. D., Reich, T., Vannier, M. et al. (1997). Subgenual prefrontal cortex abnormalities in mood disorders. *Nature, 386*, 824–827.

Evans, J. St. B. T., Newstead, S. E., & Byrne, R. M. J. (1993). *Human reasoning: The psychology of deduction*. Hove, UK: Psychology Press.

Gallagher, H. L., & Frith, C. D. (2003). Functional imaging of "theory of mind". *Trends in Cognitive Sciences, 7*, 77–83.

Gazzaniga, M. S. (1989). Organization of the human brain. *Science, 245*, 947–952.

Gazzaniga, M. S. (2000). Cerebral specialization and interhemispheric communication: Does the corpus callosum enable the human condition? *Brain, 123*, 1293–1326.

Goel, V., Stollstorff, M., Nakic, M., Knutson, K., & Grafman, J. (2009). A role for right ventrolateral prefrontal cortex in reasoning about indeterminate relations. *Neuropsychologia, 47*, 2790–2797.

Goel, V., Tierney, M., Sheesley, L., Bartolo, A., Vartanian, O., & Grafman, J. (2007). Hemispheric specialization in human prefrontal cortex for resolving certain and uncertain inferences. *Cerebral Cortex, 17*, 2245–2250.

Goldstein, W. M., & Weber, E. U. (1997). Content and discontent: Indications and implications of domain specificity in preferential decision making. In W. M. Goldstein & R. M. Hogarth (Eds.), *Research on judgment and decision making* (pp. 566–617). Cambridge, UK: Cambridge University Press.

Grice, H. P. (1975). Logic and conversation. In P. Cole & J. L. Morgan (Eds.), *Syntax and semantics: Volume 3: Speech acts* (pp. 41–58). New York: Academic Press.

Hasler, G., Fromm, S., Alvarez, R. P., Luckenbaugh, D. A., Drevets, W. C., & Grillon, C. (2007). Cerebral blood flow in immediate and sustained anxiety. *Journal of Neuroscience, 27*, 6313–6319.

Hilton, D. J., & Slugoski, B. R. (2000). Judgment and decision making in social context: Discourse processes and rational inference. In T. Connolly, H. R. Arkes, & K. R. Hammond (Eds.), *Judgment and decision making: An interdisciplinary reader* (2nd ed., pp. 651–676). Cambridge: Cambridge University Press.

Hogarth, R. M. (1981). Beyond discrete biases: Functional and dysfunctional aspects of aspects of judgmental heuristics. *Psychological Bulletin, 90*, 197–217.

Jou, J., Shanteau, J., & Harris, R. J. (1996). An information processing view of framing effects: The role of causal schemas in decision making. *Memory & Cognition, 24*, 1–15.

Jungermann, H. (2000). The two camps on rationality. In T. Connolly, H. R. Arkes, & K. R. Hammond (Eds.), *Judgment and decision making: An interdisciplinary reader* (2nd ed., pp. 575–591). Cambridge: Cambridge University Press.

Kahneman, D., & Frederick, S. (2007). Frames and brains: Elicitation and control of response tendencies. *Trends in Cognitive Sciences*, *11*, 45–46.

Kahneman, D., Knetsch, J. L., & Thaler, R. (1990). Experimental tests of the endowment effect and the Coase Theorem. *Journal of Political Economy*, *98*, 728–741.

Kahneman, D., & Tversky, A. (1979). Prospect theory: An analysis of decision under risk. *Econometrica*, *47*, 263–291.

Kahneman, D., & Tversky, A. (1984). Choices, values, and frames. *American Psychologist*, *39*, 341–350.

Kühberger, A. (1995). The framing of decisions: A new look at old problems. *Organizational Behavior and Human Decision Processes*, *62*, 230–240.

Kühberger, A. (1998). The influence of framing on risky decisions: A meta-analysis. *Organizational Behavior and Human Decision Processes*, *75*, 23–55.

Kühberger, A., Schulte-Mecklenbeck, M., & Perner, J. (1999). The effects of framing, reflection, probability, and payoff on risk preference in choice tasks. *Organizational Behavior and Human Decision Processes*, *78*, 204–231.

LeDoux, J. E. (1996). *The emotional brain: The mysterious underpinnings of emotional life*. New York: Simon and Schuster.

Macdonald, R. R. (1986). Credible conceptions and implausible probabilities. *British Journal of Mathematical and Statistical Psychology*, *39*, 15–27.

Mandel, D. R. (2001). Gain-loss framing and choice: Separating outcome formulations from descriptor formulations. *Organizational Behavior and Human Decision Processes*, *85*, 56–76.

Mandel, D. R. (2006). Economic transactions among friends: Asymmetric generosity but not agreement in buyers' and sellers' offers. *Journal of Conflict Resolution*, *50*, 584–606.

Mandel, D. R. (2008). Violations of coherence in subjective probability: A representational and assessment processes account. *Cognition*, *106*, 130–156.

Mandel, D. R. (2009). Unpublished data on framing effects and option representation.

Mandel, D. R., & Vartanian, O. (2008). Taboo or tragic: Effect of tradeoff type on moral choice, conflict, and confidence. *Mind and Society*, *7*, 115–126.

Marschner, A., Kalisch, R., Vervliet, B., Vansteenwegen, D., & Büchel, C. (2008). Dissociable roles for the hippocampus and the amygdala in human cued versus context fear conditioning. *Journal of Neuroscience*, *28*, 9030–9036.

Messick, D. M. (1967). Interdependent decision strategies in zero-sum games. *Behavioral Science*, *12*, 33–48.

Milad, M. R., Wright, C. I., Orr, S. P., Pitman, R. K., Quirk, G. J., & Rauch, S. L. (2007). Recall of fear extinction in humans activates the ventromedial prefrontal cortex and hippocampus in concert. *Biological Psychiatry*, *62*, 446–454.

Nisbett, R. E., & Wilson, T. D. (1977). Telling more than we can know: Verbal reports of mental processes. *Psychological Review*, *84*, 231–259.

Nowak, M., & Sigmund, K. (1993). A strategy of win–stay, lose–shift that outperforms tit-for-tat in the Prisoner's Dilemma game. *Nature*, *364*, 56–58.

O'Doherty, J. P. (2004). Reward representations and reward-related learning in the human brain: Insights from neuroimaging. *Current Opinion in Neurobiology*, *14*, 769–776.

O'Doherty, J., Dayan, P., Schultz, J., Deichmann, R., Friston, K., & Dolan, R. J. (2004). Dissociable roles of ventral and dorsal striatum in instrumental conditioning. *Science, 304,* 452–454.

Phillips, L. D. (1983). A theoretical perspective on heuristics and biases in probabilistic thinking. In P. C. Humphries, O. Svenson, & A. Vari (Eds.), *Analyzing and aiding decision processes* (pp. 507–513). Amsterdam: North Holland.

Pylkkanen, L., & McElree, B. (2007). An MEG study of silent meaning. *Journal of Cognitive Neuroscience, 19,* 1905–1921.

Rettinger, D. A., & Hastie, R. (2001). Content effects on decision making. *Organizational Behavior and Human Decision Processes, 85,* 336–359.

Reyna, V. F., & Brainerd, C. J. (1991). Fuzzy-trace theory and framing effects in choice: Gist extraction, truncation, and conversion. *Journal of Behavioral Decision Making, 4,* 249–262.

Savage, L. J. (1954). *The foundations of statistics.* New York: Wiley.

Stanovich, K. E., & West, R. F. (2000). Individual differences in reasoning: Implications for the rationality debate? *Behavioral and Brain Sciences, 23,* 645–665.

Tetlock, P. E., Kristel, O. V., Elson, S. B., Green, M. C., & Lerner, J. S. (2000). The psychology of the unthinkable: Taboo trade-offs, forbidden base rates, and heretical counterfactuals. *Journal of Personality and Social Psychology, 78,* 853–870.

The New Oxford Dictionary of English (2001). Cambridge: Cambridge University Press.

Tversky, A., & Kahneman, D. (1981). The framing of decisions and the psychology of choice. *Science, 211,* 453–458.

van den Bos, W., McClure, S. M., Harris, L. T., Fiske, S. T., & Cohen, J. D. (2007). Dissociating affective evaluation and social cognitive processes in the ventral medial prefrontal cortex. *Cognitive, Affective, and Behavioral Neuroscience, 7,* 337–346.

Van Veen, V., & Carter, C. S. (2006). Conflict and cognitive control in the brain. *Current Directions in Psychological Science, 15,* 237–240.

Vartanian, O., Mandel, D. R., & Duncan, M. (in press). Money or life: Context effects on risky choice. *Journal of Neuroscience, Psychology, and Economics.*

von Neumann, J., & Morgenstern, O. (1947). *Theory of games and economic behavior.* Princeton, NJ: Princeton University Press.

Wagenaar, W. A., Keren, G., & Lichtenstein, S. (1988). Islanders and hostages: Deep and surface structures of decision problems. *Acta Psychologica, 67,* 175–189.

Weingarten, G. (2007, April 8). Pearls before breakfast. *The Washington Post,* W10.

Section II

Risk and uncertainty

CHAPTER THREE

Human emotions in decision making: Are they useful or disruptive?

Antoine Bechara

INTRODUCTION

There is no question that emotion plays a major role in influencing many of our everyday cognitive and behavioral functions, including memory and decision making. The importance of emotion in human affairs is obvious. Disorders of emotion plague patients with many neurological and psychiatric conditions. Despite the fundamental role that emotion plays in many cognitive, neurological, and psychiatric disorders, scientific study of the neural correlates of emotion and its influence on thought and cognition has been largely ignored. Indeed, the study of emotion by cognitive science, neuroscience, and artificial intelligence has lagged behind the study of nearly all other major aspects of mind and brain. There is a popular notion, which most of us learn from early on in life, that logical, rational calculation forms the basis of sound decisions. Many people say, "emotion has no IQ"; emotion can only cloud the mind and interfere with good judgment. But what if these notions were wrong and had no scientific basis? What if sound, rational decision making in fact depended on prior accurate emotional processing? The studies of decision making in neurological patients who can no longer process emotional information normally suggest just that. Given the importance of emotion in the understanding of human suffering, its value in the management of disease, its role in social interactions, and its relevance to fundamental neuroscience and cognitive science, a comprehensive understanding of human cognition requires far greater knowledge of the neurobiology of emotion. In this chapter, we outline recent progress in understanding the role of emotion in cognition. Specifically, we will outline experiments supporting the argument that: (1) decision making is a process critically dependent on neural systems important for the processing of emotions; (2) conscious knowledge alone is not sufficient for making advantageous decisions; and (3) emotion is not always beneficial to decision making: Sometimes it can be disruptive.

A BRIEF HISTORY

One of the first and most famous cases of the so-called "frontal lobe syndrome" was the patient Phineas Gage, described by Harlow (1848, 1868). Phineas Gage was a dynamite worker, and survived an explosion that blasted an iron-tamping bar through the front of his head. Before the accident, Gage was a man of normal intelligence, energetic and persistent in executing all his plans of operation. He was responsible, sociable, and popular among peers and friends. After the accident, his medical recovery was remarkable! He survived the accident with normal intelligence, memory, speech, sensation, and movement. However, his behavior changed completely. He became irresponsible, untrustworthy, and impatient of restraint or advice when it conflicted with his desires.

Using modern neuroimaging techniques, Damasio and colleagues reconstituted the accident by relying on measurements taken from Gage's skull, which is currently kept at a museum at Harvard (Damasio, Grabowski, Frank, Galburda, & Damasio, 1994). The key finding of this neuroimaging study was that the most likely placement of Gage's lesion was the ventral and medial region of the front of the brain (i.e., the VM region of the prefrontal cortex) on both sides. Interestingly, the case of Phineas Gage, and similar cases that were described after him, received little attention for many years. The revival of interest in this case, and in various aspects of "frontal lobe syndrome", came in recent studies by several investigators of patients like Phineas Gage (Benton, 1991; Eslinger & Damasio, 1985; Stuss, Gow, & Hetherington, 1992). The modern counterpart to Phineas Gage is the patient described by Eslinger and Damasio (1985). Over the years, many patients with VM lesions have been studied. Such patients develop severe impairments in personal and social decision making, in spite of otherwise largely preserved intellectual abilities. Patients with bilateral damage to the VM prefrontal cortex develop severe impairments in personal and social decision making. They have difficulties planning their workday, as well as difficulties in choosing friends, partners, and activities. The actions they elect to pursue often lead to losses of diverse order; for example, financial losses, losses in social standing, losses of family and friends. The choices they make are no longer advantageous—the patients often decide against their best interests—and are remarkably different from the kinds of choices they were known to make in the pre-morbid period. They are unable to learn from previous mistakes, as reflected by repeated engagement in decisions that lead to negative consequences. In striking contrast to this real-life decision-making impairment, problem-solving abilities in laboratory settings remain largely normal. As noted, the patients have normal intellect, as measured by a variety of conventional neuropsychological tests (Bechara, Damasio, Tranel, & Anderson, 1998; Damasio, Tranel, & Damasio, 1990; Eslinger & Damasio, 1985), a fact that made it difficult to explain these patients' disturbance in terms of defects in knowledge pertinent to the situation, general intellectual compromise, defects in language comprehension or expression, working memory, or attention (Anderson, Bechara, Damasio, Tranel, & Damasio, 1999; Anderson, Damasio, Jones, & Tranel, 1991; Bechara et al., 1998; Saver & Damasio, 1991). While these VM patients were intact on standard neuropsychological tests, they did have a compromised ability to express emotion and experience feelings in appropriate situations. That is, despite normal intellect, there were abnormalities in emotion and feeling, along with the abnormalities in decision making.

For many years, this particular class of patients presented a puzzling defect, because it was difficult to explain their disturbance in terms of defects in knowledge pertinent to the situation or deficient general intellectual ability. The disturbance also could not be explained in terms of impaired language comprehension or expression, working memory or attention. Therefore, the condition of these patients posed a double challenge. First, although the decision-making impairment was obvious in the real-world behavior life of these patients, there was no effective laboratory probe to detect and measure this impairment. Second, there was no satisfactory theoretical account of the neural and cognitive mechanisms underlying the impairment. However, these challenges were eventually overcome. First, the development of the "Iowa gambling task (IGT)" enabled the detection of these patients' elusive impairment in the laboratory, its measurement, and the investigation of its possible causes (Bechara, Damasio, Damasio, & Anderson, 1994). Second, progress was made in understanding the nature of this impairment at the behavioral, psychophysiological, and cognitive levels.

Why was the IGT successful in detecting the decision-making impairment in VM patients, and why is it important for the study of the neurology of decision making? Perhaps this is because the IGT mimics real-life decisions so closely. The task is carried out in real-time and it resembles real-world contingencies. It factors reward and punishment (i.e., winning and losing money) in such a way that it creates a conflict between an immediate, luring reward and a delayed, probabilistic punishment. There-fore, the task engages the subject in a quest to make advantageous choices. As in real-life choices, the task offers choices that may be risky, and there is no obvious explanation of how, when, or what to choose. Each choice is full of uncertainty because a precise calculation or prediction of the out-come of a given choice is not possible. The way that one can do well on this task is to follow one's "hunches" and "gut feelings".

THE SOMATIC MARKER HYPOTHESIS

While these VM patients were intact on most neuropsychological tests, the patients did have a compromised ability to express emotion and to experi-ence feelings in appropriate situations. In other words, despite normal intellect, there were abnormalities in emotion and feeling, along with the abnormalities in decision making. Based on these observations, the *som-atic marker hypothesis* was proposed (Damasio, 1994). The somatic marker hypothesis posits that the neural basis of the decision-making impairment characteristic of patients with VM prefrontal lobe damage is defective activation of somatic states (emotional signals) that attach value to given options and scenarios. These emotional signals function as covert, or overt, biases for guiding decisions. Deprived of these emotional signals, patients must rely on slow cost-benefit analyses of various conflicting options. These options may be too numerous, and their analysis may be too lengthy, to permit rapid, on-line decisions to take place appropriately. Patients may resort to deciding based on the immediate reward of an option, or may fail to decide altogether if many options have the same basic value. The failure to enact somatic states (or activate these emotional biases), and consequently to decide advantageously, results from dysfunc-tion in a neural system in which the VM prefrontal cortex is a critical component. However, the VM prefrontal cortex is not the only region. Other neural regions, including the amygdala and somatosensory cortices (SI, SII, and insula) (Figure 3.1), are also components of this same neural system, although the different regions may provide different contributions to the overall process of decision making (Bechara, Damasio, Damasio, & Lee, 1999).

In essence, when we make decisions, mechanisms of arousal, attention, and memory are necessary to evoke and display the representations of various options and scenarios in our mind's eye. However, another mech-anism is necessary for weighing these various options and for selecting the most advantageous response. This mechanism for selecting good from bad options is referred to as *decision making*, and the physiological changes occurring in association with the behavioral selection constitute a part of *somatic states* (or somatic signals).

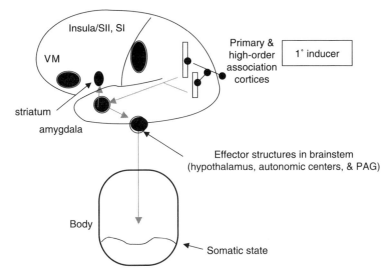

Figure 3.1   A schematic of the brain areas critical for the processing of somatic (emotional) states. The position of the amygdala is the dark circle near the label "amygdala"). The elongated circle labeled "Insula/SII, SI" represents the position of the somatosensory/insular cortex. The ventromedial prefrontal cortex is represented by the circle VM.

EVIDENCE THAT EMOTION GUIDES DECISIONS

Situations involving personal and social matters are strongly associated with positive and negative emotions. Reward or punishment, pleasure or pain, happiness or sadness all produce changes in body states, and these changes are expressed as emotions. Such prior emotional experiences often come into play when we are deliberating a decision. Whether these emotions remain unconscious, or are perceived consciously in the form of *feelings*, they provide the go, stop, and turn signals needed for making advantageous decisions. In other words, the activation of these somatic states provides "biasing" signals that covertly, or overtly, mark various options and scenarios with a value. Accordingly, these biases assist in the selection of advantageous responses from among an array of available options. Deprived of these biases or somatic markers, response options become more or less equalized, and decisions become dependent on a slow reasoned cost-benefit analysis of numerous and often conflicting options. At the end, the result is an inadequate selection of a response. Several studies were conducted in our laboratory that support the idea that decision making is a process guided by emotions.

The first set of studies involved the IGT. This task involves four decks of cards named A, B, C, and D. The goal in the task is to maximize profit on a loan of play money. Subjects are required to make a series of 100 card selections. However, they are not told ahead of time how many card selections they are going to make. Subjects can select one card at a time from any deck they choose, and they are free to switch from any deck to another at any time, and as often as they wish. However, the subject's decision to select from one deck versus another is largely influenced by various schedules of immediate reward and future punishment. These schedules are pre-programmed and known to the examiner, but not to the subject, and they entail the following principles.

Every time the subject selects a card from deck A or deck B, the subject gets $100. Every time the subject selects a card from deck C or deck D, the subject gets $50. However, in each of the four decks, subjects encounter unpredictable punishments (money loss). The punishment is set to be higher in the high-paying decks A and B, and lower in the low-paying decks C and D. For example, if 10 cards were picked from deck A, one would earn $1000. However, in those 10 card picks, 5 unpredictable punishments would be encountered, ranging from $150 to $350, bringing a total cost of $1250. Deck B is similar: Every 10 cards that were picked from deck B would earn $1000; however, these 10 card picks would encounter one high punishment of $1250. On the other hand, every 10 cards from deck C or D earn only $500, but only cost $250 in punishment. Hence, decks A and B are disadvantageous because they cost more in the long run; i.e., one loses $250 every 10 cards. Decks C and D are advantageous because they result in an overall gain in the long run; i.e., one wins $250 every 10 cards.

The performance of normal controls and patients with VM prefrontal cortex lesions were investigated on this task. Normal subjects avoided the bad decks A and B and preferred the good decks C and D. In sharp contrast, the VM patients did not avoid the bad decks A and B; indeed, they preferred decks A and B (Figure 3.2). These results suggested that the patients' performance profile is comparable to their real-life inability to decide advantageously. This is especially true in personal and social matters, a domain for which in life, as in the task, an exact calculation of the future outcomes is not possible and choices must be based on hunches and gut feelings.

In light of the finding that the IGT is an instrument that detects the decision-making impairment of VM patients in the laboratory, the next question involved whether the impairment is linked to a failure in somatic (emotional) signaling (Bechara, Tranel, Damasio, & Damasio, 1996). Motivated to address this question, a physiological measure was added to the IGT. The goal was to assess somatic state activation (or generation of emotional signals) while subjects were making decisions during the IGT. Bechara et al. (1996) studied two groups: Normal subjects and VM

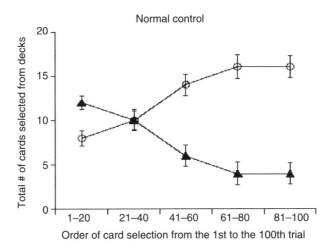

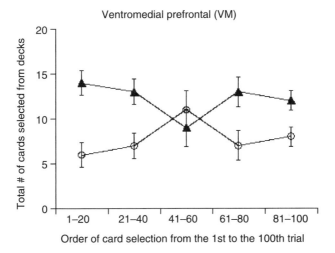

Figure 3.2 Card selection on the Iowa gambling task (IGT) as a function of group (normal control, ventromedial (VM) prefrontal), deck type (disadvantageous versus advantageous), and trial block. Normal control subjects shifted their selection of cards toward the advantageous decks. The VM prefrontal patients did not make a reliable shift and opted for the disadvantageous decks.

patients. The subjects performed the IGT while their electrodermal activity (skin conductance response; SCR) was recorded. As the body begins to change after a thought, and as a given emotion begins to be enacted, the autonomic nervous system begins to increase the activity in the skin's sweat glands. Although this sweating activity is relatively small and not observable by the naked eye, it can be amplified and recorded by a polygraph as a wave. The amplitude of this wave can be measured, and thus provides an indirect measure of the emotion experienced by the subject.

Both normal subjects and VM patients generated SCRs after they had picked a card and were told that they won or lost money. The most important difference, however, was that normal subjects, as they became experienced with the task, began to generate SCRs *prior* to the selection of any cards; that is, during the time when they were pondering from which deck to choose. These anticipatory SCRs were more pronounced before picking a card from the risky decks A and B compared with the safe decks C and D, where risk was defined as greater variability of possible outcomes around the expected outcome. In other words, these anticipatory SCRs were like "gut feelings" that warned the subject against picking from the bad decks. Frontal patients failed to generate such SCRs before picking a card. This failure to generate anticipatory SCRs *before* picking cards from the bad decks correlates with their failure to avoid these bad decks and choose advantageously in this task (Figure 3.3). These results provide strong support for the notion that decision making is guided by emotional signals (gut feelings) that are generated in anticipation of future events.

EMOTIONAL SIGNALS NEED NOT BE CONSCIOUS

Further experiments revealed that these biasing somatic signals (gut feelings) do not need to be perceived consciously. Bechara, Damasio, Tranel, and Damasio (1997) carried out an experiment similar to the previous one, which tested normal subjects and VM patients on the IGT while recording their SCRs. However, every time the subject picked 10 cards from the decks, the experimenters would stop the game briefly, and ask the subject to declare whatever they knew about what was going on in the game. From the answers to the questions, the experimenters were able to distinguish four periods as subjects went from the first to the last trial in the task. The first was a pre-punishment period, when subjects sampled the decks, and before they had yet encountered any punishment. The second was a pre-hunch period, when subjects began to encounter punishment, but when asked about what was going on in the game, they had no clue. The third was a hunch period, when subjects began to express a hunch about which decks were riskier, but were not sure. The fourth was a conceptual period,

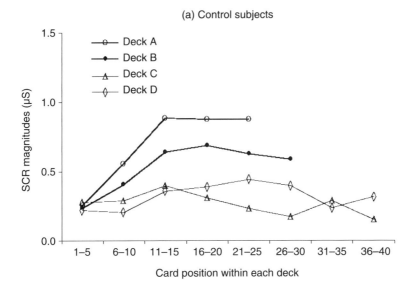

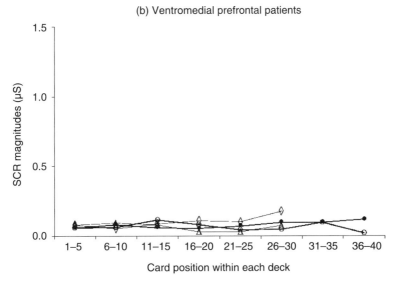

Figure 3.3 Magnitudes of anticipatory skin conductance response (SCR) as a function of group (control [a] versus ventromedial prefrontal [b]), deck, and card position within each deck. Note that control subjects gradually began to generate high-amplitude SCRs to the disadvantageous decks. The ventromedial prefrontal patients failed to do so.

when subjects knew very well the contingencies in the task, and which decks were the good ones, which decks were the bad ones, and why this was so (Figure 3.4).

When examining the anticipatory SCRs from each period, Bechara et al. (1997) found that there was no significant activity during the pre-punishment period. These were expected results because, at this stage, the subjects were picking cards and gaining money, and had not encountered any losses yet. Then there was a substantial rise in anticipatory responses during the pre-hunch period; that is, after encountering some money losses, but still before the subject had any clue about what was going on in the game. This SCR activity was sustained for the remaining periods (i.e., during the hunch and then during the conceptual period). When examining the behavior during each period, Bechara et al. (1997) found that there was a preference for the high-paying decks (A and B) during the pre-

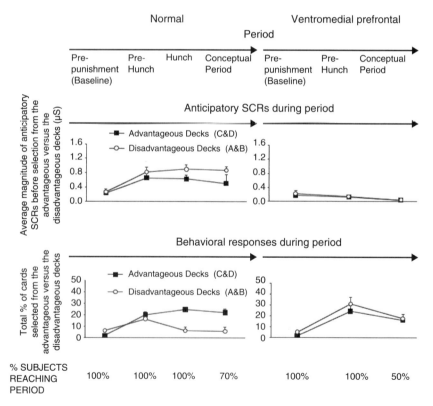

Figure 3.4 Anticipatory SCRs and behavioral responses (card selection) as a function of four periods (pre-punishment, pre-hunch, hunch, and conceptual) from normal control subjects and ventromedial prefrontal patients.

punishment period. Then there was a hint of a shift in the pattern of card selection, away from the bad decks, even in the pre-hunch period. This shift in preference for the good decks became more pronounced during the hunch and conceptual periods. The VM patients, on the other hand, never reported a hunch about which of the decks were good or bad. Furthermore, they never developed anticipatory SCRs, and they continued to choose more cards from the bad decks A and B relative to the good decks C and D.

An especially intriguing observation was that not all the normal control subjects were able to figure out the task, explicitly, in the sense that they did not reach the conceptual period. Only 70% of them were able to do so. Although 30% of controls did not reach the conceptual period, they still performed advantageously. On the other hand, 50% of the VM patients were able to reach the conceptual period and state explicitly which decks were good and which ones were bad and why. Although 50% of the VM patients did reach the conceptual period, they still performed disadvantageously. After the experiment, when these VM patients were confronted with the question: "Why did you continue to pick from the decks you thought were bad?" they would resort to excuses such as "I was trying to figure out what happens if I kept playing the $100 decks . . ." or "I wanted to recover my losses fast, and the $50 decks are too slow . . .".

These results show that VM patients continue to choose disadvantageously in the IGT, even after realizing explicitly the consequences of their action. This suggests that the anticipatory SCRs represent unconscious biases derived from prior experiences with reward and punishment. These biases (or gut feelings) help deter the normal subject from pursuing a course of action that is disadvantageous in the future. This occurs even before the subject becomes aware of the goodness or badness of the choice he or she is about to make. Without these biases, the knowledge of what is right and what is wrong may still become available. However, by itself, this knowledge is not sufficient to ensure an advantageous behavior. Therefore, although the VM patient may manifest declarative knowledge of what is right and what is wrong, he or she fails to act accordingly. The VM patients may "say" the right thing, but they "do" the wrong thing.

Thus "knowledge" without "emotion/somatic signaling" leads to dissociation between what one knows or says and how one decides to act. This dissociation is not restricted to neurological patients, but also applies to neuropsychiatric conditions with suspected pathology in the VM cortex or other components of the neural circuitry that process emotion. Addiction is one example, where patients know the consequences of their drug-seeking behavior, but they still take the drug. Psychopathy is another example, where the psychopaths can be fully aware of the consequences of their actions, but they still go ahead and plan the killing or the rape of a victim.

THE NEUROLOGY OF EMOTION AND DECISION MAKING

The VM prefrontal cortex receives projections from all sensory modalities, directly or indirectly. In addition, the VM cortex has extensive bidirectional connections with the amygdala, an almond-shaped structure that is important for emotion. Also, the VM cortex has extensive bidirectional connections with the somatosensory (SI and SII) and insular cortices. As proposed by the somatic marker hypothesis framework (Damasio, 1994), when confronted with a decision and the VM prefrontal cortex is engaged, one or both of the following two chains of physiological events take place (Figure 3.5). In one chain, an appropriate emotional (somatic) state is actually re-enacted, and signals from its activation are then relayed back to subcortical and cortical somatosensory processing structures, especially in the somatosensory (SI and SII) and insular cortices. This anatomical system is described as the "body loop" within the somatic marker hypothesis (Damasio, 1994). The enacted somatic state can then act consciously or nonconsciously on the neural processes that enable the person to do or to avoid doing a certain action.

However, after emotions have been expressed and experienced at least

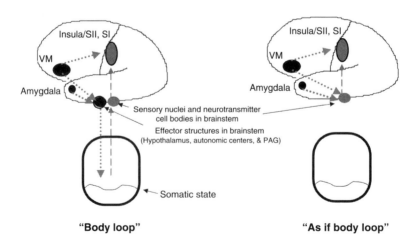

Figure 3.5   Simple diagrams illustrating the "body loop" and "as if loop" chain of physiologic events. In both "body loop" and "as if loop" panels, the brain is represented by the top black perimeter and the body by the bottom one.

once, one can also form representations of these emotional experiences in the somatosensory/insular cortices. Therefore, after emotions are learnt, one possible chain of physiological events is to bypass the body altogether, activate the insular/somatosensory cortices directly, and create a fainter image of an emotional body state than if the emotion were actually expressed in the body. This anatomical system is described in the somatic marker hypothesis framework as the "as if body loop" (Damasio, 1994). Thus, the neural network mediating the activation of emotional (somatic) states involves numerous neural regions. The VM prefrontal cortex is one critical region. However, there are other critical components in this neural network. Two critical structures in this neural system are the amygdala and the somatosensory/insular cortices. Next, I discuss the contribution of the amygdala and the somatosensory/insular cortices to the activation of emotional (somatic) states.

AMYGDALA

Central autonomic structures, such as the amygdala, can activate somatic responses in the viscera, vascular bed, endocrine system, and nonspecific neurotransmitter systems (LeDoux, 1996). Therefore, the amygdala plays an important role in emotion, and also in decision making (Bechara, Damasio, & Damasio, 2003). In fact, the amygdala triggers emotion from specific sets of stimuli referred to as *primary inducers* (Bechara & Damasio, 2005). Primary inducers are stimuli or entities that are either innately pleasurable or aversive or else learned to be so. Once they are encountered, they automatically, quickly, and necessarily elicit an emotional response. Examples of primary inducers include the encounter of a fear object (e.g., a snake) or a stimulus predictive of a snake (e.g., movement through a grassy patch that appears "snake-like"). Even well-learned concepts such as winning or losing a large sum of money, which instantly, automatically, and necessarily elicit a somatic response, are examples of primary inducers.

The function of the amygdala is to couple the features of the object with its emotional attribute. For example, a snake is simply an object with certain features. However, this object is linked to some emotional attributes such as fear, which make people run away from the snake and perhaps experience fear. The amygdala binds the features of the snake to the emotion of fear. Without an amygdala, a person can look at a snake and know what it is, but the snake no longer elicits an emotional reaction of fear. In fact, this outcome is strikingly demonstrated in monkeys who have an innate extreme fear of snakes; they go crazy when they see a snake. However, after removing its amygdala, the monkey can look at the snake and attempt to pick it up. In other words, the object of fear can no longer elicit fear; there is a disconnection between the object and its emotional attribute.

Thus a primary inducer is something that triggers an emotion via the amygdala before one can figure out what the fuss is about. The amygdala is evolutionarily the part of the brain that embraces one instantly for a "fight or flight" response, and it has evolved during a time when probably there was no harm in confusing false alarms and real ones: If the amygdala sent a person scrambling up a tree to escape a bear, the person was safe! Even if this turned out to be a false alarm (e.g., a rock that looked like a bear), the person was still safe, and there was no harm in responding to a false alarm (see also Friedrich, 1993). Therefore the emotional reactions triggered by the amygdala are beneficial and serve a very good purpose in life. In fact, Bechara et al. (2003) have shown that this highly emotional part of the brain could help the person make more rational decisions.

Using the IGT as a tool for measuring decision making, Bechara et al. (1999) investigated a group of patients with bilateral amygdala lesions, and a group of demographically and educationally matched normal subjects. The experimenters monitored the SCR activity of these subjects during their performance of the IGT. The results showed that normal controls selected more cards from the advantageous decks C and D (low immediate gain, but larger future yield), and fewer cards from the disadvantageous decks A and B (high immediate gain, but larger future loss). Similar to the patients with bilateral lesions of the VM prefrontal cortex, the amygdala patients did the opposite and selected more cards from the disadvantageous decks as compared with the advantageous decks. When examining the anticipatory SCRs, the amygdala patients were similar to the VM patients in that they also failed to generate anticipatory SCRs before the selection of a card. However, what was different was that the amygdala patients also failed to generate SCRs when they were told that they lost large sums of money.

These results suggest that when the amygdala is damaged, the patient can no longer signal how painful it feels when one loses money. This in turn fools the VM cortex about how painful it should feel if a decision led to monetary loss. Together, the results provide strong support for the notion that decision making is guided by emotional signaling (or somatic states) generated in anticipation of future events. Without the ability to generate these emotional/somatic signals, the patients fail to avoid the decks that lead to painful losses—so they sample the wrong decks until they go broke—in a manner that is very similar to how they behave in real life. Thus both emotional parts of the brain, the amygdala and VM cortex, help people make more rational decisions.

SOMATOSENSORY AND INSULAR CORTICES

The somatosensory and insular cortices receive signals from the soma (the body). Furthermore, based on studies from patients with lesions in the right somatosensory and insular cortices, it has been proposed that these areas may hold representations of the body states such as those occurring during the experience of an emotion (Damasio, 1994). Indeed, anosognosia is a neurological condition resulting from dysfunction of the right hemisphere (damage to somatosensory and insular cortices), in which the patient is paralyzed on the left side of the body. The anosognosic patient cannot move the left hand and arm, or the left leg and foot. The left half of the face may also be immobile, and the patient is unable to stand or walk. Yet, this same patient is oblivious to the entire problem, reporting that nothing is wrong, and it is only when confronted with their blatant problem that they begin to admit that something may be wrong. In other words, these patients are unable to sense the defect automatically, rapidly, and internally through the body sensory system. Not only this, anosognosics are unable to make appropriate decisions on personal and social matters, just as in the case of VM patients, except that this defect is less noticeable than in VM patients. The reason is that VM patients appear neurologically normal, and thus can engage in a variety of social interactions that can easily expose their impaired judgment and decision making. On the other hand, patients with anosognosia are considered sick because of their motor and sensory impairments, and are thus limited in the range of social interactions in which they can engage. In other words, their opportunity to place themselves in situations that lead to negative consequences is reduced. On the basis of these clinical observations, it has been hypothesized that these somatosensory structures are critical for decision making, in that they hold representations of somatic (emotional) states. In other words, they signal "what it feels like" to do this action or that action. Without this emotional signaling, the person will not have a sense or a feeling of what their action will bring, and therefore may choose the wrong action.

THE VM PREFRONTAL CORTEX

I have described how the VM cortex is important for decision making and activation of somatic (emotional) states. However, I have not described what the VM cortex actually does. Yes, the VM cortex is important for decision making. However, decision making is a very complex function that depends on many simpler functions. The VM cortex carries one of these functions. Its function is almost similar to that of the amygdala, in that it couples information to emotional representations, except that this coupling function is a bit more complex than that of the amygdala.

More specifically, throughout development, suppose that the representations of somatic (emotional) states associated with the encounter of a primary inducer (e.g., a fear object like a snake or painful stimulus such as burning a hand on a stove) develop normally in the somatosensory and insular cortices, then accessing these representations of somatic/emotional states from secondary inducers is dependent on a neural circuitry in which the VM cortex is a critical substrate. The VM cortex is a *trigger* structure for somatic/emotional states from secondary inducers. Secondary inducers are entities generated by the recall of a personal or hypothetical emotional event (i.e., "thoughts" and "memories" about the primary inducer), which, when they are brought to working memory, elicit an emotional response (Bechara & Damasio, 2005). The emotional responses elicited by remembering instances such as encountering a snake or losing a large sum of money are examples of secondary inducers, as are the thoughts generated by even the idea of being attacked by a bear, winning an award, or losing a large sum of money. So to repeat, encountering a real snake or something that looks like a snake is a *primary inducer* and it depends on the amygdala. Thinking or worrying that a snake may attack you is a *secondary inducer* and it depends on the VM cortex (Bechara et al., 2003).

Neurologically speaking, the VM cortex serves as a convergence–divergence zone, which couples: (1) a certain category of event based on memory records in high-order association cortices to (2) the effector structures that induce the emotional response (these structures are in more primitive areas of the brain, i.e., the brainstem), and to (3) the substrates that hold representations of the nonconscious or conscious (e.g., the somatosensory and insular cortices) *feeling* of the emotional state (Damasio, 1994). In other words, the VM cortex couples knowledge to representations of "what it feels like" to be in a given situation.

Several lines of studies support the notion just presented, that the VM cortex is a trigger structure for somatic states from secondary inducers. First, lesions of the VM cortex interfered with the generation of somatic responses (SCRs and heart rate) from internally generated images of emotional situations (e.g., recalling a happy wedding, or the death of a loved one) (Bechara et al., 2003). This was true for emotional situations that occurred in the life of these patients before, as well as after, the onset of their brain damage. It was clear that the patients had a vivid memory of each emotional event. That is, they were able to retrieve and recall previous happy, sad, anger, and fear experiences, such as weddings, funerals, car accidents, and family disputes. However, they had difficulties re-experiencing the emotion of these situations as reflected by low physiological activity and low subjective rating of feeling the emotion, relative to normal control subjects (Bechara et al., 2003). In other words, the patients had a memory of the emotional event, but lacked the emotion of that memory (i.e., a disconnection between the memory and the somatic state representation of that memory).

INTERPLAY BETWEEN VM AND AMYGDALA SYSTEMS

While the amygdala is engaged in emotional situations requiring a rapid response—that is, "lower-order" emotional reactions arising from relatively automatic processes (Berkowitz, 1993; LeDoux, 1996)—the VM cortex is engaged in emotional situations driven by thoughts and reason. Once this initial amygdala emotional response is over, "higher-order" emotional reactions begin to arise from relatively more controlled, higher-order processes involved in thinking, reasoning, and consciousness (Schneider & Shiffrin, 1977). Unlike the amygdala response, which is sudden and habituates quickly, the VM response is deliberate, slow, and lasts for a long time.

Thus the prefrontal cortex, especially the VM part, helps predict the emotion of the future, thereby forecasting the consequences of one's own actions. However, it is important to note that the amygdala system is a necessary prerequisite for the normal development of the VM system for triggering somatic/emotional states from secondary inducers (i.e., thoughts and reflections). The normal acquisition of secondary inducers requires the integrity of the amygdala, and also the somatosensory and insular neural system. When the amygdala or critical components of the somatosensory and insular system are damaged, then primary inducers cannot induce somatic states, or signals from triggered somatic states cannot be transmitted to somatosensory cortices. Consequently, secondary inducers cannot acquire somatic state representations. For instance, individuals with congenital absence of C fibers do not feel pain, and are unable to construct somatic state representations related to pain. It follows that such individuals are unable to fear situations that lead to pain, or empathize in contexts related to pain. That is, they lack somatic state representations of "what it feels like" to be in pain (Damasio, 1994, 1999). Thus the normal development of the VM system is contingent on integrity of the amygdala system, which is critical for triggering somatic states from primary inducers.

Given this neural evidence, it follows that there may be a fundamental difference between two types of abnormalities that lead to distorted somatic/emotional state representations that in turn lead to abnormal cognition and behavior, especially in the area of judgment and decision making. One abnormality is neurobiological in nature and may relate to: (1) abnormal receptors or cells concerned with the triggering, or detection of somatic/emotional signals at the level of the viscera and internal milieu; (2)

abnormal peripheral neural and endocrine systems concerned with transmission of somatic/emotional state signals from the viscera and internal milieu to the brainstem; that is, the spinal cord, the vagus nerve, and the circumventricular organs (namely, the brain areas that lack a blood–brain barrier); or (3) abnormal neural systems involved in the triggering (e.g., the amygdala, VM cortex, and effector structures in the brainstem) or building of somatic/emotional state representations (e.g., sensory nuclei in the brainstem, and somatosensory and insular cortices).

The other abnormality is environmental in nature and relates to social learning. For instance, growing up in a social environment where, for instance, "killing" another individual is glorified and encouraged leads to abnormal somatic/emotional state representations of the act of killing. Although both abnormalities may be difficult to distinguish from each other at a behavioral level, the two are distinguishable at a physiological level.

I argue that individuals with abnormal social learning are capable of triggering somatic/emotional states under a variety of laboratory conditions. These individuals have the capacity to empathize, feel remorse, and fear negative consequences. In contrast, individuals with neurobiological abnormalities demonstrate failure to activate somatic states under the same laboratory conditions. Such individuals cannot express emotions, empathize, or fear negative consequences. The distinction between the two abnormalities has important social and legal implications. Individuals whose abnormal somatic state representations relate to *faulty* social learning can reverse this abnormality and unlearn the antisocial behavior once they are exposed to proper learning contingencies. In other words, these individuals are likely to benefit from cognitive and behavioral rehabilitation. In contrast, individuals with underlying neurobiological abnormalities do not have the capacity to reverse the somatic state abnormality. Consequently, these individuals demonstrate repeated and persistent failures to learn from previous mistakes, even in the face of rising and severe punishment. It follows that these individuals are unlikely to benefit from rehabilitation.

EMOTION AND DISRUPTIONS TO DECISION MAKING

Although the somatic marker view argues that emotions are an important factor in the process of decision making, there is a popular notion that "emotions cloud the mind and interfere with good judgment" and that "wise decisions and judgments come only from cool heads". How can we reconcile these seemingly conflicting views? Do emotions help the process of making advantageous decisions or disrupt it?

The somatic marker hypothesis concerns emotion that is integral to the decision-making task at hand. For instance, when deciding to speed on a highway because you are late for an interview, the "thought" of being stopped by the police, or the "thought" of getting into an accident will trigger somatic states (e.g., some form of a fear response). However, these somatic states are integral to the decision-making task at hand, such as the decision on whether to speed or not. These somatic states are indeed beneficial, because they consciously or nonconsciously bias the decision in an advantageous manner. However, the induction of somatic states that are unrelated to the decision task at hand (for example, receiving a cell phone call while driving about someone in the family dying) may become disruptive.

Support of this hypothesis comes indirectly from clinical observations of neuropsychiatric patients with bipolar disorders, who show disturbances in decision making that include indecisiveness (during depression) or impulsiveness (during mania) (First, Spitzer, Gibbon, & Williams, 1997). Experimental evidence also suggests that the presence of such unrelated emotions shifts decisions in the direction of short-term goals (Gray, 1999). Also, preliminary evidence obtained from normal subjects suggests that the induction of strong emotional states (e.g., by the recall of personal emotional experiences) before the performance of the IGT reduced the number of choices from the advantageous decks (Preston, Buchanan, Stansfield, & Bechara, 2007).

However, this emotion-related versus emotion-unrelated distinction does not always hold true. For instance, there are instances where emotions that are integral to the task can sometimes be disruptive (Shiv, Loewenstein, Bechara, Damasio, & Damasio, 2005). In a study, Shiv et al., (2005) developed a "risky decision-making task" closely modeled on a paradigm developed in previous economic research to demonstrate "myopic loss aversion". They studied normal participants and patients with focal lesions in the VM cortex, but also patients with damage in other neuronal components known to be critical for processing emotions— namely, the amygdala and insula. Each participant was endowed with $20 of play money, which they were told to treat as real because they would cash the amount they were left with at the end of the study. Participants were told that they would be making several rounds of investment decisions, and that, in each round, they had to make a decision between two options: Invest $1 or not invest. If the decision were not to invest, the task would advance to the next round. If the decision were to invest, they would hand over a dollar bill to the experimenter. The experimenter would then toss a coin in plain view of the subject. If the outcome of the toss was heads (50% chance), they would lose the $1 that was invested; if the outcome of the toss was tails (50% chance), $2.50 would be added to the participant's account. The task would then advance to the next round. The task consisted of 20 rounds of investment decisions. The experimenters designed the investment task so that it would behoove participants to invest in all the 20 rounds because the expected value on each round is higher if one invests ($1.25) than if one does not ($1). Examination of the proportion of the 20 rounds in which participants decided to invest revealed that the target patients made decisions that were closer to a profit-maximizing viewpoint. Specifically, target patients invested in 83.7% of the rounds, on average, as compared with normal participants who invested in 57.6% of the rounds, and patient-controls who invested in 60.7% of the rounds (Shiv et al., 2005). Further, target patients earned more money over the 20 rounds of the experiment ($25.7, on average) than did normal parti-cipants ($22.8) or patient-controls ($20.1). The average amount earned by normal participants was no different from that earned by patient-controls. Even though the normal subjects intellectually knew what to do, loss aver-sion took over: Normal subjects know that the right thing to do is to invest in every single round, but when they actually get into the game, they just start reacting to the outcomes of previous rounds.

These results suggest that taking away neural systems that are import-ant for processing emotions render decisions more optimal, which is in contrast to what was shown earlier in the IGT experiments. Two key dif-ferences between the two types of experiments should be noted. First, in the IGT experiments, subjects always have to make an investment, whereas in the investment task experiments subjects can opt out of making an investment (and proceed to the next trial). In other words, whereas in the IGT the selected option must always involve an action, in the investment task the alternatives permit either an action or an inaction. Second, in the IGT the expected values (or long-term consequences) of the luring decks were negative, whereas in the investment task the expected values were positive. Had the expected values in the investment task turned negative, the target patients may have performed sub-optimally. Indeed, in sub-sequent experiments where the expected values of a risky decision were rendered negative, then VM lesion patients as well as amygdala lesion patients performed sub-optimally and took risks when they were not sup-posed to, which led to long-term losses (Weller, Levin, Shiv, & Bechara, 2007). Irrespective of these methodological differences, the fact remains that there are instances when emotions can be disruptive to decision mak-ing, and the ability to suppress or control these emotions can be advanta-geous in the long term. Thus it is not a simple issue of trusting biases and emotions as the necessary arbiter of good and bad decisions. It is a matter of discovering the circumstances in which biases and emotions can be useful or disruptive.

CONCLUSION

Emotions are a major factor in the interaction between environmental conditions and human decision processes, with these emotional systems (underlying somatic state activation) providing valuable implicit or explicit knowledge for making fast and advantageous decisions. Historically, most theories of choice have been cognitive in perspective, and they assumed that decisions derive from an assessment of the future outcomes of various options and alternatives through some type of cost-benefit analyses (for a review, see Loewenstein, Weber, Hsee, & Welch, 2001). The somatic marker hypothesis (Damasio, 1994) provides neurobiological support for the notion that people make judgments not only by evaluating the consequences and their probability of occurring, but also and even sometimes primarily at a gut or emotional level (Damasio, 1994; Loewenstein et al., 2001; Schwartz & Clore, 1983; Zajonc, 1984). However, it is important to note that emotion is not always beneficial to decision making, and sometimes it can be disruptive. Therefore, it is important to discover the various conditions and circumstances under which emotion can be helpful or disruptive. The process of decision making depends in many important ways on neural substrates that regulate homeostasis, emotion, and feeling. In other words, the process of deciding is not just logical and computational but also emotional.

ACKNOWLEDGMENT

This work was supported by NINDS Program Project Grant P01 NS19632.

REFERENCES

Anderson, S. W., Bechara, A., Damasio, H., Tranel, D., & Damasio, A. R. (1999). Impairment of social and moral behavior related to early damage in the human prefrontal cortex. *Nature Neuroscience, 2,* 1032–1037.

Anderson, S. W., Damasio, H., Jones, R. D., & Tranel, D. (1991). Wisconsin card sorting test performance as a measure of frontal lobe damage. *Journal of Clinical and Experimental Neuropsychology, 3,* 909–922.

Bechara, A., & Damasio, A. (2005). The somatic marker hypothesis: A neural theory of economic decision. *Games and Economic Behavior, 52,* 336–372.

Bechara, A., Damasio, H., & Damasio, A. (2003). The role of the amygdala in decision-making. In P. Shinnick-Gallagher, A. Pitkanen, A. Shekhar, & L. Cahill (Eds.), *The amygdala in brain function: Basic and clinical approaches* (Vol. 985, pp. 356–369). New York: Annals of the New York Academy of Science.

Bechara, A., Damasio, A. R., Damasio, H., & Anderson, S. W. (1994). Insensitivity to future consequences following damage to human prefrontal cortex. *Cognition, 50,* 7–15.

Bechara, A., Damasio, H., Damasio, A. R., & Lee, G. P. (1999). Different contributions of the human amygdala and ventromedial prefrontal cortex to decision-making. *The Journal of Neuroscience, 19,* 5473–5481.

Bechara, A., Damasio, H., Tranel, D., & Anderson, S. W. (1998). Dissociation of working memory from decision making within the human prefrontal cortex. *The Journal of Neuroscience, 18,* 428–437.

Bechara, A., Damasio, H., Tranel, D., & Damasio, A. R. (1997). Deciding advantageously before knowing the advantageous strategy. *Science, 275,* 1293–1295.

Bechara, A., Tranel, D., Damasio, H., & Damasio, A. R. (1996). Failure to respond autonomically to anticipated future outcomes following damage to prefrontal cortex. *Cerebral Cortex, 6,* 215–225.

Benton, A. L. (1991). The prefrontal region: Its early history. In H. Levin, H. Eisenberg, & A. Benton (Eds.), *Frontal lobe function and dysfunction* (pp. 3–12). New York: Oxford University Press.

Berkowitz, L. (1993). Towards a general theory of anger and emotional aggression: Implications of the cognitive-neoassociationistic perspective for the analysis of anger and other emotions. In R. S. Wyer & T. K. Srull (Eds.), *Advances in social cognition* (Vol. 6, pp. 1–46). Hillsdale, NJ: Lawrence Erlbaum Associates.

Damasio, A. R. (1994). *Descartes' error: Emotion, reason, and the human brain.* New York: Grosset/Putnam.

Damasio, A. R. (1999). *The feeling of what happens: Body and emotion in the making of consciousness.* New York: Harcourt Brace & Company.

Damasio, A. R., Tranel, D., & Damasio, H. (1990). Individuals with sociopathic behavior caused by frontal damage fail to respond autonomically to social stimuli. *Behavioral Brain Research, 41,* 81–94.

Damasio, A. R., Tranel, D., & Damasio, H. (1991). Somatic markers and the guidance of behavior: Theory and preliminary testing. In H. S. Levin, H. M. Eisenberg, & A. L. Benton (Eds.), *Frontal lobe function and dysfunction* (pp. 217–229). New York: Oxford University Press.

Damasio, H., Grabowski, T., Frank, R., Galburda, A. M., & Damasio, A. R. (1994). The return of Phineas Gage: Clues about the brain from the skull of a famous patient. *Science, 264,* 1102–1104.

Eslinger, P. J., & Damasio, A. R. (1985). Severe disturbance of higher cognition after bilateral frontal lobe ablation: Patient EVR. *Neurology, 35,* 1731–1741.

First, M. B., Spitzer, R. L., Gibbon, M., & Williams, J. B. W. (1997). *Structured clinical interview for DSM-IV axis I disorders, research version, non-patient edition (SCID-I/NP).* New York: Biometrics Research, New York State Psychiatric Institute.

Friedrich, J. (1993). Primary error detection and minimization (PEDMIN) strategies in social cognition: A reinterpretation of confirmation bias phenomena. *Psychological Review, 100,* 298–319.

Gray, J. R. (1999). A bias toward short-term thinking in threat-related negative emotional states. *Personality and Social Psychology Bulletin, 25,* 65–75.

Harlow, J. M. (1848). Passage of an iron bar through the head. *Boston Medical and Surgical Journal, 39,* 389–393.

Harlow, J. M. (1868). Recovery from the passage of an iron bar through the head. *Publications of the Massachusetts Medical Society, 2,* 327–347.

LeDoux, J. (1996). *The emotional brain: The mysterious underpinnings of emotional life*. New York: Simon and Schuster.

Loewenstein, G. F., Weber, E. U., Hsee, C. K., & Welch, N. (2001). Risk as feelings. *Psychological Bulletin, 127*, 267–286.

Preston, S. D., Buchanan, T. W., Stansfield, R. B., & Bechara, A. (2007). Effects of anticipatory stress on decision-making in a gambling task. *Journal of Behavioral Neuroscience, 121*, 257–263.

Saver, J. L., & Damasio, A. R. (1991). Preserved access and processing of social knowledge in a patient with acquired sociopathy due to ventromedial frontal damage. *Neuropsychologia, 29*, 1241–1249.

Schneider, W., & Shiffrin, R. M. (1977). Controlled and automatic human information processing. *Psychological Reviews, 84*, 1–66.

Schwartz, N., & Clore, G. L. (1983). Mood, misattribution, and judgements of well-being: Information and directive functions of affective states. *Journal of Personality and Social Psychology, 45*, 513–523.

Shiv, B., Loewenstein, G., Bechara, A., Damasio, H., & Damasio, A. R. (2005). Investment behavior and the negative side of emotion. *Psychological Science, 16*, 435–439.

Stuss, D. T., Gow, C. A., & Hetherington, C. R. (1992). "No longer Gage": Frontal lobe dysfunction and emotional changes. *Journal of Consulting and Clinical Psychology, 60*, 349–359.

Weller, J. A., Levin, I. P., Shiv, B., & Bechara, A. (2007). Neural correlates of adaptive decision-making in risky gains and losses. *Psychological Science, 18*, 958–964.

Zajonc, R. B. (1984). On the primacy of affect. *American Psychologist, 39*, 117–123.

CHAPTER FOUR

Uncertainty and neuromodulation: Acetylcholine and sustained attention

Angela J. Yu

INTRODUCTION

Decision making is an essential component of intelligent behavior. Whether interpreting sensory inputs, allocating cognitive resources, or planning actions, the brain constantly makes decisions based on noisy inputs and competing objectives. Understanding decision making at both the psychological and neurobiological levels is an important problem in neuroscience, and has received increasing theoretical attention in recent years. Of key interest is the way that uncertainty is represented and computed in cognitive processing. Uncertainty is a ubiquitous and critical component of neural computation. It arises from inherent stochasticity and nonstationarity in statistical relationships in the environment, incomplete knowledge about the state of the world (e.g., sensory receptor limitations, an observer's solitary viewpoint), neuronal processing noise, and so on. Uncertainty complicates the task of constructing and maintaining an appropriate internal representation of the world. Despite the plethora of complications induced by such uncertainty, animals adeptly negotiate a complex and changeable world. A major challenge in neuroscience is to develop a formal theory of decision making that incorporates the various types of uncertainty, and link them to both animal behavior at the phenomenological level and neurobiology at the algorithmic level.

One set of powerful mathematical tools comes from Bayesian

probability theory, which deals with the quantification and integration of noisy information sources. Bayesian statistical theory has been successfully applied to cognitive phenomena such as perception (Battaglia, Jacobs, & Aslin, 2003; Clark & Yuille, 1990; Ernst & Banks, 2002; Knill & Richards, 1996), attention (Dayan, Kakade, & Montague, 2000; Dayan & Yu, 2003; Yu & Dayan, 2005a), and sensorimotor learning (Körding & Wolpert, 2004). Bayesian optimality framework formalizes the notion that efficient inference and learning depend critically on correct representation and processing of the various sorts of uncertainty associated with a behavioral context. Whether the brain performs near Bayesian optimality, and how exactly it deviates from optimality in specific contexts, can provide valuable insight into the computational principles underlying cognitive processing.

In this chapter, I shall focus on the representation of uncertainty by neuromodulators. Neuromodulatory systems are notable for their ubiquitous presence, centralized control, and potent modulatory effects on information transmission and experience-dependent plasticity in cortical neurons. Some early ideas, based on the relative promiscuity of neuromodulators, tended to associate them with rather general computational roles, such as controlling the signal to noise ratio of cells (for review, see Gu, 2002). More recently, as data suggesting more specific and heterogeneous actions for neuromodulators have emerged, there has been a flourishing of theoretical ideas inveighing them with more specific computational functions. The most well-established of these is the proposal that the dopamine system signals reward prediction errors (Schultz, Dayan, & Montague, 1997), possibly assisted by serotonin in mediating reward representation at multiple time-scales (Daw, Kakade, & Dayan, 2002). In addition to prediction errors, a critical factor controlling inference and learning is uncertainty—this is both predicted by Bayesian probability theory and evident in animal behavior (Dayan & Yu, 2003). Based on this observation, and a large and diverse body of pharmacological, physiological, anatomical, and behavioral data, I have previously proposed that the neuromodulator acetylcholine (ACh) signals *expected uncertainty* due to known variability in the behavioral context, while another neuromodulator, norepinephrine, gates the need to overhaul internal assumptions about the environment due to *unexpected uncertainty* (Yu & Dayan, 2005b). Results from a recent study confirm that ACh lesion in rats produces specific impairments in the sequential updating of statistical information that are consistent with the theory (Córdova, Yu, Dayan, & Chiba, forthcoming).

Complementing earlier work, this chapter examines the role played by ACh in a well-studied sustained attention task, which requires uncertainty-mediated information processing at a finer timescale. I will show that the assumption that ACh codes for a form of expected uncertainty, associated with stimulus frequency, produces precise effects that quantitatively match behavioral alterations due to pharmacological manipulations of ACh. In the following section, I first review the relevant anatomical, physiological, behavioral, and pharmacological data on ACh that point to its role in signaling uncertainty. In the subsequent section, I will apply these ideas to a well-studied sustained attention task by formulating a quantitative model of ACh signaling a specific type of expected uncertainty.

ACh is one of the major neuromodulatory systems found across the mammalian species, the others being norepinephrine, dopamine, serotonin, and histamine. Like ordinary neurons, the neurons in the neuromodulatory systems release neurotransmitters when activated; however, they differ from ordinary neurons in several respects: (1) they tend to reside in subcortical, localized clusters (*nuclei*); (2) they send extensive and far-reaching projections throughout the cortical and subcortical areas; (3) they tend to exert mixed actions on post-synaptic neurons, sometimes excitatory and sometimes inhibitory; and (4) they can alter the synaptic efficacy or plasticity of target neurons, thus modulating the way other neurons communicate with each other and store information.

ACh binds to two major classes of receptors, nicotinic and muscarinic, so named because nicotine (found in the leaves of the tobacco plant *Nicotiniana tabacum*) and muscarine (found in the poisonous mushroom *Amanita muscaria*) readily bind to the respective receptors and mimic the actions of ACh. Nicotinic receptors are *ionotropic*: they gate fast-acting ligand-gated ion channels; muscarinic receptors are *metabotropic*: they are coupled to G-proteins that act via second messengers and can have diverse and more sustained effects.

ACh is delivered to many cortical and subcortical areas by neurons residing in several nuclei in the basal forebrain. The most prominent among these is the nucleus basalis magnocellularis (NBM, of Meynert in humans; also referred to as the substantia innominata, SI), which provides the main cholinergic inputs to the neocortex. Another important cholinergic nucleus in the basal forebrain is the medial septum, which innervates the hippocampus. In addition, these same nuclei receive strong, topographically organized, reciprocal projections from the prefrontal cortex (Gaykema, Weeghel, Hersh, & Luiten, 1991) and the hippocampus (Alonso & Kohler, 1984). Figure 4.1 shows a schematic diagram of the projection patterns of the cholinergic system.

In the basal forebrain, ACh-releasing neurons intermingle with neurons releasing other transmitter types, including a notable population of GABAergic neurons, some of which are local interneurons, and some of which are large projection neurons (Fisher, Buchwald, Hull, & Levine,

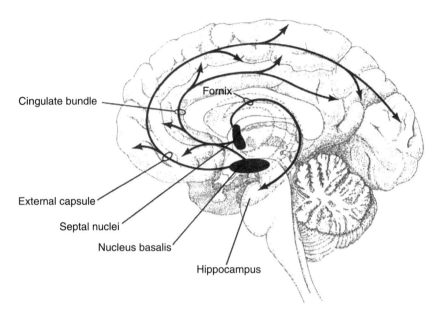

Figure 4.1   Projection pattern of the cholinergic system: Cholinergic innervation of the cortex and hippocampus by neurons in the nucleus basalis of Meynert (NBM) and the medial septum (MD), respectively. These nuclei are part of the basal forebrain, which is located at the base of the forebrain anterior to the hypothalamus and ventral to the basal ganglia (Détári et al., 1999).

1988; Gritti, Mainville, Mancia, & Jones, 1997). GABAergic terminals of basal forebrain neurons appear to synapse with GABAergic interneurons in the hippocampus and neocortex (Freund & Gulyás, 1991). This raises the interesting possibility that the cholinergic and GABAergic projections from the basal forebrain work synergistically on their cortical targets (Détári et al., 1999).

As is typical for neuromodulators, ACh has a wide array of physiological effects on downstream neurons. While the activation of nicotinic receptors is generally excitatory, effects mediated by the indirectly coupled muscarinic receptors are varied, including increases in a nonspecific cation conductance, increases or decreases in various potassium conductances, and a decrease in calcium conductance (Nicholls, Martin, & Wallace, 1992). While ACh release sites can directly target specific dendritic or somatic receptors, the majority portion of ACh release is non-specific, resulting in substantial volume transmission in the hippocampus (Umbriaco, Garcia, Beaulieu, & Descarries, 1995) and the neocortex (Umbriaco, Watkins, Descarries, Cozzari, & Hartman, 1994).

Due to anatomical and physiological heterogeneity in the basal fore-brain, direct recording of the cholinergic neurons has been difficult to verify (Détári et al., 1999). Two classes of *in vivo* experiments focusing on the effects of ACh on target cortical areas have contributed significant insights toward a more coherent understanding of cholinergic actions. One established series of studies has shown that ACh facilitates stimulus-evoked responses across sensory cortices (Metherate & Weinberger, 1990; Sillito & Murphy, 1987; Tremblay, Warren, & Dykes, 1990). For example, tetanic stimulation in the nucleus basalis increases cortical responsiveness by facilitating the ability of synaptic potentials in thalamocortical connections to elicit action potentials in the rat auditory cortex (Hars, Maho, Edeline, & Hennevin, 1993; Metherate, Asche, & Weinberger, 1993), an effect blocked by the application of atropine (an antagonist that deactivates cholinergic receptors). Similarly, iontophoretic application of ACh in the somatosensory cortex (Donoghue & Carroll, 1987; Metherate, Tremblay, & Dykes, 1987) and visual cortex (Sillito & Kemp, 1983) enhances stimulus-evoked discharges and short-term potentiation without a concomitant loss in selectivity.

Another, more recent set of experiments has shed light on the modulatory role ACh plays at the network level. At this higher level, ACh seems selectively to promote the flow of information in the feedforward pathway over that in the top–down feedback pathway (Gil, Conners, & Amitai, 1997; Hasselmo & Bower, 1992; Hsieh, Cruikshank, & Metherate, 2000; Kimura, Fukuada, & Tusomoto, 1999). Data suggest that ACh selectively enhances thalamocortical synapses via presynaptic nicotinic receptors (Gil et al., 1997) and strongly suppresses intra-cortical synaptic transmission in the visual cortex through postsynaptic muscarinic receptors (Kimura et al., 1999). In a separate study, ACh has been shown selectively to suppress synaptic potentials elicited by the stimulation of a layer in the rat piriform cortex that contains a high percentage of feedback synapses, while having little effect on synaptic potentials elicited by the stimulation of another layer that has a high percentage of feedforward synapses (Hasselmo & Bower, 1992) (see Figure 4.2).

Collectively, these data suggest ACh modulates the way that information propagates in hierarchical cortical networks, by enhancing the influences of bottom–up, sensory-bound inputs at the expense of the top–down/recurrent influence. These properties are reminiscent of the earlier discussions about the need for a signal for top–down uncertainty, which would limit the relative impact of internal knowledge/expectations on the interpretation of immediate sensory inputs.

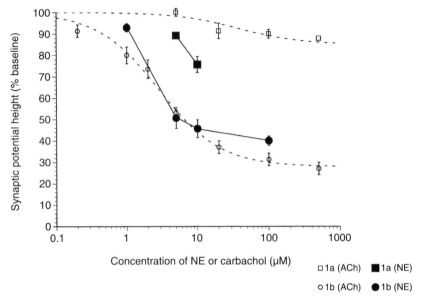

Figure 4.2   ACh effects on afferent vs. intrinsic transmission: Differential suppression of afferent (layer Ia) and intrinsic (layer Ib) synaptic transmission by ACh and norepinephrine (NE) in a dose-dependent fashion. Perfusion of carbachol (open symbols), a cholinergic agonist, into the rat piriform cortex induces a strong suppression of extracellularly recorded activities in layer Ib (mainly feedback/recurrent inputs) in response to fiber stimulation (circle); in contrast, carbachol has a much smaller suppressive effect on the afferent (feed-forward) fiber synapses to layer Ia (square). The effects are concentration-dependent (Hasselmo & Bower, 1992). Similarly, selective suppression of intrinsic but not afferent fibers has also been observed with the perfusion of norepinephrine (solid). Figure adapted from Hasselmo et al. (1997).

LITERATURE REVIEW

Direct measurements of cholinergic neuronal activities or ACh release during behavioral testing have had limited success so far. One approach involves electrophysiological recording of cholinergic neurons in awake, behaving animals. A major problem with direct recordings of ACh neurons in the basal forebrain is identification: ACh neurons are substantially intermingled with other types of neurons (mainly GABAergic) in the basal forebrain and they share similar projection patterns. For instance, a few recording studies in the NBM suggest they respond to rewarding stimuli (DeLong, 1971; Rolls, Sanghera, & Roper-Hall, 1979), but no distinction was made between cholinergic and GABAergic neurons, which have been shown through pharmacological techniques to be differentially involved in cognition and behavior (Burk & Sarter, 2001). Due to this identification problem, direct recordings of cholinergic neurons in behavioral tasks have been scarce in the literature. Were there to be a technological breakthrough in the recording of ACh neurons in behaving animals, or the unequivocal identification of neuronal type in extracellular recording, much novel insight could be gained into ACh functions during different behavioral and cognitive states. A new choline-sensing technique being developed, with temporal resolution on the order of seconds or less, seems highly promising (Parikh & Sarter, 2006).

Another approach is microdialysis of ACh in various parts of the brain. This approach suffers from the problem of temporal resolution, as typically only one measurement is taken every 20 minutes, whereas phasic events in behavioral testing typically last seconds or even less than a second. Thus, microdialysis techniques are restricted to measurements of rather tonic changes in the substance of interest. For instance, one study reported the somewhat nonspecific observation that when contingencies in an operant conditioning task are changed, ACh and norepinephrine levels are both elevated, but that ACh increases in a more sustained fashion and is less selective for the specific change in contingencies (Dalley, McGaughy, O'Connell, Cardinal, Levita, & Robbins, 2001).

Partly due to the limitations mentioned above, pharmacological manipulation of ACh in conjunction with behavioral testing has been a popular approach. Pharmacological approaches include local (ionto-phoretic) or systemic administration of agonists and antagonists, as well as certain drugs that interfere with either the production of the ACh molecule within the cholinergic neuron or the re-uptake/destruction of ACh in the extracellular medium. It is also possible to stimulate ACh neurons directly, or lesion them through incisions or neurotoxins. Through these techniques, ACh has been found to be involved in a variety of attentional tasks, such as versions of sustained attention and spatial attention tasks. Importantly for theoretical analyses, the attentional tasks studied in association with ACh can generally be viewed as top–down/bottom–up inferential tasks with elements of uncertainty.

One behavioral paradigm involving ACh is what is known as a sustained attention task, which elicits in subjects a prolonged state of readiness to respond to rarely and unpredictably occurring signals (Sarter, Givens, & Bruno, 2001). Data from experiments in which cortical ACh levels are pharmacologically manipulated (Holley, Turchi, Apple, & Sarter, 1995; McGaughy, Kaiser, & Sarter, 1996; Turchi & Sarter, 2001) show an interesting double dissociation: Abnormally low levels of ACh lead to a selective increase in error rate on signal trials, while abnormally high ACh levels lead to an increase in error rate on no-signal trials. Here, I will pursue the interpretation of these results that the rare occurrence of signals leads to an implicit top–down expectation of the signal being infrequent. If ACh signals the uncertainty about that information, then low ACh levels may be interpreted by the brain as less uncertainty about that top–down expectation, and thus even lower perceived stimulus frequency; conversely, high ACh levels may signal greater uncertainty about that expectation, equivalent to higher perceived stimulus frequency. Thus, pharmacologically suppressing ACh leads to over-confidence in the "rarity" prior and therefore a tendency not to detect a signal when it is actually present. In contrast, pharmacologically elevating ACh corresponds to under-valuation of the "rarity" prior, which can result in an over-processing of the bottom–up, noisy sensory input, leading to a high number of false signal detections. Of course, this is a somewhat over-simplified view of the problem. In the next section, I will consider a quantitative model of ACh in this task.

The second class of attention tasks, the Posner probabilistic spatial cueing task (Posner, 1980), is a well-studied paradigm for exploring the attentional modulation of visual discrimination by manipulating the top–down expectation of the location of a target stimulus. In a typical rendition of Posner's task, a subject is presented with a cue that indicates the likely location of a subsequent target, on which a detection or discrimination task must be performed. The cue is considered valid if it correctly predicts the target location, and invalid otherwise. Subjects typically respond more rapidly and accurately on a valid-cue trial than an invalid one (Downing, 1988; Posner, 1980). This difference in reaction time or accuracy, termed validity effect, has been shown to be inversely related to ACh levels through pharmacological manipulations (Phillips, McAlonan, Robb, & Brown, 2000; Witte, Davidson, & Marrocco, 1997) and lesions of the cholinergic nuclei (Chiba, Bushnell, Oshiro, & Gallagher, 1999; Voytko, Olton, Richardson, Gorman, Tobin, & Price, 1994). Validity effect has also been shown to be elevated in Alzheimer's disease patients (Parasuraman, Greenwood, Haxby, & Grady, 1992) with characteristic cholinergic depletions (Whitehouse, Price, Struble, Clark, Coyle, & DeLong, 1982), and depressed in smokers after nicotine consumption (Witte et al., 1997). Again, if ACh signals the top–down uncertainty associated with the cued location, then increasing ACh would correspond to an underestimation of the validity of the cue and therefore a decrease in the cue-induced attentional effect.

Finally, certain neurological conditions are associated with abnormal levels of specific neuromodulatory substances. In addition to the higher validity effect exhibited by Alzheimer's disease patients as mentioned above, there is a tendency toward hallucination common among patients diagnosed with Lewy Body dementia, Parkinson's disease, and Alzheimer's disease, all of which are accompanied by some degree of cortical cholinergic deficit (Perry, Walker, Grace, & Perry, 1999). In the Bayesian framework, this route to hallucination might reflect over-processing of top–down information due to an ACh deficit. The cholinergic nature of hallucination is supported by the observed correlation between the severity of hallucination and the extent of cholinergic depletion (Perry et al., 1999). Consistent with the notion that hallucination is antagonistic to sensory processing, hallucinatory experiences induced by plant chemicals containing anti-muscarinic agents such as scopolamine and atropine (Schultes & Hofmann, 1992) are enhanced during eye closure and suppressed by visual input (Fisher, 1991). Many patients with Lewy Body dementia and Alzheimer's disease also exhibit the related condition of pereidolias (also referred to as a misidentification syndrome), or the discernment of images such as faces or animals in wallpaper, curtains, or clouds (Perry & Perry, 1995), which can be interpreted as the inappropriate dominance of a top–down sensory percept over bottom–up inputs. This condition is also cholinergic in nature, as it is ameliorated by the administration of physostigmine, an ACh reuptake-inhibitor (Cummings, Gorman, & Shapira, 1993). In addition to hallucinations related to the basal forebrain cholinergic system listed here, there are also other conditions, notably due to hyperactivities of cholinergic neurons in the pedunculopontine nucleus (Ch5) and dorsolateral tegmental nucleus (Ch6) (Perry & Perry, 1995), as well as via serotonin receptors (e.g., Jacobs, 1978). As the focus of this chapter is a computational theory of basal forebrain cholinergic system, a wider discussion is beyond the current scope of this chapter.

COMPUTATIONAL MODEL

In this section, I consider a concrete behavioral task, the sustained attention task (McGaughy & Sarter, 1995) described in the previous section, to elucidate some of the computations involved in coping with a non-stationary environment. Sustained attention typically refers to a prolonged state of readiness to respond to brief, hard-to-detect signals that occur infrequently and unpredictably (Sarter et al., 2001). This element of non-stationarity leads to state uncertainty that depends on observations. Pharmacological manipulations of ACh in a rodent version of the sustained attention task have shown that suppressing and elevating ACh result in specific and distinct patterns of impairment that are dose-dependent (Holley et al., 1995; McGaughy et al., 1996; Turchi & Sarter, 2001). I will identify ACh with a form of top–down uncertainty in the model, and demonstrate that bi-directional modulation of ACh in the model has similar consequences to those observed in the experiments (Holley et al., 1995; McGaughy et al., 1996; Turchi & Sarter, 2001).

In the sustained attention experiment, rats are required to press one lever in response to a hard-to-detect light stimulus, and another lever when no light stimulus has been presented (McGaughy & Sarter, 1995). On half of the trials, no stimulus is present; the remaining half is divided into trials with signals of varying length. Figure 4.3a schematically illustrates the

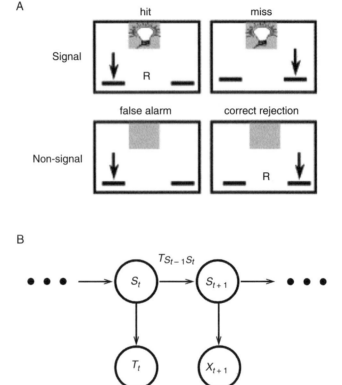

Figure 4.3   (a) Schematic illustration of a sustained attention task in rodents. Rats were trained to discriminate between signal (center light illuminated for 25, 50, or 500 ms), and nonsignal conditions. Two seconds following either stimulus, the levers were extended. The animal is rewarded only if it responds correctly (left for signal, called hits; right for non-signal, called correct rejection) within 4000 ms of lever extension. Right lever press for signal and left lever press for nonsignal trials constitute "miss" and "false alarm" responses, respectively. Figure adapted from Turchi and Sarter (2001). (b) An HMM that captures the basic stimulus properties in this task. The hidden variable s can take on one of two values: 0 for signal off, 1 for signal on. The transition matrix T controls the evolution of s. The observation x_t is generated from s_t under a Gaussian distribution.

task, as well as the classification of the different correct and incorrect responses. As might be expected, the ability of the rats to detect a stimulus drops with shorter stimuli. In an extensive series of experiments, Sarter and colleagues have shown that the basal forebrain cholinergic system plays an important role in this task. Cortical ACh elevation, via the administration of either benzodiazepine receptor inverse agonists (Holley et al., 1995) or an NMDA agonist into the basal forebrain (Turchi & Sarter, 2001), results in the decrease of the number of correct rejections (CR) but no changes to the number of hits. In contrast, infusion of 192 IgG-saporin (McGaughy et al., 1996), an ACh-specific neurotoxin, or an NMDA antagonist (Turchi & Sarter, 2001) into the basal forebrain adversely affects hits but not CR. These doubly-dissociated effects are moreover dose-dependent on the drug concentration (Turchi & Sarter, 2001). Figures 4.4a and 4.5a show these interesting behavioral impairments from NMDA agonist/antagonist manipulations (Turchi & Sarter, 2001).

In the experiment, a trial consists of a 9000±3000 ms inter-trial interval (ITI), followed by the stimulus presentation, and, 2 s later, the extension of the two levers on one of which the animal is required to make a response (left lever for signal, right lever for nonsignal). The response is then reinforced (depending on its rectitude), before another variable ITI and a new trial. The nonsignal stimulus is presented on 50% of the trials, and the remaining trials are equally divided among stimulus durations of 25, 50, and 500 ms. All trial types, including the different stimuli lengths and the no-signal trials, are inter-mixed and presented in a pseudo-random fashion (Turchi & Sarter, 2001).

Let us consider a computational characterization of this sustained attention task in the Bayesian framework. The hidden variable of interest is the presence (or absence) of the light stimulus. It undergoes transitions between two different states (signal on and signal off). There is uncertainty about both when the transitions occur and how long the stimulus variable persists in each of these states. These properties of the task suggest that a form of hidden Markov model (HMM) would be an appropriate generative model for the task, allowing the rarity (in total time) and unpredictability of the signal to be captured.

In the HMM, the hidden stimulus variable s_t takes on the value 1 if the signal is on at time t and 0 otherwise. It is assumed that the observation x_t is directly generated by s_t under a Gaussian distribution, whose mean and variance are determined by s_t:

$$p(x_t | s_t = i) = N(\mu_i, \sigma_i^2)$$

For simulations in this section, the following parameters are used: $\mu_0 = 1$, $\mu_1 = 2$, $\sigma_0 = 0.75$, $\sigma_1 = 1.5$. While this is clearly a simplifying model that

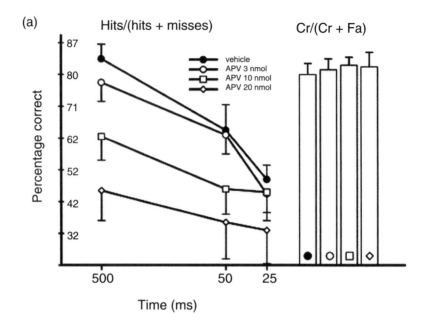

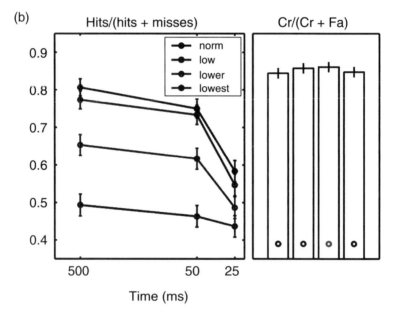

Figure 4.4 Effects of cholinergic depletion on a sustained attention task. (a) Infusion of DL-2-amino-5-phophonovaleric acid (APV) into the basal forebrain, an NMDA antagonist known to block corticopetal ACh release, dose-dependently decreases the animals' ability to detect brief, infrequent, unpredictably occurring light stimuli (line graph), but does not affect the number of correct rejections (CR) relative to false alarms (FA) on no-signal trials (bars). Error bars: Standard errors of the mean. Adapted from Turchi and Sarter (2001). (b) Simulated ACh depletion, corresponding to an over-heightened expectation of signal rarity, leads to a similar dose-dependent decrease in hits (relative to misses), while sparing CR (relative to FA). Second line from top: $a = 0.98$, third line from top: $a = 0.90$, bottom line: $a = 0.80$ (see text for more information on a). Error bars: Standard errors of the mean. See color plate.

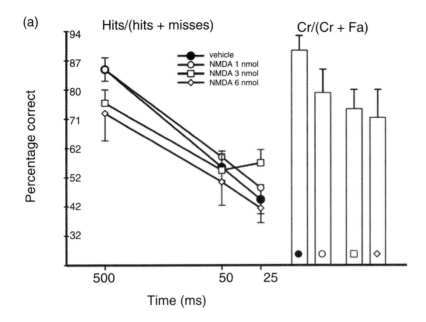

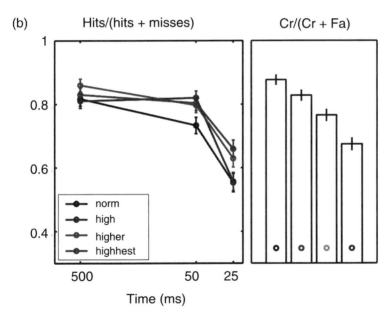

Figure 4.5 Effects of cholinergic elevation on a sustained attention task. (a) Infusion of NMDA into the basal forebrain, known to elevate corticopetal ACh release, dose-dependently decreases the fraction CRs, but has no effect on the number of hits relative to misses. Error bars: Standard errors of the mean. Adapted from Turchi and Sarter (2001). (b) Simulated ACh elevation, corresponding to a suppressed expectation of signal rarity, leads to a similar dose-dependent decrease CR, while sparing hits (relative to misses). Second line from top: $a = 1.10$, third line from top: $a = 1.15$, bottom line: $a = 1.20$ (see text for more information on a). Error bars: Standard errors of the mean. See color plate.

assumes that all sensory inputs at time t can be summarized into a single scalar x_t, it captures the properties that there is a baseline activity level (reflecting the constantly lit house light, neuronal noise, etc.) associated with the nonsignal state, and a heightened activity level associated with the signal state, as well as multiplicative noise. Figure 4.3b illustrates the generative model with a graphical model; Figure 4.6a illustrates the noise generation process.

The dynamics of s between one time step and the next are controlled by the transition matrix T_{ij}:

$$T_{ij} = P(s_t = j | s_{t-1} = i).$$

The number of consecutive time-steps $<l_i>$ that the hidden variable spends in a particular state $s = i$ is determined by the self-transition probabilities:

$$<l_i> = \frac{T_{ii}}{1 - T_{ii}}.$$

Thus, the average signal length being $(500 + 50 + 25)/3 \approx 200$ ms translates into a signal self-transition probability of $P(s_t = 1 | s_{t-1} = 1) = 0.9756$ (each timestep in the model represents 5 ms). In addition, the average duration of no-signal being 9000 ms translates into a no-signal self-transition probability of $P(s_t = 0 | s_{t-1} = 0) = 0.9994$. These quantities completely specify the Markov transition matrix T:

$$T = P(s_t | s_{t-1}) = \begin{bmatrix} 0.9994 & 0.0006 \\ 0.0244 & 0.9756 \end{bmatrix}$$

where the entry T_{ij} in row i and column j specifies $P(s_t = i | s_{t-1} = j)$. Note that Markovian state dynamics lead to exponential distributions of dwell-time in each state, which may or may not be the case for a particular experiment.

Here, I focus on the inference problem and not the learning process, and assume that the animal will have learned the parameters of the generative model (the transition matrix, the prior distribution of s, and the noise distributions of x) at the outset of the experimental session. In addition, since the onset of the ITI resets internal belief ($s_1 = 1$) at the beginning of each trial, it is assumed that the animal knows with perfect certainty that there is no signal: $P(s_1 = 1) = 0$.

When the animal is confronted with the levers at the end of t time steps (for simplicity, I assume that the animal can recall perfectly the inferential state 2000 ms before lever extension, and therefore do not model the 2000 ms delay explicitly), the animal must decide whether a signal was present or not depending on the relative probabilities of $s_t = 1$ versus $s_t = 0$, given all observations $D_t = \{x_1, x_2, \ldots, x_t\}$. In other words, $P(s_t = 1 | D_t) > P(s_t = 0 | D_t)$

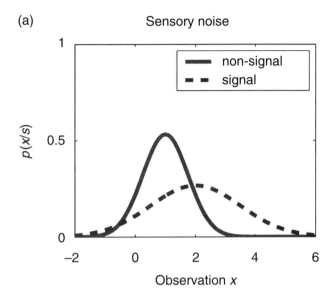

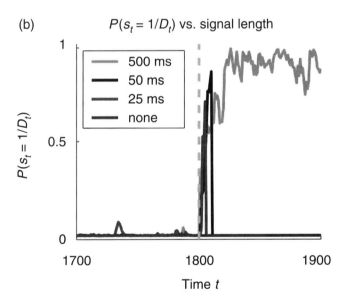

Figure 4.6 Generative noise and posterior inference in an HMM model of the sustained attention task. (a) "Sensory" noise generated by nonsignal (red: $\mu_0 = 1$, $\sigma_0 = 0.75$) and signal (blue: $\mu_1 = 2$, $\sigma_1 = 1.5$). (b) Posterior probability of signal $P(s_t = 1 \mid D_t)$ for different signal lengths, aligned at stimulus onset (dashed line at 1800 ms). Traces averaged over five trials generated from the noise parameters in (a), stimulus durations are specified as in the legend. See color plate.

would lead to the decision $s_t = 1$, and the opposite would lead to the decision $s_t = 0$, since the prior probability of there being a light stimulus on a given trial is exactly 0.5 and the reward structure of hits and correct rejections is symmetric. The computation of this posterior is iterative and straightforward given Bayes' Theorem:

$$P(s_t|D_t) \propto p(x_t|s_t)P(s_t|D_{t-1}) = p(x_t|s_t)\sum_{s_t-1} T_{s_{t-1}s_t}P(s_{t-1}|D_{t-1}).$$

As usual, there is a critical balance between the bottom–up likelihood term, $p(x_t|s_t)$, and the top–down prior term $P(s_{t-1}|D_{t-1})$. If the prior term favors one hypothesis (e.g., $s_t = 0$), and the likelihood term favors the other (e.g., $s_t = 1$), then this prediction error would shift the posterior (and the prior for the next time-step) a bit more in favor of $s_t = 1$. Multiple observations of inputs favoring $s_t = 1$ in a row would shift the dynamic prior increasingly toward $s_t = 1$. Note that the influence of the prior on the inference step relative to the likelihood is determined by a constant component (the transition matrix T) and a dynamic component $P(s_{t-1}|D_{t-1})$ driven by observations.

Such an inferential/decision process is optimal according to Bayesian theory, but it still can result in an error when the posterior distribution based on a finite amount of noisy data favors the "wrong" hypothesis by chance. In addition to these "inferential" errors, we assume that the animal makes some noninferential (e.g., motor or memory) errors that occur in addition to any in the inferential process. So even though the animals ideally should always choose the left lever when $P(s_t = 1|D_t) > .5$, and the right lever otherwise, they are modeled as pressing the opposite lever with a small probability (.15).

RESULTS

As can be seen in Figure 4.6a, there is a substantial amount of "sensory" noise due to the overlap in the distributions: $p(x|s = 0)$ and $p(x|s = 1)$. Consequently, each observation x_t tends to give relatively little evidence for the true state of the stimulus s_t. The initial condition of $P(x_1 = 0) = 1$ and the high nonsignal self-transition probability (T_{00}) together ensure a "conservative" stance about the presence of a stimulus. If s persists in one state (e.g., the "on" state) for longer, however, the bottom–up evidence can overwhelm the prior. The accumulation of these effectively i.i.d. (independently and identically distributed) samples when the stimulus is turned on drives the posterior probability mass in the "on" state $(s = 1)$, and underlies the monotonic relationship between stimulus duration and hit rate (see Figures 4.4a and 4.5a). Figure 4.6b shows the evolution of the iterative posterior probability of $s_t = 1$ for stimuli that appear for different lengths of time. As evident from the traces (averaged over five random trials each), the posterior probabilities stay close to 0 when there is no signal, and start rising when the signal appears. The length of stimulus duration has a strong influence on the height of the final posterior probability at the end of the stimulus presentation. The black trace in the line plot of Figure 4.4b shows this more systematically, where we compare the averages from 300 trials of each stimulus duration. The results qualitatively replicate the duration-dependent data from the sustained attention experiment (filled circles in Figure 4.4a).

A strong component of the top–down information here is the rarity of the signal "on" state: $s_t = 0$ is almost two orders of magnitude more likely than $s_t = 1$ at any particular time t, in both the experimental setting and the generative model. In accordance with the proposition that ACh signals expected uncertainty, it seems natural to identify the ACh signal to be the uncertainty associated with the predominant expectation $s_t = 0$, or $1 - P(s_t = 0 | D_t) = P(s_t = 1 | D_t)$.

With this identification of ACh to a specific probabilistic quantity in place, it becomes possible to explore the consequences of manipulating ACh levels (or the corresponding probabilities) in the model. ACh depletion, for instance, is equivalent to decreasing $P(s_t = 1 | D_t)$, which is modeled here as multiplying it by a constant a less than 1 (lower-bounded at 0). Similarly, ACh elevation can be modeled as multiplying $P(s_t = 1 | D_t)$ by a constant a greater than 1 (the probability is upper-bounded at 1). Consequently, ACh depletion in the model results in an underestimation of the probability of the stimulus being present and a drop in hit rate. However, the CR rate is already saturated, with a false alarm (FA) rate reflecting the noninferential error rate of .15, and cannot fall substantially lower despite the overestimation of nonsignal trials. It makes little sense that the animals should be more likely to report "no signal" on true signal trials but not on true nonsignal trials, when the substantial error rates indicate that a number of the trials, both signal and no-signal, must be inferentially confusable. One explanation for the lack of improvement in the number of CR is that there is a base rate of noninferential errors, either motor or memory-related, which do not depend on the difficulty of sensory discrimination or the perceptual decision criterion.

In contrast, ACh elevation in the model is equivalent to an overestimation of the probability of the stimulus being present, resulting in a rise of FAs relative to CRs. The benefits to hit rate, also close to saturation, are relatively small. Figures 4.4b and 4.5b show that under these assumptions, the model can produce simulation results that qualitatively replicate experimental data (Turchi & Sarter, 2001) for ACh depletion and elevation, respectively. Although there is some flexibility in the formal implementation of ACh manipulations (different values of a or altogether a different functional form), the monotonic (dose-dependent) and doubly dissociated properties of ACh depletion/elevation observed experimentally are clearly demonstrable in the model. The exact quantitative effects of NMDA drugs on ACh release, and more importantly on the processing of downstream neurons, are not precisely known in any case.

DISCUSSION

In this chapter, I introduced the concept of uncertainty in cortical processing, and suggested that the neuromodulator ACh is a critical component of the neural strategy to cope with uncertainty in sensory processing and attentional control. This builds on my previous work on neuromodulatory representation of uncertainty (Yu & Dayan, 2005b). It also complements a growing body of work on the coding of uncertainty in cortical neuronal populations (Barber, Clark, & Anderson, 2003; Deneve, 2005; Deneve, Latham, & Pouget, 1999; Pouget, Zhang, Deneve, & Latham, 1998; Rao, 2004; Sahani & Dayan, 2003; Weiss & Fleet, 2002; Yu, 2007; Yu & Dayan, 2005a; Zemel, Dayan, & Pouget, 1998).

To illustrate the theoretical concepts, I used a simple two-state HMM with Gaussian noise to model a sustained attention task. In the model, I identify ACh level as the moment-by-moment internal belief of the stimulus being present. As observed in experiments (McGaughy & Sarter, 1995), shorter stimuli lead to poorer detection performance in the model. Moreover, I simulated pharmacological manipulations of ACh by artificially altering the posterior probability in the inference model. Similar to experimental data (Turchi & Sarter, 2001), ACh depletion leads to a dose-dependent decrease of hit rate while sparing CRs, and ACh elevation selectively impairs CR while having little effect on hit rate. The strength of this model is its simplicity and its ability to capture the experimental data quantitatively.

It is possible that animals can actually learn and utilize a more complex internal model than the HMM assumed here, which is one of the simplest models that can capture information about the frequency and timing of the stimulus presentation. The HMM is limited in its capacity to represent arbitrary distributions of signal duration and onset times. A two-state HMM has only two free parameters, T_{00} and T_{11}, which can be used to mold the distributions. I discussed the relationship between the mean duration of the two signal states (on and off) and the two self-transition probabilities in the "Computational model" section. It can also be shown that these probabilities determine the *variance* of the signal durations: $\mathrm{var}(l_i) = T_{ii}^3/(1 - T_{ii})^2$. This limits the capacity of the HMM in modeling the experimental settings. For instance, the transition matrix used makes the standard deviation of the inter-signal interval (8300 ms) much larger than the experimental value (1750 ms). Moreover, the stimulus cannot actually occur within 6000 ms of ITI onset, nor can it appear more than once per trial. These additional pieces of information can be helpful for signal detection, but not captured by the simple HMM, as they require longer-range temporal contingencies and richer representations.

Another hint that the HMM formulation may be overly simple comes from a discrepancy between Figures 4.5a and 4.5b. One qualitative difference is that the animals' performance on intermediate signal (50 ms) trials is significantly worse than on the long signal (500 ms) trials, whereas in the model, the performance is already near saturation at 50 ms, and it is this saturation property that prevents the hit rate from rising when ACh is elevated in the model. This may be empirical evidence that the animals might be employing a more complex computational model than the HMM.

Despite these shortcomings, the HMM coupled with ACh modulation has been shown to capture the core characteristics of the experimental data, indicating that the representation of these additional experimental contingencies is not fundamental to induce the general pattern of deficits observed in the animals. Even in richer Bayesian models, identifying ACh with the on-line posterior probability of signal presence should give qualitatively similar results as those presented here. Of course, it is possible that other, non-Bayesian models might equally well explain some of the experimental phenomena explored here. Without richer experimental data, however, it is not possible currently to distinguish between this Bayesian formulation and other potentially suitable models.

ACh is one of several major neuromodulatory systems that strongly interact in their influence on cortical processing. In particular, norepinephrine has been found to have similar physiological properties as ACh: Across primary sensory areas, norepinephrine selectively suppresses intracortical and feedback synaptic transmission, while sparing thalamo-cortical processing (Hasselmo, Wyble, & Wallenstein, 1996; Kobayashi, 2000). ACh and norepinephrine also play a synergistic role in experience-dependent plasticity in the neocortex and the hippocampus (reviewed in Gu, 2002), enabling the revision of internal representations based on new experiences. Behavioral data suggest, however, that norepinephrine plays a somewhat different role than ACh: It has been shown to be important in tasks in which the animal must learn about new environmental contingencies (such as in reversal or extinction manipulations), or when encountering novel stimuli and situations. Boosting norepinephrine with the drug idazoxan (Curet, Dennis, & Scatton, 1987) in one such task accelerates the detection of the cue-shift and learning of the new cues in rodents

(Devauges & Sara, 1990). This contrasts with the involvement of ACh in tasks in which there is inherent stochasticity (e.g., stimulus onset, stimulus type, cue validity).

Based on these data, I previously proposed that ACh signals *expected uncertainty* corresponding to known variability or stochasticity in an environment, while norepinephrine signals *unexpected uncertainty* due to drastic changes in the environment that requires substantial revamping of the internal representation of the world (Yu & Dayan, 2005b). That formulation is consistent with a wealth of physiological, pharmacological, and behavioral data implicating ACh and norepinephrine in specific aspects of a range of cognitive processes. Moreover, that work proposed a novel class of attentional cueing tasks that would involve both neuromodulators, and predicts their interactions to be semi-antagonistic (Yu & Dayan, 2005b). In particular, how much unexpected observations should be allowed to modify an internal model depends on how much known variability is expected in the first place.

The distinction of expected and unexpected uncertainty, motivated by Bayesian probabilistic modeling, is related to the notions of external (disposition) and internal (ignorance) attributes of uncertainty in behavioral economics (Kahneman & Tversky, 1982). The former makes the distinction based on the observer's expectations, the latter is defined in terms of the source of the uncertainty. The two are related because uncertainty due to external factors is often unexpected in nature, whereas internal uncertainty is known to the observer and therefore often expected. However, expected uncertainty can also arise from external sources, such as inherent stochasticity in the environment like the imperfectly valid cues in the Posner task discussed above (Posner, 1980). Likewise, unexpected uncertainty can be fundamentally internal, as when an observer lacks a good model of a new environment due to deliberate/voluntary change (e.g. moving to a foreign country). From a computational point of view, it is useful to define variants of uncertainty according to how they impact subsequent inference and learning. Of course, the source of uncertainty is also important, so that new observations can be used appropriately to update the various types of uncertainty. Bayesian probability theory also provides convenient tools for these purposes (Dayan & Yu, 2003).

Another closely related dissection of uncertainty is aleatory versus epistemic, concepts in philosophy with Greek and Egyptian roots. Aleatory uncertainty refers to irreducible uncertainty due to inherent randomness in nature. Epistemic uncertainty refers to reducible uncertainty due to lack of knowledge or ignorance. The emphasis there, therefore, is on the reducibility of uncertainty. Expected uncertainty is much like aleatory uncertainty, since it often refers to inherent, irreducible uncertainty; how-

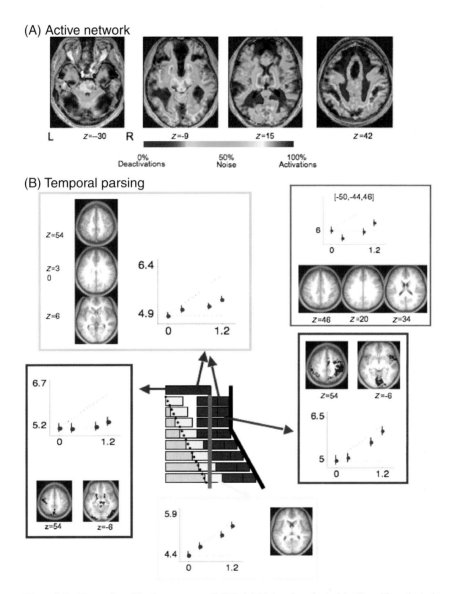

(A) Active network

L   z=−30   R   z=−9   z=15   z=42

0%   50%   100%
Deactivations   Noise   Activations

(B) Temporal parsing

Figure 1.5 Dynamics of brain processes: fMRI. (a) Network activated (red) and inactivated (blue) during dual-task performance as identified by a phase coherence analysis. (b) Parsing the brain network in distinct dynamic processing stages, according to their phase profile. Blue: The brain network involved exclusively in task 1. Yellow: The brain network involved in the perceptual component of task 2. Red: The brain network involved in the central and motor components of task 2. Cyan: Regions involved in both tasks. Green: The brain network involved in executive coordination of both tasks.

(A) Introspective RT is a reliable measure

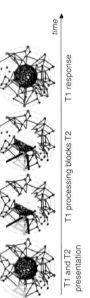

(B) The dual-task delay is inaccessible to introspection

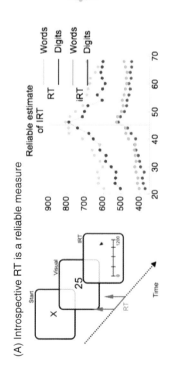

Figure 1.6 Temporal dynamics of processes. Introspection of response time and its failure during dual-task processing. (a) A number comparison task followed by an estimate of introspective response time (IRT) indicated that, although there is a consistent under-estimation (reflecting a poor calibration of absolute IRT), subjects' estimate of IRT is very tightly correlated with RT. (b) On the contrary, the 300 ms delay of the PRP was unnoticed in introspection. Subjects always thought that they were taking a constant time for task 2, regardless of SOA.

ATTENTIONAL BLINK

- T2 is masked, resulting in extinction.
- The second stimulus does not access consciousness.

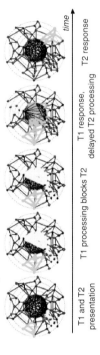

| T1 and T2 presentation | T1 processing blocks T2 | T1 response |

PSYCHOLOGICAL REFRACTORY PERIOD

- T2 is sustained and thus can access the workspace after a delay.
- This delay is inaccessible to introspection.

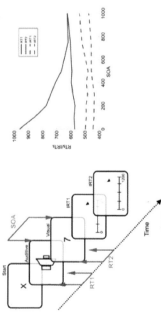

| T1 and T2 presentation | T1 processing blocks T2 | T1 response, delayed T2 processing | T2 response |

Figure 1.7 A simple sketch of the dynamics of modular and workspace processing during the PRP and the attentional blink.

(a)   (b)

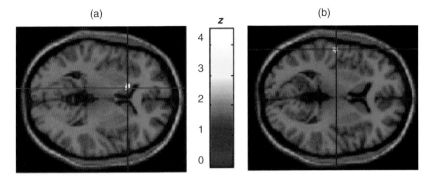

Figure 2.3 Neural activation for choice as a function of context. From Vartanian et al. (2009). The anterior caudate nucleus was activated more when subjects made choices in life problems (a). The posterior insula was activated more when subjects made choices in cash problems (b).

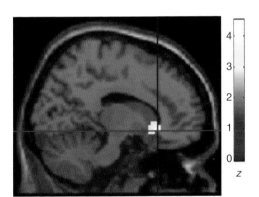

Figure 2.4 Neural activation as a function of negative feedback and context. From Vartanian et al. (2009). The subgenual anterior cingulate was activated more when subjects received negative feedback in life domain than when they received negative feedback in the cash domain.

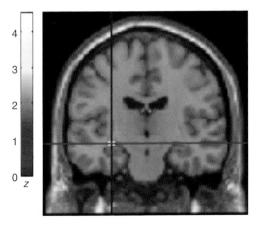

Figure 2.5 Neural activation as a function of negative feedback, subsequent choice, and context. From Vartanian et al. (2009). The dorsal hippocampus (bordering on posterior amygdala) was activated more in the life than cash domain when subjects opted to return to the uncertain deck on trial n following negative feedback on trial $n-1$.

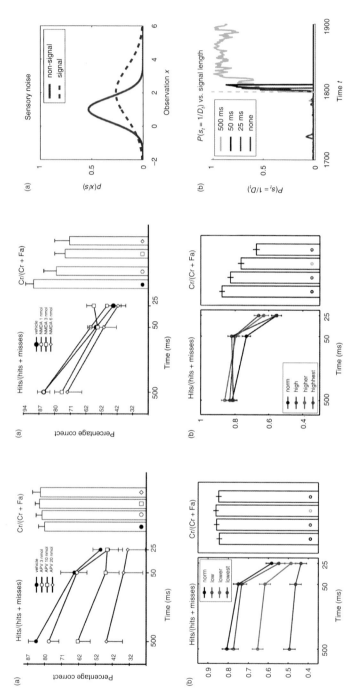

Figure 4.4 Effects of cholinergic depletion on a sustained attention task. (a) Infusion of DL-2-amino-5-phophonovaleric acid (APV) into the basal forebrain, an NMDA antagonist known to block corticopetal ACh release, dose-dependently decreases the animals' ability to detect brief, infrequent, unpredictably occurring light stimuli (line graph), but does not affect the number of correct rejections (CR) relative to false alarms (FA) on no-signal trials (bars). Error bars: Standard errors of the mean. Adapted from Turchi and Sarter (2001). (b) Simulated ACh depletion, corresponding to an over-heightened expectation of signal rarity, leads to a similar dose-dependent decrease in hits (relative to misses), while sparing CR (relative to FA). Second line from top: $a = 0.90$, bottom line: $a = 0.80$ (see text for more information on a). Error bars: Standard errors of the mean.

Figure 4.5 Effects of cholinergic elevation on a sustained attention task. (a) Infusion of NMDA into the basal forebrain, known to elevate corticopetal ACh release, dose-dependently decreases the fraction CRs, but has no effect on the number of hits relative to misses. Error bars: Standard errors of the mean. Adapted from Turchi and Sarter (2001). (b) Simulated ACh elevation, corresponding to a suppressed expectation of signal rarity, leads to a similar dose-dependent decrease CR, while sparing hits (relative to misses). Second line from top: $a = 1.10$, third line from top: $a = 1.15$, bottom line: $a = 1.20$ (see text for more information on a). Error bars: Standard errors of the mean.

Figure 4.6 Generative noise and posterior inference in an HMM model of the sustained attention task. (a) "Sensory" noise generated by nonsignal (red: $\mu_0 = 1$, $\sigma_0 = 0.75$) and signal (blue: $\mu_1 = 2$, $\sigma_1 = 1.5$). (b) Posterior probability of signal $P(s_t = 1|D_t)$ for different signal lengths, aligned at stimulus onset (dashed line at 1800 ms). Traces averaged over five trials generated from the noise parameters in (a), stimulus durations are specified as in the legend.

(1) Parietal "analytic" ROIs

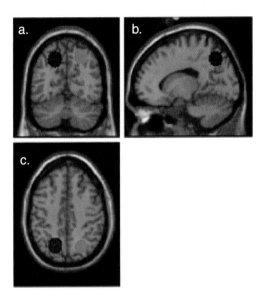

(2) Temporal "heuristic" ROIs

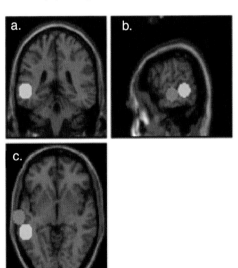

Figure 5.1 Location of the ROI assumed to be involved in analytic and heuristic decision making superimposed on to coronal (a), sagittal (b), and transverse (c) sections of a magnetic resonance image, which is itself in standard space. Left-hand panels (1) shows the position of the superior parietal ROI (BA7; left in dark blue, right in light blue). Right-hand panels (2) show the position of the posterior (light green) and additional anterior (orange) left lateral temporal ROI (BA 21/22).

(a) 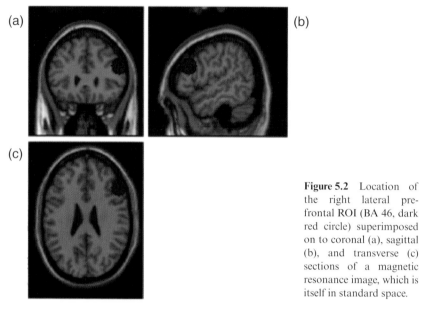 (b)

(c)

Figure 5.2 Location of the right lateral prefrontal ROI (BA 46, dark red circle) superimposed on to coronal (a), sagittal (b), and transverse (c) sections of a magnetic resonance image, which is itself in standard space.

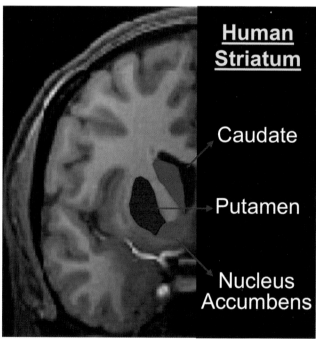

Figure 6.1 Coronal section of human brain roughly depicting striatal subdivisions. The caudate (light purple region), putamen (dark purple region) and nucleus accumbens (orange region) are highlighted.

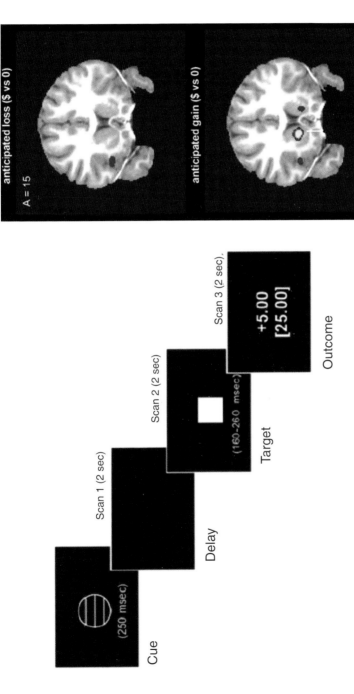

Figure 6.2 The Monetary Incentive Delay task. Participants view a cue that represents the valence (reward or loss) and magnitude ($0–$5.00) of the outcome. Increases in BOLD response in the ventral striatum are observed when participants anticipate potential rewards, but not losses. Reprinted with permission from Knutson, Adams et al. (2001).

A. Probabilistic gambling task

Condition 1
Reward $1.00

Condition 2
Punishment –$0.50

Condition 3
Neutral –

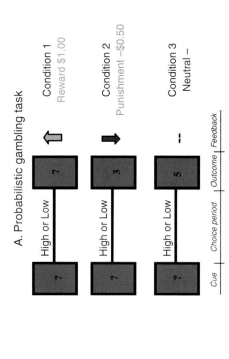

Cue | Choice period | Outcome | Feedback

B. Striatum hemodynamic response during probabilistic gambling task

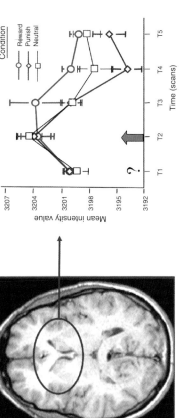

Figure 6.3 The card-guessing task. (a) Participants are asked to guess if the value of the card is higher or lower than the number 5. A correct response leads to a monetary reward (e.g., $1.00), while an incorrect response leads to a monetary loss (e.g., −$0.50). When the card number is 5, a neutral outcome occurs and money is neither gained nor lost. (b) Activation of the striatum, particularly the head of the caudate nucleus (pictured) is observed when participants are engaged in this paradigm. The hemodynamic response is higher for reward trials, while it decreases sharply below baseline when the outcome is a loss. Reprinted with permission from Delgado et al. (2000).

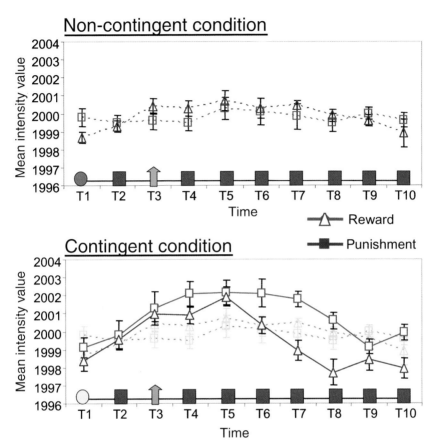

Figure 6.4 The affective oddball paradigm. Participants are instructed to detect the oddball (monetary arrow) which is delivered either contingently (yellow circle) or non-contingently (blue circle) on the participant's action. Contingent, but not non-contingent, affective outcomes recruit activation in the head of the caudate nucleus. Reprinted with permission from Tricomi et al. (2004).

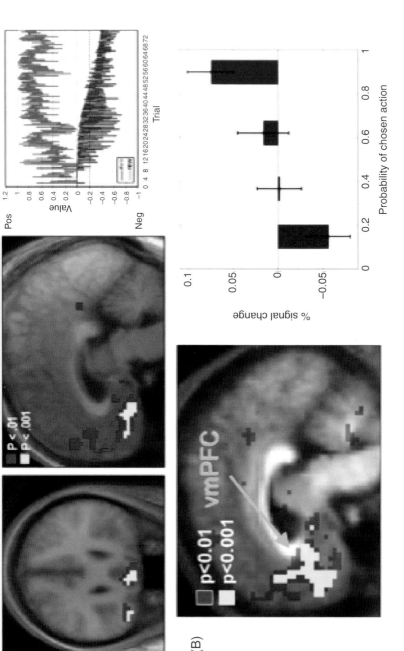

Figure 7.1 Reward prediction signals in the vmPFC during reward-based action-selection in humans. (a) Regions of the vmPFC (medial and central orbitofrontal cortex extending into medial prefrontal cortex) correlating with expected value signals generated by a variant of a reinforcement learning model during an fMRI study of instrumental choice of reward and avoidance (left and middle panels). The model-predicted expected value signals are shown for one subject in the right panel for both the reward (top line) and avoidance (bottom line) conditions. Data from Kim et al. (2006). (b) Similar regions of the vmPFC correlating with model-predicted expected value signals during performance of a four-armed bandit task with nonstationary reward distributions (left panel). BOLD signal changes in this region are shown plotted against model predictions (right panel), revealing an approximately linear relationship between expected value and BOLD signal changes in this region. Data from Daw et al. (2006).

(A)

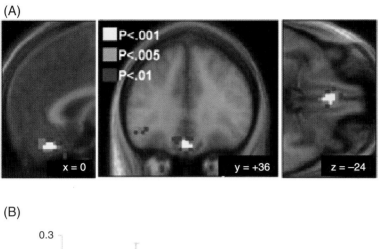

(B)

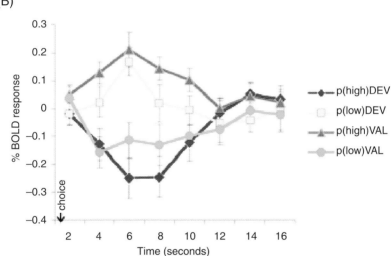

Figure 7.2 Regions of the vmPFC and OFC showing response properties consistent with action-outcome learning. Neural activity during action selection for reward showing a change in response properties as a function of the value of the outcome with each action. Choice of an action leading to a high probability of obtaining an outcome that had been devalued (p(high)DEV) led to a decrease in activity in these areas, whereas choice of an action leading to a high probability of obtaining an outcome that was still valued led to an increase in activity in the same areas. Devaluation was accomplished by means of feeding the subject to satiety on that outcome prior to the test period. (a) A region of the medial OFC showing a significant modulation in its activity during instrumental action selection as a function of the value of the associated outcome. (b) Time-course plots derived from the peak voxel (from each individual subject) in the mOFC during trials in which subjects chose each one of the four different actions (choice of the high vs. low probability action in either the Valued or Devalued conditions). Data from Valentin et al. (2007).

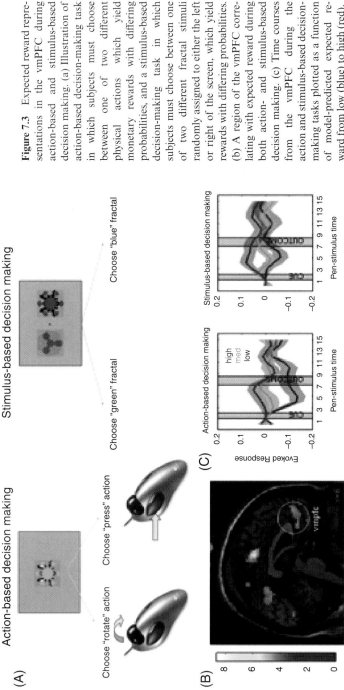

Figure 7.3 Expected reward representations in the vmPFC during action-based and stimulus-based decision making. (a) Illustration of action-based decision-making task in which subjects must choose between one of two different physical actions which yield monetary rewards with differing probabilities, and a stimulus-based decision-making task in which subjects must choose between one of two different fractal stimuli randomly assigned to either the left or right of the screen, which yield rewards with differing probabilities. (b) A region of the vmPFC correlating with expected reward during both action- and stimulus-based decision making. (c) Time courses from the vmPFC during the action and stimulus-based decision-making tasks plotted as a function of model-predicted expected reward from low (blue) to high (red).

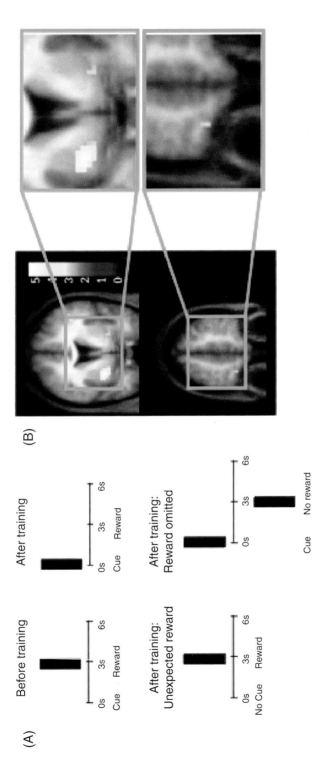

Figure 7.4 Temporal difference prediction error signals during Pavlovian reward conditioning in humans. (a) Properties of the temporal difference prediction error signal. This signal responds positively at the time of reward presentation before training, shifts to responding at the time of presentation of the predictive cue after training, and shows a decrease from baseline (negative signal) if an expected reward is omitted. (b) Results from an fMRI study testing for brain regions correlating with a temporal difference prediction error signal during classical conditioning in humans. Significant correlations with the TD prediction error signal were found in the ventral striatum bilaterally (top panel) and in the OFC (bottom panel).

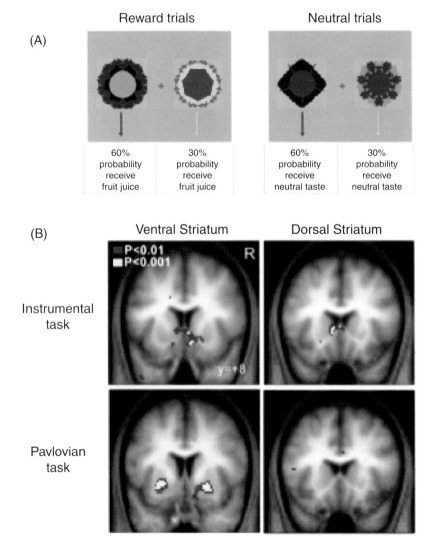

Figure 7.5 Prediction error signals underlying action selection for reward. (a) Schematic of instrumental choice task used by O'Doherty et al. (2004). On each trial of the reward condition the subject chooses between two possible actions, one associated with a high probability of obtaining juice reward (60%), the other a low probability (30%). In a neutral condition, subjects also choose between actions with similar probabilities, but in this case they receive an affectively neutral outcome (tasteless solution). Prediction error responses during the reward condition of the instrumental choice task were compared with prediction error signals during a yoked Pavlovian control task. (b) Significant correlations with the reward prediction error signal generated by an actor/critic model were found in the ventral striatum (ventral putamen extending into nucleus accumbens proper) in both the Pavlovian and instrumental tasks, suggesting that this region is involved in stimulus–outcome learning. In contrast, a region of the dorsal striatum (anteromedial caudate nucleus) was found to be correlated with prediction error signals only during the instrumental task, suggesting that this area is involved in stimulus–response or stimulus–response–outcome learning. Data from O'Doherty et al. (2004).

ever, just after the detection of an unexpected global change in the environment, expected uncertainty also rises due to known ignorance (and may be eventually reducible to a certain extent). Unexpected uncertainty is roughly analogous to epistemic uncertainty—uncertainty due to unexpected changes in the environment may be ultimately reducible with greater familiarity, but it does not need to be. Our emphasis is on current expectations, rather than eventual reducibility of uncertainty.

Ultimately, there are many different ways to slice the pie of uncertainty, and the brain may need to use different configurations depending on the task at hand. Indeed, there is ongoing investigation of how cortical neural populations also contribute to the neural representation of uncertainty. Theoretical models of neural coding span from simpler population codes that can also encode restricted aspects of uncertainty (Zemel et al., 1998; Pouget et al., 1998; Deneve et al., 1999) to more exotic interpretations of codes as representing complex featural distributions (Barber et al., 2003; Rao, 2004; Sahani & Dayan, 2003; Weiss & Fleet, 2003). Previously, we proposed a hierarchical neural architecture for Bayes-optimal sensory processing spatial attentional selection (Yu & Dayan, 2005a). The work represents one possible reconciliation of cortical and neuromodulatory representations of uncertainty. The sensory-driven cortical activities themselves encode bottom-up sensory stimulus-dependent uncertainty. The top-down information involves two kinds of uncertainty: one determines the locus and spatial extent of visual attention, and the other specifies the relative importance of this top-down bias compared to the bottom-up stimulus-driven input. The first is highly specific in modality and featural dimension, presumably originating from higher visual cortical areas (e.g. parietal cortex for spatial attention, inferotemporal cortex for complex featural attention). The second is more generic and may affect different featural dimensions and maybe even different modalities simultaneously, and is thus more appropriately signaled by a diffusely-projecting neuromodulator such as ACh. A major challenge for future research is to develop an integrated theory of how different subsystems in the brain interact and reconfigure to represent different variants of uncertainty across a range of task demands.

ACKNOWLEDGMENTS

Many thanks to Jonathan Cohen, Peter Dayan, Jill McGaughy, Iain Murray, and Martin Sarter for helpful discussions.

REFERENCES

Alonso, A., & Kohler, C. (1984). A study of the reciprocal connections between the septum and the entorhinal area using anterograde and retrograde axonal transport methods in the rat brain. *Journal of Comparative Neurology, 225*, 327–343.

Barber, M. J., Clark, J. W., & Anderson, C. H. (2003). Neural representation of probabilistic information. *Neural Computation, 15*, 1843–1864.

Baskerville, K. A., Schweitzer, J. B., & Herron, P. (1997). Effects of cholinergic depletion on experience-dependent plasticity in the cortex of the rat. *Neuroscience, 80*, 1159–1169.

Battaglia, P. W., Jacobs, R. A., & Aslin, R. N. (2003). Bayesian integration of visual and auditory signals for spatial localization. *Journal of the Optical Society of America. A, Optics, Image Science, and Vision, 20*, 1391–1397.

Bear, M. F., & Singer, W. (1986). Modulation of visual cortical plasticity by acetylcholine and noradrenaline. *Nature, 320*, 172–176.

Burk, J. A., & Sarter, M. (2001). Dissociation between the attentional functions mediated via basal forebrain cholinergic and gabaergic neurons. *Neuroscience, 105*, 899–909.

Chiba, A. A., Bushnell, P. J., Oshiro, W. M., & Gallagher, M. (1999). Selective removal of ACh neurons in the basal forebrain alters cued target detection. *Neuroreport, 10*, 3119–3123.

Clark, J. J., & Yuille, A. L. (1990). *Data fusion for sensory information processing systems*. London: Kluwer Academic Press.

Córdova, C. A., Yu, A. J., Dayan, P., & Chiba, A. A. (forthcoming). *Attention, uncertainty, and acetylcholine: Effects of nucleus basalis cholinergic lesions on probabilistic inference*. Manuscript submitted for publication.

Cummings, J. L., Gorman, D. G., & Shapira, J. (1993). Physostigmine ameliorates the delusions of Alzheimer's disease. *Biological Psychiatry, 33*, 536–541.

Curet, O., Dennis, T., & Scatton, B. (1987). Evidence for the involvement of presynaptic alpha-2 adrenoceptors in the regulation of norepinephrine metabolism in the rat brain. *Journal of Pharmacology and Experimental Therapeutics, 240*, 327–336.

Dalley, J. W., McGaughy, J., O'Connell, M. T., Cardinal, R. N., Levita, L., & Robbins, T. W. (2001). Distinct changes in cortical acetylcholine and noradrenaline efflux during contingent and noncontingent performance of a visual attentional task. *Journal of Neuroscience, 21*, 4908–4914.

Daw, N. D., Kakade, S., & Dayan, P. (2002). Opponent interactions between serotonin and dopamine. *Neural Networks, 15*, 603–616.

Dayan, P., Kakade, S., & Montague, P. R. (2000). Learning and selective attention. *Nature Reviews Neuroscience, 3*, 1218–1223.

Dayan, P., & Yu, A. J. (2002). ACh, uncertainty, and cortical inference. In T. G. Dietterich, S. Becker, & Z. Ghahramani (Eds.), *Advances in neural information processing systems 14* (pp. 189–196). Cambridge, MA: MIT Press.

Dayan, P., & Yu, A. J. (2003). Uncertainty and learning. *IETE Journal of Research, 49*, 171–181.

DeLong, M. R. (1971). Activity of pallidal neurons during movement. *Neurophysiology, 34*, 414–427.

Deneve, S. (2005). Bayesian inference in spiking neurons. In L. K. Saul, Y. Weiss, & L. Bottou (Eds.), *Advances in neural information processing systems 17* (pp. 353–360). Cambridge, MA: MIT Press.

Deneve, S., Latham, P., & Pouget, A. (1999). Reading population codes: A neural implementation of ideal observers. *Nature Neuroscience, 2*, 740–745.

Détári, L., Rasmusson, D. D., & Semba, K. (1999). The role of basal forebrain neurons in tonic and phasic activation of the cerebral cortex. *Progress in Neurobiology, 58*, 249–277.

Devauges, V., & Sara, S. J. (1990). Activation of the noradrenergic system facilitates an attentional shift in the rat. *Behavioural Brain Research, 39*, 19–28.

Dickinson, A. (1980). *Contemporary animal learning theory*. Cambridge: Cambridge University Press.

Donoghue, J. P., & Carroll, K. L. (1987). Cholinergic modulation of sensory responses in rat primary somatic sensory cortex. *Brain Research, 408*, 367–371.

Downing, C. J. (1988). Expectancy and visual-spatial attention: Effects on perceptual quality. *Journal of Experimental Psychology: Human Perception and Performance, 14*, 188–202.

Ernst, M. O., & Banks, M. S. (2002). Humans integrate visual and haptic information in a statistically optimal fashion. *Nature, 415*, 429–433.

Fisher, C. M. (1991). Visual hallucinations on eye closure associated with atropine toxicity. *Canadian Journal of Neurological Sciences, 18*, 18–27.

Fisher, R. S., Buchwald, N. A., Hull, C. D., & Levine, M. S. (1988). GABAergic basal forebrain neurons project to the neocortex: The localization of glutamic acid decarboxylase and choline acetyltransferase in feline corticopetal neurons. *Journal of Comparative Neurology, 272*, 489–502.

Freund, T. F., & Gulyás, A. I. (1991). GABAergic interneurons containing calbindin D28K or somatostatin are major targets of GABAergic basal forebrain afferents in the rat neocortex. *Journal of Comparative Neurology, 314*, 187–199.

Gaykema, R. P. A., Weeghel, R. V., Hersh, L. B., & Luiten, P. G. M. (1991). Prefrontal cortical projections to the cholinergic neurons in the basal forebrain. *Journal of Comparative Neurology, 303*, 563–583.

Gil, Z., Conners, B. W., & Amitai, Y. (1997). Differential regulation of neocortical synapses by neuromodulators and activity. *Neuron, 19*, 679–686.

Greuel, J. M., Luhmann, H. J., & Singer, W. (1988). Pharmacological induction of use-dependent receptive field modifications in the visual cortex. *Science, 242*, 74–77.

Gritti, I., Mainville, L., Mancia, M., & Jones, B. E. (1997). GABAergic and cholinergic basal forebrain and GABAergic preoptic-anterior hypothalamic neurons to the posterior lateral hypothalamus of the rat. *Journal of Comparative Neurology, 339*, 251–268.

Gu, Q. (2002). Neuromodulatory transmitter systems in the cortex and their role in cortical plasticity. *Neuroscience, 111*, 815–835.

Gu, Q., & Singer, W. (1993). Effects of intracortical infusion of anticholinergic drugs on neuronal plasticity in kitten visual cortex. *European Journal of Neuroscience*, *5*, 475–485.

Hars, B., Maho, C., Edeline, J. M., & Hennevin, E. (1993). Basal forebrain stimulation facilitates tone-evoked responses in the auditory cortex of awake rat. *Neuroscience*, *56*, 61–74.

Hasselmo, M. E., & Bower, J. M. (1992). Cholinergic suppression specific to intrinsic not afferent fiber synapses in rat piriform (olfactory) cortex. *Journal of Neurophysiology*, *67*, 1222–1229.

Hasselmo, M. E., Linster, C., Patil, M., Ma, D., & Cekicm, M. (1997). Noradrenergic suppression of synaptic transmission may influence cortical signal-to-noise ratio. *Journal of Neurophysiology*, *77*, 3326–3339.

Hasselmo, M. E., Wyble, B. P., & Wallenstein, G. V. (1996). Encoding and retrieval of episodic memories: Role of cholinergic and GABAergic modulation in the hippocampus. *Hippocampus*, *6*, 693–708.

Holley, L. A., Turchi, J., Apple, C., & Sarter, M. (1995). Dissociation between the attentional effects of infusions of a benzodiazepine receptor agonist and an inverse agonist into the basal forebrain. *Psychopharmacology*, *120*, 99–108.

Hsieh, C. Y., Cruikshank, S. J., & Metherate, R. (2000). Differential modulation of auditory thalamocortical and intracortical synaptic transmission by cholinergic agonist. *Brain Research*, *800*, 51–64.

Jacobs, B. L. (1978). Dreams and hallucinations: A common neurochemical mechanism mediating their phenomenological similarities. *Neuroscience & Biobehavioral Reviews*, *2*, 59–69.

Kahneman, D., & Tversky, A. (1982). Variants of uncertainty. *Cognition*, *11*, 143–157.

Kilgard, M. P., & Merzenich, M. M. (1998). Cortical map reorganization enabled by nucleus basalis activity. *Science*, *279*, 1714–1718.

Kimura, F., Fukuada, M., & Tusomoto, T. (1999). Acetylcholine suppresses the spread of excitation in the visual cortex revealed by optical recording: Possible differential effect depending on the source of input. *European Journal of Neuroscience*, *11*, 3597–3609.

Knill, D. C., & Richards, W. (Eds.). (1996). *Perception as Bayesian inference*. Cambridge: Cambridge University Press.

Kobayashi, M. (2000). Selective suppression of horizontal propagation in rat visual cortex by norepinephrine. *European Journal of Neuroscience*, *12*, 264–272.

Körding, K. P., & Wolpert, D. M. (2004). Bayesian integration in sensorimotor learning. *Nature*, *427*, 244–247.

McGaughy, J., Kaiser, T., & Sarter, M. (1996). Behavioral vigilance following infusion of 192 IgG-saporin into the basal forebrain: Selectivity of the behavioral impairment and relation to cortical AChE-positive fiber density. *Behavioral Neuroscience*, *110*, 247–265.

McGaughy, J., & Sarter, M. (1995). Behavioral vigilance in rats: Task validation and effects of age, amphetamine, and benzodiazepine receptor ligands. *Psychopharmacology*, *117*, 340–357.

Metherate, R., Asche, J. H., & Weinberger, N. M. (1993). Nucleus basalis stimulation facilitates thalamocortical synaptic transmission in the rat auditory cortex. *Synapse, 14,* 132–143.

Metherate, R., Tremblay, N., & Dykes, R. W. (1987). Acetylcholine permits long-term enhancement of neuronal responsiveness in cat primary somatosensory cortex. *Neuroscience, 22,* 75–81.

Metherate, R., & Weinberger, N. M. (1990). Cholinergic modulation of responses to single tones produces tone-specific receptive field alterations in cat auditory cortex. *Synapse, 6,* 133–145.

Nicholls, J. G., Martin, A. R., & Wallace, B. G. (1992). *From neuron to brain: A cellular and molecular approach to the function of the nervous system* (3rd ed.). Sunderland, MA: Sinauer Associates.

Parasuraman, R., Greenwood, P. M., Haxby, J. V., & Grady, C. L. (1992). Visuospatial attention in dementia of the Alzheimer type. *Brain, 115,* 711–733.

Parikh, V., & Sarter, M. (2006). Cortical choline transporter function measured in vivo using choline-sensitive microelectrodes: Clearance of endogenous and exogenous choline and effects of removal of cholinergic terminals. *Journal of Neurochemistry, 97,* 488–503.

Perry, E., Walker, M., Grace, J., & Perry, R. (1999). Acetylcholine in mind: A neurotransmitter correlate of consciousness? *Trends in Neurosciences, 22,* 273–280.

Perry, E. K., & Perry, R. H. (1995). Acetylcholine and hallucinations: Disease-related compared to drug-induced alterations in human consciousness. *Brain and Cognition, 28,* 240–258.

Phillips, J. M., McAlonan, K., Robb, W. G. K., & Brown, V. (2000). Cholinergic neurotransmission influences covert orientation of visuospatial attention in the rat. *Psychopharmacology, 150,* 112–116.

Posner, M. I. (1980). Orienting of attention. *Quantitative Journal of Experimental Psychology, 32,* 3–25.

Pouget, A., Zhang, K., Deneve, S., & Latham, P. E. (1998). Statistically efficient estimation using population codes. *Neural Computation, 10,* 373–401.

Rao, R. P. (2004). Bayesian computation in recurrent neural circuits. *Neural Computation, 16,* 1–38.

Rasmusson, D. D., & Dykes, R. W. (1988). Long-term enhancement of evoked potentials in cat somatosensory cortex produced by co-activation of the basal forebrain and cutaneous receptors. *Experimental Brain Research, 70,* 276–286.

Rolls, E. T., Sanghera, M. K., & Roper-Hall, A. (1979). The latency of activation of neurones in the lateral hypothalamus and substantia innominata during feeding in the monkey. *Brain Research, 164,* 121–135.

Sahani, M., & Dayan, P. (2003). Doubly distributional population codes: Simultaneous representation of uncertainty and multiplicity. *Neural Computation, 15,* 2255–2279.

Sarter, M., Givens, B., & Bruno, J. P. (2001). The cognitive neuroscience of sustained attention: Where top-down meets bottom-up. *Brain Research Reviews, 35,* 146–160.

Schultes, R. E., & Hofmann, A. (1992). *Plants of the gods.* Rochester, VT: Healing Arts Press.

Schultz, W., Dayan, P., & Montague, P. R. (1997). A neural substrate of prediction and reward. *Science, 275*, 1593–1599.

Sillito, A. M., & Kemp, J. A. (1983). Cholinergic modulation of the functional organization of the cat visual cortex. *Brain Research, 289*, 143–155.

Sillito, A. M., & Murphy, P. C. (1987). The cholinergic modulation of cortical function. In E. G. Jones & A. Peters (Eds.), *Cerebral cortex* (pp. 161–185). New York: Plenum Press.

Sutton, R. S. (1992). Gain adaptation beats least squares? In K. S. Narendra (Ed.), *Proceedings of the 7th Yale workshop on adaptive and learning systems* (pp. 161–166). New Haven, CT: Yale University Press.

Tremblay, N., Warren, R. A., & Dykes, R. W. (1990). Electrophysiological studies of acetylcholine and the role of the basal forebrain in the somatosensory cortex of the cat. II. Cortical neurons excited by somatic stimuli. *Journal of Neurophysiology, 64*, 1212–1222.

Turchi, J., & Sarter, M. (2001). Bidirectional modulation of basal forebrain NMDA receptor function differentially affects visual attention but not visual discrimination performance. *Neuroscience, 104*, 407–417.

Umbriaco, D., Garcia, S., Beaulieu, C., & Descarries, L. (1995). Relational features of acetylcholine, noradrenaline, serotonin and gaba axon terminals in the stratum radiatum of adult rat hippocampus (CA1). *Hippocampus, 5*, 605–620.

Umbriaco, D., Watkins, K. C., Descarries, L., Cozzari, C., & Hartman, B. K. (1994). Ultrastructural and morphometric features of the acetylcholine innervation in adult rat parietal cortex: An electron microscopic study in serial sections. *Journal of Comparative Neurology, 348*, 351–373.

Voytko, M. L., Olton, D. S., Richardson, R. T., Gorman, L. K., Tobin, J. R., & Price, D. L. (1994). Basal forebrain lesions in monkeys disrupt attention but not learning and memory. *Journal of Neuroscience, 14*, 167–186.

Weiss, Y., & Fleet, D. J. (2002). Velocity likelihoods in biological and machine vision. In R. P. N. Rao, B. A. Olshausen, & M. S. Lewicki (Eds.), *Probabilistic models of the brain: Perception and neural function* (pp. 77–96). Cambridge, MA: MIT Press.

Whitehouse, P. J., Price, D. L., Struble, R. G., Clark, A. W., Coyle, J. T., & DeLong, M. R. (1982). Alzheimer's disease and senile dementia: Loss of neurons in the basal forebrain. *Science, 215*, 1237–1239.

Wiesel, T. N., & Hubel, D. H. (1963). Single-cell responses in striate cortex of kittens deprived of vision in one eye. *Journal of Neurophysiology, 26*, 1003–1017.

Witte, E. A., Davidson, M. C., & Marrocco, R. T. (1997). Effects of altering brain cholinergic activity on covert orienting of attention: Comparison of monkey and human performance. *Psychopharmacology, 132*, 324–334.

Yu, A. J. (2007). Optimal change-detection and spiking neurons. In B. Schölkopf, J. Platt, & T. Hoffman (Eds.), *Advances in neural information processing systems 19* (pp. 1545–1552). Cambridge, MA: MIT Press.

Yu, A. J., & Dayan, P. (2005a). Inference, attention, and decision in a Bayesian neural architecture. In L. K. Saul, Y. Weiss, & L. Bottou (Eds.), *Advances in neural information processing systems 17* (pp. 1577–1584). Cambridge, MA: MIT Press.

Yu, A. J., & Dayan, P. (2005b). Uncertainty, neuromodulation, and attention. *Neuron, 46*, 681–692.

Zemel, R. S., Dayan, P., & Pouget, A. (1998). Probabilistic interpretation of population codes. *Neural Computation, 10*, 403–430.

CHAPTER FIVE

Heuristics and biases in the brain: Dual neural pathways for decision making

Wim De Neys and Vinod Goel

INTRODUCTION

One of the most striking findings of cognitive reasoning research over recent decades is that human judgment frequently violates traditional normative standards: In a wide range of reasoning tasks, people often do not give the answer that is correct according to logic or probability theory (e.g., Evans, 2002; Kahneman, Slovic, & Tversky, 1982). Influential dual process theories of thinking have explained this "rational thinking failure" by positing two different human reasoning systems (e.g., Epstein, 1994; Evans, 2003; Goel, 1995; Kahneman, 2002; Sloman, 1996; Stanovich & West, 2000). The common failure to provide the correct answer on reasoning tasks has been attributed to the pervasiveness of the heuristic system. It is argued that human thinking typically relies on the operation of intuitive heuristics instead of a deliberate, controlled reasoning process. Whereas the fast and undemanding heuristics provide us with useful responses in many situations, they may also bias reasoning in tasks that require more elaborate, analytic processing. That is, both systems will sometimes cue different responses. In these cases the logical, analytic system will need to override the intuitive belief-based response generated by the heuristic system (De Neys, 2006; Stanovich & West, 2000). Since the analytic operations heavily burden our limited executive resources, the analytic override will frequently fail and the heuristic system will dominate our thinking.

The claim that there are two different human reasoning systems received substantial support from imaging studies pointing to dual neural pathways during deductive reasoning (e.g., Goel, Buchel, Frith, & Dolan, 2000; Goel & Dolan, 2003). For some deductive reasoning problems the logical status of the conclusion conflicts with background beliefs (i.e., incongruent items, for example, a valid but unbelievable syllogism like "All mammals can walk. Whales are mammals. Therefore, whales can walk"). The heuristic, belief-based system thus triggers a logically erroneous response and providing the correct response requires demanding analytic computations. For other syllogisms the logical status of the problem is consistent with its believability (i.e., congruent items, for example, a syllogism with a valid and believable conclusion like "All fruits can be eaten. Apples are fruits. Therefore, apples can be eaten"). Here, the heuristic system cues the correct response and solving the problem can be based on mere belief-based thinking without any need for an additional analytic intervention.

Goel et al. repeatedly observed that reasoning with congruent items activated a left temporal system, whereas a bilateral parietal system was activated when people tried to solve the incongruent problems. The parietal system was also specifically engaged when people reasoned with belief-neutral problems where beliefs neither biased nor helped reasoning (e.g., "All X are Y. Z is an X. Therefore, Z is a Y") and people could only rely on logical, analytic thinking to solve the problem. This leads to the suggestion that the left temporal pathway corresponds to the heuristic system, while the bilateral parietal pathway corresponds to the analytic system (e.g., Goel, 2005).

The neuroimaging studies of Goel and colleagues have focused on deductive reasoning tasks (e.g., categorical syllogisms). Deductive reasoning and decision making are both components of our system of rationality, although the two literatures remain somewhat disparate (Evans, 2002, 2003). Reasons for the sharp division are not very clear, but they may in part have to do with the different normative theories the two domains draw on; formal logic for deductive reasoning and probability theory for decision making. However, dual process theories have the potential of bringing the two fields together. Within a dual process framework it can be suggested that people's deductive reasoning and decision making is governed by exactly the same machinery: The heuristic and analytic reasoning system (e.g., Evans, 2003).

In this chapter we present a neuroimaging study that examines the generalizability of the dual pathway findings to decision-making tasks. We are interested in answering the following two questions: (1) Is there a dissociation in the neural systems underlying analytic and heuristic decision making as there is for deductive reasoning? (2) Will the same neural systems that underlie deductive reasoning underwrite decision making? Affirmative answers to these questions will serve to reinforce the case for dual process theories.

We scanned participants while they were solving judgment problems that were modeled after Kahneman and Tversky's infamous (1973) base-rate neglect problems. The base rate or "Lawyer-engineer" task is a classic task in the field but, despite decades of behavioral studies, its neural foundations have not been explored. In the task, the normative answer is given by the base rates. However, an accompanying description engages heuristic processes that often override the normative response. Consider the following example:

> *Base rate*: A psychologist wrote thumbnail descriptions of a sample of 1000 participants consisting of 5 engineers and 995 lawyers. The description below was chosen at random from the 1000 available descriptions.
>
> *Description*: Jack is a 45-year-old man. He is married and has four children. He is generally conservative, careful, and ambitious. He shows no interest in political and social issues and spends most of his free time on his many hobbies, which include home carpentry, sailing, and mathematical puzzles.
>
> *Question*: Which one of the following two statements is most likely?
> a. Jack is an engineer.
> b. Jack is a lawyer.

Logically speaking, given the size of the two groups in the sample, it will be more likely that a randomly drawn individual will be a lawyer. Hence, the normative response based on the group size information is (b). However, many people will be tempted to respond (a) on the basis of stereotypical beliefs cued by the description. Just as in the incongruent syllogisms, the logical response will conflict with the cued heuristic response and solving the problem will call for an analytic intervention. In the case of the base-rate problems it is assumed that the heuristic response is based on the operation of the infamous representativeness heuristic (e.g., Kahneman & Tversky, 1973).

We constructed four types of base-rate problems to test our hypotheses: *incongruent*, *congruent*, *neutral-heuristic*, and *neutral-analytic* problems. For incongruent problems, the heuristic response cued by the description conflicted with the base rates as in the classic, standard version. For congruent problems, the base rates were switched around (e.g., 5 lawyers and 995 engineers) so that the heuristic response was consistent with the normative response. Hence, contrary to the classic problems, base rates and description will not conflict and the response can be right based on the cued heuristic without any need for further analytic intervention. For neutral-heuristic problems, the description was completely neutral (e.g., "Jack has brown hair and green eyes"). Hence, the problem will not trigger a stereotypical heuristic response and participants should have little trouble to reason analytically and rely on the base rates to solve the problem. Finally, for neutral-analytic problems, we presented neutral base rates (e.g., "a sample with 500 lawyers and 500 engineers"). This control problem does not trigger an analytic response and solving it will rely on mere heuristic thinking about the description. Table 5.1 presents examples of the different items.

In sum, we expected that solving the incongruent and neutral-heuristic problems would be based on analytic thinking, whereas solving the congruent and neutral-analytic problems would be based on heuristic thinking. Contrasting brain activations while reasoning about the different problem types should help identify the regions engaged in heuristic and

Table 5.1
Examples of the different item types

Incongruent
Study with 5 men and 995 women.
Jo is 23 and is finishing a degree in engineering. On Friday nights, Jo likes to go out cruising with friends while listening to loud music and drinking beer.
What is most likely?
a. Jo is a man
b. Jo is a woman

Congruent
Study with 5 Swedish people and 995 Italians.
Marco is 16. He loves to play soccer with his friends, after which they all go out for pizza or to someone's house for homemade pasta.
What is most likely?
a. Marco is Swedish
b. Marco is Italian

Neutral heuristic
Study with 5 people who campaigned for Bush and 995 who campaigned for Kerry.
Jim is 5 ft 8 in tall, has black hair, and is the father of two young girls. He drives a yellow van that is completely covered with posters.
What is most likely?
a. Jim campaigned for Bush
b. Jim campaigned for Kerry

Neutral analytic
Study with 500 40-year-olds and 500 17-year-olds.
Rylan lives in Buffalo. He hangs out with his buddies every day and likes watching MTV. He is a big Korn fan and is saving to buy his own car.
What is most likely?
a. Rylan is 40
b. Rylan is 17

---

analytic decision making. Based on the Goel et al. findings from the deductive reasoning tasks, we predict activations in bilateral posterior parietal areas (BA 7) during analytic thinking and left lateral temporal activation (BA 21/22) during heuristic thinking.

METHOD

Participants

Thirteen right-handed participants (seven females and six males) with a mean age of 27.9 years ($SD = 3.7$) and mean education level of 16.1 years ($SD = 1.1$) gave informed consent to participate in the study in return for a monetary reimbursement. All participants had lived in Canada or the United States for at least 10 years.

Stimuli

We presented four types of base-rate problems: (1) incongruent; (2) congruent; (3) neutral heuristic; and (4) neutral analytic. Participants solved 24 problems of each type resulting in a total of 96 presented problems. Examples of each problem type appear in Table 5.1.

The problems were based on a wide range of stereotypes (e.g., gender, age, race, or profession). Material was selected on the basis of an extensive pilot study where a large number of stereotypical and neutral descriptions were constructed and rated. Selected descriptions for the incongruent, congruent, and neutral-analytic problems moderately but consistently cued one of the two groups, whereas ratings for the neutral-heuristic problems had to be as similar as possible. This point is not trivial. We are assuming that the response cued by the base rates is the correct response in our task. Since the base rates are not informative for the neutral-analytic problems, the response that matches the description was considered correct for these problems. Note that especially in the case of the classic, incongruent problems, the actual normative status of the "correct" response is debated (e.g., Gigerenzer, Hell, & Blank, 1988). If reasoners adopt a formal Bayesian approach and combine the base rates with the diagnostic value of the description, this can lead to complications when the description is extremely diagnostic. Imagine that we have a sample of males and females and the description would state that the randomly drawn individual "is the pope of the catholic church". Now, by definition, no matter what the base rates in the sample are, one would always need to conclude that the person is a man. We limited the impact of this problem by only selecting descriptions that were judged to have a moderate diagnostic value. By combining these with quite extreme base rates (e.g., 995/5) one may conclude that the response that is cued by the base rates should be selected if participants engage in a minimal form of formal, analytic thinking.

All 96 selected problems had a different content. The average length of the 24 selected problems for each of the four conditions was matched. The order of the two response options ("a" and "b") was also counterbalanced. For half of the problems the correct response was option "a", whereas for the other half the second response option ("b") was the correct one.

There were also 12 rest trials that were presented at the beginning and end of the experimental session. These rest trials showed series of Xs in place of each of the lines where the base rates, description, and question were otherwise presented. Participants answered these trials by pressing any of the two response keys.

Instructions

Before going into the scanner, participants were familiarized with the task format. They were given the following instructions:

> In a big research project a number of studies were carried out where short personality descriptions of the participants were made. In every study there were participants from two population groups (e.g., carpenters and policemen). In this experiment you will have to solve problems based on these studies.

> First, you'll get information about the composition of the population groups tested in the study in question. Next, you'll get to see the personality description of **a randomly chosen** participant of the study. You'll be asked to indicate to which population group the participant most likely belongs.

> Once you've made a decision press the corresponding key on the response box. After you pressed the key, you just wait until the next problem is presented.

To avoid repetition and to limit the amount of text presented on the screen, we did not explicitly repeat the classic lines about the total sample size and random sampling in the problems (e.g., "A total of 1000 people were tested . . . The description was drawn at random from the sample . . ."). However, this information was clearly stressed in the instructions. To make sure that participants grasped the concept of random sampling, they could observe the actual drawing of descriptions from an urn with an example problem (e.g., Gigerenzer et al., 1988). We also clarified that participants needed to think as statisticians when solving the problems (e.g., Schwartz, Strack, Hilton, & Naderer, 1991). These simple manipulations have been shown to minimize possible task misinterpretations.

Stimuli presentation

The items were presented in one of two random orders. The beginning of a base-rate trial was signaled by a fixation cross that was presented for 500 ms. Next, the problem was presented in three parts. First, the line with the base-rate information was presented for 4000 ms. Next, the description was presented for 5000 ms (base rates remained on the screen). Afterwards, the question and two response alternatives appeared. Once the question appeared the whole problem remained on the screen for another 8500 ms. Hence, each trial lasted exactly 18,000 ms.

Participants responded by pressing one of two buttons on a keypad (half the participants used their left hand, the other half the right) after the appearance of the question. Hence, participants had 8500 ms to enter their response. Participants were instructed to respond naturally and efficiently so as to be prepared to read the next trial. They were also told to let the trial pass and to focus on the upcoming problem in the event they could not respond quickly enough.

Before or after the base-rate problems had been solved, participants were presented with a block of rest trials. The rest trials only lasted 9 s each. The trials started with the presentation of a fixation cross for 500 ms. Next, the first and second line of Xs were presented for 2500 ms each. Participants were simply asked to press a key once the third line (corresponding to the question) appeared on the screen.

fMRI scanning technique

Participants were scanned in a 4-Tesla Oxford Magnet Technologies magnet with a Siemens Sonata gradient coil at the Robarts Institute in London, Ontario (Canada). Twenty-three T2*-weighted interleaved multi-shot contiguous echo-planar images, 5-mm thick ($3.44 \times 3.44 \times 5.0$ mm voxels), were acquired axially positioned to cover the whole brain. Data were recorded during a single acquisition period. A total of 624 volume images were acquired over two sessions (312 volumes per session) with a repetition time (TR) of 3 s/volume. The first six volumes in each session were discarded (leaving 306 volumes per session). Each session lasted 15.6 min. The scanner was synchronized with the presentation of each trial.

fMRI data analysis

Data were analyzed using Statistical Parametric Mapping (SPM2; Friston, Holmes, Worsley, Poline, Frith, & Frackowiak, 1995). Each volume was realigned to the first image of the session. Head movement was less than 2 mm in all cases. The images were smoothed with an isotropic Gaussian kernel with full-width half-maximum (FWHM) of 12 mm to allow for between-subject comparisons (Worseley & Friston, 1995).

Condition effects at each voxel were estimated using the general linear model and regionally specific effects compared using linear contrasts. Each contrast produced a statistical parametric map of the t-statistic at each voxel, which was subsequently transformed to a unit normal Z-distribution. The blood oxygen level dependent (BOLD) signal was modeled as a hemodynamic response function during the interval between the presentation of the description and the motor response, on a trial-by-trial, subject-by-subject basis. This epoch covers the crucial time interval of interest. On one hand, the crucial conflict between the base rates and conclusion can only start arising once the description is presented. On the other hand, the decision-making process should be terminated once the response is entered. The presentation of the base rates and the motor response were modeled out of the analysis.

We selected specific parietal and temporal regions of interest (ROI) for the present analyses based on the original activations in Goel et al. (2000). These ROI were spheres with a 12 mm radius centered on the voxels that showed peak activation in the Goel et al. study: A right superior parietal ROI in BA 7 (center voxel coordinates = 26, −66, 50), a left superior parietal ROI in BA 7 (center = −18, −64, 46), and a left lateral temporal ROI in BA 21/22 (center = −54, −40, −2). Figure 5.1 shows an illustration of the location of these ROI. Activations in the ROI that are reported here survived a voxel-level intensity threshold of $p < .05$ (uncorrected) using a random effect model.

RESULTS

Behavioral results

Behavioral scores were in keeping with expectations. As Table 5.2 shows, the two problem types that could be solved by relying on mere heuristic thinking, the congruent and neutral-analytic problems, were solved best (93% accuracy for each). Performance on the neutral-heuristic problems for which analytic thinking was required but where thinking could not be biased by heuristic activations decreased slightly in accuracy, $F(1, 12) = 196.73$, $p < .001$, but remained at a high level (88% accuracy).

(1) Parietal "analytic" ROIs

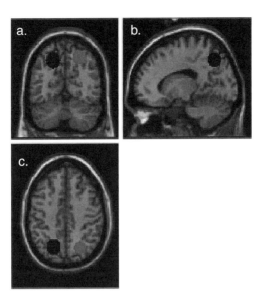

(2) Temporal "heuristic" ROIs

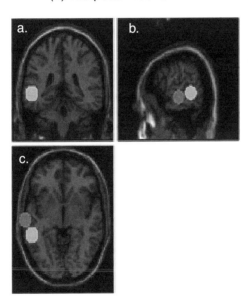

Figure 5.1 Location of the ROI assumed to be involved in analytic and heuristic decision making superimposed onto coronal (a), sagittal (b), and transverse (c) sections of a magnetic resonance image, which is itself in standard space. Top (1) shows the position of the superior parietal ROI (BA7; left in dark blue, right in light blue). Bottom (2) shows the position of the posterior (light green) and additional anterior (orange) left lateral temporal ROI (BA 21/22). See color plate.

Table 5.2
Behavioral scores

Trial type	Scores (%)	Reaction time (ms)
Neutral heuristic	88 (18)	3290 (1336)
Neutral analytic	93 (8)	2996 (1442)
Congruent	93 (11)	3008 (1480)
Incongruent	45 (32)	3553 (1515)

Note: SD in parentheses.

However, consistent with Kahneman and Tversky's (1973) original observations, solving the incongruent problems where the problem solutions cued by analytic and heuristic thinking conflicted was a lot harder, $F(1, 12) = 616.81$, $p < .001$. Only 45% of these problems were solved correctly. These findings were mirrored in the problem-solving latencies. The congruent and neutral-analytic problems were solved fastest. Reasoning latencies increased somewhat for the neutral-heuristic problems, $F(1, 12) = 29.02$, $p < .001$, whereas the incongruent problems took longest to solve, $F(1, 12) = 50.39$, $p < .001$.

Initial fMRI analysis

To establish whether our a priori ROI were generally involved in decision making, we first looked at the common activations over the different decision-making items (i.e., main effect of decision making or [(incongruent trials+congruent trials+neutral-heuristic trials+neutral-analytic trials) −rest trials]). Results showed that both parietal ROI (left: −28, −62, 52; $z = 3.90$, and right: 34, −64, 50; $z = 3.56$) and the temporal (−64, −42, −4; $z = 2.52$) ROI were activated. The coordinates of the peak activations were also very close to the exact locations observed by Goel et al. (2000). Nevertheless, closer inspection of the left lateral temporal lobe indicated that there was also a second, more anterior temporal cluster that was activated in the main analysis (−66, −18, −8; $z = 1.90$). This fits with Goel and Dolan (2003) who already reported heuristic activations in the more anterior part of the left temporal lateral lobe. For completeness, we decided to include this second temporal region as an additional heuristic ROI in the remaining analyses.

Contrasting heuristic and analytic activations

The crucial question for us is whether the parietal and temporal system specifically mediate analytic versus heuristic decision making. The following set of contrasts allowed us to address this question. First, we compared activations for the two neutral problem versions. Recall that for neutral-heuristic problems the description was completely neutral. Hence, the item did not trigger a stereotypical heuristic response and participants had to reason analytically and rely on the base rates to solve the problem. The neutral-analytic problems on the other hand had neutral base rates. Hence, participants had to rely on mere heuristic thinking about the description to answer it. Subtracting the neural activity while people are solving neutral-analytic items from the activations while people are solving neutral-heuristic items should point to those regions that mediate analytic thinking (or more specifically those regions that are activated when people rely on the sample size information to make a decision). The reversed contrast (neutral-analytic trials–neutral-heuristic trials) should identify regions that mediate heuristic thinking (or more specifically regions that are activated when people rely on the stereotypical description to make a decision). Table 5.3 shows that, as expected, analytic thinking in the first case activated the parietal ROI, whereas heuristic thinking in the later case resulted in temporal activation.

Data from the congruent problems allow a further validation of the hypotheses. On these problems the base rates and description are consistent and the response can be rightly based on the cued heuristic response without any need for further analytic intervention. As expected, heuristic thinking on the congruent problems resulted in temporal activations when the analytic activations in the neutral-heuristic problems were subtracted (i.e., the congruent–neutral-heuristic contrast). Not surprisingly, comparing congruent and neutral-analytic items where people are both assumed to be engaged in heuristic thinking did not reveal any differences in neural activation.

Finally, we contrasted activations for the incongruent problems and neutral control trials. The conflict between the responses cued by the base rates and description in the incongruent problems will result in increased analytic processing in addition to the default heuristic processing of the description. That is, both systems should be activated while people are solving the incongruent problems. Hence, in line with the above findings, subtracting the heuristic activations during thinking about the neutral-analytic problems (i.e., incongruent trials–neutral-analytic trials) should show activation of the parietal, analytic ROI. Alternatively, subtracting the analytic activations during thinking about the neutral-heuristic problems (i.e., incongruent trials–neutral-heuristic trials) should result in temporal, heuristic activation. Table 5.3 shows that these predictions were confirmed. Interestingly, as Table 5.3 indicates, the final contrast (incongruent trials–neutral-heuristic trials) also resulted in additional parietal activation. For the incongruent problems, people will need to rely on the base rates just as in the neutral-heuristic problems. However, because the

Table 5.3

Location (MNI coordinates) of significant activation within the different regions of interest (ROI) when contrasting heuristic and analytic decision making

Contrast	Expected system	Superior parietal ROIs		Left lateral temporal ROIs	
		Left	*Right*	*Posterior*	*Anterior*
Neutral heuristic–neutral analytic	Analytic	$-10, -72, 42; z = 1.80$	$34, -58, 54; z = 1.77$	n.s.	n.s.
Neutral analytic–neutral heuristic	Heuristic	n.s.	n.s.	n.s.	$-66, -12, -12; z = 2.04$
Congruent–neutral heuristic	Heuristic	n.s.	n.s.	$-62, -32, -2; z = 1.74$	$-66, -24, -2; z = 1.94$
Congruent–neutral analytic	–	n.s.	n.s.	n.s.	n.s.
Incongruent–neutral analytic	Analytic	$-24, -64, 54; z = 2.27$	$34, -62, 58; z = 2.25$	n.s.	n.s.
Incongruent–neutral heuristic	Heuristic/analytic	$-28, -60, 44; z = 2.13$	$28, -62, 60; z = 2.41$	$-64, -46, 0; z = 2.06$	n.s.

Note: n.s. denotes that there were no significant activations in the specific ROI.

base rates also conflict with the description, solving the incongruent problems will be far more demanding. The greater parietal activation may reflect the increased analytic requirements.

The role of the right lateral prefrontal cortex

The above findings support the claim that the dual parietal and temporal pathway findings can be generalized to decision making. In this last section we focus on the activation pattern of the right lateral prefrontal cortex (rLPFC) during decision making. In their deductive reasoning studies, Goel and colleagues (e.g., Goel et al., 2000; Goel & Dolan, 2003; Stollstorff, Vartanian, & Goel, 2010) observed that the rLPFC (BA 46) was specifically activated when participants managed to inhibit the erroneous beliefs and correctly completed incongruent problems. Goel argued that the rLPFC would mediate the successful resolution of the belief–logic conflict during deductive reasoning. This is consistent with the general suggestion that this area is typically involved in inhibitory control and conflict resolution (e.g., Aron, Robbins, & Poldrack, 2004; Van Veen & Carter, 2006). We wanted to examine whether the rLPFC plays a similar role during decision making.

As with the parietal and temporal activations, we defined an additional rLPFC ROI based on the original Goel et al. (2000) study (i.e., sphere with 12 mm radius centered on voxel coordinates 54, 28, 26; see Figure 5.2). Next, we contrasted activations for correctly and incorrectly solved incongruent trials. The direct comparison (incongruent correct trials–incongruent incorrect trials) indeed demonstrated that the rLPFC showed greater activation when the erroneous heuristic response was successfully overridden and people solved the incongruent problem correctly (60, 24, 20; $z = 2.51$). This finding was further supported when the rLPFC activation for correctly and incorrectly solved incongruent problems was contrasted with the congruent items where heuristic inhibition was never required. When people failed to block the conflicting heuristic response and erred on the incongruent items, the rLPFC did not show any differential activation compared with the congruent problems (i.e., incongruent incorrect trials–congruent trials). However, as expected, the same comparison for correctly solved incongruent trials (incongruent correct trials–congruent trials) showed that when the heuristic response was correctly inhibited the rLPFC was clearly activated (60, 22, 22; $z = 2.11$).

DISCUSSION

In this chapter we presented a study that examined whether the imaging findings on deductive reasoning could be generalized to decision making.

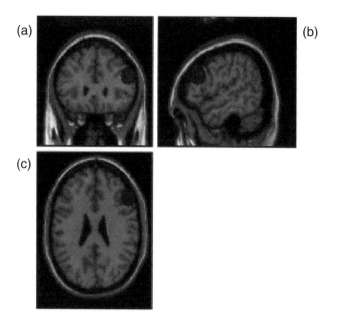

Figure 5.2 Location of the right lateral prefrontal ROI (BA 46, dark red circle) super-imposed onto coronal (a), sagittal (b), and transverse (c) sections of a magnetic resonance image, which is itself in standard space. See color plate.

We observed that the dual neural systems that have been previously found to underlie deductive reasoning also underwrite decision making. Heuristic thinking that was based on a stereotypical description activated the left lateral temporal lobe (BA 21/22) whereas the bilateral superior parietal lobe (BA 7) was activated when people reasoned analytically. Consistent with the deductive reasoning findings, we also observed that in addition to the parietal and temporal activations the right lateral prefrontal cortex was activated when people successfully resisted the heuristic temptations on the incongruent base-rate problems and correctly completed the decision-making task.

Although the present findings are encouraging for the dual systems view, one should bear in mind that the study is one of the first that focused on the neural foundations of the base-rate problems. Ideally, the present findings will need to be further replicated with other classic tasks from the judgment and decision-making literature (e.g., the notorious "Linda" problem or conjunction fallacy). One might note, for example, that whereas analytic thinking in the present study always resulted in activation of both bilateral parietal regions, heuristic thinking covered a wide region of the lateral temporal lobe with peak activations shifting between the more anterior and posterior temporal region. Future studies might want to establish whether this temporal distribution could reflect a further functional subdivision in the heuristic system.

With respect to the generality of the findings, it is interesting to note that the present results on decision making show some similarities with findings in the field of social cognition. Lieberman and colleagues (e.g., Lieberman, 2007; Satpute & Lieberman, 2006) recently proposed a neuro-cognitive dual process model of social cognition. Such dual process models postulate different neural systems for automatic and controlled social processes (i.e., the X-system and C-system in Lieberman's work). The theoretical link between the dual process systems of social cognition and judgment and decision making has already been stressed (e.g., Barrett, Tugade, & Engle, 2004). At a general level one could argue that the automatic X-system is linked to the heuristic system, whereas the controlled C-system is linked to the analytic system. Interestingly, consistent with the present work, Lieberman also suggested that the automatic X-system encompasses the lateral temporal lobes, whereas the superior parietal lobes would be part of the controlled C-system.

Finally, we want to point to the link between the rLPFC activation in the present study and some recent imaging findings on the neural basis of risk and uncertainty computation (e.g., Huettel, Song, & McCarthy, 2005; Hsu, Bhatt, Adolphs, Tranel, & Camerer, 2005; Volz, Schubotz, & von Cramon, 2004) and the emotional modulation of decision making (e.g., Bechara, Damasio, & Damasio, 2000; Sanfey, Rilling, Aronson, Nystrom, & Cohen, 2003). Although these studies have not directly addressed the dual system claims about the processing architecture of the human reasoning engine, they nevertheless show some support for the postulated role of the rLPFC in decision making. Sanfey et al., for example, observed lateral prefrontal activations when people reasoned economically in the Ultimatum Game and accepted an offer that was perceived as unfair (e.g., you get $2, your opponent gets $8, if you refuse both of you get nothing). Likewise, the rLPFC has been shown to be involved in accepting rationally favorable gambles about which people have negative emotions (e.g., De Martino, Kumaran, Seymour, & Dolan, 2006). This is consistent with the idea that the lateral prefrontal cortex might play a more general role in overcoming inappropriate heuristic intuitions during thinking.

In sum, the study we presented in this chapter reinforces the case for dual process theories of thinking and indicates that deductive reasoning and decision making are more similar than the disparate behavioral literatures may suggest.

ACKNOWLEDGMENTS

Wim De Neys is a senior research scientist at the Centre National de la Recherche Scientifique (CNRS), France. This collaboration was made possible through an FWO (Fonds Wetenschappelijk Onderzoek) travel grant awarded to Wim De Neys and a National Science and Engineering Council of Canada (NSERC) grant to Vinod Goel. We would like to thank Oshin Vartanian and David Mandel for their advice and their comments on an earlier draft of this chapter. We also thank Melanie Stollstorff, Lisa Casagrande, Marie Arsalidou, Randy Waechter, Kathleen Smith, Gorka Navarette, and Elaine Lam for their help running this study.

REFERENCES

Aron, A. R., Robbins, T. W., & Poldrack, R. A. (2004). Inhibition and the right inferior frontal cortex. *Trends in Cognitive Sciences, 8*, 170–177.

Barrett, L. F., Tugade, M. M., & Engle, R. W. (2004). Individual differences in working memory capacity and dual-process theories of the mind. *Psychological Bulletin, 130*, 553–573.

Bechara, A., Damasio, H., & Damasio, A. R. (2000). Emotion, decision making, and the orbitofrontal cortex. *Cerebral Cortex, 10*, 295–307.

De Martino, B., Kumaran, D., Seymour, B., & Dolan, R. J. (2006). Frames, biases, and rational decision making in the human brain. *Science, 313*, 684–687.

De Neys, W. (2006). Dual processing in reasoning: Two systems but one reasoner. *Psychological Science, 17*, 428–433.

Epstein, S. (1994). Integration of the cognitive and psychodynamic unconscious. *American Psychologist, 49*, 709–724.

Evans, J. St. B. T. (2002). Logic and human reasoning: An assessment of the deduction paradigm. *Psychological Bulletin, 128*, 978–996.

Evans, J. St. B. T. (2003). In two minds: Dual process accounts of reasoning. *Trends in Cognitive Sciences, 7*, 454–459.

Friston, K., Holmes, A., Worsley, K., Poline, J.-B., Frith, C., & Frackowiak, R. (1995). Statistical parametric maps in functional imaging: A general approach. *Human Brain Mapping, 2*, 189–210.

Gigerenzer, G., Hell, W., & Blank, H. (1988). Presentation and content: The use of base rates as a continuous variable. *Journal of Experimental Psychology: Human Perception and Performance, 14*, 513–525.

Goel, V. (1995). *Sketches of thought.* Cambridge, MA: MIT Press.

Goel, V. (2005). Cognitive neuroscience of deductive reasoning. In K. J. Holyoak & R. G. Morrison (Eds.), *Cambridge handbook of thinking & reasoning* (pp. 475–492). Cambridge, MA: Cambridge University Press.

Goel, V., Buchel, C., Frith, C., & Dolan, R. J. (2000). Dissociation of mechanisms underlying syllogistic reasoning. *Neuroimage, 12*, 504–514.

Goel, V., & Dolan, R. J. (2003). Explaining modulation of reasoning by belief. *Cognition, 87*, B11–B22.

Hsu, M., Bhatt, M., Adolphs, R., Tranel, D., & Camerer, C. F. (2005). Neural systems responding to degrees of uncertainty in human decision making. *Science, 310*, 1680–1683.

Huettel, S. A., Song, A. W., & McCarthy, G. (2005). Decisions under uncertainty: Probabilistic context influences activation of prefrontal and parietal cortices. *Journal of Neuroscience, 25*, 3304–3311.

Kahneman, D. (2002, December). *Maps of bounded rationality: A perspective on intuitive judgement and choice.* Nobel Prize Lecture. Retrieved January 11, 2006, from http://nobelprize.org/nobel_prizes/economics/laureates/2002/kahnemann-lecture.pdf

Kahneman, D., Slovic, P., & Tversky, A. (1982). *Judgement under uncertainty: Heuristics and biases.* Cambridge: Cambridge University Press.

Kahneman, D., & Tversky, A. (1973). On the psychology of prediction. *Psychological Review, 80*, 237–251.

Lieberman, M. D. (2007). The X- and C-systems: The neural basis of automatic and controlled social cognition. In E. Harmon-Jones & P. Winkelman (Eds.), *Fundamentals of social neuroscience* (pp. 290–315). New York: Guilford.

Sanfey, A. G., Rilling, J. K., Aronson, J. A., Nystrom, L. E., & Cohen, J. D. (2003). The neural basis of economic decision making in the ultimatum game. *Science, 300*, 1755–1758.

Satpute, A. B., & Lieberman, M. D. (2006). Integrating automatic and controlled processes into neurocognitive models of social cognition. *Brain Research, 1079*, 86–97.

Schwartz, N., Strack, F., Hilton, D., & Naderer, G. (1991). Base rates, representativeness, and the logic of conversation: The contextual relevance of "irrelevant" information. *Social Cognition, 9*, 67–84.

Sloman, S. A. (1996). The empirical case for two systems of reasoning. *Psychological Bulletin, 119*, 3–22.

Stanovich, K. E., & West, R. F. (2000). Individual differences in reasoning: Implications for the rationality debate. *Behavioral and Brain Sciences, 23*, 645–726.

Stollstorff, M., Vartanian, O., & Goel, V. (2010). *Levels of conflict in reasoning modulate right lateral prefrontal cortex.* Manuscript submitted for publication.

Van Veen, V., & Carter, C. S. (2006). Conflict and cognitive control in the brain. *Current Directions in Psychological Science, 15*, 237–240.

Volz, K. G., Schubotz, R. I., & von Cramon, D. Y. (2004). Why am I unsure? Internal and external attributions of uncertainty dissociated by fMRI. *Neuroimage, 21*, 848–857.

Worsley, K. J., & Friston, K. J. (1995). Analysis of fMRI time-series revisited—Again. *Neuroimage, 2*, 173–181.

Section III
Reward and loss

CHAPTER SIX

Reward processing and decision making in the human striatum

Mauricio R. Delgado and Elizabeth Tricomi

INTRODUCTION

Making a decision is an elaborate process involving the assessment of potential benefits (e.g., rewards or gains) and costs (e.g., punishments or losses). A child, for example, may approach a cookie jar before dinner because of the potential reward and positive feelings associated with that decision, but may not actually retrieve a cookie due to probable parental reprimand. Evaluating the consequences of our decisions enables us to learn and determine whether we should make similar decisions in the future or choose to alter our behavior instead. There are many computations at the neural level necessary to not only make decisions, but also to appraise and learn from decisions to shape future behavior. As research has advanced toward identifying a circuit involved in day-to-day decision making, one brain structure has emerged as a key contributor across species. The striatum, the input unit of the basal ganglia, plays a crucial role in our ability to process information about positive and negative outcomes, and therefore is an essential structure in the decision-making process. This chapter will describe research on how the striatum responds to reward-related information, and will attempt to underscore how it is able to flexibly learn from this information while efficiently guiding resources toward those stimuli which are most relevant to one's current goals.

A stimulus that has a positive hedonic value, that is, one that has pleasurable properties, can be loosely labeled as a "reward" (Cannon & Bseikri,

2004). Typically, the unexpected delivery of a reward will lead to increased expectations of future rewards and associations with behaviors or decisions that may lead to such rewards. Thus, rewards act as reinforcers, which are events that increase the frequency of a behavior (Hill, 1997; Skinner, 1938; White, 1989). With respect to decision making, a reward represents a desirable outcome that leads to repetition of the same decision on its presentation (e.g., child reaching for cookie jar). Punishments, on the other hand, such as the loss of something of value, tend to have negative hedonic value, and decrease the frequency of a behavior. If a decision leads to an unpleasant outcome, one would want to avoid making the same decision in the future (e.g., child grounded for eating cookie before dinner may not make a similar decision in the future).

Therefore, in order for reward-related information to appropriately steer decision making, the brain must be able not only to register the hedonic aspects of reward or punishment, but also to learn from the experience of reward and punishment. Yet evaluative and decision-making processes can be time-consuming and energy-demanding, so an efficient reward processing system should also be able to bypass these costs when possible. For example, if someone already has extensive experience with a particular decision, the outcome will be known and will require less processing than the consequences of an uncertain decision (e.g., a child who has successfully eaten cookies before dinner without reprimand in the past may reach for the cookie jar more quickly than a child who has had no positive or negative experience). Additionally, it is important that actions not be swayed by spurious associations between events and outcomes. Ideally, then, a reward processing system must only allow rewards and punishments to influence behavior to which they are contingently linked.

In this chapter, we will discuss how the striatum may be able to process reward-related information in a way that allows it to meet these demands. Although we will touch on relevant findings across species, the goal of the chapter is to focus on the role of the human striatum in reward-related processing and decision making. The first section will briefly review the anatomy of the striatum, delineating the functional and anatomical divisions within this region. The contributions of the subregions of the striatum to reward and punishment will then be discussed. The ventral striatum, the head of the caudate nucleus, and the dorsolateral striatum have all been implicated in various aspects of reward processing, and the proposed functional roles of each will be considered in turn. An emphasis will be placed on how contextual influences affect reward processing in the striatum, with special consideration of the relationship between reward processing and decision making. In the final section of the chapter, we will discuss unresolved questions and future directions for research in this area.

ANATOMICAL DIVISIONS WITHIN THE STRIATUM

The striatum is the primary input structure of the basal ganglia, a group of brain structures that also includes the globus pallidus, the subthalamic nucleus, and the dopamine neuron-containing substantia nigra (pars compacta), located in the midbrain (Alexander & Crutcher, 1990; Graybiel, 2000; Graybiel, Aosaki, Flaherty, & Kimura, 1994; Middleton & Strick, 1997). The striatum receives highly convergent projections from the prefrontal cortex, as well as afferents from the amygdala, hippocampal formation, and the midbrain (Bar-Gad, Morris, & Bergman, 2003; Haber, 2003; Parent & Hazrati, 1995; Robbins & Everitt, 1996). It sends information back to the prefrontal cortex by way of the globus pallidus and parts of the substantia nigra (pars reticulata) via the thalamus, forming a frontal–striatal–thalamic loop (Alexander, DeLong, & Strick, 1986; Robbins & Everitt, 1996). The connectivity between basal ganglia and frontal cortex allows for flexible involvement in motor, cognitive, and affective components of behavior. This is supported by the existence of parallel, partially segregated basal ganglia–thalamocortical loops, which can be functionally distinguished from one another (Alexander & Crutcher, 1990; Alexander et al., 1986). Importantly, anatomical tracing work done in primates also highlights the role of midbrain dopaminergic structures (both substantia nigra and ventral tegmental area) in modulating information processed in corticostriatal loops. Specifically, this work has suggested that an ascending spiral of projections connecting the striatum and midbrain dopaminergic centers supports a hierarchy of information flow from the ventromedial to the dorsolateral portions of the striatum (Haber, Fudge, & McFarland, 2000).

The striatum is functionally and anatomically divided into the dorsal and ventral striatum in both rodents and primates (Figure 6.1; Gerfen & Wilson, 1996; Lynd Balta & Haber, 1994; Robbins & Everitt, 1992; Voorn, Vanderschuren, Groenewegen, Robbins, & Pennartz, 2004). The internal capsule further divides the dorsal striatum (DS) into the caudate and the putamen in primates (Haber et al., 2000). Although there is no clear anatomical division between the caudate and putamen in rodents, the dorsal striatum is still functionally subdivided into the dorsomedial striatum (DMS, roughly equivalent to the caudate in primates) and the dorsolateral striatum (DLS, roughly equivalent to the putamen in primates; Yin & Knowlton, 2006). In primates, the caudate nucleus can be further subdivided into the head (more anterior portions), body, and tail, whose functional distinction is a current research question (Cincotta & Seger, 2007; Seger & Cincotta, 2005). The primary structure in the ventral striatum is the nucleus accumbens (NAcc), although the ventral portions of the putamen and caudate are also considered parts of the ventral striatum

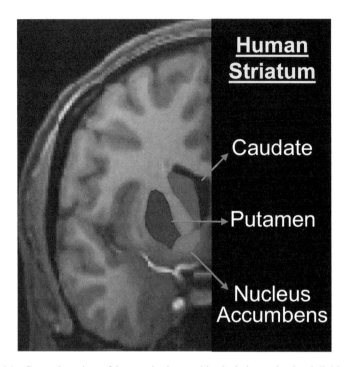

Figure 6.1   Coronal section of human brain roughly depicting striatal subdivisions. The caudate (light purple region), putamen (dark purple region), and nucleus accumbens (orange region) are highlighted. See color plate.

(Gerfen & Wilson, 1996; Haber & McFarland, 1999). The NAcc in both rodents and primates can be further subdivided into a more ventromedial shell subregion and a more dorsolateral core subregion, which can be distinguished histochemically (Groenewegen, Wright, Beijer, & Voorn, 1999; Haber et al., 2000; Meredith, Pattiselanno, Groenewegen, & Haber, 1996; Voorn et al., 2004; Zahm & Brog, 1992). Although the functional roles of these subregions are still a topic of much debate, it has been suggested that the shell may play an especially important role in hedonic processing, due to its particularly high number of opiate receptors (Berridge, 2004; Berridge & Robinson, 1998; Kelley et al., 2002), whereas research on the function of the core has focused on the role of dopamine in ascribing incentive value to particular outcomes (Ikemoto & Panksepp, 1999; Ito, Robbins, & Everitt, 2004). Unfortunately, these subregions are not readily distinguishable in human functional imaging studies, and so consideration of their particular roles in decision making is beyond the scope of this chapter. Finally, there is deliberation with respect to the existence of sharp functional divisions within the striatum. For instance, dorsal and ventral distinctions in terms of affective processing are apparent in many experiments, as will be described in the next few sections (e.g., for review, see O'Doherty, 2004; Robbins & Everitt, 1992; see also O'Doherty, this volume). The presence of a dorsomedial gradient with respect to function, however, also suggests that boundaries within the striatum can be delineated differently (Voorn et al., 2004).

Although traditionally thought of as governing motor function, more recently the basal ganglia have been found to serve cognitive functions as well (Graybiel, 1995; Packard & Knowlton, 2002). In addition to receiving inputs from motor regions of the brain, such as the premotor cortex and supplementary motor area, the striatum also receives input from an array of other prefrontal brain regions which are associated with cognitive and affective functions. The dorsolateral prefrontal cortex (DLPFC), associated with a role in executive function and working memory (Fellows & Farah, 2005; Levy & Goldman-Rakic, 2000), projects to the dorsal caudate and medial putamen (Haber, Kim, Mailly, & Calzavara, 2006). The ventromedial prefrontal cortex (vmPFC), orbitofrontal cortex (OFC), and anterior cingulate cortex (ACC) also project to the striatum, and these regions play important roles in reward processing and decision making (Botvinick, Braver, Barch, Carter, & Cohen, 2001; Fellows, 2007; O'Doherty, Kringelbach, Rolls, Hornak, & Andrews, 2001; Rolls, 2000). Although much research has focused on the projections of these regions to the ventral striatum, recent work indicates that "reward-related" projections to the striatum are actually more widespread, with projections from the OFC and ACC terminating in the dorsal striatum and converging with inputs from the DLPFC (Haber et al., 2006). This connectivity suggests that the striatum may be in an excellent position to integrate reward-related information with cognitive information to help the decision-making process.

In addition to the reward-related prefrontal input to the striatum, there are also important reward-related signals carried by dopaminergic neurons, which project from the midbrain (substantia nigra and ventral tegmental area) to the dorsal and the ventral striatum (Schultz, 1998; Schultz, Dayan, & Montague, 1997). In primates, clusters of cells in the substantia nigra pars compacta (SNC) projecting to caudate are interspersed with clusters projecting to the putamen (Haber & Fudge, 1997), with neurons in the medial SNC tending to innervate the more medial "associative" striatum and neurons in the lateral SNC innervating the more lateral, "motor" striatum (Joel & Weiner, 2000). Electrophysiological recording studies of dopaminergic neurons in nonhuman primates demonstrate that they respond to unpredicted rewards such as food and fluid; however, if the reward is preceded by a conditioned, predictive stimulus, the neuronal activity occurs following this learned stimulus and is absent following the actual reward. If a predicted reward does not actually occur, then the neurons are depressed at the time at which the reward would have occurred (Schultz, 2004; Schultz et al., 1997; Schultz, Tremblay, & Hollerman, 1998). These findings led researchers to postulate that dopaminergic neurons play a role in reward processing, but not as a hedonic indicator. Rather, the dopaminergic signal can be thought of as coding for both positive and negative "prediction errors", that is, the difference between the reward received and the expected reward (Schultz & Dickinson, 2000), a vital signal to learning and shaping of decisions.

CRAVING AND PREDICTING REWARDS: THE VENTRAL STRIATUM AND REWARD-RELATED RESPONSES

The ventral striatum, particularly the nucleus accumbens, has been implicated in various aspects of reward processing and motivation. The general concept of "wanting", a prevalent theory of dopamine function, was quickly adapted and extended to the ventral striatum (Berridge & Robinson, 2003). For instance, increases in dopamine release, as measured by microdialysis, are observed in the nucleus accumbens during presentation of a conditioned stimulus associated with cocaine (Ito, Dalley, Howes, Robbins, & Everitt, 2000), with the core but not the shell also being involved in aspects of drug-seeking behavior acquisition (Ito et al., 2004). In humans, positron emission tomography (PET) studies show increases in dopamine release in the ventral striatum (as measured by displacement of the radioligand raclopride, which selectively binds to D2 receptors) when participants are playing a game for monetary incentives (Koepp et al., 1998), or are hungry for chocolate (Small, Zatorre, Dagher, Evans, & Jones-Gotman, 2001). However, due to temporal limitations in PET and microdialysis, it is difficult to isolate the involvement of the ventral striatum to a specific aspect of reward processing and motivation. The advent of functional magnetic resonance imaging (fMRI) allowed probing of specific rewards (e.g., cocaine) with striatal function (Breiter & Rosen, 1999). In one such study, addicts exposed to blind infusions of cocaine show increases in blood oxygenated level dependent (BOLD) responses in the ventral striatum that correlate with increased levels of craving (Breiter et al., 1997), suggesting a strong link between ventral striatum function and motivational concepts such as "wanting".

The inclusion of motivational processes ("wanting") with the affective properties of a stimulus (hedonic value) leads to an expectation of reward that aids learning and goal-directed behavior. Central to decision making therefore is the role of the ventral striatum in the brain's computation of reward expectation—that is, anticipating a potential reward and predicting when a reward will become available. Numerous neuroimaging studies have reported activation of the ventral striatum when anticipating a potential reward (Breiter, Aharon, Kahneman, Dale, & Shizgal, 2001; Ernst et al., 2004; Galvan et al., 2006; Kirsch et al., 2003; Knutson, Adams, Fong, & Hommer, 2001; Knutson & Cooper, 2005; O'Doherty, Rolls, Francis, Bowtell, & McGlone, 2001). One well-known paradigm, the Monetary Incentive Delay task, was developed by Brian Knutson to measure centers of the brain involved in monetary reward anticipation (Knutson, Adams et al., 2001). In the paradigm, participants are presented with a visual cue that signifies different valence (positive, negative) and magnitude ($0–$5.00) and then perform a target detection task (i.e., press button before target disappears) to earn or avoid the outcome represented by the cue. Increases in BOLD signal are typically observed in the ventral striatum in response to the reward cues that parametrically order according to magnitude (i.e., higher responses when anticipating higher rewards), suggesting that the ventral striatum is involved in reward anticipation and is sensitive to magnitude (Figure 6.2).

Interestingly, no increases in the ventral striatum were observed to cues signaling losses (only the dorsal striatum) or even probability (Knutson & Cooper, 2005), and less response in the ventral striatum is observed in adolescents (Bjork, Knutson, Fong, Caggiano, Bennett, & Hommer, 2004). The findings of anticipatory responses to different magnitudes of reward in the ventral striatum were also replicated in a different paradigm (Galvan, Hare, Davidson, Spicer, Glover, & Casey, 2005). The main differences between the two paradigms were that the Galvan study included presentation of the various levels of magnitude as just three amounts of reward ranging from low to high (as opposed to actual value price $0–$5.00), in turn decreasing the amount of variability in the subjective appraisal of reward, a direct comparison between groups (adults, adolescents), and a stronger learning component. Yet, such differences influenced the results, highlighting how context can be important. While the Bjork study reported decreased signals in the adolescent ventral striatum, Galvan and colleagues (Galvan et al., 2006) showed that adolescents actually have higher responses in the ventral striatum during anticipation of rewards of different magnitudes compared with adults, suggesting an overactive ventral striatum (with less prefrontal inhibition) during development that may underlie risky decision making (Galvan, Hare, Voss, Glover, & Casey, 2007). This result is mirrored in other studies (May et al., 2004), and with adolescents classified with behavioral inhibition (Guyer et al., 2006), but there are also studies that report no differences between adolescents and adults in ventral striatum during risky decision making (Eshel, Nelson, Blair, Pine, & Ernst, 2007), suggesting further research is needed to clarify how ventral striatum function is modulated during development.

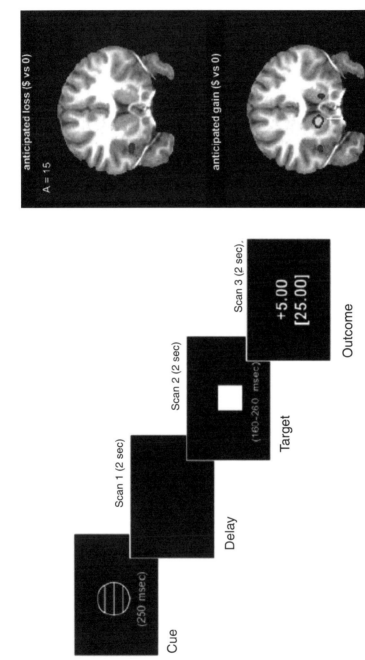

Figure 6.2 The Monetary Incentive Delay task. Participants view a cue that represents the valence (reward or loss) and magnitude ($0–$5.00) of the outcome. Increases in BOLD response in the ventral striatum are observed when participants anticipate potential rewards, but not losses. Reprinted with permission from Knutson, Adams et al. (2001). See color plate.

Recent neuroimaging data implicate the ventral striatum in reward-related learning and specifically prediction-error learning, another prominent theory on the potential role of dopamine neurons. Much like dopamine neurons (Fiorillo, Tobler, & Schultz, 2003), activity in the ventral striatum is modulated by uncertainty (Berns, McClure, Pagnoni, & Montague, 2001; see also Yu, this volume). Indeed, in the previously discussed paradigms (Galvan et al., 2005; Knutson, Adams et al., 2001) there was always a potential, but not certain reward, suggesting the involvement of the ventral striatum in prediction-based learning. Using primary reinforcers (e.g., juice rewards), studies have also shown that BOLD signals in the ventral striatum correlate with the prediction-error signal (McClure, Berns, & Montague, 2003; O'Doherty, Dayan, Friston, Critchley, & Dolan, 2003). That is, unexpected rewards lead to a rise in activation that transfers to the earliest predictor of the reward, while unexpected withdrawal of rewards leads to decreases in response signaling a prediction error. Finally, prediction-error signals can be coded in the ventral striatum during both Pavlovian and instrumental conditioning, suggesting the involvement of the ventral striatum during various forms of reward-related learning (O'Doherty, Dayan, Schultz, Deichmann, Friston, & Dolan, 2004).

Although the role of the ventral striatum in craving and prediction-based learning of positive stimuli is well documented, it is unclear how aversive stimuli are processed in the ventral striatum. While some studies suggest that the ventral striatum does not code for anticipation of monetary loss (Knutson, Adams et al., 2001), others suggest that anticipation of pain does in fact recruit the ventral striatum (Jensen, McIntosh, Crawley, Mikulis, Remington, & Kapur, 2003). Monetary loss *per se* seems to lead to decreases in ventral striatum activation (Breiter et al., 2001; Delgado, Nystrom, Fissell, Noll, & Fiez, 2000; Liu, Powell, Wang, Gold, Corbly, & Joseph, 2007) supporting the idea of a negative prediction error (subjects might predict a win in such trials), although a study recently suggested that prediction errors in the loss domain lead to positive signals (Seymour, Daw, Dayan, Singer, & Dolan, 2007). More research is needed to further understand ventral striatum function in the aversive domain.

THE HEAD OF THE CAUDATE NUCLEUS: GUIDING DECISIONS THROUGH LEARNING FROM CONSEQUENCES

The caudate nucleus has been shown to process information about positive and negative outcomes during decision making (e.g., Delgado et al., 2000; Elliott, Friston, & Dolan, 2000; Hikosaka, Sakamoto, & Usui, 1989; Kawagoe, Takikawa, & Hikosaka, 1998; Knutson, Fong, Adams, Varner,

& Hommer, 2001; Lauwereyns, Takikawa et al., 2002; McDonald & White, 1993; Packard, Hirsh, & White, 1989; Poldrack, Prabhakaran, Seger, & Gabrieli, 1999). The involvement of the head of the caudate nucleus in decision making, however, is very context-dependent. Specifically, reward-related information seems to be processed in the caudate primarily when the information is relevant to one's goal. This section will highlight the main contextual influences on reward processing in this region (see also Mandel & Vartanian, this volume).

Electrophysiological work in monkeys has found caudate activity related to the expectation of reward, as well as activity that is time-locked to reward presentation (Hikosaka et al., 1989). The firing of such caudate neurons is context-dependent, changing when environmental conditions change (Graybiel, 1995; Kawagoe et al., 1998; Lauwereyns, Takikawa et al., 2002; Lauwereyns, Watanabe, Coe, & Hikosaka, 2002; Ragozzino, 2003). In one study, monkeys were required to make visual saccades to one of four locations. Different caudate neurons showed preferential activation to each of the four locations when saccades to all four were rewarded. However, when just one location was rewarded, the preferred direction of some caudate neurons changed to be whichever direction was rewarded, while other caudate neurons began to fire preferentially for non-rewarded directions (Kawagoe et al., 1998). Further work has shown that caudate neurons display feature-based activity in anticipation of reward during performance of behavioral tasks, and that this activity appears to bias goal-directed behavior (Lauwereyns, Takikawa et al., 2002; Lauwereyns, Watanabe et al., 2002). Moreover, activity of a second class of neurons in the striatum, the cholinergic interneurons known as tonically active neurons (TANs), is also context-sensitive. Their activity is modulated by motivational state, the spatial location of rewarded movement, and other circumstances of reward presentation (Apicella, 2007). This research in nonhuman primates suggested that the caudate nucleus may play a role in integrating contextual information with reward-related dopaminergic signals from the midbrain to guide motivated action.

Using neuroimaging techniques such as fMRI, reports of the involvement of the human caudate nucleus in processing positive and negative feedback soon surfaced (Elliott et al., 2000; Elliott, Frith, & Dolan, 1997; Poldrack et al., 2001; Poldrack et al., 1999). One paradigm in particular, involving a guessing game with monetary incentives, successfully established a link between reward processing and the head of the caudate nucleus (Delgado et al., 2000). In the card-guessing paradigm, participants viewed a "card" on the screen with a question mark, and were asked to guess whether the number on the back of the card was higher or lower than five (Figure 6.3a). After entering their response with a key press, the actual number (ranging from 1 to 9) was shown, followed by a green upwards arrow for correct guesses, a red downwards arrow for incorrect guesses, or blue dashed lines for neutral trials in which the number was exactly 5. Participants were instructed that their payment would depend on these outcomes; they received $1.00 for each correct guess, lost $0.50 for each incorrect guess, and neither won nor lost money for the neutral trials. The monetary discrepancy reflects the loss aversion notion in prospect theory—namely, the tendency for losses (or punishments) to loom larger than gains (or rewards) in decision making under risk (Kahneman & Tversky, 1979). Both the dorsal and ventral striatum were identified as showing a significant outcome valence by time effect; that is, these regions differentiated between monetary gains and losses, with the most robust signals observed in the head of the caudate (Figure 6.3b). The time courses of activation in these regions reveal a response that begins to rise before the outcome is presented and that is then sustained following wins, while decreasing below baseline on trials involving monetary loss. This differential response to positive and negative outcomes in the striatum may reflect a learning signal similar to the previously discussed dopaminergic cell firings in nonhuman primates during appetitive learning (Schultz et al., 1997), whose primary output is the striatum, although input from the frontal cortex may also modulate the caudate signal.

As with the findings of electrophysiological studies of caudate neurons, early fMRI studies also suggested that the BOLD signal in the caudate nucleus to reward and punishment is not absolute, but that it varies depending on the task context. This led to the idea that the caudate signal shows "counterfactual comparison" effects; that is, it is dependent not only on the outcome that is experienced, but also on the other possible outcomes. For instance, the response profile to winning $0.00 is significantly greater when the other alternative is losing money than when the alternative is gaining money (Nieuwenhuis, Heslenfeld, Alting von Geusau, Mars, Holroyd, & Yeung, 2005). In a clever design that allowed participants to discover what the outcomes of unchosen actions "would have been" as well as what the outcomes of the chosen action were, Lohrenz and colleagues found that activation in the ventral caudate is correlated with a "fictive error signal", that is, a learning signal that provides information about the consequences of actions not taken (Lohrenz, McCabe, Camerer, & Montague, 2007). When such information is available, it may be useful in guiding future decision making, and indeed, the experiment showed that participants' choices were significantly influenced by the fictive error from their previous choice.

Another influence on activity in the head of the caudate is whether the outcome is perceived as contingently linked with the individual's action (Tricomi, Delgado, & Fiez, 2004). One study that illustrates this effect used an "oddball" paradigm, in which a standard stimulus (a purple square)

A. Probabilistic gambling task

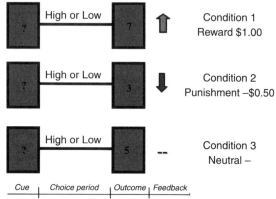

Cue | Choice period | Outcome | Feedback

B. Striatum hemodynamic response during probabilistic gambling task

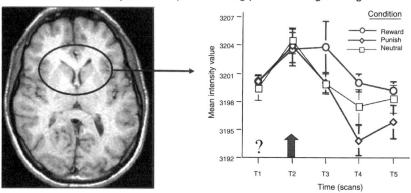

Figure 6.3 The card-guessing task. (a) Participants are asked to guess if the value of the card is higher or lower than the number 5. A correct response leads to a monetary reward (e.g., $1.00), while an incorrect response leads to a monetary loss (e.g., –$0.50). When the card number is 5, a neutral outcome occurs and money is neither gained nor lost. (b) Activation of the striatum, particularly the head of the caudate nucleus (pictured) is observed when participants are engaged in this paradigm. The hemodynamic response is higher for reward trials, while it decreases sharply below baseline when the outcome is a loss. Reprinted with permission from Delgado et al. (2000). See color plate.

was presented once every 1.5 s, interrupted by infrequent "oddballs". These oddballs were an upwards green arrow, indicating a $1.50 gain, a downwards red arrow, indicating a $0.75 loss, or a blue sideways arrow, indicating a neutral trial with no monetary consequence. The participants simply responded to the oddballs with a button press to indicate they noticed them. Interestingly, the wins and losses did not significantly activate the caudate nucleus. Significant activation in the caudate was found, however, in a follow-up study, in which participants had to respond to a cue (a yellow circle) that preceded the "oddball" by choosing one of two buttons and they were told that the outcome would depend on whether they chose the "correct" response (Figure 6.4). In this condition, the perception of contingency between action and outcome led to a replication of the previously observed response in the caudate nucleus during the card-guessing task. In a second condition, participants responded to a different cue (a blue circle) by pressing a third button and were told that although this button press would also be followed by an arrow indicating monetary reward or loss, it did not determine which outcome would occur. The lack of a contingency in this condition led to nondistinct responses in the head of the caudate nucleus.

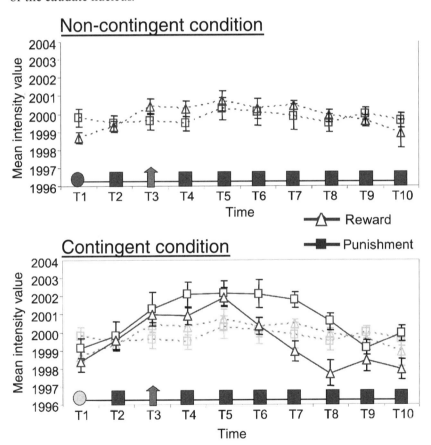

Figure 6.4   The affective oddball paradigm. Participants are instructed to detect the oddball (monetary arrow) which is delivered either contingently (yellow circle) or non-contingently (blue circle) on the participant's action. Contingent, but not non-contingent, affective outcomes recruit activation in the head of the caudate nucleus. Reprinted with permission from Tricomi et al. (2004). See color plate.

Further studies have also supported the observation that reward-related caudate activity is linked to action. The behavioral relevance of stimuli has been shown to affect activity in the caudate, whether those stimuli represent typical rewards, such as money, or not (Zink, Pagnoni, Martin-Skurski, Chappelow, & Berns, 2004; Zink, Pagnoni, Martin, Dhamala, & Berns, 2003). Additionally, the roles of the caudate and the ventral striatum have been distinguished with respect to their dependency on action (O'Doherty et al., 2004). Whereas recruitment of the caudate is more prominent during appetitive instrumental conditioning where rewards are dependent on behavioral responses, the ventral striatum is active during both instrumental and Pavlovian conditioning where rewards are linked to predictive stimuli rather than actions. These results also fit within the context of recent behavioral neuroscience work done in animals, which has found that the dorsomedial portion of the rat striatum (roughly equivalent to the caudate in primates) is critical for action–outcome learning in instrumental conditioning (Yin, Knowlton, & Balleine, 2005; Yin, Ostlund, Knowlton, & Balleine, 2005). Moreover, neurons in the primate dorsal striatum have been shown to code for the value of particular action choices, rather than for the expected value of the outcome independent of action (Samejima, Ueda, Doya, & Kimura, 2005).

What purpose might these contextual effects in the caudate serve? One possibility is that these influences on caudate activity serve to focus its processing only on relevant information. If activity in this region is to reflect the consequences of a decision, it makes sense for it to be based only on the possible consequences. Thus, choosing the "lesser of two evils" may sometimes be the best possible option, and the caudate's tendency to respond in a counterfactual manner reflects this. Further, rewards and punishments are only useful in guiding behavior to the extent that one has control over them. The caudate's sensitivity to action–outcome contingency suggests that this region may play an important role in learning from the consequences of one's actions.

Other contextual factors that have been found to influence caudate activation are: (1) the type of incentive, with more valuable incentives producing greater signal in the caudate and (2) the context in which the incentive is presented. The hemodynamic response in the head of the caudate nucleus, for example, has been found to order parametrically according to the magnitude of the reward or punishment (Delgado, Locke, Stenger, & Fiez, 2003) and with respect to type of incentive (e.g., monetary×nonmonetary; Delgado, Stenger, & Fiez, 2004). Interestingly, however, outcomes with no extrinsic reward value can under certain circumstances produce robust caudate responses. When the goal of a task is to earn positive feedback rather than to earn money, the presence of feedback that guides future decisions can elicit caudate activation, even if it does not signify the receipt of an extrinsic reward (Elliott et al., 1997; Nieuwenhuis, Slagter, Geusau, Heslenfeld, & Holroyd, 2005; Poldrack et al., 2001). One study compared caudate activity within-subjects for receipt of performance-dependent feedback in a learning task and extrinsic monetary rewards in the card-guessing task. The caudate signal was similarly modulated by the positive and negative outcomes in the two tasks, with overlapping portions of the caudate showing a significant effect (Tricomi, Delgado, McCandliss, McClelland, & Fiez, 2006). These studies indicate that the incentive value of an outcome may be best thought of as the degree to which it reflects goal achievement, whether that goal is to obtain extrinsic rewards, or something more abstract, such as mastering a task.

Finally, activity in the head of the caudate is also sensitive to predictability or how well a task is learned. Early during the learning process, behavioral consequences provide more information than they do later in learning, once those consequences are fully expected. Reflecting this, experiments in both animals and humans have shown that activity in the caudate decreases as learning progresses (Delgado, Miller, Inati, & Phelps, 2005; Haruno & Kawato, 2006; Haruno et al., 2004; Jueptner, Stephan, Frith, Brooks, Frackowiak, & Passingham, 1997; Law et al., 2005; Pasupathy & Miller, 2005; Poldrack et al., 1999; Seger & Cincotta, 2005; Williams & Eskandar, 2006). For example, in an adaptation of the card-guessing task, predictive cues were shown that indicated the probability that the card value would be high or low (Delgado, Miller et al., 2005). When the cues were 100% predictive of the card value, participants easily learned to respond appropriately, and caudate activity was only high early in the task session, when the cue–outcome associations were being learned. When the relationship between the cues and card value was less predictive (predicting a high value 67% or 50% of the time), the caudate's response did not significantly decrease over the course of the session. In these conditions, the outcome of the participants' decisions remained uncertain, and therefore the outcome provided new information. These results support the idea that caudate activity does not simply reflect reward and loss, but that it instead serves to process the information provided by rewards and punishments. In doing so, it may support the use of this information to guide future decisions.

From a decision-making perspective, it is more efficient for a reward-processing system to be more sensitive to and learn from outcomes that are goal-relevant than those that are not. After all, if one doesn't care about a particular outcome of a decision, or if one already knows what it will be, there is no reason for it to influence future behavior. For example, imagine someone who is faced with the choice of which meal to order at a new restaurant. He would like to eat a good-tasting meal and decides to order fish, which he normally enjoys. If it turns out that the fish is served undercooked, his goal will not have been met, and it wouldn't matter if the fish is beautifully presented or that it is low in fat. Rather than being overly sensitive to all the unimportant consequences of a decision, the caudate is able to hone in on the consequences that matter most: those that reflect goal achievement.

DECIDING WITHOUT THINKING: THE DORSOLATERAL STRIATUM AND HABIT-BASED BEHAVIOR

Although acting according to habit is not generally thought of as decision making in the traditional sense, it could be viewed as making decisions without consciously considering the possible options. Once one knows what decision to make in order to reach a goal, making this decision each time a similar situation arises takes less and less effort. Following a certain course of action eventually shifts from being a conscious choice to a habit, which can then be executed without thinking about the consequences of the behavior. For example, imagine someone looking for a friend's apartment in a new building. She would have to consider which way to turn when stepping out of the elevator. When coming home to her own apartment, however, she may have turned left when getting out of the elevator so many times that she no longer has to consider the decision of which way to turn. In fact, once this action has become a full-fledged habit, it is no longer even necessary to mentally represent the goal of finding the apartment at all; the stimulus of the elevator door opening in the familiar hallway may be enough to cause the habitual left turn to be executed automatically.

Behavioral neuroscience work with animals has explored this behavioral shift from goal-directed to habit-based behavior. Early in learning, rats will decrease their response rate if the outcome of the response becomes undesirable (e.g., if the rat has been allowed to eat a food reward until it is satiated). After extensive training, however, the response to a stimulus becomes independent of the outcome; even if the outcome is devalued, response rates remain high (Dickinson & Balleine, 2002). Recent work has suggested that these two types of behavior may be controlled by distinct subregions of the striatum, with the dorsomedial striatum (DMS) subserving goal-directed action, and the dorsolateral striatum (DLS) supporting habit-based behavior (Devan, McDonald, & White, 1999; Ragozzino, 2003; Yin & Knowlton, 2006).

The DLS receives cortical input from sensory-motor areas, as well as dopaminergic input from the substantia nigra, and projects to the globus pallidus, the output unit of the striatum (Bar-Gad et al., 2003). This connectivity puts it in a prime position to influence motor output (i.e., behavioral responses). In rats with lesions to the DLS, habit learning is disrupted. For example, although normal taste aversion learning occurs,

DLS-lesioned rats decrease lever pressing after taste aversion, unlike controls or rats with lesions to the DMS, who continue to lever press (Yin, Knowlton, & Balleine, 2004). Additionally, when rats in a water maze were given a choice between escaping to a visible platform or hidden platform with a learned location, DLS and sham-lesioned rats showed no preference, but DMS-lesioned rats escaped to the visible platform significantly more than to the hidden one. This suggests that without an intact DMS, tendencies to respond to a stimulus cue are enhanced. This finding is consistent with a role of the DLS in mediating stimulus–response habits, since without an intact DMS, the DLS could exert more influence over behavior (Devan et al., 1999). Electrophysiological work with rhesus monkeys also supports the conclusion that the relative contributions of the caudate and putamen to behavioral control shifts over the course of learning. Caudate activity peaks early in learning, whereas putamen activity increases over the course of learning, with the most activity once the task was well-learned (Williams & Eskandar, 2006; but see Carelli, Wolske, & West, 1997).

In humans, activation of the posterior putamen increases when free operant responses to cues become outcome-insensitive (Tricomi, Balleine, & O'Doherty, 2009). This fits with the work on animals, which suggests that the relative activity of the dorsal putamen compared with the caudate should increase as response-outcome contingency learning gives way to stimulus-response habit learning. As mentioned previously, caudate activation decreases over the course of learning, which would serve to decrease its contribution to behavioral control relative to the putamen. One PET study found that the putamen, but not other striatal subregions, was more strongly activated during execution of a well-learned motor task compared with a baseline task with similar motor demands but no learning component (Jueptner, Frith, Brooks, Frackowiak, & Passingham, 1997). A more recent neuroimaging study using fMRI found that putamen activity increases over the course of learning, which is consistent with the animal work indicating that the putamen may exert more control over behavior with experience (Seger & Cincotta, 2005). Finally, Haruno and Kawato (2006) found that learning was associated with BOLD signal increases in the putamen to stimuli indicating which action would be rewarded, along with decreases in the outcome-related signal in the caudate.

Executing a habit automatically, without having to consciously think about a decision's consequences, frees up valuable resources which could then be used to attend to something else. As long as one's goals remain constant, habitual behavior remains adaptive. However, one interesting implication of the research on habit formation is that once behaviors are well learned, they may become impervious to negative consequences. If the outcome of a decision changes, or if it is no longer in line with one's goals, then responding to a familiar stimulus habitually is no longer adaptive.

For instance, cues, such as the sight of drug paraphernalia, can become strongly linked with addictive behaviors (Childress et al., 1999). When such cues tend to elicit a habitual response, it may be difficult for people trying to overcome addiction to break these habits, even if using a drug is no longer rewarding (Cardinal & Everitt, 2004; Everitt & Robbins, 2005). People sometimes make poor decisions, it seems, at least in part because they may not consciously be making a decision, but instead simply executing a habit.

NEXT FRONTIERS OF REWARD AND DECISION-MAKING RESEARCH

As the field continues to evolve, research has started to focus on a variety of remaining issues ranging from anatomical to functional considerations of the role of the striatum in reward-related processing and decision making. A clearer delineation of the human striatum's anatomical and functional boundaries, for example, could aid interpretation of many neuroimaging studies. Moreover, while this chapter has focused on the striatum, there are a number of other brain structures involved in affective learning and decision making, such as the orbitofrontal cortex and amygdala. It is imperative to probe the interactions between the striatum and different components of a circuit involved in reward processing during various phases of learning and decision making.

Another topic of great interest is the role of the striatum during processing of aversive information, such as losses, and its effect on decision making. As previously discussed, BOLD signals in the caudate nucleus have been found to increase in anticipation of both reward and loss (Knutson, Adams et al., 2001), although conflicting data exist in the ventral striatum; while some studies find no anticipatory responses to losses (Knutson, Adams et al., 2001), others report sensitivity to aversive outcomes (Jensen et al., 2003). The interpretation of aversive outcomes, however, can be confounded in some paradigms where the opportunity to avoid the potentially negative outcome exists. Indeed, some studies suggest that the successful avoidance of a punishment (e.g., monetary loss) can also be interpreted by the striatum as rewarding (Breiter et al., 2001; Nieuwenhuis, Heslenfeld et al., 2005; Rogan, Leon, Perez, & Kandel, 2005), while a missed opportunity for monetary gain seems to act as a punishment (Breiter et al., 2001; Nieuwenhuis, Heslenfeld et al., 2005). However, additional studies are necessary to carefully assess the role of the human striatum in processing the complexities of avoidance and aversive learning. Some neuropsychological studies with patients afflicted with Parkinson's disease suggest, for example, that levels of dopamine in the striatum modulate learning and decision making according to the context of learning (Frank, Seeberger, & O'Reilly, 2004). That is, patients off medication are able to learn better from negative or punishment feedback, while patients on medication are more influenced by positive or reward feedback. Future work will endeavor to demonstrate how different brain structures interact in the processing of positive versus negative outcomes. For example, one recent study indicates that inhibitory input from the lateral habenula, a structure within the thalamus, may cause the characteristic pause in the firing of dopaminergic neurons following stimuli indicating the absence of reward, suggesting that further study of this region may reveal important clues about networks supporting the processing of negative outcomes (Matsumoto & Hikosaka, 2007).

Finally, the interdisciplinary interest in the field of decision making from both a social and economic perspective also promotes a natural extension from the more basic and simple decision processes to more complex decisions that typically occur in everyday life. Recent studies have found involvement of the striatum, particularly the caudate nucleus, during social interactions such as cooperation (Rilling, Gutman, Zeh, Pagnoni, Berns, & Kilts, 2002), social feedback (Rilling, Sanfey, Aronson, Nystrom, & Cohen, 2004a, 2004b), and even revenge (de Quervain et al., 2004; Singer, Seymour, O'Doherty, Stephan, Dolan, & Frith, 2006; see also Sanfey & Rilling, this volume). Interestingly, during a social interaction experiment where participants must learn to trust one another for greater benefits, the caudate nucleus is involved in acquiring reputations, or learning that an individual is trustworthy (King-Casas, Tomlin, Anen, Camerer, Quartz, & Montague, 2005). In society, however, biases and previous information often inhibit updating and learning of social signals. Thus, the complexity of how social information is acquired and interpreted by the brain in order to influence future decisions is an important research question.

One study examined more deeply how biases based on prior knowledge and beliefs influence activity in the caudate (Delgado, Frank, & Phelps, 2005). Participants read brief biographies of three fictional players, which described these players' moral character as praiseworthy, neutral, or suspect. The participants then played an investment game in which they could choose on each trial to keep $1.00 or give it to the other player, in which case the investment grew to $3.00, which the other player would either split or keep. Throughout the experiment, participants chose to share the money with the praiseworthy player more often than the player with suspect moral character, despite the fact that for all three players, the investment was returned 50% of the time. This behavioral bias, however, did not preclude the participants from explicitly learning that the three players were equally trustworthy; ratings of the trustworthiness of the three players indicate that this learning occurred. Like the players' behavior, activation in the caudate nucleus was biased by the initial impression created by the biographies. Whereas the responses in this region following the neutral partner's decisions to share or keep the investment showed the typical pattern for reward and punishment, the responses following the praiseworthy partner's decisions did not. Instead, activation was similar following both share and keep decisions by the praiseworthy partner, indicating that the participants' initial bias in favor of this player tended to prevent the caudate from differentially responding to the information provided by the outcomes of this player's decisions. As with other contextual influences on caudate activity, this could be seen as an example of the caudate responding to outcome-related information only when this information is relevant. Having already decided that the praiseworthy player was "good", participants did not use the information provided by this player's actions to alter future decisions. In contrast, with little prior information about the neutral player available to bias decisions, the information provided by his actions becomes more important, and the caudate becomes more sensitive to this information.

SUMMARY

There are obvious next steps for understanding how the brain computes decisions, including understanding the role of the striatum in conjunction with different brain regions, and how such reward-related circuits may subserve decisions and goal-directed behavior. The goal of this chapter was to highlight the anatomical and functional subdivisions within the striatum with respect to learning and decision-making research. To broadly illustrate how the human striatum may be involved in reward-related decision-making processes, let us return to the example of a child deciding whether to take a cookie from a cookie jar. In what ways might the striatum be contributing to this decision? The ventral striatum may play a role in the child's "wanting" the cookie and the anticipation of the reward that the cookie would bring. Both the ventral striatum and the head of the caudate might have been involved in learning from previous experiences involving a similar decision. For example, the child may have sometimes opened the jar to find a batch of freshly baked cookies, but other times may have been disappointed by finding the cookie jar empty. The ventral and dorsal striatum may have processed different aspects of those experiences, with the ventral striatum involved in processing whether the outcome was better or worse than expected, and the caudate processing the causal relationship between the action of opening the cookie jar and the reward of the cookie. Finally, if the child has become accustomed to sneaking a cookie each time he sees the jar unguarded, the dorsolateral striatum may cause him to habitually open the jar even if he's just eaten plenty of cake at a birthday party and is no longer hungry. The striatum is thus doing much more than simply processing whether something is "good" or "bad", but is involved in many different aspects of goal-directed behavior. Through this involvement, it is able to efficiently guide the individual toward making decisions that are most likely to lead to valuable outcomes, given the current context and goals. While traditional economic models, such as the self-interest model, assume a singular goal for rational behavior (e.g. maximize monetary gain), the context of the transaction can change our goals, leading to "irrational" behavior (e.g., being nice and cooperative due to personal beliefs or expectations for future interactions), with such contextual changes being modulated by cortico-striatal circuits in the human brain.

REFERENCES

Alexander, G. E., & Crutcher, M. D. (1990). Functional architecture of basal ganglia circuits: Neural substrates of parallel processing. *Trends in Neurosciences, 13*, 266–271.

Alexander, G. E., DeLong, M. R., & Strick, P. L. (1986). Parallel organization of functionally segregated circuits linking basal ganglia and cortex. *Annual Review of Neuroscience, 9*, 357–381.

Apicella, P. (2007). Leading tonically active neurons of the striatum from reward detection to context recognition. *Trends in Neurosciences, 30*, 299–306.

Bar-Gad, I., Morris, G., & Bergman, H. (2003). Information processing, dimensionality reduction and reinforcement learning in the basal ganglia. *Progress in Neurobiology, 71*, 439–473.

Berns, G. S., McClure, S. M., Pagnoni, G., & Montague, P. R. (2001). Predictability modulates human brain response to reward. *Journal of Neuroscience, 21*, 2793–2798.

Berridge, K. C. (2004). Motivation concepts in behavioral neuroscience. *Physiology and Behavior, 81*, 179–209.

Berridge, K. C., & Robinson, T. E. (1998). What is the role of dopamine in reward: Hedonic impact, reward learning, or incentive salience? *Brain Research Reviews, 28*, 309–369.

Berridge, K. C., & Robinson, T. E. (2003). Parsing reward. *Trends in Neurosciences, 26*, 507–512.

Bjork, J. M., Knutson, B., Fong, G. W., Caggiano, D. M., Bennett, S. M., & Hommer, D. W. (2004). Incentive-elicited brain activation in adolescents: Similarities and differences from young adults. *Journal of Neuroscience, 24*, 1793–1802.

Botvinick, M. M., Braver, T. S., Barch, D. M., Carter, C. S., & Cohen, J. D. (2001). Conflict monitoring and cognitive control. *Psychological Review, 108*, 624–652.

Breiter, H. C., Aharon, I., Kahneman, D., Dale, A., & Shizgal, P. (2001). Functional imaging of neural responses to expectancy and experience of monetary gains and losses. *Neuron, 30*, 619–639.

Breiter, H. C., Gollub, R. L., Weisskoff, R. M., Kennedy, D. N., Makris, N., Berke, J. D. et al. (1997). Acute effects of cocaine on human brain activity and emotion. *Neuron, 19*, 591–611.

Breiter, H. C., & Rosen, B. R. (1999). Functional magnetic resonance imaging of brain reward circuitry in the human. *Annals of the New York Academy of Sciences, 877*, 523–547.

Cannon, C. M., & Bseikri, M. R. (2004). Is dopamine required for natural reward? *Physiology and Behavior, 81*, 741–748.

Cardinal, R. N., & Everitt, B. J. (2004). Neural and psychological mechanisms underlying appetitive learning: Links to drug addiction. *Current Opinion in Neurobiology, 14*, 156–162.

Carelli, R. M., Wolske, M., & West, M. O. (1997). Loss of level press-related firing of rat striatal forelimb neurons after repeated sessions in a lever pressing task. *Journal of Neuroscience, 17*, 1804–1814.

Childress, A. R., Mozley, P. D., McElgin, W., Fitzgerald, J., Reivich, M., & O'Brien, C. P. (1999). Limbic activation during cue-induced cocaine craving. *American Journal of Psychiatry, 156*, 11–18.

Cincotta, C. M., & Seger, C. A. (2007). Dissociation between striatal regions while learning to categorize via feedback and via observation. *Journal of Cognitive Neuroscience, 19*, 249–265.

de Quervain, D. J., Fischbacher, U., Treyer, V., Schellhammer, M., Schnyder, U., Buck, A. et al. (2004). The neural basis of altruistic punishment. *Science, 305*, 1254–1258.

Delgado, M. R., Frank, R. H., & Phelps, E. A. (2005). Perceptions of moral character modulate the neural systems of reward during the trust game. *Nature Neuroscience, 8*, 1611–1618.

Delgado, M. R., Locke, H. M., Stenger, V. A., & Fiez, J. A. (2003). Dorsal striatum responses to reward and punishment: Effects of valence and magnitude manipulations. *Cognitive, Affective, and Behavioral Neuroscience, 3*, 27–38.

Delgado, M. R., Miller, M. M., Inati, S., & Phelps, E. A. (2005). An fMRI study of reward-related probability learning. *Neuroimage, 24*, 862–873.

Delgado, M. R., Nystrom, L. E., Fissell, C., Noll, D. C., & Fiez, J. A. (2000). Tracking the hemodynamic responses to reward and punishment in the striatum. *Journal of Neurophysiology, 84*, 3072–3077.

Delgado, M. R., Stenger, V. A., & Fiez, J. A. (2004). Motivation-dependent responses in the human caudate nucleus. *Cerebral Cortex, 14*, 1022–1030.

Devan, B. D., McDonald, R. J., & White, N. M. (1999). Effects of medial and lateral caudate-putamen lesions on place- and cue-guided behaviors in the water maze: Relation to thigmotaxis. *Behavioural Brain Research, 100*, 5–14.

Dickinson, A., & Balleine, B. (2002). The role of learning in the operation of motivational systems. In C. R. Gallistel (Ed.), *Stevens' handbook of experimental psychology: Learning, motivation, and emotion* (Vol. 3, pp. 497–534). New York: Wiley and Sons.

Elliott, R., Friston, K. J., & Dolan, R. J. (2000). Dissociable neural responses in human reward systems. *Journal of Neuroscience, 20*, 6159–6165.

Elliott, R., Frith, C. D., & Dolan, R. J. (1997). Differential neural response to positive and negative feedback in planning and guessing tasks. *Neuropsychologia, 35*, 1395–1404.

Ernst, M., Nelson, E. E., McClure, E. B., Monk, C. S., Munson, S., Eshel, N. et al. (2004). Choice selection and reward anticipation: An fMRI study. *Neuropsychologia, 42*, 1585–1597.

Eshel, N., Nelson, E. E., Blair, R. J., Pine, D. S., & Ernst, M. (2007). Neural substrates of choice selection in adults and adolescents: Development of the ventrolateral prefrontal and anterior cingulate cortices. *Neuropsychologia, 45*, 1270–1279.

Everitt, B. J., & Robbins, T. W. (2005). Neural systems of reinforcement for drug addiction: From actions to habits to compulsion. *Nature Neuroscience, 8*, 1481–1489.

Fellows, L. K. (2007). Advances in understanding ventromedial prefrontal function: The accountant joins the executive. *Neurology, 68*, 991–995.

Fellows, L. K., & Farah, M. J. (2005). Different underlying impairments in decision-making following ventromedial and dorsolateral frontal lobe damage in humans. *Cerebral Cortex, 15*, 58–63.

Fiorillo, C. D., Tobler, P. N., & Schultz, W. (2003). Discrete coding of reward probability and uncertainty by dopamine neurons. *Science, 299*, 1898–1902.

Frank, M. J., Seeberger, L. C., & O'Reilly R, C. (2004). By carrot or by stick: Cognitive reinforcement learning in Parkinsonism. *Science, 306*, 1940–1943.

Galvan, A., Hare, T. A., Davidson, M., Spicer, J., Glover, G., & Casey, B. J. (2005). The role of ventral frontostriatal circuitry in reward-based learning in humans. *Journal of Neuroscience, 25*, 8650–8656.

Galvan, A., Hare, T. A., Parra, C. E., Penn, J., Voss, H., Glover, G. et al. (2006). Earlier development of the accumbens relative to orbitofrontal cortex might underlie risk-taking behavior in adolescents. *Journal of Neuroscience, 26*, 6885–6892.

Galvan, A., Hare, T., Voss, H., Glover, G., & Casey, B. J. (2007). Risk-taking and the adolescent brain: Who is at risk? *Developmental Science, 10*, F8–F14.

Gerfen, C. R., & Wilson, C. J. (1996). The basal ganglia. In L. W. Swanson, A. Bjorklund, & T. Hokfelt (Eds.), *Handbook of chemical neuroanatomy* (Vol. 12, part III, pp. 371–468). Amsterdam: Elsevier Science.

Graybiel, A. M. (1995). Building action repertoires: Memory and learning functions of the basal ganglia. *Current Opinion in Neurobiology, 5*, 733–741.

Graybiel, A. M. (2000). The basal ganglia. *Current Biology, 10*, R509–511.

Graybiel, A. M., Aosaki, T., Flaherty, A. W., & Kimura, M. (1994). The basal ganglia and adaptive motor control. *Science, 265*, 1826–1831.

Groenewegen, H. J., Wright, C. I., Beijer, A. V., & Voorn, P. (1999). Convergence and segregation of ventral striatal inputs and outputs. *Annals of the New York Academy of Sciences, 877*, 49–63.

Guyer, A. E., Nelson, E. E., Perez-Edgar, K., Hardin, M. G., Roberson-Nay, R., Monk, C. S. et al. (2006). Striatal functional alteration in adolescents characterized by early childhood behavioral inhibition. *Journal of Neuroscience, 26*, 6399–6405.

Haber, S. N. (2003). The primate basal ganglia: Parallel and integrative networks. *Journal of Chemical Neuroanatomy, 26*, 317–330.

Haber, S. N., & Fudge, J. L. (1997). The primate substantia nigra and VTA: Integrative circuitry and function. *Critical Reviews in Neurobiology, 11*, 323–342.

Haber, S. N., Fudge, J. L., & McFarland, N. R. (2000). Striatonigrostriatal pathways in primates form an ascending spiral from the shell to the dorsolateral striatum. *Journal of Neuroscience, 20*, 2369–2382.

Haber, S. N., Kim, K.-S., Mailly, P., & Calzavara, R. (2006). Reward-related cortical inputs define a large striatal region in primates that interface with associative cortical connections, providing a substrate for incentive-based learning. *Journal of Neuroscience, 26*, 8368–8376.

Haber, S. N., & McFarland, N. R. (1999). The concept of the ventral striatum in nonhuman primates. *Annals of the New York Academy of Sciences, 877*, 33–49.

Haruno, M., & Kawato, M. (2006). Different neural correlates of reward expectation and reward expectation error in the putamen and caudate nucleus during stimulus–action–reward association learning. *Journal of Neurophysiology, 95*, 948–959.

Haruno, M., Kuroda, T., Doya, K., Toyama, K., Kimura, M., Samejima, K. et al. (2004). A neural correlate of reward-based behavioral learning in caudate nucleus: A functional magnetic resonance imaging study of a stochastic decision task. *Journal of Neuroscience, 24*, 1660–1665.

Hikosaka, O., Sakamoto, M., & Usui, S. (1989). Functional properties of monkey caudate neurons. III. Activities related to expectation of target and reward. *Journal of Neurophysiology, 61*, 814–832.

Hill, W. F. (1997). *Learning* (6th ed.). New York: Addison-Wesley Educational.

Ikemoto, S., & Panksepp, J. (1999). The role of nucleus accumbens dopamine in motivated behavior: A unifying interpretation with special reference to reward-seeking. *Brain Research Reviews, 31*, 6–41.

Ito, R., Dalley, J. W., Howes, S. R., Robbins, T. W., & Everitt, B. J. (2000). Dissociation in conditioned dopamine release in the nucleus accumbens core and shell in response to cocaine cues and during cocaine-seeking behavior in rats. *Journal of Neuroscience, 20*, 7489–7495.

Ito, R., Robbins, T. W., & Everitt, B. J. (2004). Differential control over cocaine-seeking behavior by nucleus accumbens core and shell. *Nature Neuroscience, 7*, 389–397.

Jensen, J., McIntosh, A. R., Crawley, A. P., Mikulis, D. J., Remington, G., & Kapur, S. (2003). Direct activation of the ventral striatum in anticipation of aversive stimuli. *Neuron, 40*, 1251–1257.

Joel, D., & Weiner, I. (2000). The connections of the dopaminergic system with the striatum in rats and primates: An analysis with respect to the functional and compartmental organization of the striatum. *Neuroscience, 96*, 451–474.

Jueptner, M., Frith, C. D., Brooks, D. J., Frackowiak, R. S. J., & Passingham, R. E. (1997). Anatomy of motor learning. II. Subcortical structures and learning by trial and error. *Journal of Neurophysiology, 77*, 1325–1337.

Jueptner, M., Stephan, K. M., Frith, C. D., Brooks, D. J., Frackowiak, R. S. J., & Passingham, R. E. (1997). Anatomy of motor learning. I. Frontal cortex and attention to action. *Journal of Neurophysiology, 77*, 1313–1324.

Kahneman, D., & Tversky, A. (1979). Prospect theory: An analysis of decision under risk. *Econometrica, 47*, 263–292.

Kawagoe, R., Takikawa, Y., & Hikosaka, O. (1998). Expectation of reward modulates cognitive signals in the basal ganglia. *Nature Neuroscience, 1,* 411–416.

Kelley, A. E., Bakshi, V. P., Haber, S. N., Steninger, T. L., Will, M. J., & Zhang, M. (2002). Opioid modulation of taste hedonics within the ventral striatum. *Physiology and Behavior, 76,* 365–377.

King-Casas, B., Tomlin, D., Anen, C., Camerer, C. F., Quartz, S. R., & Montague, P. R. (2005). Getting to know you: Reputation and trust in a two-person economic exchange. *Science, 308,* 78–83.

Kirsch, P., Schienle, A., Stark, R., Sammer, G., Blecker, C., Walter, B. et al. (2003). Anticipation of reward in a nonaversive differential conditioning paradigm and the brain reward system: An event-related fMRI study. *Neuroimage, 20,* 1086–1095.

Knutson, B., Adams, C. M., Fong, G. W., & Hommer, D. (2001). Anticipation of increasing monetary reward selectively recruits nucleus accumbens. *Journal of Neuroscience, 21,* 1–5.

Knutson, B., & Cooper, J. C. (2005). Functional magnetic resonance imaging of reward prediction. *Current Opinion in Neurology, 18,* 411–417.

Knutson, B., Fong, G. W., Adams, C. M., Varner, J. L., & Hommer, D. (2001). Dissociation of reward anticipation and outcome with event-related fMRI. *Neuroreport, 12,* 3683–3687.

Koepp, M. J., Gunn, R. N., Lawrence, A. D., Cunningham, V. J., Dagher, A., Jones, T. et al. (1998). Evidence for striatal dopamine release during a video game. *Nature, 393,* 266–268.

Lauwereyns, J., Takikawa, Y., Kawagoe, R., Kobayashi, S., Koizumi, M., Coe, B. et al. (2002). Feature-based anticipation of cues that predict reward in monkey caudate nucleus. *Neuron, 33,* 463–473.

Lauwereyns, J., Watanabe, K., Coe, B., & Hikosaka, O. (2002). A neural correlate of response bias in monkey caudate nucleus. *Nature, 418,* 413–417.

Law, J. R., Flanery, M. A., Wirth, S., Yanike, M., Smith, A. C., Frank, L. M. et al. (2005). Functional magnetic resonance imaging activity during the gradual acquisition and expression of paired-associate memory. *Journal of Neuroscience, 25,* 5720–5729.

Levy, R., & Goldman-Rakic, P. S. (2000). Segregation of working memory functions within the dorsolateral prefrontal cortex. *Experimental Brain Research, 133,* 23–32.

Liu, X., Powell, D. K., Wang, H., Gold, B. T., Corbly, C. R., & Joseph, J. E. (2007). Functional dissociation in frontal and striatal areas for processing of positive and negative reward information. *Journal of Neuroscience, 27,* 4587–4597.

Lohrenz, T., McCabe, K., Camerer, C. F., & Montague, P. R. (2007). Neural signature of fictive learning signals in a sequential investment task. *Proceedings of the National Academy of Sciences of the United States of America, 104,* 9493–9498.

Lynd Balta, E., & Haber, S. N. (1994). The organization of midbrain projections to the striatum in the primate: Sensorimotor-related striatum versus ventral striatum. *Neuroscience, 59,* 625–640.

Matsumoto, M., & Hikosaka, O. (2007). Lateral habenula as a source of negative reward signals in dopamine neurons. *Nature, 447,* 1111–1115.

May, J. C., Delgado, M. R., Dahl, R. E., Stenger, V. A., Ryan, N. D., Fiez, J. A. et al. (2004). Event-related functional magnetic resonance imaging of reward-related brain circuitry in children and adolescents. *Biological Psychiatry, 55*, 359–366.

McClure, S. M., Berns, G. S., & Montague, P. R. (2003). Temporal prediction errors in a passive learning task activate human striatum. *Neuron, 38*, 339–346.

McDonald, R. J., & White, N. M. (1993). A triple dissociation of memory systems: Hippocampus, amygdala, and dorsal striatum. *Behavioral Neuroscience, 107*, 3–22.

Meredith, G. E., Pattiselanno, A., Groenewegen, H. J., & Haber, S. N. (1996). The shell and core in monkey and human nucleus accumbens identified with antibodies to calbindin-D_{28K}. *Journal of Comparative Neurology, 365*, 628–639.

Middleton, F. A., & Strick, P. L. (1997). New concepts about the organization of basal ganglia output. *Advances in Neurology, 74*, 57–68.

Nieuwenhuis, S., Heslenfeld, D. J., Alting von Geusau, N. J., Mars, R. B., Holroyd, C. B., & Yeung, N. (2005). Activity in human reward-sensitive brain areas is strongly context dependent. *Neuroimage, 25*, 1302–1309.

Nieuwenhuis, S., Slagter, H. A., Geusau, N. J. A. v., Heslenfeld, D. J., & Holroyd, C. B. (2005). Knowing good from bad: Differential activation of human cortical areas by positive and negative outcomes. *European Journal of Neuroscience, 21*, 3161–3168.

O'Doherty, J., Dayan, P., Schultz, J., Deichmann, R., Friston, K., & Dolan, R. J. (2004). Dissociable roles of ventral and dorsal striatum in instrumental conditioning. *Science, 304*, 452–454.

O'Doherty, J., Kringelbach, M. L., Rolls, E. T., Hornak, J., & Andrews, C. (2001). Abstract reward and punishment representations in the human orbitofrontal cortex. *Nature Neuroscience, 4*, 95–102.

O'Doherty, J., Rolls, E. T., Francis, S., Bowtell, R., & McGlone, F. (2001). Representation of pleasant and aversive taste in the human brain. *Journal of Neurophysiology, 85*, 1315–1321.

O'Doherty, J. P. (2004). Reward representations and reward-related learning in the human brain: Insights from neuroimaging. *Current Opinion in Neurobiology, 14*, 769–776.

O'Doherty, J. P., Dayan, P., Friston, K., Critchley, H., & Dolan, R. J. (2003). Temporal difference models and reward-related learning in the human brain. *Neuron, 28*, 329–337.

Packard, M. G., Hirsh, R., & White, N. M. (1989). Differential effects of fornix and caudate nucleus lesions on two radial maze tasks: Evidence for multiple memory systems. *Journal of Neuroscience, 9*, 1465–1472.

Packard, M. G., & Knowlton, B. J. (2002). Learning and memory functions of the basal ganglia. *Annual Review of Neuroscience, 25*, 563–593.

Parent, A., & Hazrati, L. N. (1995). Functional anatomy of the basal ganglia. I. The cortico-basal ganglia-thalamo-cortical loop. *Brain Research Reviews, 20*, 91–127.

Pasupathy, A., & Miller, E. K. (2005). Different time course of learning-related activity in the prefrontal cortex and striatum. *Nature, 433*, 873–876.

Poldrack, R. A., Clark, J., Pare-Blagoev, E. J., Shohamy, D., Creso Moyano, J.,

Myers, C. et al. (2001). Interactive memory systems in the human brain. *Nature*, *414*, 546–550.

Poldrack, R. A., Prabhakaran, V., Seger, C. A., & Gabrieli, J. D. E. (1999). Striatal activation during acquisition of a cognitive skill. *Neuropsychology*, *13*, 564–574.

Ragozzino, M. E. (2003). Acetylcholine actions in the dorsomedial striatum support the flexible shifting of response patterns. *Neurobiology of Learning and Memory*, *80*, 257–267.

Rilling, J., Gutman, D., Zeh, T., Pagnoni, G., Berns, G., & Kilts, C. (2002). A neural basis for social cooperation. *Neuron*, *35*, 395–405.

Rilling, J. K., Sanfey, A. G., Aronson, J. A., Nystrom, L. E., & Cohen, J. D. (2004a). The neural correlates of theory of mind within interpersonal interactions. *Neuroimage*, *22*, 1694–1703.

Rilling, J. K., Sanfey, A. G., Aronson, J. A., Nystrom, L. E., & Cohen, J. D. (2004b). Opposing BOLD responses to reciprocated and unreciprocated altruism in putative reward pathways. *Neuroreport*, *15*, 2539–2543.

Robbins, T. W., & Everitt, B. J. (1992). Functions of dopamine in the dorsal and ventral striatum. *Seminars in Neuroscience*, *4*, 119–127.

Robbins, T. W., & Everitt, B. J. (1996). Neurobehavioural mechanisms of reward and motivation. *Current Opinion in Neurobiology*, *6*, 228–236.

Rogan, M. T., Leon, K. S., Perez, D. L., & Kandel, E. R. (2005). Distinct neural signatures for safety and danger in the amygdala and striatum of the mouse. *Neuron*, *46*, 309–320.

Rolls, E. T. (2000). The orbitofrontal cortex and reward. *Cerebral Cortex*, *10*, 284–294.

Samejima, K., Ueda, Y., Doya, K., & Kimura, M. (2005). Representation of action-specific reward values in the striatum. *Science*, *310*, 1337–1340.

Schultz, W. (1998). Predictive reward signal of dopamine neurons. *Journal of Neurophysiology*, *80*, 1–27.

Schultz, W. (2004). Neural coding of basic reward terms of animal learning theory, game theory, microeconomics and behavioural ecology. *Current Opinion in Neurobiology*, *14*, 139–147.

Schultz, W., Dayan, P., & Montague, P. R. (1997). A neural substrate of prediction and reward. *Science*, *275*, 1593–1599.

Schultz, W., & Dickinson, A. (2000). Neuronal coding of prediction errors. *Annual Review of Neuroscience*, *23*, 473–500.

Schultz, W., Tremblay, L., & Hollerman, J. R. (1998). Reward prediction in primate basal ganglia and frontal cortex. *Neuropharmacology*, *37*, 421–429.

Seger, C. A., & Cincotta, C. M. (2005). The roles of the caudate nucleus in human classification learning. *Journal of Neuroscience*, *25*, 2941–2951.

Seymour, B., Daw, N., Dayan, P., Singer, T., & Dolan, R. (2007). Differential encoding of losses and gains in the human striatum. *Journal of Neuroscience*, *27*, 4826–4831.

Singer, T., Seymour, B., O'Doherty, J. P., Stephan, K. E., Dolan, R. J., & Frith, C. D. (2006). Empathic neural responses are modulated by the perceived fairness of others. *Nature*, *439*, 466–469.

Skinner, B. F. (1938). *The behavior of organisms: An experimental analysis*. New York: Appleton-Century-Crofts.

Small, D. M., Zatorre, R. J., Dagher, A., Evans, A. C., & Jones-Gotman, M. (2001). Changes in brain activity related to eating chocolate: From pleasure to aversion. *Brain, 124,* 1720–1733.

Tricomi, E., Balleine, B. W., & O'Doherty, J. P. (2009). A specific role for posterior dorsolateral striatum in human habit learning. *European Journal of Neuroscience, 29,* 2225–2232.

Tricomi, E., Delgado, M. R., McCandliss, B. D., McClelland, J. L., & Fiez, J. A. (2006). Performance feedback drives caudate activation in a phonological learning task. *Journal of Cognitive Neuroscience, 18,* 1029–1043.

Tricomi, E. M., Delgado, M. R., & Fiez, J. A. (2004). Modulation of caudate activity by action contingency. *Neuron, 41,* 281–292.

Voorn, P., Vanderschuren, L. J. M. J., Groenewegen, H. J., Robbins, T. W., & Pennartz, C. M. A. (2004). Putting a spin on the dorsal–ventral divide of the striatum. *Trends in Neurosciences, 27,* 468–474.

White, N. M. (1989). Reward or reinforcement: What's the difference? *Neuroscience and Biobehavioral Reviews, 13,* 181–186.

Williams, Z. M., & Eskandar, E. N. (2006). Selective enhancement of associative learning by microstimulation of the anterior caudate. *Nature Neuroscience, 9,* 562–568.

Yin, H. H., & Knowlton, B. J. (2006). The role of the basal ganglia in habit formation. *Nature Reviews Neuroscience, 7,* 464–476.

Yin, H. H., Knowlton, B. J., & Balleine, B. W. (2004). Lesions of dorsolateral striatum preserve outcome expectancy but disrupt habit formation in instrumental learning. *European Journal of Neuroscience, 19,* 181–189.

Yin, H. H., Knowlton, B. J., & Balleine, B. W. (2005). Blockade of NMDA receptors in the dorsomedial striatum abolishes action-outcome learning in instrumental conditioning. *European Journal of Neuroscience, 22,* 505–512.

Yin, H. H., Ostlund, S. B., Knowlton, B. J., & Balleine, B. W. (2005). The role of the dorsomedial striatum in instrumental conditioning. *European Journal of Neuroscience, 22,* 513–523.

Zahm, D. S., & Brog, J. S. (1992). On the significance of subterritories in the "accumbens" part of the rat ventral striatum. *Neuroscience, 50,* 751–767.

Zink, C. F., Pagnoni, G., Martin-Skurski, M. E., Chappelow, J. C., & Berns, G. S. (2004). Human striatal responses to monetary reward depend on saliency. *Neuron, 42,* 509–517.

Zink, C. F., Pagnoni, G., Martin, M. E., Dhamala, M., & Berns, G. S. (2003). Human striatal response to salient nonrewarding stimuli. *Journal of Neuroscience, 23,* 8092–8097.

CHAPTER SEVEN

Neural mechanisms underlying reward and punishment learning in the human brain: Insights from fMRI

John P. O'Doherty

INTRODUCTION

The capacity to predict when and where affectively significant events will occur is central for the survival of most organisms, including humans. Such predictions are often learned through direct experience, and facilitate the optimization of behavioral responses in order to maximize the probability of obtaining rewards and avoiding punishments. In this chapter I will review the current state of knowledge about the neural mechanisms that underpin learning about rewards and punishments through experience. This will be done with particular emphasis on research into this question using functional neuroimaging (particularly fMRI) in humans, but where appropriate I will put this human research into context alongside relevant studies being performed on this issue using animal models.

I will begin this review by differentiating between a number of types of value signal that might conceivably be used by humans and other animals. Next we will describe the putative computational mechanisms by which predictive valuation signals might be learned through experience, and review evidence for the operation of such mechanisms in the brain. Finally, I will outline some of the main outstanding questions currently facing the field of learning and decision making.

MULTIPLE VALUATION SIGNALS

There is evidence to suggest the existence of a number of distinct types of valuation signal in the brain. Perhaps the most fundamental of these signals is the outcome value.

Outcome values

Outcome values report the reward value of stimuli as they are perceived or experienced by the organism. For example the flavor, taste, or odor of a food stimulus as it is being consumed will elicit outcome valuation signals that denote the incentive value of that food stimulus to the organism at that point in time. Such outcome valuations can be modified by the motivational state of the organism: When hungry the outcome value of the food flavor may be high, whereas if the animal is satiated, the outcome value of the food stimulus will be decreased. Outcome valuation signals have been found in the orbitofrontal cortex (OFC) in single-unit recording studies of nonhuman primates, as well as in human neuroimaging studies (O'Doherty, 2004; Rolls, 2000). In humans, regions of the OFC, particularly its medial and central aspects, have been found to correlate positively with the experienced reward value of a diverse range of stimuli in different sensory modalities including tastes, odors, flavors, and somatosensory, auditory, and visual stimuli (Blood et al., 1999; Kringelbach, O'Doherty, Rolls, & Andrews, 2003; O'Doherty et al., 2000; O'Doherty, Winston, Critchley, Perrett, Burt, & Dolan, 2003; Rolls, O'Doherty, Kringelbach, Francis, Bowtell, & McGlone, 2003; Rolls, Kringelbach, & de Araujo, 2003). This region has also been shown to encode the value of more abstract reinforcers not tied to a specific sensory modality such as winning money (O'Doherty, Kringelbach, Rolls, Hornak, & Andrews, 2001). Regions of the OFC have also been found to respond following the receipt of aversive as well as rewarding outcomes (Gottfried, Deichmann, Winston, & Dolan, 2002; O'Doherty, Rolls, Francis, Bowtell, & McGlone, 2001; Rolls, Kringelbach et al., 2003), with activity in some parts of the lateral OFC correlating positively with increasing magnitudes of monetary loss (O'Doherty, Kringelbach et al., 2001), showing increasing activity the more unattractive a visual stimulus such as a face is reported to be (O'Doherty, Winston et al., 2003; Cloutier, Heatherton, Whalen, & Kelley, 2008), or showing increasing activity during the consumption of food stimuli as subjects become satiated and the pleasantness of those stimuli decreases (Small, Zatorre, Dagher, Evans, & Jones-Gotman, 2001).

Pavlovian predictive values

Another form of value signal, Pavlovian values emerge from the detection of statistical regularities in the environment, and give an animal advance notice of when and where an outcome is likely to occur. These signals are stimulus-dependent, and are elicited by those stimuli whose presentation is correlated with the subsequent delivery of a rewarding or punishing outcome. Such predictions can come to be learned through experience, through repeated observation of the contingent pairing of that stimulus with a given outcome, and are hence formed through the acquisition of learned stimulus–outcome associations. Following learning, such Pavlovian stimuli elicit a variety of preparatory and consumatory behaviors related to the outcome (and its value to the organism). So for example, Pavlovian stimuli associated with the subsequent presentation of food outcomes might elicit approach and anticipatory licking, while stimuli associated with the subsequent delivery of an aversive outcome might elicit withdrawal and avoidance behaviors.

Studies of the neural basis of stimulus-based Pavlovian reward-prediction signals have focused on three brain regions in particular: (1) the amygdala in the medial temporal lobes; (2) the OFC on the ventral surface of the frontal lobes; and (3) the ventral striatum in the basal ganglia. Single-unit recording studies in both rodents and nonhuman primates have implicated neurons in these areas in encoding stimulus–reward associations (Cromwell & Schultz, 2003; Day, Wheeler, Roitman, & Carelli, 2006; Paton, Belova, Morrison, & Salzman, 2006; Schoenbaum, Chiba, & Gallagher, 1998; Shidara, Aigner, & Richmond, 1998; Tremblay & Schultz, 1999). Consistent with these findings in both rodents and nonhuman primates, functional neuroimaging studies in humans have also revealed activations in some of these areas during both appetitive and aversive Pavlovian conditioning in response to conditioned stimulus (CS) presentation. For example, O'Doherty, Deichmann, Critchley, and Dolan (2002) found activity in the amygdala, OFC, and striatum in response to cues signaling the subsequent delivery of a sweet taste reward. Furthermore, Gottfried, O'Doherty, and Dolan (2002) reported activity in both the amygdala and OFC following presentation of visual stimuli predictive of the subsequent delivery of both a pleasant and an unpleasant odor.

Gottfried, O'Doherty, and Dolan (2003) aimed to investigate the nature of such predictive representations in order to establish whether such responses are related to the sensory properties of the unconditioned stimulus irrespective of its underlying reward value, or whether such responses are directly related to the reward value of the associated unconditioned stimulus. To address this, Gottfried et al. trained subjects to associate visual stimuli with one of two food odors, vanilla and peanut butter, while being scanned with fMRI. Subjects were then subsequently removed from the scanner and fed to satiety on a food corresponding to one of the food odors in order to devalue that odor, similar to the devaluation procedures used in other animals. For example, to decrease the value of the vanilla odor subjects were fed to satiety on vanilla ice cream. Due to the selectivity of such a devaluation procedure, the value of the odor not eaten shows no such decrease, a phenomenon known as sensory-specific satiety (Rolls, Rolls, Rowe, & Sweeney, 1981). Following the devaluation procedure subjects were then placed back in the scanner and presented with the conditioned stimuli in a further conditioning session. Neural responses to presentation of the CS paired with the devalued odor were found to decrease in the OFC, amygdala, and ventral striatum from before to after the satiation procedure, whereas no such decrease was evident for the CS paired with the nondevalued odor. These results provide evidence that predictive representations related to presentation of a particular conditioned stimulus in the amygdala, OFC, and ventral striatum encode the value of the associated unconditioned stimulus (US) and not merely its sensory properties. When taken together, the above findings implicate a network of brain regions involving the amygdala, ventral striatum, and OFC in the expression of stimulus-based reward predictions.

Action-based value predictions

The predictive Pavlovian value signals described above are purely passive associations (i.e., they emerge from the observation of stimulus–outcome associations in the environment without any action on behalf of the animal on that environment in order to increase or decrease the probability of those outcomes). However, in many cases, it is useful for an animal to be able to learn to perform particular behavioral responses in order to increase or decrease the probability of obtaining those outcomes, a form of learning termed instrumental conditioning in behavioral psychology (Thorndike, 1898). This raises the question as to where in the brain predictive value signals tied to performance of instrumental actions are located.

A number of fMRI studies in humans have found evidence for expected reward signals during action selection in a specific brain region, the ventromedial prefrontal cortex (vmPFC). Kim, Shimojo, and O'Doherty (2006) used a computational reinforcement learning model (which will be explained later in the chapter) to generate trial-by-trial predictions of expected reward as subjects made decisions between which of two possible actions to choose in order to obtain monetary reward, as well as in a different condition, to avoid losing money. Different actions were associated with distinct probabilities of either winning or losing money, such that in the reward condition one action was associated with a 60% probability of winning money, and the other action with only a 30% probability of winning. To maximize their cumulative reward, subjects should learn to choose the action associated with the higher reward probability. In the avoidance condition, subjects were presented with a choice between the same probabilities, except in this context 60% of the time after choosing one action they avoided losing money, whereas this only occurred 30% of the time after choosing the alternative action. To minimize their losses, subjects should learn to choose the action associated with the 60% probability of loss avoidance. Model-generated expected value signals for the action chosen were found to be correlated on a trial-by-trial basis with BOLD responses in the bilateral OFC and adjacent medial prefrontal cortex in both the reward and avoidance conditions, such that activity in these areas increased under situations where greater reward was expected for the action chosen (according to the learning algorithm), and decreased under conditions where less reward was expected for a given action (Figure 7.1). Similar results were obtained by Daw, O'Doherty, Dayan, Seymour, and Dolan (2006), who used a four-armed bandit task in which "points" (that would later be converted into money) were paid out on each bandit. Again, activity in the vmPFC correlated with the trial-by-trial estimate of expected reward attributable to the action (in this case bandit) chosen on that trial.

However, although the above studies provide evidence of expected reward signals during reward-based action-selection in the vmPFC, they do not delineate the underlying associations on which such signals depend. A modern perspective on instrumental conditioning is that this form of learning can be fractionated into two distinct components: A goal-directed component grounded in action–outcome associations, and a habitual component depending on stimulus–response associations. To address whether the human vmPFC is involved in encoding response–outcome or stimulus–response associations, Valentin, Dickinson, and O'Doherty (2007) used an experimental design inspired by the animal-learning literature. One of the key manipulations used in the animal literature to discriminate whether action-selection is under goal-directed or habitual control is to selectively devalue the outcome associated with that action, by for example feeding the animal to satiety on that outcome, and then testing the degree to which the animal persists in choosing that action following the devaluation process (Balleine & Dickinson, 1998). If action selection is goal-directed (and therefore dependent on action–outcome associations), then the animal should immediately stop responding with the action associated with the devalued outcome. If, on the other hand, behavioral control is habitual, then the animal will persist in responding.

In the Valentin et al. study, subjects were scanned while they learned to

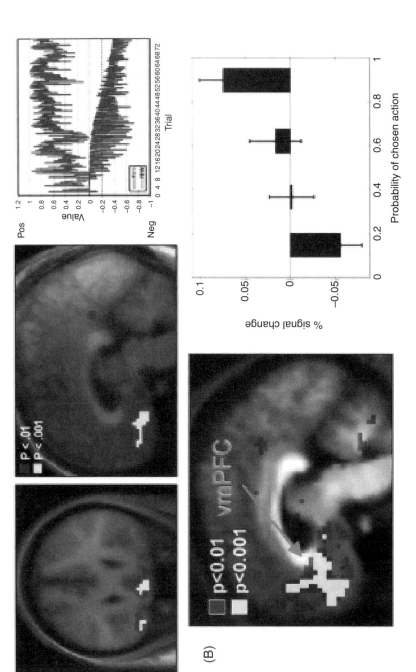

Figure 7.1 Reward prediction signals in the vmPFC during reward-based action-selection in humans. (a) Regions of the vmPFC (medial and central orbitofrontal cortex extending into medial prefrontal cortex) correlating with expected value signals generated by a variant of a reinforcement learning model during an fMRI study of instrumental choice of reward and avoidance (left and middle panels). The model-predicted expected value signals are shown for one subject in the right panel for both the reward (top line) and avoidance (bottom line) conditions. Data from Kim et al. (2006). (b) Similar regions of the vmPFC correlating with model-predicted expected value signals during performance of a four-armed bandit task with nonstationary reward distributions (left panel). BOLD signal changes in this region are shown plotted against model predictions (right panel), revealing an approximately linear relationship between expected value and BOLD signal changes in this region. Data from Daw et al. (2006). See color plate.

choose instrumental actions associated with the subsequent delivery of different food rewards. Following training, one of these foods was devalued by feeding the subject to satiety on that food (similar to the approach used in Gottfried et al., 2003). The subjects were then scanned again, while being re-exposed to the instrumental choice procedure (in extinction). By testing for regions of the brain showing a change in activity during selection of the devalued action compared with that elicited during selection of the valued action from pre to post satiety, it was possible to identify regions that track the current incentive value of the outcome, thereby identifying candidate areas responsible for goal-directed instrumental learning. The regions found to show such a response profile included a part of the vmPFC as well as an additional region of the central OFC (Figure 7.2). These findings appear to implicate this region in tracking the current incentive value of the outcome, ruling out a role for this area in habitual stimulus–response learning.

The aforementioned results would therefore appear to implicate the vmPFC in encoding action–outcome and not stimulus–response associations. However, another possibility that cannot be ruled out on the basis of the Valentin et al. study alone is that the vmPFC may instead contain a representation of the discriminative stimulus (in this case the fractals) used to signal the different available actions, and that the learned associations in this region may be formed between these stimuli and the outcomes obtained. In other words, the design of the Valentin et al. study does not allow us to rule out a possible contribution of the vmPFC to purely Pavlovian stimulus valuation.

Direct evidence of a role for the vmPFC in encoding action-related value signals has come from an fMRI study by Glascher, Hampton, and O'Doherty (2009). In this study, the possible contribution of discriminative stimuli in driving expected-reward signals in the vmPFC was probed using a specific design in which in one "action-based" condition subjects had to choose between performing one of two different physical motor responses (rolling a tracker-ball versus pressing a button) in the absence of explicit discriminative stimuli signaling those actions. Subjects were given monetary rewards on a probabilistic basis according to their choice of the different physical actions, and the rewards available on the different actions changed over time. Using an extension of a simple Rescorla-Wagner (RW) model, trial-by-trial model-predictive expected reward signals were generated for each action choice made by the subjects. Similar to the results found in studies where both discriminative stimulus information and action-selection components are present, activity in the vmPFC was found to track the expected reward corresponding to the chosen action (Figure 7.3). These results suggest that activity in the vmPFC does not necessarily depend on the presence of discriminative stimuli,

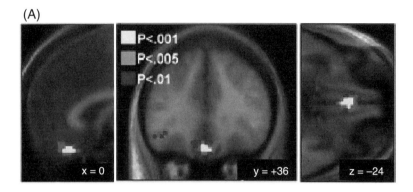

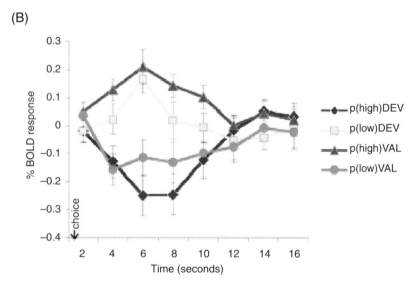

Figure 7.2   Regions of the vmPFC and OFC showing response properties consistent with action-outcome learning. Neural activity during action selection for reward showing a change in response properties as a function of the value of the outcome with each action. Choice of an action leading to a high probability of obtaining an outcome that had been devalued (p(high)DEV) led to a decrease in activity in these areas, whereas choice of an action leading to a high probability of obtaining an outcome that was still valued led to an increase in activity in the same areas. Devaluation was accomplished by means of feeding the subject to satiety on that outcome prior to the test period. (a) A region of the medial OFC showing a significant modulation in its activity during instrumental action selection as a function of the value of the associated outcome. (b) Time-course plots derived from the peak voxel (from each individual subject) in the mOFC during trials in which subjects chose each one of the four different actions (choice of the high vs. low probability action in either the Valued or Devalued conditions). Data from Valentin et al. (2007). See color plate.

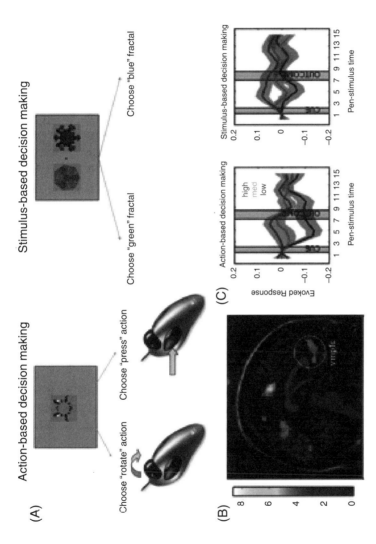

Figure 7.3 Expected reward representations in the vmPFC during action-based and stimulus-based decision making. (a) Illustration of action-based decision-making task in which subjects must choose between one of two different physical actions which yield monetary rewards with differing probabilities, and a stimulus-based decision-making task in which subjects must choose between one of two different fractal stimuli randomly assigned to either the left or right of the screen, which yield rewards with differing probabilities. (b) A region of the vmPFC correlating with expected reward during both action- and stimulus-based decision making. (c) Time courses from the vmPFC during the action and stimulus-based decision-making tasks plotted as a function of model-predicted expected reward from low (blue) to high (red). See color plate.

indicating that this region contributes to encoding of action-related value signals. In another "stimulus-based" condition, subjects performed action-selection where decision options are denoted by the presence of specific discriminative stimuli; however, the two physical actions denoting the different choice options were randomly assigned (depending on random spatial position of the two discriminative stimuli). In common with the action-based reversal task, expected reward signals were also observed in the vmPFC while subjects performed the stimulus-based task, consistent with a number of previous reports (Daw et al., 2006; Hampton, Bossaerts, & O'Doherty, 2006; Kim et al., 2006; Valentin et al., 2007). Furthermore, in a conjunction analysis to test for regions commonly activated in both the action-based and stimulus-based choice conditions, robust activity was found in the vmPFC.

Overall, these findings could be taken to indicate that the vmPFC contributes to both stimulus-based and action-based processes. An alternative possibility is that activity in the vmPFC during the stimulus-based condition (in common with that in the action-based condition) is being driven by goal-directed action–outcome associations. Although in the stimulus-based task the particular physical motor response required to implement a specific decision varied on a trial-by-trial basis (depending on where the stimuli are presented), it is possible for associations to be learned between a combination of visual stimuli locations, responses, and outcomes. Thus, the common involvement of the vmPFC in both the action- and stimulus-based reversal learning could be attributable to the possibility that this region is generally involved in encoding values of chosen actions but that those action–outcome relationships are encoded in a more abstract and flexible manner than concretely mapping specific physical motor responses to outcomes. The more flexible encoding of "actions" that this framework would entail may have parallels with computational theories of goal-directed learning in which action selection is proposed to occur via a flexible forward model system (discussed in more detail later on in the chapter), which explicitly encodes the states of the world, the transition probabilities between those states, and the outcomes obtained in those states (Daw, Niv, & Dayan, 2005). Overall therefore, these findings suggest that vmPFC may play a role in encoding the value of chosen actions irrespective of whether those actions denote physical motor responses or more abstract decision options. Next we consider how predictive reward signals are acquired by the brain, with reference to theoretical models of learning.

THEORETICAL MODELS OF PREDICTION LEARNING

Modern theories of reward learning suggest that such learning proceeds by means of a signal called a prediction error, which encodes the difference between the reward that is predicted and the actual reward that is delivered. This notion was originally instantiated in the Rescorla-Wagner (RW) model of classical conditioning (Rescorla & Wagner, 1972). In the RW model, the process by which a CS comes to produce a conditioned response (CR), is represented by two variables: v_t, which is the strength of the conditioned response elicited on trial t, or more abstractly the value of the CS, and u, which is the mean value of the US. For conditioning to occur, through repeated contingent presentations of the CS and US, the variable v_t (which may be initially zero at $t = 1$) should, as trials progress, converge toward the value of u. On any given trial if the reward is presented we can set $u_t = 1$, and if the reward is not presented $u_t = 0$.

At the core of the RW model is the aforementioned prediction error signal δ_t, which represents the difference between the current value of u_t and v_t ($\delta_t = u_t - v_t$) on each conditioning trial. Under these circumstances δ_t will be positive because $v_t < u_t$. The value of v_t is then updated in proportion to δ_t. Assuming that the reward is always delivered when the CS is presented, then over the course of learning, v_t eventually converges to u_t, δ_t will tend to zero, and once this happens learning is complete. In a stochastic learning situation, the reward is delivered on a probabilistic basis and v_t will tend to approximate the mean expected value u. For example, if the reward is delivered on 50% of occasions after the CS is presented, v_t will tend to oscillate around the mean expected value u (i.e., in this case 0.5). In those situations, δ_t can take on a very different form depending on whether the reward is delivered ($u_t = 1$) or omitted ($u_t = 0$). On trials where the reward is delivered, there will be positive prediction error as discussed above, whereas on trials where the reward is omitted, but yet v_t is positive (e.g., $v_t = 0.5$), the prediction error will take a negative form (i.e., a decrease from zero: $\delta_t = 0-0.5 = -0.5$) because less reward was delivered on that trial than expected on average. This notion that prediction error signals can take on both positive and negative response characteristics is the central feature of this form of learning model, and as we shall see is at the core of modern views on how such learning might be implemented in the brain.

An important extension of the RW model is the so-called temporal difference (TD) learning model (Sutton, 1988). This model overcomes some of the initial limitations of the RW model such as an inability to learn sequential stimulus-based predictions (e.g., when one stimulus predicts another stimulus, which in turn predicts reward), and a lack of sensitivity to the timing between stimulus presentation and reward delivery, which is known to be a critical factor in modulating the efficacy of conditioning (Dayan & Abbott, 2001). The key difference between the TD model and the earlier RW model is that, whereas the RW model is trial-based and only concerned with estimating predicted reward pertaining to a particular stimulus across trials, the TD model is also concerned with estimating predicted-reward at discrete time points i within a trial. Each time point within a trial can be thought of as a separate event, during which a stimulus is either present or not, or a reward is delivered or not. An individual time point can therefore take on a predictive value V_i indicative of the sum of the subsequent rewards that are predicted to occur from the next time point $i + 1$ until the end of the trial. The prediction error updates these predictions by computing the difference between successive predictions of reward within a trial $\delta_i = V_{i+1} - V_i + r(i)$, including the reward actually delivered at that time point. As a consequence, the TD prediction error signal has a much richer temporal profile than does its RW cousin. In particular, the TD error would first generate a strong positive signal at the time of presentation of the US before learning is established, but this positive prediction error signal would then shift back in time within a trial over the course of learning. By the time learning is complete the TD error would be positive only at the time of presentation of the earliest predictive cue stimulus. Furthermore, on any occasion in the trial where greater reward is delivered than expected (or if the reward is delivered sooner or later than expected), then a positive prediction error would be elicited. Similarly, if less reward is delivered than expected at the specific time that it has previously been found to occur, then a negative prediction error will be elicited (Figure 7.4a).

Prediction error signals in the brain

The first empirical evidence for reward-prediction error signals in the brain emerged from the work of Wolfram Schultz and colleagues who observed such signals by recording from the phasic activity of dopamine neurons in awake, behaving, nonhuman primates undergoing simple instrumental or classical conditioning tasks (Mirenowicz & Schultz, 1994; Schultz, 1998). The response profile of these neurons does not correspond to a simple RW model but rather has strong similarities to the response profile predicted by temporal difference learning, showing each of the temporal response properties within a trial described above. Just like the TD error signal, these neurons increase their firing from baseline when a reward is presented unexpectedly, but they decrease their firing from baseline when a reward is unexpectedly omitted. In addition, they respond initially at the time of the US before learning is established but shift back in time within a trial to respond instead at the time of presentation of the cue once learning has taken place.

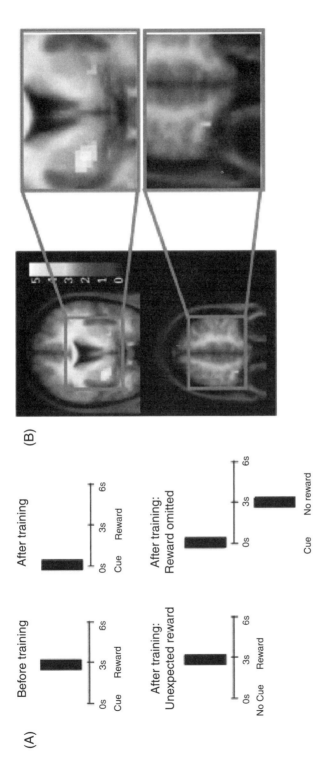

Figure 7.4 Temporal difference prediction error signals during Pavlovian reward conditioning in humans. (a) Properties of the temporal difference prediction error signal. This signal responds positively at the time of reward presentation before training, shifts to responding at the time of presentation of the predictive cue after training, and shows a decrease from baseline (negative signal) if an expected reward is omitted. (b) Results from an fMRI study testing for brain regions correlating with a temporal difference prediction error signal during classical conditioning in humans. Significant correlations with the TD prediction error signal were found in the ventral striatum bilaterally (top panel) and in the OFC (bottom panel). See color plate.

Further evidence in support of this hypothesis has been garnered from recent studies using fast cyclical voltammetry assays of dopamine release in the ventral striatum during Pavlovian reward conditioning, in which timing of dopamine release in the ventral striatum was also found to exhibit a shifting profile, occurring initially at the time of reward presentation but gradually shifting back to occur at the time of presentation of the reward-predicting cue (Day & Carelli, 2007). To test for evidence of a temporal difference prediction error signal in the human brain, O'Doherty, Dayan, Friston, Critchley, and Dolan (2003) scanned human subjects while they underwent a classical conditioning paradigm in which associations were learned between arbitrary visual fractal stimuli and a pleasant sweet taste reward (glucose). One cue was followed most of the time by the taste reward, whereas another cue was followed most of the time by no reward. However, in addition, subjects were exposed to low frequency "error" trials in which the cue associated with reward was presented but the reward was omitted, and the cue associated with no reward was presented but a reward was unexpectedly delivered. The specific trial history that each subject experienced was next fed into a temporal difference model to generate a time series that specified the model-predicted prediction error signal during the trial. This time series was then convolved with a canonical hemodynamic response function and regressed against the fMRI data for each individual subject, to identify brain regions correlating with the model-predicted time series. This analysis revealed significant correlations with the model-based predictions in a number of brain regions, most notably the ventral striatum (ventral putamen bilaterally) and OFC (Figure 7.4b), both prominent target regions of dopamine neurons. These results suggest that prediction error signals are present in the human brain during reward learning, and that these signals conform to a response profile consistent with a specific computational model: Temporal difference learning. Another study by McClure and colleagues also revealed activity in the ventral striatum consistent with a reward-prediction error signal using an event-related trial-based analysis (McClure, Berns, & Montague, 2003).

The next obvious question is whether such signals can be found to underlie learning about punishing as well as rewarding events. Evidence of a role for dopamine neurons in responding during aversive learning is mixed. Single-unit studies have generally failed to observe strong dopaminergic activity in response to aversive events (Schultz, 1998), and indeed it has been found that dopamine neurons may in fact inhibit responding during aversive stimulation such as tail pinch in rats (Ungless, Magill, & Bolam, 2004). On the other hand, a number of studies measuring dopamine release in the striatum in rats have found evidence for increased dopamine levels during aversive as well as appetitive conditioning (Pezze & Feldon, 2004). However, as termination of an aversive stimulus can in itself be rewarding, the implications of these studies for understanding the role of dopamine in aversive learning are still debated. Irrespective of whether dopamine will turn out to play a role in aversive learning or not, existing evidence appears to rule out a role for phasic dopamine in encoding prediction errors for aversive events in the same way as appears to be the case during learning with rewards. This then raises the question of whether prediction error signals for aversive learning are present anywhere else in the brain, for example in the phasic activity of neurons carrying another neuromodulatory neurotransmitter. Although the suggestion that another neurotransmitter system such as serotonin may be involved in mediating aversive learning is intuitively and computationally appealing (Daw, Kakade, & Dayan, 2002), to date no direct evidence has emerged to support such a hypothesis.

In spite of this, neuroimaging studies have revealed strong evidence for the presence of prediction error signals in the human brain during aversive as well as appetitive learning. Seymour et al. (2004) scanned human subjects while they underwent a second-order conditioning paradigm in which the sequential presentation of two visual cues led to the subject receiving a mild but painful electric stimulation to the foot, whereas the sequential presentation of two other cues led to the subject obtaining a tickling but nonpainful electrical stimulation. On most trials the first cue signaling shock was followed by the second cue signaling shock and similarly for the stimuli signaling nonshock. However, on some rare trials in which the first cue presented signaled shock, the second cue to be presented unexpectedly signaled nonshock, thereby inducing a negative prediction error. Similarly on occasional trials in which the first cue presented signaled nonshock, the second cue presented signaled shock, inducing a positive prediction error. A full temporal difference prediction error signal was then generated for each subject based on the trial-by-trial experience of that subject and correlated against the fMRI data. Significant correlation with TD prediction errors was found in the ventral striatum bilaterally, in a region very close to that found to respond during prediction errors for reward. These results demonstrate that prediction signals are also present in the brain during aversive conditioning, a finding that has been replicated a number of times subsequently (e.g., Seymour et al., 2005). Given that such aversive signals in the striatum are unlikely to depend on the afferent input of dopamine neurons, these findings also show that BOLD activity in the ventral striatum should not be considered to be a pure reflection of the afferent input of dopamine neurons, an interpretation implicitly assumed in some of the reward imaging literature. Rather, activity in the striatum is likely to also reflect the influence of a number of different neuromodulatory systems in addition to dopamine, input from other cortical and sub-cortical areas, as well as intrinsic computations within this region.

The studies discussed above demonstrate that prediction error signals are present during learning to predict both appetitive and aversive events, a finding consistent with the tenets of a prediction error-based account of associative learning. However, merely demonstrating the presence of such signals in the striatum during learning does not establish whether such signals are causally related to learning or merely an epi-phenomenon. The first study aiming to uncover a causal link was that of Pessiglione, Seymour, Flandin, Dolan, and Frith (2006), who manipulated systemic dopamine levels by delivering a dopamine agonist and antagonist while subjects were being scanned with fMRI during performance of a reward-learning task. Prediction error signals in the striatum were boosted following administration of the dopaminergic agonist, and diminished following administration of the dopaminergic antagonist. Moreover, behavioral performance followed the changes in striatal activity, being increased following administration of the dopamine agonist and decreased following administration of the antagonist. These findings therefore support a causal link between prediction error activity in the striatum and the degree of behavioral learning for reward.

LEARNING OF ACTION-BASED PREDICTIONS

We now consider computational theories about how instrumental associations, be they goal-directed or habitual, might be acquired. Previously, we reviewed the RW model and its real-time extensions and showed how these models appear to provide a good characterization of neural signals underlying learning of stimulus–outcome associations. For instrumental conditioning, a related class of models can be invoked, collectively known as reinforcement learning (RL) models. The core feature of RL models is that in order to choose optimally between different actions, an agent needs to maintain internal representations of the expected reward available on each action, and then subsequently choose the action with the highest expected value. Also central to these algorithms is the notion of a prediction error signal that is used to learn and update expected values for each action through experience, just as in the RW learning model for Pavlovian conditioning described earlier.

In one such model—the actor/critic model—action selection is conceived as involving two distinct components: A critic, which learns to predict future reward associated with particular states in the environment, and an actor, which chooses specific actions in order to move the agent from state to state according to a learned policy (Barto, 1992, 1995). The critic encodes the value of particular states in the world and as such has the characteristics of a Pavlovian reward-prediction signal described above. The actor stores a set of probabilities for each action in each state of the world, and chooses actions according to those probabilities. The goal of the model is to modify the policy stored in the actor such that over time, those actions associated with the highest predicted reward are selected more often. This is accomplished by means of the aforementioned prediction error signal that computes the difference in predicted reward as the agent moves from state to state. This signal is then used to update value predictions stored in the critic for each state, but also to update action probabilities stored in the actor such that if the agent moves to a state associated with greater reward (and thus generates a positive prediction error), then the probability of choosing that action in the future is increased. Conversely, if the agent moves to a state associated with less reward, this generates a negative prediction error and the probability of choosing that action again is decreased.

Some computational neuroscientists have drawn analogies between the anatomy and connections of the basal ganglia, and possible neural architectures for implementing reinforcement learning models including the actor/critic. Montague, Dayan, and Sejnowski (1996) proposed that the ventral and dorsal striatum implemented the critic and actor respectively, on the grounds of extant knowledge of the putative functions of these structures at the time, derived primarily from animal lesion studies. In order to test these hypotheses, O'Doherty, Dayan, Schultz, Deichmann, Friston, and Dolan (2004) scanned hungry human subjects with fMRI while they performed a simple instrumental conditioning task in which they were required to choose one of two actions leading to juice reward with either a high or low probability (Figure 7.5a). Neural responses corresponding to the generation of prediction error signals during performance of the instrumental task were compared with those elicited during a control Pavlovian task in which subjects experienced the same stimulus–reward contingencies but did not actively choose which action to select. This comparison was designed to isolate the actor, which was hypothesized to be engaged only in the instrumental task, from the critic, which was hypothesized to be engaged in both the instrumental and Pavlovian control tasks. Consistent with the proposal of a dorsal versus ventral actor/critic architecture, activity in dorsal striatum was found to be specifically correlated with prediction error signals when subjects were actively performing instrumental responses in order to obtain reward. By contrast, ventral striatum was found to be active in both the instrumental and Pavlovian tasks (Figure 7.5b). However, while the above findings establish the presence of prediction error activity in the dorsal striatum during instrumental conditioning, they do not establish the causal role of such signals in learning these associations.

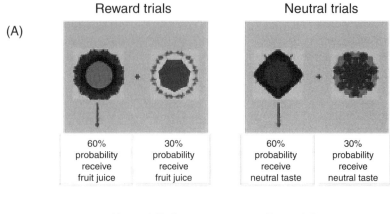

Reward trials | Neutral trials

(A)

60% probability receive fruit juice | 30% probability receive fruit juice | 60% probability receive neutral taste | 30% probability receive neutral taste

(B)

Ventral Striatum | Dorsal Striatum

Instrumental task

Pavlovian task

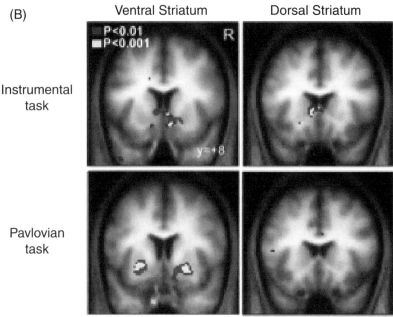

Figure 7.5 Prediction error signals underlying action selection for reward. (a) Schematic of instrumental choice task used by O'Doherty et al. (2004). On each trial of the reward condition the subject chooses between two possible actions, one associated with a high probability of obtaining juice reward (60%), the other a low probability (30%). In a neutral condition, subjects also choose between actions with similar probabilities, but in this case they receive an affectively neutral outcome (tasteless solution). Prediction error responses during the reward condition of the instrumental choice task were compared with prediction error signals during a yoked Pavlovian control task. (b) Significant correlations with the reward prediction error signal generated by an actor/critic model were found in the ventral striatum (ventral putamen extending into nucleus accumbens proper) in both the Pavlovian and instrumental tasks, suggesting that this region is involved in stimulus–outcome learning. In contrast, a region of the dorsal striatum (anteromedial caudate nucleus) was found to be correlated with prediction error signals only during the instrumental task, suggesting that this area is involved in stimulus–response or stimulus–response–outcome learning. Data from O'Doherty et al. (2004). See color plate.

A study that at least partly addresses this issue was conducted by Schonberg, Daw, Joel, and O'Doherty (2007). This study made use of an instrumental reward conditioning task that has the interesting property that there is a high degree of variance across the population in the degree to which human subjects can successfully learn the task. In this task approximately 50% fail to converge in their choices toward the two options (out of the four available options) that yield the greatest probability of reward over 150 trials, whereas the other 50% tend to converge quite rapidly on the optimal choices. Whatever the underlying reasons for this variance in performance, this property of the task provides a useful means of testing the degree to which reward-prediction error signals in the dorsal striatum can distinguish between those subjects who successfully learn the instrumental associations and those who do not. To address this, both "learner" and "nonlearner" groups were scanned while performing this task. Consistent with the possibility that reward-prediction errors in the dorsal striatum are causally related to acquisition of instrumental reward associations, activity in the dorsal striatum was significantly better correlated with reward-prediction error signals in learners than in nonlearners. On the other hand, consistent with the actor/critic proposal, while reward-prediction error activity in ventral striatum was also weaker in the nonlearners, this ventral striatum prediction error activity did not differ significantly between groups. These results suggest a dorsal/ventral distinction within the striatum, whereby the ventral striatum is more concerned with Pavlovian or stimulus–outcome learning, while the dorsal striatum is more engaged during learning of stimulus–response or stimulus–response–outcome associations.

An obvious question at this juncture is how does a model such as the actor/critic model map onto the distinction between goal-directed and habitual reward-predictions described earlier? One possibility proposed by Daw et al. (2005) is that a reinforcement learning model such as the actor/critic is concerned purely with learning of habitual S-R value signals (see also Balleine, Daw, & O'Doherty, 2008). According to this interpretation, action-value signals learned by an actor/critic would not be immediately updated following a change in the value of the reward outcome (such as by devaluation). Instead such an update would occur only after the model re-experiences the reward in its now devalued state and generates prediction errors that would incrementally modulate action-values. Alternatively, action-values learned by the actor/critic could reflect the strength of an association not only between stimuli and responses, but also between actions and outcomes. In that event, such a representation would show devaluation effects, and hence meet the criteria of being goal-directed. There is currently insufficient empirical data to distinguish between these possibilities. One way potentially to address this is to determine whether the reward-prediction error signal generated by dopamine neurons (which should be at the core of any reinforcement learning-like process) is sensitive to devaluation effects. If not, this would support the idea that RL models and the associated error signal are involved in learning habitual stimulus–response associations, otherwise the idea that dopamine neurons may contribute to the goal-directed component learning will have to be entertained.

Daw et al. (2005) also proposed an alternative to the actor/critic model to account for the goal-directed component of instrumental learning: A forward model. In the "forward model" values for different actions are worked out on-line by taking into account knowledge about the rewards available in each state and the transition probabilities between each state. These state representations are then used to iteratively compute the value of each available option, analogous to how a chess player works out which chess move to make next by explicitly thinking through the consequences of all possible moves. One property of this model is that value representations should be modulated not only incrementally, but also instantaneously following detection of a change in the underlying state-space or structure of the decision problem.

Evidence that predictive reward representations in the brain are sensitive to changes in state has emerged from a study by Hampton et al. (2006). In this study subjects were asked to participate in a decision problem called probabilistic reversal learning in which two different actions yield reward with distinct probabilities. The key feature of the task is that the rewards available on the two actions are anti-correlated; that is, when one action has a high value, the other has a low value in terms of the amount of rewards that are obtained probabilistically on the two actions, and that after an unpredictable series of trials the reward probabilities on the two actions reverse. Hampton et al. compared two computational models in terms of how well they could account for human choice behavior on the task and for the pattern of neural activity in the vmPFC during task performance. One of these algorithms incorporated the rules or structure of the decision problem as would be expected for a state-based inference mechanism, such that following a reversal the value of the two actions was instantly updated to reflect knowledge of the abstract structure. The other model was a simple reinforcement learning algorithm that did not incorporate the structure and thus would only learn to slowly and incrementally update values following successive reinforcements. Consistent with a role for the vmPFC in state-based inference, predicted reward signals in this region were found to reflect the structure of the decision problem, such that activity was updated instantly following a reversal, rather than being updated incrementally as might be expected for a simple nonstate-based reinforcement learning mechanism.

These findings are compatible with the "forward-model" proposal of Daw et al. (2005), according to which reward-predictions in the vmPFC would be computed exclusively by a forward-model (without any contribution from the reward-prediction error). However, these findings could also be consistent with the proposal that reward representations in the vmPFC are updated by two distinct but not necessarily incompatible mechanisms: Incrementally via a reward-prediction error signal, and instantaneously following detection of a change in the state of the decision problem. This latter proposal would be consistent with a hybrid model in which a state-based inference mechanism is combined with incremental reinforcement learning. It should now be clear from our brief review of computational models for instrumental conditioning that empirical evidence in support of such models is still preliminary. Perhaps the only substantive conclusion that can be reached on the basis of the current evidence is that prediction error signals certainly seem to play a role in the acquisition of instrumental associations, particularly through input into the dorsal striatum, and that changes in state representations can result in the direct modulation of value signals in the vmPFC. Further studies both at the level of human imaging and single-unit neurophysiology in other animals will be needed to establish the extent to which such signals contribute to learning of goal-directed value signals, habitual values, or both.

CONCLUSIONS

In this chapter I have reviewed evidence for the existence for multiple types of value signal in the human brain and for a number of different possible learning mechanisms that might underlie their acquisition. Outcome values report the value of an incoming stimulus as it is experienced by the organism; these signals are found predominantly in the OFC for a range of stimuli in different sensory modalities as well as for more abstract reinforcers. Pavlovian or stimulus-bound reward predictions appear to be present in three principal brain regions: (1) the OFC (particularly central and lateral areas); (2) the amygdala; and (3) the ventral striatum. Such signals appear to be learned via a stimulus-based prediction error signal projecting to the ventral striatum and elsewhere. In addition, reward predictions based on instrumental action–outcome associations appear to be encoded in the vmPFC which incorporate the medial OFC and adjacent medial prefrontal cortex, as well as possibly in the anterior medial striatum. Finally, there is now considerable evidence to suggest that prediction error signals into the dorsal striatum may play a direct role in the acquisition of instrumental reward associations. Although much progress has already been made in understanding the neural encoding of reward predictions, some of the outstanding issues highlighted in this chapter suggest a very clear agenda for future research. Most prominently among these out-standing issues will be to establish clearly the extent to which stimulus-bound and action-bound predictions are neurally dissociable, and to determine the extent to which neural signals responsible for the habitual component of instrumental conditioning can be isolated and segregated from those signals mediating goal-directed learning.

Another issue, not touched on in the present chapter, is that once the neural systems responsible for each different type of reward prediction have been delineated, it will also be important to begin to understand how these different types of reward-prediction systems interact in order to ultimately control behavior. Although this question has already been extensively studied in the animal literature, it has of yet only received preliminary treatment in humans (Bray, Rangel, Shimojo, Balleine, & O'Doherty, 2008; Talmi, Seymour, Dayan, & Dolan, 2008). Furthermore, a fundamental issue for the field of decision neuroscience will be to under-stand how value signals can be computed through the provision of explicit "descriptive" information about magnitudes and probabilities (e.g., "this option will give $10 with probability 0.2"), and to address the extent to which value signals acquired explicitly are handled differently from value signals learned through direct experience, such as those discussed in this chapter. Finally, a key question for future research will be to address how value signals for different decision options are actually compared in order to reach a decision, where this comparison process takes place, and the computational mechanism used to make the comparison.

REFERENCES

Balleine, B. W., Daw, N. D., & O'Doherty, J. P. (2008). Multiple forms of value learning and the function of dopamine. In P. W. Glimcher, C. F. Camerer, R. A. Poldrack, & E. Fehr (Eds.), *Neuroeconomics: Decision making and the brain* (pp. 367–388). New York: Academic Press.

Balleine, B. W., & Dickinson, A. (1998). Goal-directed instrumental action: Con-tingency and incentive learning and their cortical substrates. *Neuropharmacol-ogy, 37*, 407–419.

Barto, A. G. (1992). Reinforcement learning and adaptive critic methods. In D. A. White & D. A. Sofge (Eds.), *Handbook of intelligent control: Neural, fuzzy, and adaptive approaches* (pp. 469–491). New York: Van Nostrand Reinhold.

Barto, A. G. (1995). Adaptive critics and the basal ganglia. In J. C. Houk, J. L. Davis, & B. G. Beiser (Eds.), *Models of information processing in the basal ganglia* (pp. 215–232). Cambridge, MA: MIT Press.

Blood, A. J., Zatorre, R. J., Bermudez, P., & Evans, A. C. (1999). Emotional responses to pleasant and unpleasant music correlate with activity in paralimbic brain regions. *Nature Neuroscience, 2*, 382–387.

Bray, S., Rangel, A., Shimojo, S., Balleine, B., & O'Doherty, J. P. (2008). The neural mechanisms underlying the influence of Pavlovian cues on human decision making. *Journal of Neuroscience, 28,* 5861–5866.

Cloutier, J., Heatherton, T. F., Whalen, P. J., & Kelley, W. M. (2008). Are attractive people rewarding? Sex differences in the neural substrates of facial attractiveness. *Journal of Cognitive Neuroscience, 20,* 941–951.

Cromwell, H. C., & Schultz, W. (2003). Effects of expectations for different reward magnitudes on neuronal activity in primate striatum. *Journal of Neurophysiology, 89,* 2823–2838.

Daw, N. D., Kakade, S., & Dayan, P. (2002). Opponent interactions between serotonin and dopamine. *Neural Networks, 15,* 603–616.

Daw, N. D., Niv, Y., & Dayan, P. (2005). Uncertainty-based competition between prefrontal and dorsolateral striatal systems for behavioral control. *Nature Neuroscience, 8,* 1704–1711.

Daw, N. D., O'Doherty, J. P., Dayan, P., Seymour, B., & Dolan, R. J. (2006). Cortical substrates for exploratory decisions in humans. *Nature, 441,* 876–879.

Day, J. J., & Carelli, R. M. (2007). The nucleus accumbens and Pavlovian reward learning. *Neuroscientist, 13,* 148–159.

Day, J. J., Wheeler, R. A., Roitman, M. F., & Carelli, R. M. (2006). Nucleus accumbens neurons encode Pavlovian approach behaviors: Evidence from an autoshaping paradigm. *European Journal of Neuroscience, 23,* 1341–1351.

Dayan, P., & Abbott, L. (2001). *Theoretical neuroscience.* Boston, MA: MIT Press.

Glascher, J., Hampton, A. N., & O'Doherty, J. P. (2009). Determining a role for ventromedial prefrontal cortex in encoding action-based value signals during reward-related decision making. *Cerebral Cortex, 19,* 483–495.

Gottfried, J. A., Deichmann, R., Winston, J. S., & Dolan, R. J. (2002). Functional heterogeneity in human olfactory cortex: An event-related functional magnetic resonance imaging study. *Journal of Neuroscience, 22,* 10819–10828.

Gottfried, J. A., O'Doherty, J. P., & Dolan, R. J. (2002). Appetitive and aversive olfactory learning in humans studied using event-related functional magnetic resonance imaging. *Journal of Neuroscience, 22,* 10829–10837.

Gottfried, J. A., O'Doherty, J. P., & Dolan, R. J. (2003). Encoding predictive reward value in human amygdala and orbitofrontal cortex. *Science, 301,* 1104–1107.

Hampton, A. N., Bossaerts, P., & O'Doherty, J. P. (2006). The role of the ventromedial prefrontal cortex in abstract state-based inference during decision making in humans. *Journal of Neuroscience, 26,* 8360–8367.

Kim, H., Shimojo, S., & O'Doherty, J. P. (2006). Is avoiding an aversive outcome rewarding? Neural substrates of avoidance learning in the human brain. *PLoS Biology, 4,* e233.

Kringelbach, M. L., O'Doherty, J. P., Rolls, E. T., & Andrews, C. (2003). Activation of the human orbitofrontal cortex to a liquid food stimulus is correlated with its subjective pleasantness. *Cerebral Cortex, 13,* 1064–1071.

McClure, S. M., Berns, G. S., & Montague, P. R. (2003). Temporal prediction errors in a passive learning task activate human striatum. *Neuron, 38,* 339–346.

Mirenowicz, J., & Schultz, W. (1994). Importance of unpredictability for reward responses in primate dopamine neurons. *Journal of Neurophysiology, 72,* 1024–1027.

Montague, P. R., Dayan, P., & Sejnowski, T. J. (1996). A framework for mesencephalic dopamine systems based on predictive Hebbian learning. *Journal of Neuroscience, 16*, 1936–1947.

O'Doherty, J., Deichmann, R., Critchley, H. D., & Dolan, R. J. (2002). Neural responses during anticipation of a primary taste reward. *Neuron, 33*, 815–826.

O'Doherty, J. P. (2004). Reward representations and reward-related learning in the human brain: Insights from neuroimaging. *Current Opinion in Neurobiology, 14*, 769–776.

O'Doherty, J. P., Dayan, P., Friston, K., Critchley, H., & Dolan, R. J. (2003). Temporal difference models and reward-related learning in the human brain. *Neuron, 38*, 329–337.

O'Doherty, J. P., Dayan, P., Schultz, J., Deichmann, R., Friston, K., & Dolan, R. J. (2004). Dissociable roles of ventral and dorsal striatum in instrumental conditioning. *Science, 304*, 452–454.

O'Doherty, J. P., Kringelbach, M. L., Rolls, E. T., Hornak, J., & Andrews, C. (2001). Abstract reward and punishment representations in the human orbitofrontal cortex. *Nature Neuroscience, 4*, 95–102.

O'Doherty, J. P., Rolls, E. T., Francis, S., Bowtell, R., & McGlone, F. (2001). Representation of pleasant and aversive taste in the human brain. *Journal of Neurophysiology, 85*, 1315–1321.

O'Doherty, J. P., Rolls, E. T., Francis, S., Bowtell, R., McGlone, F., Kobal, G. et al. (2000). Sensory-specific satiety-related olfactory activation of the human orbitofrontal cortex. *Neuroreport, 11*, 893–897.

O'Doherty, J. P., Winston, J., Critchley, H., Perrett, D., Burt, D. M., & Dolan, R. J. (2003). Beauty in a smile: The role of medial orbitofrontal cortex in facial attractiveness. *Neuropsychologia, 41*, 147–155.

Paton, J. J., Belova, M. A., Morrison, S. E., & Salzman, C. D. (2006). The primate amygdala represents the positive and negative value of visual stimuli during learning. *Nature, 439*, 865–870.

Pessiglione, M., Seymour, B., Flandin, G., Dolan, R. J., & Frith, C. D. (2006). Dopamine-dependent prediction errors underpin reward-seeking behaviour in humans. *Nature, 442*, 1042–1045.

Pezze, M. A., & Feldon, J. (2004). Mesolimbic dopaminergic pathways in fear conditioning. *Progress in Neurobiology, 74*, 301–320.

Rescorla, R. A., & Wagner, A. R. (1972). A theory of Pavlovian conditioning: Variations in the effectiveness of reinforcement and nonreinforcement. In A. H. Black & W. F. Prokasy (Eds.), *Classical conditioning II: Current research and theory* (pp. 64–99). New York: Appleton Crofts.

Rolls, B. J., Rolls, E. T., Rowe, E. A., & Sweeney, K. (1981). Sensory specific satiety in man. *Physiology & Behavior, 27*, 137–142.

Rolls, E. T. (2000). The orbitofrontal cortex and reward. *Cerebral Cortex, 10*, 284–294.

Rolls, E. T., Kringelbach, M. L., & de Araujo, I. E. (2003). Different representations of pleasant and unpleasant odours in the human brain. *European Journal of Neuroscience, 18*, 695–703.

Rolls, E. T., O'Doherty, J. P., Kringelbach, M. L., Francis, S., Bowtell, R., &

McGlone, F. (2003). Representations of pleasant and painful touch in the human orbitofrontal and cingulate cortices. *Cerebral Cortex, 13*, 308–317.

Schoenbaum, G., Chiba, A. A., & Gallagher, M. (1998). Orbitofrontal cortex and basolateral amygdala encode expected outcomes during learning. *Nature Neuroscience, 1*, 155–159.

Schonberg, T., Daw, N. D., Joel, D., & O'Doherty, J. P. (2007). Reinforcement learning signals in the human striatum distinguish learners from nonlearners during reward-based decision making. *Journal of Neuroscience, 27*, 12860–12867.

Schultz, W. (1998). Predictive reward signal of dopamine neurons. *Journal of Neurophysiology, 80*, 1–27.

Seymour, B., O'Doherty, J. P., Dayan, P., Koltzenburg, M., Jones, A. K., Dolan, R. J. et al. (2004). Temporal difference models describe higher-order learning in humans. *Nature, 429*, 664–667.

Seymour, B., O'Doherty, J. P., Koltzenburg, M., Wiech, K., Frackowiak, R., Friston, K. et al. (2005). Opponent appetitive-aversive neural processes underlie predictive learning of pain relief. *Nature Neuroscience, 8*, 1234–1240.

Shidara, M., Aigner, T. G., & Richmond, B. J. (1998). Neuronal signals in the monkey ventral striatum related to progress through a predictable series of trials. *Journal of Neuroscience, 18*, 2613–2625.

Small, D. M., Zatorre, R. J., Dagher, A., Evans, A. C., & Jones-Gotman, M. (2001). Changes in brain activity related to eating chocolate: From pleasure to aversion. *Brain, 124*, 1720–1733.

Sutton, R. S. (1988). Learning to predict by the methods of temporal differences. *Machine Learning, 3*, 9–44.

Talmi, D., Seymour, B., Dayan, P., & Dolan, R. J. (2008). Human Pavlovian-instrumental transfer. *Journal of Neuroscience, 28*, 360–368.

Thorndike, E. L. (1898). *Animal intelligence: An experimental study of the associative processes in animals.* New York: Macmillan.

Tremblay, L., & Schultz, W. (1999). Relative reward preference in primate orbitofrontal cortex. *Nature, 398*, 704–708.

Ungless, M. A., Magill, P. J., & Bolam, J. P. (2004). Uniform inhibition of dopamine neurons in the ventral tegmental area by aversive stimuli. *Science, 303*, 2040–2042.

Valentin, V. V., Dickinson, A., & O'Doherty, J. P. (2007). Determining the neural substrates of goal-directed learning in the human brain. *Journal of Neuroscience, 27*, 4019–4026.

CHAPTER EIGHT

Reward and punishment processing in the human brain: Clues from affective neuroscience and implications for depression research

Diego A. Pizzagalli, Daniel G. Dillon, Ryan Bogdan, and Avram J. Holmes

INTRODUCTION

A substantial amount of research has investigated how two fundamental dimensions of behavior—approach and avoidance—influence emotions, reasoning, and decision making. Catalyzed by improved neuroimaging techniques, behavioral investigations in both healthy subjects and individuals with selected brain lesions, and animal studies, our understanding of the neural circuitry supporting reward and punishment processing has grown rapidly (Berridge, 2007; Knutson & Cooper, 2005; Schultz, 2007). Though much remains unknown, we now possess insight into neural pathways implicated in distinct components of incentive processing. In addition to its basic scientific value, this knowledge promises to improve our understanding of various forms of psychopathology characterized by abnormal incentive processing, including depression.

This chapter begins with an overview of basic research on the neural correlates of reward and punishment processing. We summarize animal and human findings indicating that the ventral striatum and amygdala code the incentive properties of stimuli and are critical for outcome anticipation, while the orbitofrontal cortex (OFC) and anterior cingulate cortex (ACC) link incentive properties to stimulus and action representations, respectively (Holland & Gallagher, 2004; Rushworth, Behrens, Rudebeck, & Walton, 2007). Next, we review behavioral and neuroimaging studies suggesting that depression is characterized by abnormal incentive

199

processing. Findings derived from laboratory-based assessments, rather than self-report measures, will be emphasized to facilitate integration of behavioral and neuroimaging research. We particularly focus on reports of reduced hedonic capacity and abnormal processing of internal (e.g., error monitoring) and external (e.g., negative feedback) signals of poor performance. Based on several converging lines of evidence, we speculate that ventral striatal dysfunction may lead to deficits in reward anticipation and reward-based learning, thus contributing to one of the cardinal features of depression: Anhedonia. Hyperactivity in the amygdala, combined with dysfunction of prefrontal cortical (PFC) regions implicated in cognitive control, may contribute to the emergence and maintenance of negative processing biases. We conclude by highlighting important issues for future investigations, and suggest that objective assessments of incentive processing may provide an especially powerful tool for improving the phenotypic definition of depression.

THE NEURAL BASIS OF INCENTIVE PROCESSING

The role of the ventral striatum in incentive anticipation

The ventral striatum (e.g., nucleus accumbens) receives dopaminergic (DA) afferents from midbrain structures, including the ventral tegmental area and substantia nigra (Bannon & Roth, 1983). In nonhuman primates, midbrain DA neurons projecting to the ventral striatum show phasic bursts in response to unexpected rewards and reward-predicting cues, but decreased activity on omission of expected rewards (Schultz, 2007). Building on these findings, early functional magnetic resonance (fMRI) studies in humans revealed that the ventral striatum is activated by a wide range of rewarding stimuli, including drugs of abuse (e.g., Breiter et al., 1997) and attractive opposite-sex faces (Aharon et al., 2001). Knutson and colleagues extended this work by using a monetary incentive delay task to investigate the anticipatory versus consummatory phases separately, and consistently found that the ventral striatum is activated by anticipation of monetary rewards (e.g., Knutson, Adams, Fong, & Hommer, 2001; for review, see Knutson & Cooper, 2005). This activity is positively correlated with the size of potential reward (Knutson, Fong, Bennett, Adams, & Hommer, 2003) and self-reported happiness elicited by reward cues (Knutson et al., 2001).

There is controversy over whether the ventral striatum specifically codes reward, as studies have reported activation of this region during anticipation of aversive stimuli (e.g., painful heat: Jensen, McIntosh, Crawley, Mikulis, Remington, & Kapur, 2003), as well as by salient neutral stimuli (Zink, Pagnoni, Martin, Dhamala, & Berns, 2003). However, omission of expected rewards consistently elicits decreased firing in this structure, and novel or especially salient stimuli may have rewarding properties (Ungless, 2004). Thus, although this issue warrants more research, the current consensus is that the ventral striatum is particularly important for reward anticipation. Also, while ventral striatal responses to rewarding outcomes have been described (e.g., Bjork & Hommer, 2007), several studies report that monetary gains more strongly activate mesial PFC and OFC regions (Dillon, Holmes, Jahn, Bogdan, Wald, & Pizzagalli, 2008; Knutson et al., 2003; O'Doherty, Kringelbach, Rolls, Hornak, & Andrews, 2001). These findings support the hypothesis that the ventral striatum and the mesolimbic DA system in general are more important for reward anticipation than consumption (Berridge, 2007).

The role of the amygdala in encoding predictive incentive value

In contrast to the ventral striatum, the amygdala is best known for its role in aversive learning—specifically, the acquisition of conditioned fear (LeDoux, 1995). During acquisition of conditioned fear, contingent pairing of a neutral conditioned stimulus (CS) with an aversive unconditioned stimulus (US) results in the CS acquiring the ability to elicit fear. This can be conceptualized as anticipatory learning, as the organism appears to expect the US on presentation of the CS. In rodents, the neural mechanisms underlying fear acquisition are well understood (LeDoux, 1995). Briefly, sensory information about the CS and US is transmitted to the basolateral amygdaloid complex (BLA), where CS–US associations are formed. This information is then transmitted to the central nucleus of the amygdala, which is connected to a number of effector sites that control various aspects of the fear response (e.g., freezing behavior).

Research confirms a similar role for the amygdala in humans, as the amygdala is activated during fear conditioning in healthy participants (e.g., LaBar, Gatenby, Gore, LeDoux, & Phelps, 1998; for review, see Buchel & Dolan, 2000) and conditioned fear acquisition is impaired in patients with amygdala damage, despite normal responses to the US (LaBar, LeDoux, Spencer, & Phelps, 1995). This dissociation—amygdala damage leaves US processing intact but disrupts conditioned fear expectancy—suggests that the amygdala may be more critical for cued fear anticipation than for the experience of fear.

Although the role of the amygdala in processing negative information is well known, this structure is also connected to the ventral striatum and is critical for representing the reward value of stimuli. Reward devaluation studies illustrate the amygdala's role in reward anticipation (Baxter & Murray, 2002; Holland & Gallagher, 2004). In a typical Pavlovian devaluation paradigm, two different foods are initially paired with distinct CSs, which come to elicit conditioned appetitive responses. Next, the value of one of the two foods is reduced (devalued), generally either through a selective satiation procedure or through taste-aversion learning. In the test phase, the two CSs are presented again. Healthy animals do not show an appetitive response to the CS previously paired with the now-devalued food but show intact responding to the other CS. This indicates that animals form CS–outcome representations that control anticipatory responding and can be manipulated via devaluation.

Studies in rodents and monkeys indicate that the BLA is critical for the formation of stimulus–outcome value representations (e.g., Hatfield, Han, Conley, Gallagher, & Holland, 1996; Malkova, Gaffan, & Murray, 1997). If the BLA is lesioned before training, the typical devaluation effect is not observed: Lesioned animals are motivated to obtain food rewards and show reduced consumption of the devalued food when it is directly presented, but their response to the CS that was previously paired with the now-devalued food remains unchanged at test. Functional imaging suggests a similar role for the amygdala in humans. Gottfried, O'Doherty, and Dolan (2003) paired two CSs with two food odors and identified a network of brain regions supporting the acquisition of conditioned responses to the CSs, including the amygdala, ventral midbrain, and OFC. Next, participants were sated on one of the two foods whose odors had been presented. The CSs were then presented a second time. Significantly decreased responses to the CS previously paired with the now-devalued food were observed in the amygdala and OFC, whereas responses in these regions to the other CS were unchanged. In sum, animal and human findings indicate the amygdala is critical for encoding predictive incentive value.

The role of the OFC in stimulus-reinforcement representations

While the BLA has been implicated in the formation of stimulus–outcome representations, the OFC appears to be more important in using those representations to guide behavior (Holland & Gallagher, 2004). A recent study functionally dissociated these regions by making lesions of the BLA or OFC after CS–food pairings but before devaluation (Pickens, Saddoris, Setlow, Gallagher, Holland, & Schoenbaum, 2003). Rodents with BLA lesions performed normally at test, consistent with the hypothesis that the BLA is most important for formation of stimulus–outcome representations. By contrast, the OFC lesion group showed impaired performance, similar to what is observed if BLA lesions are made before training (see also Baxter, Parker, Lindner, Izquierdo, & Murray, 2000). These findings suggest that the OFC uses updated stimulus–outcome representations to guide behavior (for a conceptual replication in humans, see Gottfried et al., 2003); if the OFC is lesioned, perseverative responding based on outdated representations is observed.

Neuroimaging studies demonstrate that the human OFC codes incentive (rather than the sensory) properties of gustatory (e.g., O'Doherty, Rolls, Francis, Bowtell, & McGlone, 2001), olfactory (e.g., Anderson et al., 2003), somatosensory (e.g., Rolls et al., 2003), auditory (e.g., Blood, Zatorre, Bermudez, & Evans, 1999), and visual (e.g., Aharon et al., 2001) stimuli. However, particularly strong evidence for conservation of OFC function across species comes from investigations of individuals with selective brain lesions. Humans with OFC damage show perseverative responding in a reversal-learning paradigm, in which a previously rewarded stimulus becomes associated with punishment after a switch in stimulus–outcome contingencies (Hornak et al., 2004). Similarly, individuals with OFC damage appear to be unable to update stimulus–outcome representations in a gambling task (Bechara, Damasio, Damasio, & Lee, 1999).

The role of the ACC in action-reinforcement representations

Although the OFC and ACC are both connected to the ventral striatum and amygdala and thus well positioned to make use of incentive information, the ACC's stronger connections to the motor system give it a primary role in linking outcome representations to actions (Rushworth et al., 2007). In humans, large literatures link dorsal ACC activity to response conflict (e.g., Botvinick, Cohen, & Carter, 2004) and error processing (e.g., Holroyd & Coles, 2002). However, proponents of both the response conflict (e.g., Kerns, Cohen, MacDonald, Cho, Stenger, & Carter, 2004) and error processing hypotheses (e.g., Gehring & Willoughby, 2002) have seated their formulations in larger conceptions of ACC function, suggesting that these are special cases of the structure's role in monitoring internal states for signs that behavior is not leading to desired outcomes.

Consistent with this hypothesis, recent findings indicate a broad role for the ACC in maximizing adaptive behavior. For example, multiple studies suggest that rather than simply detecting errors or response conflict, the ACC is involved in optimizing behavior so as to avoid errors before they occur (Brown & Braver, 2005; Magno, Foxe, Molhom, Robertson, & Garavan, 2006). In a related vein, studies by Walton and colleagues demonstrate that the ACC is involved in effort-related decision making (e.g., Walton, Kennerley, Bannerman, Phillips, & Rushworth, 2006). Compared with control animals, rodents with ACC lesions are reluctant to expend effort to obtain large rewards when smaller rewards are easily obtained, a result that is hypothesized to reflect the loss of top–down excitatory signals from the ACC to mesolimbic DA neurons (Walton et al., 2006).

A critical role for the dorsal ACC in using reinforcement history to guide action has been established in nonhuman primates (Kennerley, Walton, Behrens, Buckley, & Rushworth, 2006). In a voluntary choice task in which the identity of the rewarded response was intermittently switched, both control animals and monkeys with dorsal ACC lesions quickly adjusted their behavior in response to errors by switching from the unrewarded response (which had previously been rewarded) to the rewarded response (which was previously unrewarded). Controls maintained this behavior over a series of rewarded trials. By contrast, animals with dorsal ACC lesions showed a tendency to repeatedly switch back to the now-unrewarded response. This ineffective behavior suggests that the ACC may guide action by integrating response history over time, a function that is often necessary for maintaining adaptive behavior in the absence of explicit instructions or in an environment with fluctuating reinforcements. Similar conclusions have emerged from functional neuroimaging studies that have described dorsal ACC activation in paradigms requiring representation of both gains and losses, as well as integration of reinforcements across trials (e.g., Akitsuki et al., 2003; Rogers et al., 2004).

Section summary

Evidence from functional neuroimaging, human lesion, and animal studies suggests that distinct aspects of incentive processing preferentially recruit specific brain regions. The ventral striatum and amygdala code the incentive properties of stimuli and are important for the initial formation of stimulus–outcome representations. The OFC is implicated in updating these representations, as illustrated by the perseverative behavior of subjects with OFC lesions in reversal-learning paradigms. The dorsal ACC uses outcome representations to guide voluntary actions; damage to this structure impairs the ability to use reinforcement history as a guide for goal-directed behavior. As reviewed in the next section, dysfunction within these structures may contribute to disruptions of incentive processing in depression.

ABNORMAL INCENTIVE PROCESSING IN DEPRESSION

Major depressive disorder (MDD) is a highly recurrent and prevalent mood disorder characterized by affective (e.g., depressed mood, loss of pleasure), cognitive (e.g., feelings of worthlessness, decreased ability to concentrate), vegetative (e.g., sleep disturbance, appetite disturbance), and motor (e.g., psychomotor retardation or agitation) symptoms (American

Psychiatric Association, 2000). The diagnosis of MDD, which is based on clusters of symptoms, has been criticized for its heterogeneous nature (e.g., Hasler, Drevets, Manji, & Charney, 2004). A major goal of affective neuroscience research is to reduce this complexity by identifying a smaller number of core components, which might provide novel insights into the etiology and pathophysiology of this debilitating disorder. Inspired by early theoretical work emphasizing the importance of anhedonia (Costello, 1972; Meehl, 1975) and hypersensitivity to negative information (Beck, Rush, Shaw, & Emery, 1979), recent research has specifically investigated dysfunctional reward and punishment processing in depression.

Reward processing in depression: Behavioral studies

Depression is associated with reduced approach-related behavior and blunted reward processing. For example, we have employed a probabilistic reward task that allowed us to objectively assess participants' propensity to modulate behavior as a function of reward (Pizzagalli, Jahn, & O'Shea, 2005; see also Henriques & Davidson, 2000; Henriques, Glowacki, & Davidson, 1994). In each trial, participants choose between two responses that are linked to different probabilities of reward. Due to the probabilistic nature of the reinforcement schedule, participants cannot infer which stimulus is more advantageous based on the outcome of a single trial but need to integrate reinforcement history over time for optimal performance. Healthy controls are able to do this (Bogdan & Pizzagalli, 2006), resulting in a significant response bias for the more frequently rewarded stimulus. In comparison, controls reporting elevated depressive symptoms (Pizzagalli, Jahn et al., 2005), unmedicated individuals with MDD (Pizzagalli, Iosifescu, Hallett, Ratner, & Fava, 2009), and euthymic patients with bipolar disorder (Pizzagalli, Goetz, Ostacher, Iosifescu, & Perlis, 2009) develop a weak response bias, indicative of reduced responsivity to rewards. Moreover, in two independent nonclinical samples, reward responsiveness negatively correlated with self-reported anhedonic symptoms (Bogdan & Pizzagalli, 2006; Pizzagalli, Jahn et al., 2005), and predicted these symptoms one month later (Pizzagalli, Jahn et al., 2005).

These findings are consistent with work highlighting reduced affective, behavioral, and physiological responses to positive cues in depressed and/ or anhedonic subjects (cf. Must, Szabo, Bodi, Szasz, Janka, & Keri, 2006). Depressed and/or anhedonic participants: (1) fail to distinguish between options yielding large versus small rewards (Forbes, Shaw, & Dahl, 2006); (2) experience diminished affective (e.g., Berenbaum & Oltmanns, 1992), behavioral (e.g., Sloan, Strauss, & Wisner, 2001), and physiological (e.g.,

Pierson, Ragot, Ripoche, & Lesevre, 1987) responses to pleasant stimuli; (3) underestimate the frequency of correct feedback and positive reinforcement received in experimental tasks (e.g., Nelson & Craighead, 1977; Wener & Rehm, 1975); (4) self-reinforce less frequently for "good" or "correct" responses (Nelson & Craighead, 1977; Rozensky, Rehm, Pry, & Roth, 1977); and (5) incorrectly label happy facial expressions as neutral and require greater emotional intensity to correctly identify happy facial expressions (e.g., Joormann & Gotlib, 2006; Surguladze, Young, & Senior, 2004).

Reward processing in depression: Neuroimaging and electrophysiological studies

To the best of our knowledge, only two neuroimaging studies have directly investigated reward processing in MDD (Forbes, Christopher et al., 2006; Tremblay, Naranjo, Graham, Herrmann, Mayberg, Hevenor, & Busto, 2005). Using a task involving choices associated with varying magnitude and probabilities of reward and punishment, Forbes, Christopher et al. (2006) reported that, relative to healthy controls, depressed children displayed reduced activation in the ACC, caudate, and right OFC during the decision/anticipation and outcome phases (particularly for punishment and low-magnitude rewards), but increased amygdala and OFC activation in response to high-magnitude rewards. Although these findings demonstrate altered activation of incentive coding regions in depression, the significance of differences between reward magnitudes are not immediately clear.

Extending their initial observation of increased response to a dopaminergic agonist in depression (Tremblay, Naranjo, Cardenas, Herrmann, & Busto, 2002), Tremblay and coworkers (2005) recently reported that, relative to healthy controls, participants with MDD showed increased self-reported affective responses to a dopaminergic agonist along with decreased blood oxygenation level dependent (BOLD) signals in the OFC, caudate, and putamen. The decreased BOLD signal in these regions was interpreted as possibly resulting from the disinhibition of DA neurons. Thus, both the self-reported hyper-response to the drug and the fMRI results were interpreted as suggesting hypofunction in the brain's reward system in MDD.

Indirect evidence of dysfunctional reward pathways in depression arises from two additional sources. First, neuroimaging studies of individuals with MDD reveal reduced responses to positive stimuli in reward-related regions, including the ventral striatum (e.g., Epstein et al., 2006; Lawrence et al., 2004), medial PFC/OFC (e.g., Elliott, Rubinsztein, Sahakian, & Dolan, 2002; Lawrence et al., 2004; Mitterschiffthaler et al., 2003), and amygdala (e.g., Lawrence et al., 2004). Of particular relevance, a recent study using a gambling task reported that medicated MDD participants failed to show the behavioral (RT reduction) and neural (ventral striatum activation) pattern displayed by controls on receiving positive feedback (Steele, Kumar, & Ebmeier, 2007). Finally, anhedonic symptoms have been negatively correlated with activation in the ventral striatum, dorsolateral prefrontal cortex (DLPFC), and amygdala in response to visual stimuli and facial expressions (Epstein et al., 2006; Harvey, Pruessner, Czechowska, & Lepage, 2007; Keedwell, Andrew, Williams, Brammer, & Phillips, 2005).

Second, electroencephalographic (EEG) studies assessing resting brain activity indicate that depression is associated with relatively reduced activity over left PFC regions (for review, see Thibodeau, Jorgensen, & Kim, 2006), which have been implicated in supporting approach-related motivation (Davidson, 1992). Because resting activity within left prefrontal regions has been found to predict reward responsiveness in healthy participants (Pizzagalli, Sherwood, Henriques, & Davidson, 2005), reduced left PFC activity may reflect reduced hedonic capacity in depression. Consistent with this hypothesis, a recent EEG study found that early-onset (but not late-onset) depressed subjects showed reduced activity over left PFC regions while anticipating a potential reward (Shankman, Klein, Tenke, & Bruder, 2007).

Section summary

A variety of behavioral findings indicate that depression is characterized by reduced hedonic responses and a blunted propensity to modulate behavior as a function of positive reinforcement. Albeit preliminary, evidence from functional neuroimaging suggests that these deficits may reflect reduced responses to rewarding stimuli in the ventral striatum, ACC, left PFC, and OFC. Because positive reinforcers increase the likelihood of behavior (Rescorla & Wagner, 1972), blunted responsiveness to reward-related cues may lead to reduced motivational drive to pursue pleasurable activities, which may in turn contribute to depressive symptoms. Indeed, reduced hedonic capacity and low scores on self-report measures of sensitivity to reward-related cues have been found to: (1) characterize both currently depressed and remitted depressed individuals (Kasch, Rottenberg, Arnow, & Gotlib, 2002; Pinto-Meza, Caseras, Soler, Puigdemont, Perez, & Torrubia, 2006); and (2) predict depressive symptoms (Hundt, Nelson-Gray, Kimbrel, Mitchell, & Kwapil, 2007), time to recovery (McFarland, Shankman, Tenke, Bruder, & Klein, 2006), and poor treatment outcome (Kasch et al., 2002; Spijker, Bijl, de Graaf, & Nolen, 2001).

Punishment processing in depression: Behavioral studies

Results from several early behavioral studies indicate that depressed individuals are especially sensitive to negative cues and are prone to self-administer punishments, although inconsistencies have emerged. Asked to retrospectively estimate the number of times they had received positive or negative feedback for their performance in a perceptual vigilance task, students with elevated depressive symptoms reported significantly higher amounts of punishments but significantly lower amounts of rewards received relative to healthy controls (Nelson & Craighead, 1977). Interestingly, group differences in the punishment condition emerged due to the fact that controls underestimated the amount of negative feedback received, whereas dysphoric participants' estimation closely matched the number of delivered punishments. In the reward condition, on the other hand, dysphoric participants underestimated the amount of positive feedback received, whereas controls' estimation closely matched the number of delivered rewards.

However, whereas dysphoric subjects self-reinforced less often for "good" responses, the two groups did not differ in rate of self-punishments. By contrast, Roth, Rehm, and Rozensky (1980) found that dysphoric students self-administered more punishments than did controls while rewarding themselves at an equivalent rate. Moreover, severely (but not moderately) depressed individuals self-administered fewer rewards and more punishments following their responses in a memory task (Rozensky et al., 1977). Increased sensitivity to punishments (monetary loss) was also observed in a dysphoric sample that performed a verbal memory task under neutral, reward, and punishment incentive conditions (Henriques et al., 1994). However, this finding was not replicated when a clinical MDD sample was tested with the same task (Henriques & Davidson, 2000).

Indirect evidence of increased sensitivity to negative cues in MDD comes from investigations of interpretive and attentional biases. Depressed individuals are susceptible to increased interference from negative distractors (Gotlib, Traill, Montoya, Joormann, & Chang, 2005) and demonstrate impaired ability to disengage attention from negative stimuli (Koster, De Raedt, Goeleven, Franck, & Crombez, 2005), suppress failure-related thoughts (Conway, Howell, & Giannopoulos, 1991), and inhibit negative information (Goeleven, De Raedt, Baert, & Koster, 2006).

Furthermore, a growing body of work suggests that depressed subjects display abnormal responses to negative feedback and errors. Several studies reveal that negative task-relevant feedback can lead to a deterioration of performance in depressed patients (e.g., Beats, Sahakian, & Levy, 1996; Elliott, Sahakian, McKay, Herrod, Robbins, & Paykel, 1996; Elliott, Sahakian, Herrod, Robbins, & Paykel, 1997). In particularly important studies on this topic, Elliott and coworkers (Elliott et al., 1996, 1997) reported that abnormal response to errors was specific to depression (as compared with schizophrenia and Parkinson's disease) and persisted after clinical recovery, indicating that oversensitivity to errors may be a trait-like marker of depression. Findings from two independent studies from our laboratory have extended this line of work by showing that abnormal reactions to errors can also be observed in nonclinical samples and in the absence of overt feedback about task performance. Specifically, subjects with elevated depressive symptoms showed significantly impaired performance in trials immediately following incorrect—but not correct— responses in Eriksen (Pizzagalli, Peccoralo, Davidson, & Cohen, 2006) and Stroop (Holmes & Pizzagalli, 2007) tasks that required internal monitoring of errors.

Punishment processing in depression: Neuroimaging and electrophysiological studies

Few neuroimaging studies involving depressed participants have utilized negative cues. In a reinforced decision-making task, Forbes, Christopher, and colleagues (2006) reported decreased activation in response to losses in the ACC, caudate, and OFC in depressed children, relative to healthy controls. Along similar lines, Steele et al. (2007) reported that, unlike matched controls, medicated MDD participants failed to show RT slowing and medial PFC/dorsal ACC activation after receiving negative feedback in a gambling task. Finally, relative to healthy controls, individuals with MDD showed reduced blood flow in the medial caudate and ventromedial OFC, in response to both positive and negative feedback delivered across multiple cognitive tasks (Elliott, Sahakian, Michael, Paykel, & Dolan, 1998).

Surprisingly, as of 2007, no studies have investigated brain activity during the anticipation of negative cues in MDD. This type of investigation might uncover dysfunctional activation in paralimbic regions (e.g., amygdala) that have been associated with excessive worry and rumination (e.g., Siegle, Steinhauer, Thase, Stenger, & Carter, 2002). Indeed, depressed individuals show increased paralimbic and amygdalar activation in response to: (1) passive viewing of negative images (Anand et al., 2005); (2) sad targets in a go/no-go task (Elliott et al., 2002); and (3) subliminally presented negative facial expressions (Sheline, Barch, Donnelly, Ollinger, Snyder, & Mintun, 2001). Intriguingly, increased and sustained amygdala activity has been linked to reduced DLPFC activity in both healthy (Dolcos & McCarthy, 2006) and depressed individuals (Siegle, Thompson, Carter, Steinhauer, & Thase, 2007), and MDD subjects have been found to have relatively decreased DLPFC activity compared with healthy participants during negative mood induction (Fitzgerald, Laird, Maller, & Daskalakis, 2008). These findings raise the possibility that, in depression, increased paralimbic/amygdala activation during anticipation or in response to a negative cue may be associated with failure to recruit PFC regions that play important roles in cognitive control and emotion regulation (Botvinick et al., 2004; Ochsner & Gross, 2005).

Recent studies have utilized electrophysiological techniques to explore abnormal responses to errors and negative feedback in depression. Most studies have focused on two ERP waveforms, the error-related negativity (ERN) and the feedback-related negativity (FRN). The ERN is a response-locked, negative waveform that peaks over frontocentral scalp regions approximately 50–100 ms following error commission (Falkenstein, Hohnsbein, Hoormann, & Blanke, 1991; Gehring, Goss, Coles, Meyer, & Donchin, 1993). The FRN is also a negative deflection with a frontocentral scalp distribution, but it peaks approximately 200–400 ms following feedback that a mistake has occurred (Miltner, Braun, & Coles, 1997). Although it is currently unclear whether the ERN and FRN are functionally related, it has been postulated that these waveforms might originate from the ACC when a signal indicating a negative prediction error (e.g., errors or negative feedback) is conveyed through the mesencephalic dopaminergic system (e.g., Holroyd & Coles, 2002).

Relative to healthy controls, larger amplitude ERNs have been observed in both medicated and unmedicated MDD samples (Alexopoulos et al., 2007; Chiu & Deldin, 2007; Holmes & Pizzagalli, 2008). Relative to controls, individuals with MDD also display a significantly increased medial frontal negativity after receiving negative feedback (Tucker, Luu, Frishkoff, Quiring, & Poulsen, 2003). Finally, in a geriatric MDD sample, increased ERN predicted poor response to antidepressant (citalopram) treatment (Kalayam & Alexopoulos, 2003).

Intriguingly, relative to healthy controls, individuals with MDD generate a *decreased* ERN on error trials immediately following a prior mistake (e.g., Ruchsow, Herrnberger, Wiesend, Gron, Spitzer, & Kiefer, 2004), a finding that might be associated with dysregulated performance immediately following error commission. Recent ERP findings from our laboratory are in line with this hypothesis (Holmes & Pizzagalli, 2008). Consistent with an early fMRI study in depression reporting increased error signal in the rostral ACC (Steele, Meyer, & Ebmeier, 2004), we observed impaired post-error performance, increased ERN, and potentiated error-related activation in the rostral ACC in depressed individuals relative to controls. When considered in conjunction with prior reports (e.g., Siegle et al., 2007), these findings indicate that impaired performance after errors might arise due to increased activation in regions coding affective responses to errors and/or an inability to adjust behavior after a perceived failure.

Section summary

Depression is characterized by increased sensitivity to negative cues, impaired ability to inhibit or disengage from negative information, and difficulty adjusting performance following errors or negative performance feedback. Although few neuroimaging studies of punishment processing have been performed in depressed samples, initial evidence suggests that increased sensitivity to negative cues may reflect hyperactivation in ventral paralimbic and limbic regions implicated in affective responses and/or abnormal recruitment of DLPFC regions subserving cognitive control (Holmes & Pizzagalli, 2008; Mayberg, 1997; Siegle et al., 2007). Future studies will be required to evaluate whether abnormal sensitivity to punishments and errors might represent cognitive diatheses increasing vulnerability to depression.

CONCLUSION

The past two decades have witnessed remarkable progress in understanding the neural systems that code rewards and punishments and use that information to guide behavior. This work has much to offer the study of psychopathology, as more precise, mechanistic dissection of the core components of affective illness may help overcome the many limitations of the current nosological system (e.g., Hasler et al., 2004; Hyman, 2007; Meyer-Lindenberg & Weinberger, 2006).

A particular case in point is depression, the focus of this chapter. Growing evidence indicates that MDD is characterized by reduced sensitivity to positive cues (including rewards) and increased sensitivity to negative reinforcers (including punishments). However, it is only recently that these deficits have been linked to their neural substrates. Initial data suggest that decreased reward sensitivity in depression is associated with impaired function of the mesolimbic DA system, evident in altered function of striatal regions and PFC targets of the dopaminergic neurons, including the OFC and ACC (e.g., Epstein et al., 2006; Tremblay et al., 2005).

However, many questions remain unanswered. For example, although depression has been associated with decreased resting EEG activity over left PFC regions, it is unclear whether this finding is related to putative asymmetries (left > right) in DA innervation of the PFC (Wittling, 1995). In addition, it will be important to determine whether anhedonia is more closely tied to neural deficits in reward anticipation or consumption, which are supported by different neural structures (Berridge, 2007). More importantly, it is unclear what causes anhedonia (and the associated dysfunction in striatal and OFC regions). Work from several labs, including our own, suggests an important role for stressors in the manifestation of anhedonia (e.g., Anisman & Matheson, 2005; Bogdan & Pizzagalli, 2006; Pizzagalli, Bogdan, Ratner, & Jahn, 2007), but few studies have investigated this hypothesis in humans, particularly with respect to chronic (as opposed to acute) stressors.

To date, the excessive negative processing biases/rumination characteristic of MDD have been associated primarily with hyperactivity in the amygdala (e.g., Siegle et al., 2002). This finding provides a sound foundation for future investigation, but again, many issues remain unresolved. For example, the animal literature suggests that the amygdala is primarily involved in coding the anticipation of both positive and negative reinforcers, but whether amygdala hyperactivity in MDD affects anticipation (of punishment and/or reward) is currently unknown. On another note, we have provided evidence suggesting that depression is characterized by diminished functional connectivity within fronto-cingulate pathways (Holmes & Pizzagalli, 2008; Pizzagalli, Oakes, & Davidson, 2003), which might lead to difficulties recruiting cognitive control in situations requiring flexible behavioral adjustments (e.g., after errors or receiving negative feedback). The cause of this reduction in functional connectivity remains unclear. In addition, cognitive control is a complex construct that involves many regions beyond the DLPFC. Thus, the decision-making and motivational deficits that are characteristic of MDD, and that are thought to underlie impaired post-error performance, are also likely to be quite complex.

In short, there is much work to be done. However, understanding of the neural circuitry underlying reward and punishment processing now provides a foundation on which to build an improved affective neuroscience of depression. Ultimately, this approach is expected to provide more objective phenotypic characterizations, and hopefully yield improved treatments for individuals suffering from this all-too-common and debilitating disease.

ACKNOWLEDGMENTS

Preparation of this chapter was supported by grants from NIH (NIMH R01 MH68376 and NCCAM R21 AT002974) and Talley Fund (Harvard University) awarded to Diego A. Pizzagalli.

REFERENCES

Aharon, I., Etcoff, N., Ariely, D., Chabris, C. F., O'Connor, E., & Breiter, H. C. (2001). Beautiful faces have variable reward value: fMRI and behavioral evidence. *Neuron, 32,* 537–551.

Akitsuki, Y., Sugiura, M., Watanabe, J., Yamashita, K., Sassa, Y., Awata, S. et al. (2003). Context-dependent cortical activation in response to financial reward and penalty: An event-related fMRI study. *Neuroimage, 19,* 1674–1685.

Alexopoulos, G. S., Murphy, C. F., Gunning-Dixon, F. M., Kalayam, B., Katz, R., Kanellopoulos, D. et al. (2007). Event-related potentials in an emotional go/no-go task and remission of geriatric depression. *Neuroreport, 12,* 217–221.

American Psychiatric Association. (2000). *Diagnostic and statistical manual of mental disorders, DSM-IV-TR.* Washington, DC: American Psychiatric Association.

Anand, A., Li. Y., Wang, Y., Wu, J., Gao, S., Bukhari, L. et al. (2005). Activity and connectivity of brain mood regulating circuit in depression: a functional magnetic resonance study. *Biological Psychiatry, 57,* 1079–1088.

Anderson, A. K., Christoff, K., Stappen, I., Panitz, D., Ghahremani, D. G., Glover, G. et al. (2003). Dissociated neural representations of intensity and valence in human olfaction. *Nature Neuroscience, 6,* 196–202.

Anisman, H., & Matheson, K. (2005). Stress, depression, and anhedonia: Caveats concerning animal models. *Neuroscience and Biobehavioral Reviews, 29,* 525–546.

Bannon, M. J., & Roth, R. H. (1983). Pharmacology of mesocortical dopamine neurons. *Pharmacological Reviews, 35,* 53–68.

Baxter, M. G., & Murray, E. A. (2002). The amygdala and reward. *Nature Reviews Neuroscience, 3,* 563–572.

Baxter, M. G., Parker, A., Lindner, C. C. C., Izquierdo, A. D., & Murray, E. A. (2000). Control of response selection by reinforcer value requires interaction of amygdala and orbitofrontal cortex. *Journal of Neuroscience, 20,* 4311–4319.

Beats, B. C., Sahakian, B. J., & Levy, R. (1996). Cognitive performance in tests sensitive to frontal lobe dysfunction in the elderly depressed. *Psychological Medicine, 26,* 591–603.

Bechara, A., Damasio, H., Damasio, A. R., & Lee, G. P. (1999). Different contributions of the human amygdala and ventromedial prefrontal cortex to decision-making. *Journal of Neuroscience, 19,* 5473–5481.

Beck, A. T., Rush, A. J., Shaw, B. F., & Emery, G. (1979). *Cognitive therapy of depression.* New York: Guilford Press.

Berenbaum, H., & Oltmanns, T. F. (1992). Emotional experience and expression in schizophrenia and depression. *Journal of Abnormal Psychology, 101,* 37–44.

Berridge, K. C. (2007). The debate over dopamine's role in reward: the case for incentive salience. *Psychopharmacology, 191,* 391–431.

Bjork, J. M., & Hommer, D. (2007). Anticipating instrumentally obtained and passively-received rewards: A factorial fMRI investigation. *Behavioural Brain Research, 177,* 165–170.

Blood, A. J., Zatorre, R. J., Bermudez, P., & Evans, A. C. (1999). Emotional responses to pleasant and unpleasant music correlate with activity in paralimbic brain regions. *Nature Neuroscience, 2,* 382–387.

Bogdan, R., & Pizzagalli, D. A. (2006). Acute stress reduces hedonic capacity: Implications for depression. *Biological Psychiatry, 60,* 1147–1154.

Botvinick, M. M., Cohen, J. D., & Carter, C. S. (2004). Conflict monitoring and anterior cingulate cortex: An update. *Trends in Cognitive Sciences, 8,* 539–546.

Breiter, H. C., Gollub, R. L., Weisskoff, R. M., Kennedy, D. N., Makris, N., Berke, J. D. et al. (1997). Acute effects of cocaine on human brain activity and emotion. *Neuron, 19*, 591–611.

Brown, J. W., & Braver, T. S. (2005). Learned predictions of error likelihood in the anterior cingulate cortex. *Science, 307*, 1118–1121.

Buchel, C., & Dolan, R. J. (2000). Classical fear conditioning in functional neuroimaging. *Current Opinion in Neurobiology, 10*, 219–223.

Chiu, P., & Deldin, P. (2007). Neural evidence for enhanced error detection in major depressive disorder. *American Journal of Psychiatry, 164*, 608–616.

Conway, M., Howell, A., & Giannopoulos, C. (1991). Dysphoria and thought suppression. *Cognitive Therapy and Research, 15*, 153–166.

Costello, C. G. (1972). Depression: Loss of reinforcers or loss of reinforcer effectiveness? *Behavior Therapy, 3*, 240–247.

Davidson, R. J. (1992). Anterior cerebral asymmetry and the nature of emotion. *Brain & Cognition, 20*, 125–151.

Dillon, D. G., Holmes, A. J., Jahn, A. L., Bogdan, R., Wald, L. L., & Pizzagalli, D. A. (2008). Dissociation of neural regions associated with anticipatory versus consummatory phases of incentive processing. *Psychophysiology, 45*, 36–49.

Dolcos, F., & McCarthy, G. (2006). Brain systems mediating cognitive interference by emotional distraction. *Journal of Neuroscience, 26*, 2072–2079.

Elliott, R., Sahakian, B. J., McKay, A. P., Herrod, J. J., Robbins, T. W., & Paykel, E. S. (1996). Neuropsychological impairments in unipolar depression: The influence of perceived failure on subsequent performance. *Psychological Medicine, 26*, 975–989.

Elliott, R., Sahakian, B. J., Herrod, J. J., Robbins, T. W., & Paykel, E. S. (1997). Abnormal response to negative feedback in unipolar depression: Evidence for a diagnosis specific impairment. *Journal of Neurology, Neurosurgery, and Psychiatry, 63*, 74–82.

Elliott, R., Sahakian, B. J., Michael, A., Paykel, E. S., & Dolan, R. J. (1998). Abnormal neural response to feedback on planning and guessing tasks in patients with unipolar depression. *Psychological Medicine, 28*, 559–571.

Elliott, R., Rubinsztein, J. S., Sahakian, B. J., & Dolan, R. J. (2002). The neural basis of mood-congruent processing biases in depression. *Archives of General Psychiatry, 59*, 597–604.

Epstein, J., Pan, H., Kocsis, J. H., Yang, Y., Butler, T., Chusid, J. et al. (2006). Lack of ventral striatal response to positive stimuli in depressed versus normal subjects. *American Journal of Psychiatry, 163*, 1784–1790.

Falkenstein, M., Hohnsbein, J., Hoormann, J., & Blanke, L. (1991). Effects of crossmodal divided attention on late ERP components. II. Error processing in choice reaction tasks. *Electroencephalography and Clinical Neurophysiology, 78*, 447–455.

Fitzgerald, P. B., Laird, A. R., Maller, J., & Daskalakis, Z. J. (2008). A meta-analytic study of changes in brain activation in depression. *Human Brain Mapping, 29*, 683–695.

Forbes, E. E., Shaw, D. S., & Dahl, R. E. (2006). Alterations in reward-related decision making in boys with recent and future depression. *Biological Psychiatry, 61*, 633–639.

Forbes, E. E., Christopher, M. J., Siegle, G. J., Ladouceur, C. D., Ryan, N. D., Carter, C. S. et al. (2006). Reward-related decision-making in pediatric major depressive disorder: An fMRI study. *Journal of Child Psychology and Psychiatry*, *47*, 1031–1040.

Gehring, W. J., Goss, B., Coles, M. G. H., Meyer, D. E., & Donchin, E. (1993). A neural system for error detection and compensation. *Psychological Science*, *4*, 385–390.

Gehring, W. J., & Willoughby, A. R. (2002). The medial frontal cortex and the rapid processing of monetary gains and losses. *Science*, *295*, 2279–2282.

Goeleven, E., De Raedt, R., Baert, S., & Koster, E. H. (2006). Deficient inhibition of emotional information in depression. *Journal of Affective Disorders*, *93*, 149–157.

Gottfried, J. A., O'Doherty, J., & Dolan, R. J. (2003). Encoding predictive reward value in human amygdala and orbitofrontal cortex. *Science*, *301*, 1104–1107.

Gotlib, I. H., Traill, S. K., Montoya, R. L., Joormann, J., & Chang, K. (2005). Attention and memory biases in the offspring of parents with bipolar disorder: Indications from a pilot study. *Journal of Child Psychology & Psychiatry*, *46*, 84–93.

Harvey, P. O., Pruessner, J., Czechowska, Y., & Lepage, M. (2007). Individual differences in trait anhedonia: A structural and functional magnetic resonance imaging study in non-clinical subjects. *Molecular Psychiatry*, *12*, 767–775.

Hasler, G., Drevets, W. C., Manji, H. K., & Charney, D. S. (2004). Discovering endophenotypes for major depression. *Neuropsychopharmacology*, *29*, 1765–1781.

Hatfield, T., Han, J.-S., Conley, M., Gallagher, M., & Holland, P. (1996). Neurotoxic lesions of the basolateral, but not central, amygdala interfere with Pavlovian second-order conditioning and reinforcer devaluation effects. *Journal of Neuroscience*, *16*, 5256–5265.

Henriques, J. B., & Davidson, R. J. (2000). Decreased responsiveness to reward in depression. *Cognition & Emotion*, *14*, 711–724.

Henriques, J. B., Glowacki, J. M., & Davidson, R. J. (1994). Reward fails to alter response bias in depression. *Journal of Abnormal Psychology*, *103*, 460–466.

Holland, P. C., & Gallagher, M. (2004). Amygdala-frontal interactions and reward expectancy. *Current Opinion in Neurobiology*, *14*, 148–155.

Holmes, A. J., & Pizzagalli, D. A. (2007). Task feedback effects on conflict monitoring and executive control: Relationship to subclinical measures of depression. *Emotion*, *7*, 68–76.

Holmes, A. J., & Pizzagalli, D. A. (2008). Spatio-temporal dynamics of error processing dysfunctions in major depressive disorder. *Archives of General Psychiatry*, *65*, 179–188.

Holroyd, C. B., & Coles, M. G. (2002). The neural basis of human error processing: Reinforcement learning, dopamine, and the error-related negativity. *Psychological Review*, *109*, 679–709.

Hornak, J., O'Doherty, J., Bramham, J., Rolls, E. T., Morris, R. G., Bullock, P. R. et al. (2004). Reward-related reversal learning after surgical excisions in orbito-frontal or dorsolateral prefrontal cortex in humans. *Journal of Cognitive Neuroscience*, *16*, 463–478.

Hundt, N. E., Nelson-Gray, R. O., Kimbrel, N. A., Mitchell, J. T., & Kwapil, T. R. (2007). The interaction of reinforcement sensitivity and life events in the prediction of anhedonic depression and mixed anxiety-depression symptoms. *Personality and Individual Differences*, *43*, 1001–1012.

Hyman, S. E. (2007). Can neuroscience be integrated into the DSM-V? *Nature Reviews Neuroscience*, *8*, 725–732.

Jensen, J., McIntosh, A. R., Crawley, A. P., Mikulis, D. J., Remington, G., & Kapur, S. (2003). Direct activation of the ventral striatum in anticipation of aversive stimuli. *Neuron*, *40*, 1251–1257.

Joormann, J., & Gotlib, I. H. (2006). Is this happiness I see? Biases in the identification of emotional facial expressions in depression and social phobia. *Journal of Abnormal Psychology*, *115*, 705–714.

Kalayam, B., & Alexopoulos, G. S. (2003). A preliminary study of left frontal region error negativity and symptom improvement in geriatric depression. *American Journal Psychiatry*, *160*, 2054–2056.

Kasch, K. L., Rottenberg, J., Arnow, B. A., & Gotlib, I. H. (2002). Behavioral activation and inhibition systems and the severity and course of depression. *Journal of Abnormal Psychology*, *111*, 589–597.

Keedwell, P. A., Andrew, C., Williams, S. C., Brammer, M. J., & Phillips, M. L. (2005). The neural correlates of anhedonia in major depressive disorder. *Biological Psychiatry*, *58*, 843–853.

Kennerley, S. W., Walton, M. E., Behrens, T. E. J., Buckley, M. J., & Rushworth, M. F. S. (2006). Optimal decision making and the anterior cingulate cortex. *Nature Neuroscience*, *7*, 940–947.

Kerns, J. G., Cohen, J. D., MacDonald, A. W., Cho, R. Y., Stenger, V. A., & Carter, C. S. (2004). Anterior cingulate conflict monitoring and adjustments in control. *Science*, *303*, 1023–1026.

Knutson, B., Adams, C. M., Fong, G. W., & Hommer, D. (2001). Anticipation of increasing monetary reward selectively recruits nucleus accumbens. *Journal of Neuroscience*, *21*, RC159.

Knutson, B., & Cooper, J. C. (2005). Functional magnetic resonance imaging of reward prediction. *Current Opinion in Neurology*, *18*, 411–417.

Knutson, B., Fong, G. W., Bennett, S. M., Adams, C. M., & Hommer, D. (2003). A region of mesial prefrontal cortex tracks monetarily rewarding outcomes: Characterization with rapid event-related fMRI. *Neuroimage*, *18*, 263–272.

Koster, E. H., De Raedt, R., Goeleven, E., Franck, E., & Crombez, G. (2005). Mood-congruent attentional bias in dysphoria: Maintained attention to and impaired disengagement from negative information. *Emotion*, *5*, 446–455.

LaBar, K. S., Gatenby, J. C., Gore, J. C., LeDoux, J. E., & Phelps, E. A. (1998). Human amygdala activation during conditioned fear acquisition and extinction: A mixed-trial fMRI study. *Neuron*, *20*, 937–945.

LaBar, K. S., LeDoux, J. E., Spencer, D. D., & Phelps, E. A. (1995). Impaired fear conditioning following unilateral temporal lobectomy in humans. *Journal of Neuroscience*, *15*, 6846–6855.

Lawrence, N. S., Williams, A. M., Surguladze, S., Giampietro, V., Brammer, M. J., Andrew, C. et al. (2004) Subcortical and ventral prefrontal cortical neural responses to facial expressions distinguish patients with bipolar disorder and major depression. *Biological Psychiatry, 15*, 578–587.

LeDoux, J. E. (1995). Emotion: Clues from the brain. *Annual Review of Psychology, 46*, 209–235.

Magno, E., Foxe, J. J., Molholm, S., Robertson, I. H., & Garavan, H. (2006). The anterior cingulate and error avoidance. *Journal of Neuroscience, 26*, 4769–4773.

Malkova, L., Gaffan, D., & Murray, E. A. (1997). Excitotoxic lesions of the amygdala fail to produce impairment in visual learning for auditory secondary reinforcement but interfere with reinforcer devaluation effects in rhesus monkeys. *Journal of Neuroscience, 17*, 6011–6020.

Mayberg, H. S. (1997). Limbic-cortical dysregulation: A proposed model of depression. *Journal of Neuropsychiatry & Clinical Neurosciences, 9*, 471–481.

McFarland, B. R., Shankman, S. A., Tenke, C. E., Bruder, G. E., & Klein, D. N. (2006). Behavioral activation system deficits predict the six-month course of depression. *Journal of Affective Disorders, 91*, 229–234.

Meehl, P. E. (1975). Hedonic capacity: Some conjectures. *Bulletin of the Menninger Clinic, 39*, 295–307.

Meyer-Lindenberg, A., & Weinberger, D. R. (2006). Intermediate phenotypes and genetic mechanisms of psychiatric disorders. *Nature Review Neuroscience, 7*, 818–827.

Miltner, W. H. R., Braun, C. H., & Coles, M. G. H. (1997). Event-related brain potentials following incorrect feedback in a time-estimation task: Evidence for a "generic" neural system for error detection. *Journal of Cognitive Neuroscience, 9*, 788–798.

Mitterschiffthaler, M. T., Kumari, V., Malhi, G. S., Brown, R. G., Giampietro, V. P., Brammer, M. J. et al. (2003). Neural response to pleasant stimuli in anhedonia: An fMRI study. *Neuroreport, 10*, 177–182.

Must, A., Szabo, Z., Bodi, N., Szasz, A., Janka, Z., & Keri, S. (2006). Sensitivity to reward and punishment and the prefrontal cortex in major depression. *Journal of Affective Disorders, 90*, 209–215.

Nelson, R. E., & Craighead, W. E. (1977). Selective recall of positive and negative feedback, self-control behaviors, and depression. *Journal of Abnormal Psychology, 86*, 379–388.

Ochsner, K. N., & Gross, J. J. (2005). The cognitive control of emotion. *Trends in Cognitive Sciences, 9*, 242–249.

O'Doherty, J., Rolls, E. T., Francis, S., Bowtell, R., & McGlone, F. (2001). Representation of pleasant and aversive taste in the human brain. *Journal of Neurophysiology, 85*, 1315–1321.

O'Doherty, J., Kringelbach, M. L., Rolls, E. T., Hornak, J., & Andrews, C. (2001). Abstract reward and punishment representations in the human orbitofrontal cortex. *Nature Neuroscience, 4*, 95–102.

Pickens, C. P., Saddoris, M. P., Setlow, B., Gallagher, M., Holland, P. C., & Schoenbaum, G. (2003). Different roles for orbitofrontal cortex and basolateral amygdala in a reinforcer devaluation task. *Journal of Neuroscience, 23*, 11078–11084.

Pierson, A., Ragot, R., Ripoche, A., & Lesevre, N. (1987). Electrophysiological changes elicited by auditory stimuli given a positive or negative value: A study comparing anhedonic with hedonic subjects. *International Journal of Psychophysiology, 5,* 107–123.

Pinto-Meza, A., Caseras, X., Soler, J., Puigdemont, D., Perez, V., & Torrubia, R. (2006). Behavioural inhibition and behavioural activation systems in current and recovered major depression participants. *Personality and Individual Differences, 40,* 215–226.

Pizzagalli, D. A., Bogdan, R., Ratner, K. G., & Jahn, A. L. (2007). Increased perceived stress is associated with blunted hedonic capacity: Potential implications for depression research. *Behaviour Research and Therapy, 45,* 2742–2753.

Pizzagalli, D. A., Jahn, A. L., & O'Shea, J. P. (2005). Toward an objective characterization of an anhedonic phenotype: A signal-detection approach. *Biological Psychiatry, 57,* 319–327.

Pizzagalli, D. A., Oakes, T. R., & Davidson, R. J. (2003). Coupling of theta activity and glucose metabolism in the human rostral anterior cingulate cortex: An EEG/PET study of normal and depressed subjects. *Psychophysiology, 40,* 939–949.

Pizzagalli, D. A., Peccoralo, L. A., Davidson, R. J., & Cohen, J. D. (2006). Resting anterior cingulate activity and abnormal responses to errors in subjects with elevated depressive symptoms: A 128-channel EEG study. *Human Brain Mapping, 27,* 185–201.

Pizzagalli, D. A., Sherwood, R. J., Henriques, J. B., & Davidson, R. J. (2005). Frontal brain asymmetry and reward responsiveness: A source-localization study. *Psychological Science, 10,* 805–813.

Rescorla, R. A., & Wagner, A. R. (1972). A theory of Pavlovian conditioning: Variations in the effectiveness of reinforcement and nonreinforcement. In A. H. Black & W. F. Prokasy (Eds.), *Classical conditioning II: Current theory and research* (pp. 64–99). New York: Appleton-Century-Crofts.

Rogers, R. D., Ramnani, N., Mackay, C., Wilson, J. L., Jezzard, P., Carter, C. S. et al. (2004). Distinct portions of anterior cingulate cortex and medial prefrontal cortex are activated by reward processing in separable phases of decision-making cognition. *Biological Psychiatry, 55,* 594–602.

Rolls, E. T., O'Doherty, J., Kringelbach, M. L., Francis, S., Bowtell, R., & McGlone, F. (2003). Representations of pleasant and painful touch in the human orbitofrontal and cingulate cortices. *Cerebral Cortex, 13,* 308–317.

Roth, D., Rehm, L. P., & Rozensky, R. H. (1980). Self-reward, self-punishment and depression. *Psychological Reports, 47,* 3–7.

Rozensky, R. H., Rehm, L. P., Pry, G., & Roth, D. (1977). Depression and self-reinforcement behavior in hospitalized patients. *Journal of Behavior Therapy and Experimental Psychiatry, 8,* 35–38.

Ruchsow, M., Herrnberger, B., Wiesend, C., Gron, G., Spitzer, M., & Kiefer, M. (2004). The effect of erroneous responses on response monitoring in patients with major depressive disorder: A study with event-related potentials. *Psychophysiology, 41,* 833–840.

Rushworth, M. F. S., Behrens, T. E. J., Rudebeck, P. H., & Walton, M. E. (2007). Contrasting roles for cingulate and orbitofrontal cortex in decisions and social behavior. *Trends in Cognitive Sciences, 11,* 168–176.

Schultz, W. (2007). Behavioral dopamine signals. *Trends in Neuroscience, 30*, 203–210.

Shankman, S. A., Klein, D. N., Tenke, C.E., & Bruder, G. E. (2007). Reward sensitivity in depression: A biobehavioral study. *Journal of Abnormal Psychology, 116*, 95–104.

Sheline, Y. I., Barch, D. M., Donnelly, J. M., Ollinger, J. M., Snyder, A. Z., & Mintun, M. A. (2001). Increased amygdala response to masked emotional faces in depressed subjects resolves with antidepressant treatment: An fMRI study. *Biological Psychiatry, 50*, 651–658.

Siegle, G. J., Steinhauer, S. R., Thase, M. E., Stenger, V. A., & Carter, C. S. (2002). Can't shake that feeling: Event-related fMRI assessment of sustained amygdala activity in response to emotional information in depressed individuals. *Biological Psychiatry, 51*, 693–707.

Siegle, G. J., Thompson, W., Carter, C. S., Steinhauer, S. R., & Thase, M. E. (2007). Increased amygdala and decreased dorsolateral prefrontal BOLD responses in unipolar depression: Related and independent features. *Biological Psychiatry, 61*, 198–209.

Sloan, D. M., Strauss, M. E., & Wisner, K. L. (2001). Diminished response to pleasant stimuli by depressed women. *Journal of Abnormal Psychology, 110*, 488–493.

Spijker, J., Bijl, R. V., de Graaf, R., & Nolen, W. A. (2001). Determinants of poor 1-year outcome of DSM-III-R major depression in the general population: Results of the Netherlands Mental Health Survey and Incidence Study (NEMESIS). *Acta Psychiatrica Scandinavica, 103*, 122–130.

Steele, J. D., Kumar, P., & Ebmeier, K. P. (2007). Blunted response to feedback information in depressive illness. *Brain, 130*, 2367–2374.

Steele, J. D., Meyer, M., & Ebmeier, K. P. (2004). Neural predictive error signal correlates with depressive illness severity in a game paradigm. *Neuroimage, 23*, 269–280.

Surguladze, S. A., Young, A. W., & Senior, C. (2004). Recognition accuracy and response bias to happy and sad facial expressions in patients with major depression. *Neuropsychology, 18*, 212–218.

Thibodeau, R., Jorgensen, R. S., & Kim, S. (2006). Depression, anxiety, and resting frontal EEG asymmetry: A meta-analytic review. *Journal of Abnormal Psychology, 115*, 715–729.

Tremblay, L. K., Naranjo, C. A., Cardenas, L., Herrmann, N., & Busto, U. E. (2002). Probing brain reward system function in major depressive disorder: Altered response to dextroamphetamine. *Archives of General Psychiatry, 59*, 409–416.

Tremblay, L. K., Naranjo, C. A., Graham, S. J., Herrmann, N., Mayberg, H. S., Hevenor, S., & Busto, U. E. (2005). Functional neuroanatomical substrates of altered reward processing in major depressive disorder revealed by a dopaminergic probe. *Archives of General Psychiatry, 62*, 1228–1236.

Tucker, D. M., Luu, P., Frishkoff, G., Quiring, J., & Poulsen, C. (2003). Frontolimbic response to negative feedback in clinical depression. *Journal of Abnormal Psychology, 112*, 667–678.

Ungless, M. A. (2004). Dopamine: The salient issue. *Trends in Neurosciences, 27*, 702–706.

Walton, M. E., Kennerley, S. W., Bannerman, D. M., Phillips, P. E. M., & Rushworth, M. F. S. (2006). Weighing up the benefits of work: Behavioral and neural analyses of effort-related decision making. *Neural Networks, 19*, 1302–1314.

Wener, A. E., & Rehm, L. P. (1975). Depressive affect: A test of behavioral hypotheses. *Journal of Abnormal Psychology, 84*, 221–227.

Wittling, W. (1995). Brain asymmetry in the control of autonomic-physiological activity. In R. J. Davidson & K. Hughdal (Eds.), *Brain asymmetry* (pp. 305–357). Cambridge, MA: MIT Press.

Zink, C. F., Pagnoni, G., Martin, M. E., Dhamala, M., & Berns, G. S. (2003). Human striatal response to salient nonrewarding stimuli. *Journal of Neuroscience, 23*, 8092–8097.

Section IV

Cooperation and trust

CHAPTER NINE

Neural bases of social decision making

Alan G. Sanfey and James K. Rilling

INTRODUCTION

The study of decision making tries to understand our ability to process multiple alternatives and choose an optimal course of action, with a good decision being one that chooses the best available option in the face of characteristic uncertainty about the possible consequences. This ability has historically been studied from many perspectives, with many different disciplines examining aspects of decision making. Foremost of these research directions have been those of economics, psychology, and neuroscience.

Approaches from economics have primarily focused on describing optimal decision behavior at a market level. However, in recent times the emergence of psychological models of decision making have offered more accurate descriptive accounts of individual behavior by taking into consideration the constraints of the human information processing system. Often though, these psychological models lack the mathematical sophistication and rigor of the economic approaches. In concert, neuroscientific studies have used single-cell recording approaches to examine lower-level, perceptual choices in many animals, but these "micro-level" decisions are often difficult to reconcile with the decisions made by humans in experimental studies. These disparate approaches have all made important advances, but there has been surprisingly little integration of findings across fields, with researchers often unaware of empirical discoveries and

223

theoretical approaches from other areas that have immediate relevance for their own investigations. The recent emergence of an interdisciplinary field, popularly known as neuroeconomics (e.g., Sanfey, Loewenstein, Cohen, & McClure, 2006), has begun to redress this lack of integration, with its proponents seeking to better understand decision making by taking into account the cognitive and neural constraints on this process, as investigated by psychology and neuroscience, while in addition utilizing the mathematical decision models and tasks that have emerged from economics. By using these complementary strengths, this approach offers a promising avenue to examine decision making at different levels of analysis and, eventually, to arrive at a comprehensive account of how this process operates.

Traditional economic models of decision making, such as Subjective Expected Utility Theory, propose several aspects of a decision that must be integrated in order to choose the best option. Broadly speaking, these are the subjective values of the potential outcomes that may occur (how each possible outcome feels to us—the subjective utility) and the likelihood of these outcomes actually occurring (how probable is each outcome—the subjective probability). The subjective utility for each outcome is then weighted by its estimated probability, and the alternative with the highest expected utility should be chosen. In general, the experimental study of decision making has examined choices with rather clearly defined probabilities and outcomes, in which decision makers select between options that have direct consequences for only themselves. The typical type of decision task investigated involves choices between monetary gambles—for example, participants might be asked whether they prefer a 50% chance of $25 or a 100% chance of $10. Though the outcomes and likelihoods of these problems can be quite complex, it is important to note that these decisions are typically made in "social isolation"; that is, the outcome rarely affects anyone other than the decision maker.

However, given that humans work and play in highly complex social environments, many of our most important decisions are often made in the context of direct or indirect social interactions. Indeed many of our everyday choices are often additionally dependent on the concomitant decisions of others; for example, when we are deciding to ask someone on a date or when we are entering a business negotiation. The nature of decision making may change fundamentally when the outcome of a decision is dependent on the decisions of others. For example, the standard expected utility computation, outlined above, that underlies many of the existing theories and models of decision making is complicated by the fact that we must also attempt to infer the values and probabilities of our partner or opponent in attempting to reach the optimal decision. However, these types of situation have rarely been studied in the decision-making literature to date.

A further reason to focus on the neural basis of decisions in the context of social interactions stems from evolutionary considerations. Primate social behavior is more complex than that of most other mammals, in part because primates form social alliances and coalitions that compete with one another. On average, primates also have larger brains for their body size than other mammals (Martin, 1990). Moreover, relative neocortex size is positively correlated with social group size, a presumed proxy for social complexity, across anthropoid primates (Dunbar, 1998). These facts suggest that large primate brains may have evolved in response to social complexity in order to support greater social intelligence. If humans represent an extension of this primate trend, then a reasonable claim is that the human brain was designed in some measure to deal with complex social interactions, and that our brain's decision-making circuitry likely evolved in part to support these types of decisions.

To begin to address some of the above questions, researchers have begun to investigate the psychological and neural correlates of social decisions using tasks derived from a branch of economics known as Game Theory. These tasks, though simple and straightforward, require sophisticated reasoning about the motivations of other players in the task. Recent research has combined these paradigms with a variety of neuroscientific methods in an effort to gain a more detailed picture of social decision making.

This chapter will focus on research investigating social decision making in two person interactions, although of course social decision making often involves considerably more than this. Nevertheless, even in the course of dyadic social interactions, humans are regularly confronted with a wide range of decisions that have far-reaching consequences for the welfare of both themselves and others. Should I affiliate with or trust this person? Should I compete with or be deferential toward this person? How should I respond to a breach of trust by this person? What is the socially appropriate thing to do in this situation? Research, from across a number of different fields using different approaches and techniques, is beginning to reach answers about these important questions.

Game theory

Game Theory offers the twin advantages for the investigation of social exchange of simple, yet powerful, tasks and well-specified mathematical models. The seminal development in this field was the work of von Neumann and Morgenstern (1947) whose initial work established the foundations of the discipline. In essence, Game Theory is a collection of rigorous models attempting to understand and explain situations in which decision makers must interact with one another, with these models applicable to such diverse scenarios as bidding in auctions, salary negotiations, and jury decisions, to name but a few.

A common standard criticism of the economic modeling approach typified by Utility and Game Theories is that observed decision behavior deviates, often quite substantially, from the predictions of the standard model. This is true for the predictions of Utility Theory for individual decisions (Kahneman, Slovic, & Tversky, 1982), as well as Game Theory for social decisions. Classical Game Theory predicts that a group of rational, self-interested players will make decisions to reach outcomes, known as Nash equilibria (Nash, 1950), from which no player can increase his or her own payoff unilaterally. However, ample research has shown that players rarely play according to these strategies (e.g., Camerer, 2003). In reality, decision makers deviate from the predictions of the classical model by being both less selfish and more willing to consider factors such as reciprocity and equity.

Despite these valid criticisms of the economic approach, the well-characterized tasks and formal modeling approach offered by Game Theory provides a useful foundation for the study of decisions in a social context. From an experimental standpoint, the mathematical framework of Game Theory provides a common language in which findings from different research approaches can be compared, and deviations from model predictions quantified. Additionally, these tasks produce a surprisingly varied and rich pattern of decision making, while employing very simple rules. And importantly, behavioral and neurobiological studies of social decision making are proving instructive in understanding the nature of the discrepancies between model predictions and observed behavior. For example, the empirical observations that are being uncovered may well assist in building "better" models of economic theory. In fact, this is already occurring, with findings from behavioral economics being used to add social utility functions (e.g., Bolton & Ockenfels, 2000) to many of the existing models in order to better fit observed data.

TASKS

As mentioned above, Game Theory has provided a very useful set of tools with which to examine the processes and factors underlying social decision making, and a multitude of recent studies, using many different methodologies, have leveraged these tasks to provide a unique window onto the brain basis of choices made in a social context. In this section we review briefly the set of tasks that have been employed in this endeavor, and describe the behavioral responses that participants typically make in these situations (for a useful summary of the findings outlined in this section, see Camerer, 2003). The set of games generally used can broadly be divided into three categories—bargaining, reciprocal exchange, and coordination games.

Bargaining games

One specific focus of these games is bargaining behavior, with the family of Dictator and Ultimatum games often used to examine both how negotiations are struck, and perhaps more interestingly psychologically, how people respond to conditions of both equality and inequality. In the Dictator Game, one player (the Proposer) decides how much of an endowment to award to the second player (the Responder). Allocations in this game measure pure altruism, in that the Proposer sacrifices personal gain to share the endowment with their partner. The Ultimatum Game (Guth, Schmittberger, & Schwarze, 1982) examines strategic thinking in the context of two-player bargaining. In the Ultimatum Game, the Proposer and Responder are also asked to divide a sum of money, with the Proposer specifying how this sum should be divided between the two. In this case though, the Responder has the option of accepting or rejecting the offer. If the offer is accepted, the sum is divided as proposed. However, if it is rejected, neither player receives anything. In either event the game is over, that is, there are no subsequent rounds in which to reach agreement. If people are motivated purely by self-interest, the Responder should accept any offer and, knowing this, the Proposer will offer the smallest nonzero amount. However, this Nash equilibrium prediction is at odds with observed behavior and, at least in most industrialized cultures, low offers of less than 20% of the total amount are rejected about half of the time. There are some interesting differences in more traditional cultures (Henrich et al., 2005), but in general the probability of rejection increases substantially as offers decrease in magnitude. Thus, people's choices in the Ultimatum Game do not conform to a model in which decisions are driven purely by self-interest, and, as will be discussed below, neuroscience has begun to offer clues as to the mechanisms underlying these decisions.

Reciprocal exchange games

Reciprocal exchange games are another common focus of experimental economics, exemplified by Trust games and closely related Prisoner's Dilemma games. In the Trust Game, a player (the Investor) must decide how much of an endowment to invest with a partner (the Trustee) in the game. Prior to this investment being transferred to the Trustee, the experimenter multiplies this money by some factor (usually tripled or quadrupled), and then the Trustee has the opportunity to return some or all of this increased amount back to the Investor, but, importantly, need not return any money if he or she decides against it. If the Trustee honors trust, and returns money to the Investor, both players end up with a higher monetary payoff than was originally obtained. However, if the Trustee abuses trust and keeps the entire amount, the Investor ends up with a loss. As the Investor and Trustee interact only once during the game, Game Theory predicts that a rational and selfish Trustee will never honor the trust given by the Investor. The Investor, realizing this, should never place trust in the first place, and so will invest zero in the transaction. Despite these rather grim theoretical predictions, in most studies of the Trust Game a majority of investors do send some amount of their money to the Trustee, with this trust typically reciprocated.

The well-studied Prisoner's Dilemma Game is similar to the Trust Game, except that in the standard version both players simultaneously choose whether or not to trust each other without knowledge of their partner's choice. In the Prisoner's Dilemma Game, each player chooses to either cooperate or not with their opponent, with their payoff dependent on the interaction of the two choices. Using some standard monetary payoffs, the largest payoff for the player occurs when the player defects (D) and the partner cooperates (C), with a payoff for this combination of decisions being \$3 (DC = \$3). The second largest payoff is for mutual cooperation (CC = \$2), followed by mutual defection (DD = \$1), and finally player cooperation combined with partner defection (CD = \$0). Each outcome of the game can be said to correspond to a different outcome of a social interaction, and typically elicits a different set of social emotions. The Nash equilibrium for the Prisoner's Dilemma Game is mutual defection, which, interestingly, is in fact a worse outcome for both players than mutual cooperation, but again, in most iterations of the game players exhibit much more trust than expected, with mutual cooperation occurring about 50% of the time, especially in early rounds of the game. Mutual cooperation is often associated with friendship, love, trust, or obligation; mutual defection with feelings of rejection and hatred; cooperation by one and defection by the other typically results in the cooperator feeling anger or indignation, and in the defector feeling anxiety, guilt, or elation from successfully exploiting the partner to their advantage. The Prisoner's Dilemma Game, like the Trust Game, can be played either "single-shot", in which case there is a single interaction between the two players after which the game is over, or "iterated" where the game is made up of a number of rounds between the players.

These games are good models for the reciprocal exchange of favors. Given that favors are rarely exchanged simultaneously in real life, the Trust

Game at first seems a better model for real-life behavior than the Prisoner's Dilemma Game. However, the Prisoner's Dilemma Game choices in round n can also be viewed as a response to the partner's choice in round $n - 1$. As mentioned, both Prisoner's Dilemma Game and Trust Game can be played as either single-shot or iterated interactions. In the single-shot versions, cooperative moves by the Trustee in the Trust Game such as a large amount of money being sent over to the Investor, or by either partner in the Prisoner's Dilemma Game, are unambiguously altruistic insofar as individuals are sacrificing personal gain so that their partner can receive more. In the iterated versions of the games, in which several consecutive rounds are played with the same partner, cooperative choices are not necessarily selfless, since consistent cooperation with a reciprocating partner will generally yield the player higher cumulative earnings over the long term than will a non-cooperative strategy that often settles into the equilibrium outcome of mutual selfishness. While economists have emphasized the importance that these interactions be anonymous in order to eliminate reputation effects that could bias choices, others argue that humans are evolutionarily unprepared for such nonnaturalistic social interactions and that subjects should meet and know the identity of their playing partners. Both anonymous and nonanonymous versions of these games have been studied with neuroimaging.

A final type of game, Public Goods games, are a generalized form of the Prisoner's Dilemma Game, with each player able to invest a proportion of an endowment provided by the experimenter in a public good, which is then increased in value and shared back with all players. The self-interested solution here is to hold back on investment and hope that everyone else contributes the maximum amount, modeling situations such as environmental pollution or upkeep of a public park. However, as in Prisoner's Dilemma Games, players on average contribute about half of their endowment to the public good.

Coordination games

Finally, coordination games that typically call for mixed-strategy equilibrium solutions, such as Matching Pennies and the Inspection Game, offer insights into how we assess the preferences of others and choose accordingly. For example, in Matching Pennies, each player chooses between two alternatives (such as heads or tails, or red or black). One player (the matcher) wins if the two choices are the same (heads/heads or tails/tails), and the other (the nonmatcher) wins if they are not (heads/tails or tails/heads). The Nash equilibrium is to select the two alternatives randomly with equal probabilities, but players typically approach this game by attempting to infer the strategy of our opponent, thus providing a window into how we use Theory of Mind processes to assist our strategic decision making.

Summary

In many of the cases discussed here, such as cooperation in a Prisoner's Dilemma Game, generous offers in a Trust Game, fair offers in the Ultimatum Game, and contribution in public goods experiments, it is unclear whether the decisions emerge from strategic or altruistic motivations. Do I offer you 50% of the pot in an Ultimatum Game because I value fairness or because I fear you will reject anything less? Examining these games in a neural context can begin to offers clues as to the motivations behind the decisions. The combination of Game Theory and neuroscience, therefore, offers a useful set of tasks, a rigorous mathematical modeling approach, and techniques to allow us to begin probing the underlying processes of social decision making.

RESEARCH METHODS

Before discussing specific research findings, it is useful to outline the primary neuroscientific methods that have been employed to examine questions of how the brain processes social decisions. This section will briefly review the primary methodological tools that have been used to answer these questions.

Probably the most widely used method is that of functional neuroimaging, principally functional magnetic resonance imaging (fMRI), though several studies have employed positron emission tomography (PET). Both techniques measure blood flow in the brain, which has been reliably demonstrated as a good correlate of neural activity. Examining the neural correlates of social decision making has been a relatively recent development within the field of cognitive neuroscience, and indeed it is only in the last several years that there has been a critical mass of studies allowing inferences to be made about the brain organization of decision processes.

Many early fMRI studies used as stimuli static, two-dimensional pictures of human faces, and asked participants to either passively view these faces, or judge them on some attribute, such as age (e.g., Winston, Strange, O'Doherty, & Dolan, 2002). Similarly, other studies have examined the neural basis of social processing by instructing subjects to read stories or look at cartoons and then make assessments of these scenarios. For example, researchers have used these methods to study both moral decision making (Greene, Sommerville, Nystrom, Darley, & Cohen, 2001) and the ability to assess the mental state of another (Gallagher, Happe, Brunswick, Fletcher, Frith, & Frith, 2000).

While these methods have made interesting claims about the neural underpinnings of social decisions, valid questions can be raised regarding the ecological validity of these paradigms. Is the pattern of brain activation in response to reasoning about hypothetical, fictitious scenarios the same as when grappling with significant real-life social problems? Is thinking about the actions of another person the same as making a consequential decision based on these actions?

More recent approaches have sought to embed participants in an actual consequential social interaction with another player (e.g., McCabe, Houser, Ryan, Smith, & Trouard, 2001; Rilling, Gutman, Zeh, Pagnoni, Berns, & Kilts, 2002) while undergoing scanning using fMRI. Studies in this vein have made important progress in understanding the neural processes underlying cooperative and competitive behavior, as will be described in the next section. An additional and potentially even more useful technology has recently been developed that makes it possible to image brain function in two or more interacting partners simultaneously, by utilizing network connections between two separate scanners (e.g., Montague et al., 2002). These "hyperscanning" approaches have advantages not only in terms of the efficiency of data collection, but also will potentially allow imaging of coordinated patterns of brain activity in small groups.

Another method that has been employed in several recent studies is that of transcranial magnetic stimulation (TMS). This approach uses portable equipment. The brain area's involvement in social decisions can then be assessed directly (e.g., Van't Wout, Kahn, Sanfey, & Aleman, 2005). The potential of this method is obvious; however, some technical challenges still remain before very clear inferences can be made regarding the effect of TMS. In a similar vein, patients with circumscribed brain damage to particular regions can be tested in these tasks to see if the damaged brain area has an impact on social decision making (e.g., Koenigs & Tranel, 2007).

Other approaches have sought to manipulate the neurochemical systems of the brain, and then examine performance on social games. One good candidate neurotransmitter for involvement in these processes is serotonin, which has long been thought to help regulate social and emotional states. For example, one study that used dietary tryptophan depletion to decrease brain serotonin levels showed a corresponding decrease in cooperative behavior (e.g., Wood, Rilling, Sanfey, Bhagwagar, & Rogers, 2006). Other experiments have targeted oxytocin (OT), a neuropeptide involved in affiliative behaviors. In one study, intranasal self-administration of OT increased trust behavior (Kosfeld, Heinrichs, Zak, Fischbacher, & Fehr, 2005).

A final useful method may be to leverage the social decision-making deficits commonly seen in various psychiatric disorders. For example, depressed patients often withdraw from social interactions, choosing instead to be alone. Psychopathic individuals often manipulate and object-ify others, making it difficult for them to establish stable, long-term bonds, and patients suffering from schizophrenia typically exhibit pronounced disturbances in their social behavior. Examining the neural bases of these disorders in the context of the decision-making deficits could provide add-itional information as to the nature of these processes, and of course could have the ancillary benefit of potentially suggesting treatments that may help alleviate some of the problems suffered by these populations.

CURRENT RESEARCH DIRECTIONS

The combination of the innovative methods and novel tasks outlined in the previous sections has allowed researchers to begin to assess brain func-tion as players interact with one another while playing economic games with real consequences. Though the very recent development of this field means that there are relatively few definitive results to date, studies have outlined a number of initial findings with respect to the neural underpinnings of social decision making.

Bargaining: Deliberative and affective processing

Bargaining tasks, such as Dictator and Ultimatum Games, have helped illuminate the complex nature of processing that occurs while engaged in a social decision-making situation. These games are particularly interesting from a psychological standpoint in that they readily evoke often quite powerful feelings of competitiveness or camaraderie. Despite the fact that participants are playing with "house money", that they are typically partnered with strangers, and that rather small stakes are used in most laboratory experiments, participants often report feeling quite angry about offers made to them that they perceive as unfair (Pillutla & Murnighan, 1996). For example, as noted above, offers of $1 from a $10 Ultimatum pot are routinely rejected.

One speculation is that these emotional reactions may be a mechanism by which perceived inequity is avoided, and indeed that they may have evolved precisely to foster fairness and reputation development (Nowak, Page, & Sigmund, 2000). Interestingly, even capuchin monkeys respond negatively to unequal distributions of rewards by refusing to participate in an effortful task if they witness a conspecific receiving more reward for the same amount of work (Brosnan & de Waal, 2003).

Classical models of decision making have largely ignored the influence of affective processes on how decisions are made, but recent research using neuroscientific approaches has begun to demonstrate the powerful effect these factors play. These studies offer the potential to examine the causal relationships between affective processing and subsequent social decisions, as well as to investigate whether areas specialized for the processing of basic emotions may be co-opted for more complex affective reactions.

Early work in this domain showed that patients suffering damage to the ventromedial frontal cortex (VMPFC) who were presented with associated emotional deficits were impaired on gambling tasks (Bechara, Damasio, Tranel, & Damasio, 1997), demonstrating experimentally that emotion plays a vital role in determining decisions. Further research using both standard laboratory tasks (Mellers, Schwartz, & Ritov, 1999) and functional neuroimaging (Coricelli, Critchley, Joffily, O'Doherty, Sirigu, & Dolan, 2005) have shown the biasing effect of anticipated regret and disappointment on decision making, demonstrating that people avoid situations that they predict could cause feelings of regret, even if this behavior comes with a monetary cost to themselves.

In terms of research directly studying social decisions, an fMRI study (Sanfey, Rilling, Aronson, Nystrom, & Cohen, 2003) examined unfair behavior in the Ultimatum Game and found a brain area, namely the anterior insula, that exhibited greater activation as the unfairness (i.e., inequity) of the offer increased. Further, this area was more active when playing with another human than with a computer partner, and, importantly, the activation of this area reliably predicted the player's decision to either accept or reject the offer, with rejections associated with significantly higher activation than acceptances. In a related study involving an iterated Prisoner's Dilemma Game, the anterior insula was activated by unreciprocated cooperation, and functional connectivity between the anterior insula and lateral orbitofrontal cortex (OFC) in response to unreciprocated cooperation predicted subsequent defection (Rilling et al., 2008). Finally, the same region has been activated in relation to empathic responses when witnessing a fair Prisoner's Dilemma Game partner receive painful electric shocks (Singer, Seymour, O'Doherty, Klaas, Dolan, & Frith, 2006).

The presence of anterior insula activations in these studies is notable, as this brain region is also responsive to physically painful and disgusting stimuli (Calder, 2001; Derbyshire, Jones, & Gyulai, 1997). In addition, it is as involved in mapping physiological states of the body, including touch and visceral sensations of autonomic arousal (Critchley, Elliott, Mathias, & Dolan, 2000), as it is in aversive conditioning. These results suggest that the anterior insula and associated emotion processing areas may play a role in marking a social interaction as aversive, and thus discouraging trust of the partner in the future.

Separate measures of emotional arousal provide support for this hypothesis. An Ultimatum Game study measuring skin conductance responses, used as an autonomic index of affective state, found that the skin conductance activity was higher for unfair offers, and as with insula activation, discriminated between acceptances and rejections of these offers (Van't Wout, Kahn, Sanfey, & Aleman, 2006). Further, in recent studies both VMPFC patients (Koenigs & Tranel, 2007) and normal players primed with negative emotional state (Harle & Sanfey, 2007) reject unfair offers more frequently than controls in both cases, suggesting that the regulation of affective processing is important in decision making in games.

Activation in regions of the frontal lobes was also observed in the aforementioned Ultimatum Game fMRI study (Sanfey et al., 2003) in relation to unfair offers. One interpretation of this activation is of a mechanism by which other more deliberative goals (such as reputation maintenance or the desire to make money) can be implemented. In two novel studies (Knoch, Pascual-Leone, Meyer, Treyer, & Fehr, 2006; Van't Wout et al., 2005), TMS was used to disrupt processing in the dorsolateral prefrontal cortex while players were making decisions about offers in an Ultimatum Game. In both cases, stimulation increased acceptance rate of unfair offers as compared to a control, non-stimulated, condition providing strong evidence for a causal relationship between activation in this area and social decisions. Though TMS is still rather a crude tool, thus making clear-cut interpretations of behavior challenging, use of this technology to experimentally test hypotheses generated by this early series of studies will be important in progressing the field.

Both ethnographic evidence (Sober & Wilson, 1998) as well as experiments in behavioral economics have shown that some people will only uphold fairness norms under threat of punishment (Fehr & Gachter, 2002). Thus, sensitivity to the threat of punishment is an important motive for norm-abiding behavior in some people. In an fMRI study (Spitzer, Fischbacher, Herrnberger, Gron, & Fehr, 2007), players were scanned while playing two different games. In one game, resembling a dictator game, player A received a monetary endowment that they could distribute freely between themselves and another player (player B). In this game, player B is a passive recipient of player A's monetary transfer. In the other game, player B could choose to pay money to financially punish player A after having been informed of player A's decision. Player A transferred substantially more money to player B in the punishment compared with the nonpunishment condition. Those players who showed the largest change in monetary transfer from the nonpunishment to the punishment condition also showed the greatest increase in activation of the lateral orbitofrontal cortex (OFC) across conditions. The lateral OFC is involved in the evaluation of punishing stimuli that may lead to behavioral changes (Kringelbach & Rolls, 2004). Both studies suggest that the lateral OFC motivates norm-abiding decision making in response to the threat of punishment.

A final potentially fruitful avenue of research in these games is in using neuropeptides such as OT and vasopressin (AVP), described above, which are known to facilitate social affiliation in nonhuman animals. In a Trust Game (Kosfeld et al., 2005), intranasal administration of oxytocin led to an increase in trust placed by Investors. This effect was not general for all type of decisions, and was not observed for risk or in games with random outcomes, but rather was specific for consequential social interactions with other humans. Intranasal OT administration has recently been combined with fMRI to assess the impact of OT on the neural response to fearful/threatening faces and scenes (Kirsch et al., 2005). Compared with placebo, OT decreased activation in the amygdala for both types of fearful stimuli. These results are consistent with evidence that OT reduces stress and anxiety (Heinrichs, Baumgartner, Kirschbaum, & Ehlert, 2003; McCarthy, McDonald, Brooks, & Goldman, 1996), and suggest a potential mechanism by which OT could increase trust; namely, by reducing the fear of betrayal.

While the research reviewed here has greatly increased our understanding of the neural correlates of social decisions, it is important to note that this also has the potential to inform economic theories of interactive decision making. Recent models in behavioral economics have attempted to account for social factors, such as inequity aversion, by adding these social utility functions to the standard models (e.g., Bolton & Ockenfels, 2000; Fehr & Schmidt, 1999), and modeling these functions based on the underlying neural patterns provides a useful constraint in the effort to develop new models.

Reciprocal exchange: Reward and punishment

One promising research direction that has employed reciprocal exchange tasks such as Trust, Prisoner's Dilemma, and Public Goods games has been the investigation of how the brain's basic reward system may be implicated in social decisions. The notion of a common neural reward metric is important to broader theories of decision making, as a metric of this kind allows us to compare options offered in different forms. The neuroeconomic approach, as is featured elsewhere in this volume, has attempted to illuminate the neural processes involved in the encoding and representation of reward, usually defined as monetary amounts won or lost.

A strong candidate for this reward metric is the mesolimbic dopamine system. Single-cell recording studies in monkeys have demonstrated that midbrain dopamine neurons track reward prediction errors (Montague, Dayan, & Sejnowski, 1996; Schultz, Dayan, & Montague, 1997). Midbrain dopamine cells project to both ventral and dorsal striatum, including the caudate nucleus, and activation in the human caudate nucleus is modulated as a function of trial-and-error learning with feedback. This suggests that the caudate nucleus may allow an organism to learn contingencies between response and outcome. Indeed, in simple coordination games, researchers have uncovered compelling evidence for the existence of reinforcement-learning mechanisms in nonhuman primates (Barroclough, Conroy, & Lee, 2004). This mechanism is thought to improve choices over time, by continually updating the outcome functions according to the rewards and punishments we encounter in our environment. These results also are observed using functional neuroimaging, with activity changes in the human striatum scaling directly with the magnitude of monetary reward or punishment (e.g., Knutson & Cooper, 2005). Building from this, an important development has been the discovery that the human striatum appears to be centrally involved in social decisions, above and beyond any financial outcome that may accrue to the player.

Several neuroimaging studies using reciprocal exchange tasks have now demonstrated that the striatum tracks a social partner's decision to reciprocate or not reciprocate cooperation, appearing to encode abstract rewards such as the positive feeling garnered by mutual cooperation. One interpretation of these findings is that this area may also encode more abstract valuations, such as the positive feeling garnered by mutual cooperation, or the negative feeling of being treated poorly. For example, reciprocated cooperation with another human in a Prisoner's Dilemma Game leads to increased activation in both caudate and nucleus accumbens, as compared with a control condition where an identical amount of money is earned without social involvement. Conversely, unreciprocated cooperation, that is, cooperation by you (as the subject) while your partner defects, shows a corresponding decrease in activation in this area (Rilling et al., 2002). Additionally, the striatum may be utilized as a guide to informing future decisions in an iterated version of this game, where you must play multiple rounds with the same partner. In these situations, striatal activation is associated with increased cooperation in subsequent rounds, suggesting that the striatum may register social prediction errors to guide decisions about reciprocity.

Similar findings have been reported in a multi-round Trust Game (King-Casas, Tomlin, Anen, Camerer, Quartz, & Montague, 2005). In this study, activation in the trustee's caudate was related to how much reciprocity the investor had shown on previous trials, thus corresponding to an "intention to trust" signal of the trustee. Further, this signal gradually shifted over time—in early trials the signal occurred after the investor made his or her choice, whereas later on this signal occurred much earlier, before in fact the investor's decision was revealed. This temporal shift is strongly reminiscent of reward prediction errors in reinforcement learning models, providing further evidence that social decision making may recruit basic reward mechanisms in order to construct a model of the social domain.

Of course, social reward need not always be related to positive, mutually cooperative actions, and players also may derive satisfaction from punishing defectors for their norm violations. This was demonstrated in a PET study (de Quervain et al., 2004) in which investors were confronted with nonreciprocators in a Trust Game. Players had the option to punish these defectors by reducing their payout, though, importantly, this action also entailed a loss of money for the players themselves. Nonetheless, players made the decision to "altruistically punish" in many cases. These decisions were associated with activation in the caudate nucleus, with this activation greater when the punishment was real (involving a financial loss to the other player) than when it was merely symbolic.

Though these rather basic reward and punishment mechanisms have the potential to strongly guide behavior even in complex social decision-making tasks, these prediction error signals can be greatly modulated by "top–down" processes, such as declarative information previously learned about the partner. For example, providing general personality information about partners before playing a Trust Game led to reduced caudate activity in response to actions of partners described as either morally positive or morally negative, though responses to morally neutral players remained unchanged (Delgado, Frank, & Phelps, 2005). This suggests prior social knowledge about a partner can reduce the amount of trial-by-trial learning, demonstrating both top–down and bottom–up influences on the neural basis of social cooperation.

Finally, in a wider sense of what constitutes social decision making, two studies have examined the neural basis of social altruism. These experiments assessed brain activation when participants donated money to charitable organizations. In one study (Moll, Krueger, Zahn, Pardini, de Oliveira-Souza, & Grafman, 2006), the striatum was engaged by both receiving money and by donations to charity. Further, the magnitude of this activation was related positively to the number of decisions to donate made by players. In another study (Harbaugh, Mayr, & Burghart, 2007), these areas were also activated by receipt of money and observing a personal donation to a charity, but this activation was enhanced when this charitable donation was voluntary as opposed to forced. These latter studies offer the possibility of extending investigations of social reward beyond simple two-player interactions to interactive decision making at a societal level, which has potential implications to inform questions of public policy.

CONCLUSION

The preceding sections reviewed some general ways in which the neuro-economic approach can be harnessed to make important new contributions to the relatively understudied field of social decision making. Games offer some real advantages over standard decision-making paradigms, not least is their embedding in actual, consequential, social interactions that allow investigation of complex processes such as reputation, trust, equality, and cooperation.

There are two primary advantages to the methods and tasks outlined here. First, neuroscience can provide important biological constraints on the component processes involved, and indeed research is revealing that many of the processes underlying complex decision making may overlap with more fundamental brain mechanisms, such as reward and affective motivations. Knowledge of these "building blocks" of social decision making will greatly assist in constructing better models of this process. Second, as noted earlier, actual decision behavior in these tasks often does not conform to the predictions of Game Theory. For example, classical Game Theory predicts all players would accept even an egregiously unfair offer in an Ultimatum Game, and that players would always defect in a simultaneous one-shot Prisoner's Dilemma Game. Ample experimental data now contradict both of these positions. Therefore, more precise characterizations of behavior will be important in adapting these models to better fit how decisions are actually made. Despite the theoretical problems noted, Game Theory offers a rich, formal, principled, mathematical structure by which to investigate social decision-making behavior, and therefore has an important role to play in advancing this research.

Of course, as with any new and novel approach, and it should be noted that decision neuroscience as an interdisciplinary field is less than 10 years old, there are challenges to address. The primary component disciplines of psychology, neuroscience, and economics operate at different levels of analysis and have different theoretical assumptions. More practically, there are important differences in methodology, in particular with regard to the use of deception, generally prohibited by economics but used extensively in psychology and neuroscience. Additionally, it is important to use caution in interpreting neural activations as measured by neuroimaging. For example, the association of a brain region with either value encoding or aversive processing in previous studies does not necessarily mean that activation in this area in the context of an interactive game can automatically be interpreted as rewarding or displeasing, respectively. It would therefore be prudent for the field as a whole to buttress these claims by either converging evidence from other methodologies such as TMS or patient work, or at the very least demonstrate behavioral performance in line with the neural predictions, such as a player's preference for options that activate reward centers more strongly (e.g., de Quervain et al., 2004). Nonetheless, data generated by both this approach and other related approaches that will surely emerge in the near future will be valuable in providing additional constraints for any theory that seeks to accurately model social decision making. These constraints, based on the neural substrate, have the potential to allow discrimination and modeling of processes that may be difficult to separate at the behavioral level.

In conclusion, this chapter has examined recent attempts at combining neuroscience methodology with the theoretical framework of Game Theory. The advances outlined here illustrate the potential for this cross-disciplinary approach to further our understanding of the neural mechanisms that underpin social interactions.

REFERENCES

Barraclough, D. J., Conroy, M. L., & Lee, D. (2004). Prefrontal cortex and decision making in a mixed-strategy game. *Nature Neuroscience, 7*, 404–410.

Bechara, A., Damasio, H., Tranel, D., & Damasio, A. R. (1997). Deciding advantageously before knowing the advantageous strategy. *Science, 275*, 1293–1295.

Bolton, G. E., & Ockenfels, A. (2000). ERC: A theory of equity, reciprocity, and competition. *American Economic Review, 90*, 166–193.

Brosnan, S. F., & de Waal, F. B. M. (2003). Monkeys reject unequal pay. *Nature, 425*, 297–299.

Calder, A. J., Lawrence, A. D., & Young, A. W. (2001). Neuropsychology of fear and loathing. *Nature Reviews Neuroscience, 2*, 352–363.

Camerer, C. F. (2003). *Behavioral game theory*. Princeton, NJ: Princeton University Press.

Coricelli, G., Critchley, H. D., Joffily, M., O'Doherty, J. P., Sirigu, A., & Dolan, R. J. (2005). Regret and its avoidance: A neuroimaging study of behavior. *Nature Neuroscience, 8*, 1255–1262.

Critchley, H. D., Elliott, R., Mathias, C. J., & Dolan, R. J. (2000). Neural activity relating to generation and representation of galvanic skin conductance responses: A functional magnetic resonance imagining study. *Journal of Neuroscience, 20*, 3033–3040.

Delgado, M. R., Frank, R. H., & Phelps, E. A. (2005). Perceptions of moral character modulate the neural systems of reward during the trust game. *Nature Neuroscience, 8*, 1611–1618.

Derbyshire, S. W., Jones, A. K. P., & Gyulai, F. (1997). Pain processing during three levels of noxious stimulation produces differential patterns of central activity. *Pain, 73*, 431–445.

de Quervain, D. J., Fischbacker, U., Treyer, V., Schellhammer, M., Schnyder, U., Buck, A. et al. (2004). The neural basis of altruistic punishment. *Science, 305*, 1254–1258.

Dunbar, R. I. M. (1998). The social brain hypothesis. *Evolutionary Anthropology, 6*, 178–190.

Fehr, E., & Gachter, S. (2002). Altruistic punishment in humans. *Nature, 415*, 137–140.

Fehr, E., & Schmidt, K. M. (1999). A theory of fairness, competition, and cooperation. *Quarterly Journal of Economics, 114*, 817–868.

Gallagher, H. L., Happe, F., Brunswick, N., Fletcher, P. C., Frith, U., & Frith, C. D. (2000). Reading the mind in cartoons and stories: An fMRI study of "theory of mind" in verbal and nonverbal tasks. *Neuropsychologia, 38*, 11–21.

Greene, J. D., Sommerville, R. B., Nystrom, L. E., Darley, J. M., & Cohen, J. D. (2001). An fMRI investigation of emotional engagement in moral judgment. *Science, 293*, 2105–2108.

Guth, W., Schmittberger, R., & Schwarze, B. (1982). An experimental analysis of ultimate bargaining. *Journal of Economic Behavior and Organization, 3*, 376–388.

Harbaugh, W. T., Mayr, U., & Burghart, D. R. (2007). Neural responses of taxation and voluntary giving reveal motives for charitable donations. *Science, 316*, 1622–1625.

Harle, K., & Sanfey, A. G. (2007). Sadness biases social economic decisions in the ultimatum game. *Emotion, 7*, 876–881.

Heinrichs, M., Baumgartner, T., Kirschbaum, C., & Ehlert, U. (2003). Social support and oxytocin interact to suppress cortisol and subjective responses to psychosocial stress. *Biological Psychiatry, 54*, 1389–1398.

Henrich, J., Boyd, R., Bowles, S., Gintis, H., Fehr, E., Camerer, C. et al. (2005). "Economic man" in cross-cultural perspective: Ethnography and experiments from 15 small-scale societies. *Behavioral and Brain Science, 28*, 795–855.

Kahneman, D., Slovic, P., & Tversky, A. (1982). *Judgment under uncertainty: Heuristics and biases*. Cambridge: Cambridge University Press.

King-Casas, B., Tomlin, D., Anen, C., Camerer, C. F., Quartz, S. R., & Montague, P. R. (2005). Getting to know you: Reputation and trust in a two-person economic exchange. *Science, 308*, 78–83.

Kirsch, P., Esslinger, C., Chen, Q., Mier, D., Lis, S., Siddhanti, S. et al. (2005). Oxytocin modulates neural circuitry for social cognition and fear in humans. *Journal of Neuroscience, 25*, 11489–11493.

Knoch, D., Pascual-Leone, A., Meyer, K., Treyer, V., & Fehr, E. (2006). Diminishing reciprocal fairness by disrupting the right prefrontal cortex. *Science, 314*, 829–832.

Knutson, B., & Cooper, J. C. (2005). Functional magnetic resonance imaging of reward prediction. *Current Opinion in Neurology and Neurosurgery, 18*, 411–417.

Koenigs, M., & Tranel, D. (2007). Irrational economic decision making after ventromedial prefrontal damage: Evidence from the ultimatum game. *Journal of Neuroscience, 27*, 951–956.

Kosfeld, M., Heinrichs, M., Zak, P. J., Fischbacher, U., & Fehr, E. (2005). Oxytocin increases trust in humans. *Nature, 435*, 673–676.

Kringelbach, M. L., & Rolls, E. T. (2004). The functional neuroanatomy of the human orbitofrontal cortex: Evidence from neuroimaging and neuro-psychology. *Progress in Neurobiology*, *72*, 341–372.

Martin, R. D. (1990). *Primate origins and evolution*. Princeton, NJ: Princeton University Press.

McCabe, K., Houser, D., Ryan, L., Smith, V., & Trouard, T. (2001). A functional imaging study of cooperation in two-person reciprocal exchange. *Proceedings of the National Academy of Sciences USA*, *98*, 11832–11835.

McCarthy, M. M., McDonald, C. H., Brooks, P. J., & Goldman, D. (1996). An anxiolytic action of oxytocin is enhanced by estrogen in the mouse. *Physiological Behavior*, *60*, 1209–1215.

Mellers, B., Schwartz, A., & Ritov, I. (1999). Predicting choices from emotions. *Journal of Experimental Psychology: General*, *128*, 332–345.

Moll, J., Krueger, F., Zahn, R., Pardini, M., de Oliveira-Souza, R., & Grafman, J. (2006). Human fronto-mesolimbic networks guide decisions about charitable donation. *Proceedings of the National Academy of Sciences USA*, *103*, 15623–15628.

Montague, P. R., Berns, G. S., Cohen, J. D., McClure, S. M., Pagnoni, G., Dhamala, M. et al. (2002). Hyperscanning: Simultaneous fMRI during linked social interactions. *NeuroImage*, *16*, 1159–1164.

Montague, P. R., Dayan, P., & Sejnowski, T. J. (1996). A framework for mesencephalic dopamine systems based on predictive Hebbian learning. *Journal of Neuroscience*, *16*, 1936–1947.

Nash, J. F. (1950). Equilibrium points in N-person games. *Proceedings of the National Academy of Sciences USA*, *36*, 48–49.

Nowak, M. A., Page, K. M., & Sigmund, K. (2000). Fairness versus reason in the ultimatum game. *Science*, *289*, 1773–1775.

Pillutla, M. M., & Murnighan, J. K. (1996). Unfairness, anger, and spite: Emotional rejections of ultimatum offers. *Organizational Behavior and Human Decision Processes*, *68*, 208–224.

Rilling, J. K., Goldsmith, D. R., Glenn, A. L., Jairam, M. R., Elfenbein, H. A., Dagenais, J. E. et al. (2008). The neural correlates of the affective response to unreciprocated cooperation. *Neuropsychologia*, *46*, 1256–1266.

Rilling, J. K., Gutman, D. A., Zeh, T. R., Pagnoni, G., Berns, G. S., & Kilts, C. D. (2002). A neural basis for social cooperation. *Neuron*, *35*, 395–405.

Sanfey, A. G., Loewenstein, G., Cohen, J. D., & McClure, S. M. (2006). Neuroeconomics: Cross-currents in research on decision making. *Trends in Cognitive Sciences*, *10*, 108–116.

Sanfey, A. G., Rilling, J. K., Aronson, J. A., Nystrom, L. E., & Cohen, J. D. (2003). The neural basis of economic decision making in the ultimatum game. *Science*, *300*, 1755–1758.

Schultz, W., Dayan, P., & Montague, P. R. (1997). A neural substrate of prediction and reward. *Science*, *275*, 1593–1599.

Singer, T., Seymour, B., O'Doherty, J., Klaas, E. S., Dolan, J. D., & Frith, C. (2006). Empathic neural responses are modulated by the perceived fairness of others. *Nature*, *439*, 466–469.

Sober, E., & Wilson, D. S. (1998). *Unto others—The evolution and psychology of unselfish behavior*. Cambridge, MA: Harvard University Press.

Spitzer, M., Fischbacher, U., Herrnberger, B., Gron, G., & Fehr, E. (2007). The neural signature of social norm compliance. *Neuron*, *56*, 185–196.

Van't Wout, M., Kahn, R. S., Sanfey, A. G., & Aleman, A. (2005). rTMS over the right dorsolateral prefrontal cortex affects strategic decision making. *Neuro-Report*, *16*, 1849–1852.

Van't Wout, M., Kahn, R. S., Sanfey, A. G., & Aleman, A. (2006). Affective state and decision making in the ultimatum game. *Experimental Brain Research*, *169*, 564–568.

von Neumann, J., & Morgenstern, O. (1947). *Theory of games and economic behavior*. Princeton, NJ: Princeton University Press.

Winston, J. S., Strange, B. A., O'Doherty, J., & Dolan, R. J. (2002). Automatic and intentional brain responses during evaluations of trustworthiness of faces. *Nature Neuroscience*, *5*, 277–283.

Wood, R. M., Rilling, J. K., Sanfey, A. G., Bhagwagar, Z., & Rogers, R. D. (2006). The effects of altering 5-HT activity on the performance of an iterated prisoner's dilemma game in healthy volunteers. *Neuropsychopharmacology*, *31*, 1075–1084.

CHAPTER TEN

Social and biological evidence on motives for punishment

Daniel Houser, Robert Kurzban, and Erte Xiao

INTRODUCTION

The causes, consequences, and neurophysiology of punishment have received increasing attention in recent years. Punishment often occurs in social environments when trust is not reciprocated or when people given an opportunity to be cooperative choose to be selfish instead. In such cases, punishment can stem from formal contracts that specify specific sanctions for specific types of behavior. Often though, punishment is spontaneous, informal, and even costly to the punisher. Here we review and discuss aspects of what is known about human motives for punishment. By way of background, this section briefly discusses research on effects, both negative and positive, of formal and informal punishment on cooperation in groups.

Formal punishment

By formal punishment we refer to sanctions that reduce material well-being, as opposed to informal punishments like expressions of disapproval (discussed below). Formal punishment can be effective at promoting cooperation and compliance with norms in groups. For example, Fehr and Gächter (2002), and Yamagishi (1988), reported such effects in a "social dilemma" experiment, where the narrow self-interest of individuals conflicts with the interest of groups in which the individuals interact. These scholars reported that participants were willing to punish noncooperators and that punishment significantly increased cooperation in groups.

However, many have provided empirical evidence that imposing punishment can also reduce cooperation (see, e.g., Fehr & Falk, 2002; Frey & Oberholzer-Gee, 1997; Gneezy & Rustichini, 2000; Kreps, 1997; Pokorny, 2008; Tenbrunsel & Messick, 1999). Punishment can fail to foster cooperation for two key reasons. One is weak incentives, in the sense that after accounting for expected punishment costs, people continue to perceive the net benefit of noncooperation to be positive. "Intention effects", which refer to effects that can arise when an incentive is chosen and applied by a human rather than an external process, can be another source of detrimental punishment outcomes. The reason is that imposing sanctions might be seen as a signal of distrust (see, e.g., Dickinson & Villeval, 2008; Fehr & Falk, 2002; Frey, 1993), or might create a hostile atmosphere (Bewley, 1999) and consequently reduce cooperation. Indeed, a substantial amount of experimental research suggests that intentions play a very important role in shaping decisions (see, e.g., Blount, 1995; Brandts & Solà, 2001; Charness, 2004; Charness & Haruvy, 2002; Charness & Levine, 2007; Falk, Fehr, & Fischbacher, 2008, 2003; Falk & Kosfeld, 2006; Fehr & Gächter, 2000; Gordon & Bowlby, 1989; Greenberg & Frisch, 1972; McCabe, Rigdon, & Smith, 2003; Nelson, 2002; Offerman, 2002).

Houser, Xiao, McCabe, and Smith (2008) investigated the relative importance of punishment intentions and punishment incentives in producing noncooperative behavior in a bilateral exchange environment. Investors sent an amount to trustees and requested a return on this investment and, in some treatments, were given the option to threaten sanctions to enforce this return request. In other treatments, sanctions were threatened by a random mechanism unrelated to the investors' decisions. Threats of punishment did indeed decrease trustees' decisions to cooperate, and did so irrespective of whether the sanction was threatened intentionally or randomly. Thus, the authors conclude that the detrimental impact of punishment on cooperation in their environment stems primarily from the impact of incentives.

Informal punishment

While weak material incentives can have a detrimental impact on cooperation, an interesting recent experimental literature has documented that informal (nonmaterial) sanctions, particularly expressions of negative emotions or disapproval, can be quite effective in enforcing norms and promoting cooperation (see, e.g., Gächter & Fehr, 1999; Masclet, Noussair, Tucker, & Villeval, 2003; Noussair & Tucker, 2005; Rege & Telle, 2004).

In their recent contribution, Masclet et al. (2003) hypothesized that peer-to-peer expressions of disapproval, even absent fines for non-cooperative behavior, can promote cooperation in social dilemma environments. To obtain data on this hypothesis they asked participants to play games similar to those studied by Fehr and Gächter (2002). In one game, group members could assign monetary costs to each other, and these fines were also costly to assign. A second game was identical with the exception that punishment consisted of "disapproval points" instead of monetary fines. Participants were instructed that points represented the level of a sender's disapproval regarding a target's behavior. Participants also knew that disapproval points were costless to send, and if received had no payoff consequence. The key finding from Masclet et al. is that nonmonetary sanctions had a significant positive impact on cooperation.

Although informal sanctions seem to promote cooperation, there is no consensus for why this is the case. Factors playing a role include communication, coordination, reactions to disapproval, and attempts to avoid disapproval. The first three can refer to effects that arise subsequent to receiving an informal sanction (see, e.g., Miller, Butts, & Rode, 2002; Noussair & Tucker, 2005), while the latter refers exclusively to effects prior to the occurrence of communication, and in particular those effects motivated by an effort to avoid receiving an informal sanction. This is relevant to economic institution design because opportunities for expressions of disapproval can be provided to varying degrees within institutional frameworks. In particular, if people make systematic efforts to avoid disapproval, then mechanisms can be designed to discourage norm violations even within economic contexts that include partially anonymous trade with strangers (e.g., some types of internet exchange).

The role of "avoidance" in the effects of informal sanctions is informed by two closely related and independent investigations. Xiao and Houser (2009) and Ellingsen and Johannesson (2008) studied "dictator games", where one participant (the "dictator") determines a division of a sum of money between her and another anonymous participant (the "receiver"). In both studies receivers were provided an opportunity to write messages, in natural language, to their respective dictators. The messages were not monitored by the experimenters and could have no effect on dictators' division decisions or ultimate earnings. Importantly though, dictators were informed before they made their decision that the receiver could write a message after they learned the dictator's allocation. Compared with dictator games without messaging opportunities, both studies found significant evidence for disapproval-avoidance effects, in that dictators were significantly more generous when they knew receivers would have *ex post* opportunities to respond to their division decisions with natural language messages.

Some light has been shed on the effects of punishment on cooperation, both when punishment is likely to be effective and when it is not. We pointed out that punishment can promote cooperation in groups. However, this need not be a primary motive for punishment. Obviously, even if punishment often has the *effect* of eliciting cooperation, the inference is not licensed that the motive behind punishment is to bring about this effect. Below we review additional studies informing motives for punishment. The literature in this area is very large, and our review is unfortunately but necessarily narrow. We comment on motives including norm expression, egalitarianism (fairness), and emotion expression.

Norm expression

Various scholars in law and economics have argued that one important reason to punish is to express social norms (see, e.g., Cooter, 1998; Kahan, 1998, Sunstein, 1996; Tyran & Feld, 2006). Xiao and Houser (in press) noted that, because punishment not only threatens misbehavior but also reinforces norms, publicly and privately implemented punishment should have different effects because norms direct behavior more effectively when they are the focus of attention (see, e.g., Berkowitz, 1972; Cialdini, Kallgren, & Raymond, 1990; Harvey & Enzle, 1981). Because public implementation of punishment expresses the relevant norms, not only to those who receive punishment but also to observers, the norm should be relatively more salient when punishment is publicly implemented. In this light, Xiao and Houser (in press) hypothesized that publicly implemented punishment would be more effective in enforcing norm compliance than its privately implemented counterpart, especially in cases where punishment incentives are weak.

To investigate this issue, variants of public goods games with punishment were used. One of their games included privately implemented punishment, and in another punishment was publicly implemented. In both treatments, each of 30 rounds had a 50% chance of being monitored. If a round was monitored, then the lowest contributor to the public good in that round received a very small sanction. The only difference between treatments is that in the public treatment punishment was announced to all group members whenever it occurred, while in the private treatment only the punished person knew that punishment occurred. The particular person who was punished remained at all times anonymous.

The key finding reported by Xiao and Houser (in press) is that privately implemented weak punishment reduced cooperation in relation to their baseline treatment without punishment. However, and in line with their hypothesis, when that same incentive was implemented publicly, cooperation was sustained at significantly higher rates than in either the baseline or private punishment treatments.

Egalitarianism

In experimental environments such as public goods games, those who contribute less than others are simultaneously violating a norm of cooperation by free riding, and generating an inequality in outcomes because free riders earn more than those who contribute. Therefore, punishment of free riders could, in principle, be driven either by a motive to reduce inequalities *per se* or to enforce a social norm of cooperating in these types of contexts (see, e.g., Fowler, Johnson, & Smirnov, 2005).

The motive to reduce inequities has been formalized by a number of researchers, with variations on the general theme (Bolton & Ockenfels, 2000; Charness & Rabin, 2002; Fehr & Schmidt, 1999). There is substantial controversy surrounding inequity aversion (e.g., Engelmann & Strobel, 2004), and a substantial amount of research attention has been paid to determining the strength and boundaries of this motive.

One important empirical avenue in investigating the role of egalitarianism in punishment decisions is to isolate egalitarianism from norm enforcement motivations. To take one example, in a recent effort in this direction, Dawes, Fowler, Johnson, McElreath, and Smirnov (2007) designed an experiment where participants could reduce or augment another participant's income even when there was no cooperation norm to enforce. In that game, subjects were anonymously divided into groups of four. Each subject received a randomly generated sum of money. Participants were shown the payoffs of other group members for that round and were then provided an opportunity to reduce or increase other participants' earnings for that round. Each unit spent by a participant increased or reduced a target participant's payoff by three units. New groups were randomly formed at the beginning of each round.

The results of this study indicated that participants who randomly received a high payoff were also more likely to receive high payoff deductions from other subjects. In addition, on average, the lowest earners in each group spent 96% more on payoff deductions than the top earners, and the top earner spent 77% more on payoff augmentation than the bottom earner. Finally, questionnaire data revealed that emotions toward the top earners became increasingly negative as inequality increased, and those who indicated that they felt greater negative emotions also spent more to reduce above-average earners' incomes. These results provide evidence that unequal outcomes can lead to negative emotions, which in turn affect human decisions. Subjects are motivated by egalitarianism even when there is no cooperative norm to enforce.

Compare these results with those reported by Carpenter and Matthews (2005), who had subjects play public goods games where participants in one group could, in some treatments, punish participants in other groups. In line with previous work in the area (Fehr & Gächter, 2002; Yamagishi, 1986, 1988), people punished those in their own group who failed to contribute to the public good. Importantly, however, in a critical treatment condition in which people in one group could spend money to punish low contributors in another, they did so at very low levels. This hints strongly that the motive to punish in public goods games, at least, derives less from norm enforcement than some sort of appetite for diminishing the payoff of individuals who could have made one's own payoff larger (at a cost to themselves), but chose not to (see, e.g., Price, Cosmides, & Tooby, 2002).

Clearly, a great deal more work needs to be done to understand the interaction between the desire to punish in order to bring about equality in outcomes and the desire to punish in order to enforce a norm, exact retribution, or influence subsequent decisions, though these may not always be distinct and distinguishable motives (Mandel, 2006). The relative strengths of the relevant motives and the contexts in which these motives operate remain a set of open and important research questions.

Emotion expression

We noted earlier that informal nonmaterial sanctions, particularly expressions of negative emotions or disapproval, can be effective at enforcing norms and promoting cooperation in groups. Humans typically desire to express emotions when they are aroused (see Kennedy-Moore, Watson, & Safran, 2001; Marshall, 1972). This demand for emotion expression, just as any other material demand, can potentially have important effects on human behavior. Indeed, results obtained by Xiao and Houser (2005) strongly suggest that the desire to express negative emotions can itself be an important motivation underlying costly punishment behavior.

In ultimatum game experiments reported by Xiao and Houser (2005), responders are given an opportunity to write a message to their proposer simultaneously with their decision to accept or reject the proposer's offer. They found that, compared with standard ultimatum games where the *only* action responders can take is to accept or reject the offer, responders are significantly less likely to reject the unfair offer when they can write a message to the proposers. In particular, proposers' offers of $4 (20% of the total surplus) or less are rejected 60% of the time in standard ultimatum games. However, when responders can express emotions only 32% reject unfair offers, and the reduction is statistically significant. Furthermore, the messages written in this game were independently evaluated by ten participants blind to both the research hypotheses and the offers/decisions. The vast majority of those who accepted offers of 20% or less wrote messages, and all but one of those messages were classified as expressing negative emotions.

Taken together with findings reviewed above, these results suggest that providing opportunities in markets for *ex post* emotion expression can promote efficient exchange by both reducing costly punishment activity and promoting fair economic decisions. For example, a system which facilitates expressions of dissatisfaction might reduce costly consumer boycotts, especially ones stemming from perceptions of unfair pricing (see, e.g., Friedman, 1991; Tyran & Engelmann, 2005).

In addition, the above findings lend support to the notion of restorative justice (see, e.g., Lind & Tyler, 1988; Umbreit, 1995). The theory of restorative justice emphasizes the importance of victim–offender mediation programs (VOMP), during which victims meet face-to-face with offenders in order to discuss the impact of the crime. The idea is that both victims and offenders will feel more fairly treated after having the opportunity to express their view. In addition, the data reported by Xiao and Houser (2005) are consistent with VOMP perhaps mitigating recidivism, in that a potential offender might prefer to avoid being subjected to a future victim's emotion expression.

Moreover, as discussed above, a sense of egalitarianism can lead one to experience negative emotions even when inequality is produced randomly by nature, and these negative emotions can evidently generate costly punishment behavior. An interesting question is whether the behaviors Dawes et al. (2007) observe are also sensitive to opportunities for emotion expression. Future research might explore whether income reduction decisions in an environment like Dawes et al.'s are changed when participants are able to express emotions to one another.

NEURAL EVIDENCE

The research reviewed above might be interpreted to suggest that humans punish in part out of a sense of concern for fairness. In an early study to investigate the neural underpinnings of this motivation, Sanfey, Rilling, Aronson, Nystrom, and Cohen (2003) had subjects play an ultimatum game (UG) while inside an fMRI scanner. Their particular interest was in rejections of positive UG offers. On standard theory, no such offer should be rejected, as a positive amount of money dominates zero.

Sanfey et al. scanned responders (but not proposers) in the UG, comparing data from iterations of the game in which responders were faced with a proposal that was fair (i.e., $5 for each player) versus those that were unfair ($9/$1, $8/$2, $7/$3). The unfair offers showed greater activation in the following areas: bilateral anterior insula, dorsolateral prefrontal cortex (DLPFC), and anterior cingulate cortex. Because of the use of a control condition in which people were paired with computers rather than people, the hypothesis that this difference is due to the amount of money rather than the fairness of the offer is unlikely.

The activation of the insula—implicated as having a role in distress and anger (see, e.g., Calder, Lawrence, & Young, 2001)—is of particular interest, and suggests a negative affective reaction to the unfairness of the offer. Indeed, activation of this region was positively related to the probability of rejecting the unfair offer, suggesting an important role for this region. More generally, this work indicates a neuroanatomical substrate for negative affect associated with unfairness, and a potential causal link between this region and rejections, which can be easily interpreted as a kind of costly punishment of the unfair proposer. It is interesting to note that when offers were accepted, activation in DLPFC was greater than in the anterior insula, whereas rejected offers showed less DLPFC activation than in the anterior insula. One might infer from this that DLPFC has some role in inhibiting the link between the affective computations in the anterior insula and neurophysiological systems that drive eventual behavior.

This account is complicated, however, by recent experiments using repetitive transcranial magnetic stimulation (rTMS), which suppresses activation of a particular region of the brain. Knoch, Pascual-Leone, Meyer, Treyer, and Fehr (2006) used this technique to suppress activity in DLPFC, on both the left and the right side. In particular, they had people play the UG, and once again focused on cases in which a responder received an unfair offer. Their question was whether applying rTMS to DLPFC would alter responses to such unfair offers.

Whereas the results of Sanfey et al. (2003) might have led one to expect that suppression of this area would have increased rejection (by counteracting the anterior insula's role), the results from Knoch et al. (2006) did not conform to this prediction. In the critical cases, in which subjects were made maximally unfair splits ($4/$16) from humans (rather than computers), rejection rates were roughly 10% when rTMS was applied to the left DLPFC (and in a control condition), but reached nearly 50% when rTMS was applied to right DLPFC. No such effect was found for the left DLPFC. The authors interpreted their results as suggesting that "the DLPFC plays a key role in overriding or weakening self-interested impulses" (p. 831). This leaves open the issue of the role of DLPFC, including lateralization of function—whether suppressing self-interest or the motive to punish unfairness.

The physical locations of possibly affective computations associated with unfair outcomes are beginning to be illuminated. This invites the question about what people are willing to do about unfair situations when they occur. Recent behavioral work on this question has focused on what has been termed "altruistic punishment". The leading research on this question focuses on cases in which people impose costs on others, and incur costs themselves, even when there is no way in which this costly punishment decision can lead to commensurate benefits to the one doing the punishing (e.g., Fehr & Gächter, 2002).

It is worth clarifying the term "altruistic punishment", because it might be confusing at first to those not familiar with the conventions that have been established in the behavioral economics literature on punishment. In particular, and in contrast to well-established conventions of the definition of altruism (e.g., Trivers, 1971), the meaning of the term "altruism" in this literature does not involve the direct delivery of benefits to others. It only requires an imposition of costs on others at a cost to oneself. The term "altruistic punishment" derives from the fact that the effect of punishing norm violators can be to promote cooperative behavior, and therefore improve outcomes for a broader social group. One should be careful not to understand the term "altruistic punishment" as suggesting that punishment is necessarily motivated by altruism.

In one of the first studies investigating the neural basis of "altruistic punishment", De Quervain et al. (2004) used a trust game (or investment game) (Berg, Dickhaut, & McCabe, 1995). In its basic form, player A was endowed with 10 MU (monetary units) and could send this (or not) to player B. If the money was sent, it was quadrupled, leaving B with their initial 10 MU endowment plus four times the amount sent, or 50 MU. Player B could then return 25 MU to player A, or keep all the money. If player B keeps the money, player A can then punish B at a ratio of 2:1, using up to 20 MU to do so.

There were a number of treatment conditions. Of particular interest was the comparison of activation when punishment decisions were made between two types of cases, one in which the decision to be untrustworthy (keep all 50 MU) was intentional and the other in which the decision was determined by a random device. Here, there was a significant difference in activation in the caudate nucleus between conditions, with activation greater in the former. The caudate nucleus is well known to be associated with reward (e.g., Delgado, Stenger, & Fiez, 2004). Although this is plausibly consistent with an altruistic motivation for punishment, retribution cannot be ruled out as a motive.

A second relevant study investigated the effect of observing a sequential prisoner's dilemma game in which an unfair player received a painful stimulus (Singer et al., 2006). Although the stimulus was not chosen by the scanned subject, the nucleus accumbens was implicated, as was the left ventral striatum. The authors conclude that this "echoes recent evidence for altruistic punishment" (p. 466). However, one might treat this interpretation with caution in light of the fact that the person in the scanner did not do any punishing—that is, they did not endure a cost. In fact, what the results imply is much narrower: Some people find it rewarding to see unfair people punished. In sum, in contrast to claims in this literature, the evidence that punishment observed is motivated by altruism is weak, at best, and might well be plausibly attributed to the desire for revenge at being treated unfairly. In similar fashion, seeing unfair others punished might be rewarding; this does not entail that people will find punishing people engaged in transactions in which they have not participated to be rewarding.

CONCLUSION

This chapter discussed biological and social empirical evidence on motives for punishment. It is useful to conclude by saying a few words about the connection between these results and the theory of punishment motives, and especially the well-known theories that underlie altruistic punishment (e.g., Boyd, Gintis, Bowles, & Richerson, 2003). With respect to such theories, the following particularly relevant stylized facts emerge from our discussion: (1) emotions and the desire to express emotions play an important role in decisions to punish; (2) people take pleasure in seeing unfair people punished.

How to model the decision to punish in a way that accounts for these stylized facts remains an active open question. For theories in the spirit of Boyd et al. (2003) to hold, it must be true that people generally like (or at least are willing) to bear costs to punish those who engage in untrustworthy or counter-normative behavior. To date, the behavioral evidence in support of this is mixed and inconclusive. In particular, some studies have found that people tend not to punish unrelated third-party transactions (Carpenter & Matthews, 2005), or do so in only very small amounts (Kurzban, DeScioli, & O'Brien, 2007). Moreover, third-party punishment seems quite sensitive to the social context in which it occurs, and especially with respect to whether the third-party punisher is observed.

While our view is that recent neuroscientific research offers compelling evidence supporting the role of emotion in punishment decisions, it is also the case that this evidence has been collected in environments where punishment immediately follows norm violations. Of course, in many cases of practical importance, putative judgments are separated from the violation itself by days, months, or even years. The neural substrates associated with deliberative punishment are important to identify but have received less attention. It is interesting to speculate that emotion plays an important though different role in this case as well. In particular, for a deliberative process to end in a punishment decision might require one to employ emotional resources as a personal punishment commitment device.

Whether and how such commitments are made, and their role in deliberative punishment, is an open question worthy of future research.

To understand why people punish is an important topic of enduring interest. Research in this area resides at the nexus of neuroscience, psychology, economics, and sociology. Continuing collaborative efforts among scholars within these fields will further illuminate social and biological underpinnings of punishment decisions. Such efforts could also create the foundation for improved policies that promote cooperation and norm compliance in social environments.

REFERENCES

Berg, J., Dickhaut, J., & McCabe, K. (1995). Trust, reciprocity, and social history. *Games and Economic Behavior*, *10*, 122–142.

Berkowitz, L. (1972). Social norms, feelings, and other factors affecting helping and altruism. In L. Berkowitz (Ed.), *Advances in experimental social psychology* (Vol. 6, pp. 63–108). New York: Academic Press.

Bewley, T. (1999). *Why wages don't fall during a recession*. Cambridge, MA: Harvard University Press.

Blount, S. (1995). When social outcomes aren't fair: The effect of causal attributions on preferences. *Organizational Behavior and Human Decision Process*, *63*, 131–144.

Bolton, G. E., & Ockenfels, A. (2000). ERC: A theory of equity, reciprocity, and competition. *American Economic Review*, *90*, 166–193.

Boyd, R., Gintis, H., Bowles, S., & Richerson, P. J. (2003). The evolution of altruistic punishment. *Proceedings of the National Academy of Sciences USA*, *100*, 3531–3535.

Brandts, J., & Solà, C. (2001). Reference points and negative reciprocity in simple sequential games. *Games and Economic Behavior*, *36*, 397–409.

Calder, A. J., Lawrence, A. D., & Young, A. W. (2001). Neuropsychology of fear and loathing. *Nature Reviews Neuroscience*, *2*, 352–363.

Carpenter, J. P., & Matthews, P. H. (2005). *Norm enforcement: Anger, indignation or reciprocity*. Unpublished manuscript.

Charness, G. (2004). Attribution and reciprocity in an experimental labor market. *Journal of Labor Economics*, *22*, 665–668.

Charness, G., & Haruvy, E. (2002). Altruism, fairness, and reciprocity in a gift-exchange experiment: An encompassing approach. *Games and Economic Behavior*, *40*, 203–231.

Charness, G., & Levine, D. (2007). Intention and stochastic outcomes: an experimental study. *Economic Journal*, *117*, 1051–1072.

Charness, G., & Rabin, M. (2002). Understanding social preferences with simple tests. *Quarterly Journal of Economics*, *117*, 817–869.

Cialdini, R. B., Kallgren, C. A., & Raymond, R. R. (1990). A focus theory of normative conduct: A theoretical refinement and reevaluation of the role of norms in human behavior. *Advances in Experimental Social Psychology*, *24*, 201–234.

Cooter, R. D. (1998). Expressive law and economics. *Journal of Legal Studies, 27,* 585–608.

Dawes, C. T., Fowler, J. H., Johnson, T., McElreath, R., & Smirnov, O. (2007). Egalitarian motives in humans. *Nature, 446,* 794–796.

De Quervain, D. J., Fischbacher, U., Treyer, V., Schellhammer, M., Schnyder, U., Buck, A. et al. (2004). The neural basis of altruistic punishment. *Science, 305,* 1254–1258.

Delgado, M. R., Stenger, V. A., & Fiez, J. A. (2004). Motivation-dependent responses in the human caudate nucleus. *Cerebral Cortex, 14,* 1022–1030.

Dickinson, D., & Villeval, M. (2008). Does monitoring decrease work effort? The complementarity between agency and crowding-out theories. *Games and Economic Behavior, 63,* 56–76.

Ellingsen, T., & Johannesson, M. (2008). Anticipated verbal feedback induces pro-social behavior. *Evolution and Human Behavior, 29,* 100–105.

Engelmann, D., & Strobel, M. (2007). Preferences over income distributions: Experimental evidence. *Public Finance Review, 35,* 285–310.

Falk, A., Fehr, E., & Fischbacher, U. (2008). Testing theories of fairness—intentions matter. *Games and Economic Behavior, 1,* 287–303.

Falk, A., Fehr, E., & Fischbacher, U. (2003). On the nature of fair behavior. *Economic Inquiry, 41,* 20–26.

Falk, A., & Kosfeld, M. (2004). Distrust—The hidden cost of control. *American Economic Review, 96,* 1611–1630.

Fehr, E., & Falk, A. (2002). Psychological foundation of incentives. *European Economic Review, 46,* 687–724.

Fehr, E., & Gächter, S. (2000). Fairness and retaliation: The economics of reciprocity. *Journal of Economic Perspectives, 14,* 159–181.

Fehr, E., & Gächter, S. (2002). Altruistic punishment in humans. *Nature, 415,* 137–140.

Fehr, E., & Schmidt, K. (1999). A theory of fairness, competition, and cooperation. *Quarterly Journal of Economics, 114,* 817–868.

Fowler, J. H., Johnson, T., & Smirnov, O. (2005). Egalitarian motive and altruistic punishment. *Nature, 433,* E1.

Frey, B. (1993). Does monitoring increase work effort? The rivalry between trust and loyalty. *Economic Inquiry, 31,* 663–670.

Frey, B., & Oberholzer-Gee, F. (1997). The cost of price incentives: An empirical analysis of motivation crowding-out. *American Economic Review, 87,* 746–755.

Friedman, M. (1991). Consumer boycotts: A conceptual framework and research agenda. *Journal of Social Issues, 47,* 149–168.

Gächter, S., & Fehr, E. (1999). Collective action as a social exchange. *Journal of Economic Behavior and Organization, 39,* 341–369.

Gneezy, U., & Rustichini, A. (2000). A fine is a price. *Journal of Legal Studies, 29,* 1–17.

Gordon, M., & Bowlby, R. (1989). Reactance and intentionality attribution as determinants of the intent to file a grievance. *Personal Psychology, 42,* 309–329.

Greenberg, M., & Frisch, D. (1972). Effect of intentionality on willingness to return a favor. *Journal of Experimental Social Psychology, 8,* 99–111.

Harvey, M. D., & Enzle, M. E. (1981). A cognitive model of social norms for understanding the transgression-helping effect. *Journal of Personality and Social Psychology*, *41*, 866–875.

Houser, D., Xiao, E., McCabe, K., & Smith, V. (2008). When punishment fails: Research on sanctions, intentions and non-cooperation. *Games and Economic Behavior*, *62*, 509–532.

Kahan, D. M. (1998). Social meaning and the economic analysis of crime. *Journal of Legal Studies*, *27*, 661–672.

Kennedy-Moore, E., Watson, J. C., & Safran, J. D. (2001). *Expressing emotion: Myths, realities, and therapeutic strategies*. New York: Guilford Press.

Knoch, D., Pascual-Leone, A., Meyer, K., Treyer, V., & Fehr, E. (2006). Diminishing reciprocal fairness by disrupting the right prefrontal cortex. *Science*, *314*, 829–832.

Kreps, D. (1997). Intrinsic motivation and extrinsic incentives. *American Economic Review Papers and Proceedings*, *87*, 359–364.

Kurzban, R., DeScioli, P., & O'Brien, E. (2007). Audience effects on moralistic punishment. *Evolution and Human Behavior*, *28*, 75–84.

Lind, E. A., & Tyler, T. R. (1988). *The social psychology of procedural justice*. New York: Plenum Press.

Mandel, D. R. (2006). Economic transactions among friends: Asymmetric generosity but not agreement in buyers and sellers offers. *Journal of Conflict Resolution*, *50*, 584–606.

Marshall, J. R. (1972). The expression of feelings. *Archives of General Psychiatry*, *27*, 789–790.

Masclet, D., Noussair, C., Tucker, S., & Villeval, M.-C. (2003). Monetary and nonmonetary punishment in the voluntary contributions mechanism. *American Economic Review*, *93*, 366–380.

McCabe, K., Rigdon, M., & Smith, V. (2003). Positive reciprocity and intention in trust games. *Journal of Economic Behavior and Organization*, *52*, 267–275.

Miller, J. H., Butts, C., & Rode, D. (2002). Communication and cooperation. *Journal of Economic Behavior and Organization*, *47*, 179–195.

Nelson, W. R. Jr. (2002). Equity and intention: It's the thought that counts. *Journal of Economic Behavior and Organization*, *48*, 423–430.

Noussair, C., & Tucker, S. (2005). Combining monetary and social sanctions to promote cooperation. *Economic Inquiry*, *43*, 649–660.

Offerman, T. (2002). Hurting hurts more than helping helps. *European Economic Review*, *46*, 1423–1437.

Pokorny, K. (2008). Pay—but don't pay too much: An experimental study on the impact of incentives. *Journal of Economic Behavior and Organization*, *66*, 251–264.

Price, M. E., Cosmides, L., & Tooby, J. (2002). Punitive sentiment as an anti-free rider psychological device. *Evolution and Human Behavior*, *23*, 203–231.

Rege, M., & Telle, K. (2004). The impact of social approval and framing. *Journal of Public Economics*, *88*, 1625–1644.

Sanfey, A. G., Rilling, J. K., Aronson, J. A., Nystrom, L. E., & Cohen, J. D. (2003). The neural basis of economic decision-making in the ultimatum game. *Science*, *300*, 1755–1758.

Singer, T., Seymour, B., O'Doherty, J. P., Stephan, K. E., Dolan, R. J., & Frith,

C. D. (2006). Empathic neural responses are modulated by the perceived fairness of others. *Nature*, *439*, 466–469.

Sunstein, C. R. (1996). On the expressive function of law. *University of Pennsylvania Law Review*, *144*, 2021–2031.

Tenbrunsel, A. E., & Messick, D. M. (1999). Sanctioning systems, decision frames, and cooperation. *Administrative Science Quarterly*, *44*, 684–707.

Trivers, R. (1971). The evolution of reciprocal altruism. *Quarterly Review of Biology*, *46*, 35–57.

Tyran, J.-R., & Engelmann, D. (2005). To buy or not to buy? An experimental study of consumer boycotts in retail markets. *Economica*, *72*, 1–16.

Tyran, J.-R., & Feld, L. (2006). Achieving compliance when legal sanctions are non-deterrent. *Scandinavian Journal of Economics*, *108*, 135–156.

Umbreit, M. S. (1995). *Mediating interpersonal conflicts: A pathway to peace*. Minneapolis, MN: Erickson Mediation Institute.

Xiao, E., & Houser, D. (2005). Emotion expression in human punishment behavior. *Proceedings of the National Academy of Sciences USA*, *102*, 7398–7401.

Xiao, E., & Houser, D. (2009). Avoiding the sharp tongue: anticipated written messages promote fair economic exchange. *Journal of Economic Psychology*, *30*, 393–404.

Xiao, E., & Houser, D. (in press). *Punish in public*.

Yamagishi, T. (1986). The provision of a sanctioning system as a public good. *Journal of Personality and Social Psychology*, *51*, 110–116.

Yamagishi, T. (1988). Seriousness of social dilemmas and the provision of a sanctioning system. *Social Psychology Quarterly*, *51*, 32–42.

Section V

Goal-directed decision making

CHAPTER ELEVEN

The role of spontaneous thought in human cognition

Kalina Christoff, Alan Gordon, and Rachelle Smith

INTRODUCTION

When making a decision of minor importance, I have always found it advantageous to consider all the pros and cons. In vital matters, however, the decision should come from the unconscious, from somewhere within ourselves.

Sigmund Freud

When you have to make a decision, the first step should be to get all the information necessary for the decision. Once you have the information, you have to decide, and this is best done with conscious thought for simple decisions, but left to unconscious thought—to "sleep on it"—when the decision is complex.

Ap Dijksterhuis

The benefits of deliberate, goal-directed thought processes to decision making have been understood for hundreds of years (Descartes, 1637/ 1998; Locke, 1690/1979). The idea that deliberately "thinking things through" is the best way to make a decision is at the basis of both classic (Janis & Mann, 1977; Simon, 1955) and contemporary perspectives on decision making (Bettman, Luce, & Payne, 1998; Kahneman, 2003). In contrast, our intuitions and folk wisdom often offer a different perspective, emphasizing the passage of time and the more spontaneous thought processes that occur without conscious control over the direction of the thought process (Bargh, Lee-Chai, Barndollar, & Trotschel, 2001)—a

259

perspective perhaps best captured by the notion that there is a benefit of "keeping something at the back of your mind" and even "sleeping on it".

The importance of such spontaneous thought processes to decision making has only recently begun to be recognized by experimental scientists (Dijksterhuis, 2004; Dijksterhuis, Maarten, Nordgren, & van Baaren, 2006). A growing community of psychologists is beginning to view spontaneous thought as a rich and vibrant cognitive phenomenon with distinct phenomenology and considerable influences on other aspects of cognition (Christoff, Ream, & Gabrieli, 2004; Klinger, 1990; Mason, Norton, Van Horn, Wegner, Grafton, & Macrae, 2007; Singer, 1981; Smallwood & Schooler, 2006). The prevalence of spontaneous thought is striking. Ninety-six percent of American adults report some kind of daydreaming each day (Singer & McCraven, 1961) and approximately 30% of thoughts that people experience in their daily lives can be classified as mind wandering (Kane, Brown, McVay, Silvia, Myin-Germeys, & Kwapil, 2007; Klinger & Cox, 1987). This indicates that spontaneous thought is a ubiquitous phenomenon, occupying in as much as a third of our waking life.

Findings from psychology and neuroscience indicate that spontaneous thought shares a number of common attributes with goal-directed thought. For instance, spontaneous thought competes with goal-directed thought processes, just as goal-directed thought processes compete with each other (Teasdale et al., 1995). Our capacity for spontaneous thought increases during highly practiced tasks (Cunningham, Scerbo, & Freeman, 2000; Smallwood, Davies et al., 2004; Smallwood, O'Connor, Sudberry, Haskell, & Ballantyne, 2004; Teasdale et al., 1995) and decreases with age (Giambra, 1989, 1995), just as does our capacity for goal-directed thought (Crawford, Bryan, Luszcz, Obonsawin, & Stewart, 2000; Hasher & Zacks, 1988; Schneider & Shiffrin, 1977). As well, neuroimaging evidence has demonstrated that the brain regions recruited in spontaneous mentation during rest overlap with those recruited during goal-directed thought (Andreasen et al., 1995; Christoff et al., 2004; Shulman et al., 1997; Stark & Squire, 2001). These findings have led researchers to argue that spontaneous thought should be viewed as a complex form of cognition worthy of empirical investigation (e.g., Christoff et al., 2004; Smallwood & Schooler, 2006).

This chapter focuses on the role that spontaneous thought plays in human cognition. We examine its potential place in an overarching framework of thought and compare it with other forms of thought, such as goal-directed and creative, in terms of neural and cognitive mechanisms. We argue that spontaneous mentation shares functions and mechanisms not only with other forms of thought but also with sleep-related cognition. Based on the evidence reviewed in this chapter, we propose that rather than being a futile and wasteful mental activity, spontaneous thought plays a number of important functions in human cognition including, perhaps most importantly, the consolidation and re-consolidation of past and present experiences in relation to our current concerns and emotions.

DIFFERENT FORMS OF THOUGHT AND THEIR NEURAL BASES

In this chapter, we will talk about three types of thought: (1) goal-directed; (2) spontaneous; and (3) creative. The most studied is *goal-directed* thought, which occurs frequently during reasoning, problem solving, and decision making. Indeed, it is this form of thought that psychologists most often have in mind when they refer to thinking. Goal-directed thought is achieved by consciously representing current and desired states, and linking these representations through a series of actions that attempt to transform the current state to the desired state (Unterrainer & Owen, 2006).

The other two forms of thought are studied to a much lesser extent. *Spontaneous* thought, including mind wandering, in many ways appears to be the opposite of goal-directed thought. Between these two extreme ends of a possible thought continuum lies yet another form of thinking, *creative* thought, which appears to share commonalities with both goal-directed and spontaneous thought. In this section, we examine these three forms of thought in terms of their neural and cognitive bases. We suggest that they differ in terms of the extent to which cognitive control, defocused attention, and long-term memory contribute to each.

Goal-directed thought and cognitive control

The region of the brain most tightly linked to goal-directed thought is the prefrontal cortex (PFC), which spans the anterior expanse of the lateral frontal cortical surface (Figure 11.1). Patient studies throughout the last century have repeatedly demonstrated that lesions to the PFC lead to profound deficits in goal-directed thought (e.g., Duncan, Burgess, & Emslie, 1995; Luria, 1966; Milner, 1964; Shallice, 1982). Neuroimaging findings have yielded further support for this link, arguing for a specific role of the two most anterior lateral prefrontal subregions, the dorsolateral PFC (DLPFC) and the rostrolateral PFC (RLPFC), in planning, reasoning, and problem solving (for reviews, see Christoff & Gabrieli, 2000; Unterrainer & Owen, 2006).

The crucial role the PFC plays in goal-directed thought is closely linked to its ability to influence other cortical regions—a function known as cognitive control (Miller & Cohen, 2001). Cognitive control is the process by which the PFC selectively biases currently relevant representations in other parts of the brain, thereby helping to focus attention on currently relevant

Lateral Prefronal Cortex

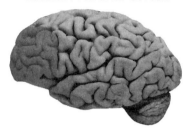

Default Network

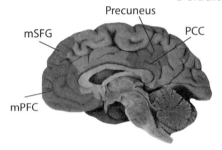
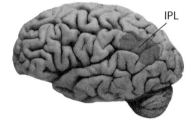

Temporal Lobe Memory Regions

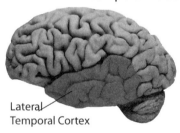
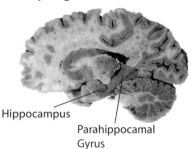

Figure 11.1   Approximate anatomical localization of the lateral prefrontal cortex, the default network, and temporal lobe memory regions. mPFC = medial prefrontal cortex; mSFG = medial superior frontal gyrus; PCC = posterior cingulate cortex; IPL = inferior parietal lobe.

stimuli while diminishing attention toward other competing stimuli (Desimone & Duncan, 1995). The PFC may play an analogous role during goal-directed thinking by biasing those thoughts that are relevant to the current goal and allowing them to be selected among other competing thoughts, thus keeping mental content "on track" and producing a logically connected train of thought. In this way, cognitive control and its implementation through the recruitment of the lateral PFC appear to be some of the characteristic features of goal-directed thinking.

Spontaneous thought, defocused attention, and memory

Mind wandering is a much less focused mental state than goal-directed thought. Although the neuroscience of mind wandering is still in its infancy, emerging evidence (Christoff, Gordon, Smallwood, Smith, & Schooler, 2009; Mason et al., 2007) is beginning to link mind wandering to a set of regions known as the "default network" (Raichle, MacLeod, Snyder, Powers, Gusnard, & Shulman, 2001), as well as to regions of the temporal lobe linked to memory processing (Christoff et al., 2004). Default network regions lie largely along the midline of the brain (Figure 11.1) and include, most prominently, the medial prefrontal cortex, the anterior and posterior cingulate cortices, the precuneus, and the posterior parietal lobule (Raichle et al., 2001; Shulman et al., 1997). This network is typically deactivated during novel, attention-demanding tasks (Raichle et al., 2001), but becomes activated when attentional demands are low, such as during a highly familiar task (Raichle, 1998) or in the absence of a task (Shulman et al., 1997). The accompanying "default" mode of thought is considered to be a state of defocused attention whereby information broadly arising in the external and internal milieu is gathered and evaluated (Raichle et al., 2001). A recent study by Mason et al. (2007) demonstrates that subjects who report a higher propensity toward mind wandering show greater default network recruitment as cognitive demands decrease. These neuroimaging findings, alongside the long-standing behavioral results demonstrating that mind wandering increases as cognitive demands decrease (Antrobus, 1968; Antrobus, Singer, & Greenberg, 1966), are consistent with the notion that mind wandering is associated with a lowering of cognitive control and a defocusing of attention. Conversely, when focused attention and cognitive control are required, activation in the default network becomes attenuated (Raichle et al., 2001; Shulman et al., 1997).

Besides the default network, spontaneous thought has also been linked to recruitment of structures of the lateral and medial temporal lobe that are associated with memory processing (Figure 11.1). Thus, periods of "rest"—an experimental condition during which subjects are typically instructed to lie still in the scanner and "do nothing"—have been associated with consistent recruitment of the temporal lobe, including medial temporal lobe regions such as the hippocampus and parahippocampus, as well as lateral temporal regions including the temporopolar cortex (Binder, Frost, Hammeke, Bellgowan, Rao, & Cox, 1999; Christoff et al., 2004; Stark & Squire, 2001). The temporal lobes have long been implicated in long-term memory phenomena such as episodic and semantic memory, and their recruitment during rest has been proposed to reflect ongoing spontaneously occurring memory retrieval and encoding (Andreasen et al., 1995; Binder et al., 1999; Christoff et al., 2004; Stark & Squire, 2001). Furthermore, recent findings suggest that the off-line processing that occurs during periods of rest is associated with the kind of memory consolidation processes that occur during sleep (Ellenbogen, Hu, Payne, Titone, & Walker, 2007; Maquet et al., 2000). These findings suggest that long-term memory processes contribute strongly to the phenomenon of spontaneous thought (Christoff et al., 2004). As we discuss later in this chapter, memory consolidation may be one of the main functions of spontaneous thought.

Creative thought: Bringing together the prefrontal, "default", and memory networks

Similar to spontaneous thought, creative thought processes are also associated with reduced cognitive control. One line of evidence supporting this association comes from studies of electroencephalography (EEG) dynamics during creative thinking. Divergent thinking tasks produce decreased beta range synchrony and increased alpha range synchrony over the frontal cortex (Fink & Neubauer, 2006; Molle, Marshall, Lutzenberger, Pietrowsky, Fehm, & Born, 1996; Molle, Marshall, Wolf, Fehm, & Born, 1999; Razumnikova, 2000, 2007), providing evidence for loosened cognitive control and lower prefrontal cortical arousal during creative thought. Another line of evidence comes from findings regarding the pattern of catecholaminergic influences on thought processes. Catecholamines, including noradrenaline and dopamine, are directly linked to cognitive control, prefrontal functioning, and cortical arousal (Chamberlain, Muller, Blackwell, Robbins, & Sahakian, 2006; Cohen & Servan-Schreiber, 1992; Robbins, 1997). Lower levels of these two catecholamines appear to be beneficial for creative thought (for review, see Heilman, Nadeau, & Beversdorf, 2003). For example, lowering levels of noradrenaline through the administration of a noradrenaline antagonist improves performance on creative problem solving such as anagram solution (Beversdorf, Hughes, Steinberg, Lewis, & Heilman, 1999; Silver, Hughes, Bornstein, & Beversdorf, 2004). Subjects are also quicker to solve anagrams when lying down than when standing (Lipnicki & Byrne, 2005), an effect linked to the lower noradrenergic system activity when lying down (Svensson, 1987). Similarly, the administration of L-Dopa, a precursor to both dopamine and noradrenaline, decreases subjects' capacity to access distant semantic relations between concepts (Kischka, Kammer, Maier, Weisbrod, Thimm, & Spitzer, 1996), thus lowering creative thinking ability. Finally, rapid eye movement (REM) sleep is marked by decreased levels of noradrenaline relative to nonREM (NREM) sleep (Rasmussen, Morilak, & Jacobs, 1986) and a corresponding decrease in cognitive control and increase in hyper-associative imagery (Fosse, Stickgold, & Hobson, 2004). Subjects awoken from REM sleep are better at solving anagrams compared with when awoken from NREM sleep (Walker, Liston, Hobson, & Stickgold, 2002) and show improved access to distant semantic relations between concepts (Stickgold, Scott, Rittenhouse, & Hobson, 1999). Thus, lowering cognitive control and arousal, as well as shifting attention from a focused state to a wider, defocused attentional state, enables a transition from a relatively goal-directed thinking mode to a more associative, creative mode. This state of defocused attention may be one of the key factors facilitating creative thought (Gabora, 2002, 2003; Heilman et al., 2003; Howard-Jones & Murray, 2003; Mendelsohn, 1976).

A further parallel between spontaneous and creative thought is the observed recruitment of regions of the default and memory networks for both types of thought processes. For example, the occurrence of insight during remote associate problems is linked to activation in temporal lobe regions, such as the anterior superior temporal gyrus (aSTG) and the parahippocampus, as well as the medial prefrontal cortex and the posterior cingulate (Jung-Beeman et al., 2004). Furthermore, in a study designed to investigate the mental set prior to solving insight problems, Kounios and colleagues (2006) found that default network regions (ACC and PCC) are more active prior to the presentation of remote associates problems that were subsequently solved with insight, compared with those solved without insight. Default network regions (anterior medial frontal cortex and ACC) are also activated when subjects generate creative compared with uncreative stories, and when they generate a story from a list of unrelated compared with related words (Howard-Jones, Blakemore, Samuel, Summers, & Claxton, 2005). This facilitation of semantic divergence and insight solutions may be linked to the wider and looser attentional focus associated with activation of default network regions, while the recruitment of temporal lobe regions may be important for the generation of associations and their semantic integration (Achim, Bertrand, Montoya, Malla, & Lepage, 2007; Lepage, Habib, Cormier, Houle, & McIntosh, 2000).

In addition to the memory and default networks, some types of creative thought—particularly those that require more control and focused attention—are associated with recruitment of the lateral PFC. For example, a typical divergent thinking task is to generate as many different uses for a brick as possible (de Bono, 1970). This task requires the evaluation of each generated use for its appropriateness and its novelty with respect to the other uses already generated (Feist, 1998). Such evaluative functions are tightly linked to lateral PFC functions, and PFC recruitment has been observed when creative individuals engage in this divergent thinking task (Carlsson, Wendt, & Risberg, 2000). In addition, the PFC is also recruited for creative thinking tasks that require shifting from traditional to more novel strategies (e.g., Camfield, 2005; Heilman et al., 2003), a finding consistent with the long-established role of the lateral PFC in task-switching (Buchsbaum, Greer, Chang, & Berman, 2005).

Other forms of creative thought may be associated with less prefrontal recruitment. One example is the state of "flow experience" characterized by the performance of a task seemingly without effort but to the best of one's ability (Csikszentmihalyi, 1990). Such flow states are considered to be accompanied by a diminished prefrontal recruitment compared with other forms of creative thought (Dietrich, 2004). It has been proposed that creative thought includes different components: First, a generative stage relying on the generation of novelty and access to remote semantic associations, which appears to be linked to "default" network and memory regions; and second, the evaluative aspects, which may be most strongly linked to lateral prefrontal recruitment.

Thus, creative thought appears to be in a unique position of involving the contribution of cognitive control (lateral PFC), defocused attention (default network), and memory (temporal lobes). In contrast, goal-directed thinking appears to require a proportionately higher contribution from cognitive control (lateral PFC) and is associated with some of the lowest contributions from the default network, presumably because the state of heightened attention it requires displaces the state of defocused attention associated with default network recruitment. Finally, mind wandering is associated with a relatively limited contribution from the lateral PFC, but relatively high default and memory network contributions (see Figure 11.2). Keeping in mind these relationships between mind wandering and other forms of thought, we next turn to the question of the possible functions of spontaneous thought.

SPONTANEOUS THOUGHT, SLEEP, AND MEMORY CONSOLIDATION

Spontaneous thought may appear to occupy one extreme end of a thought continuum in terms of cognitive control. However, if we view it as part of

Forms of thought

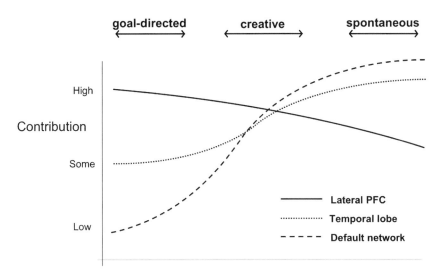

Figure 11.2 Proposed relative contribution of the lateral PFC, temporal lobe memory regions, and the default network to goal-directed, creative, and spontaneous thought.

a broader continuum of wake–sleep mental states (Fosse, Stickgold, & Hobson, 2001), it would represent only a mid-point between the highly focused attention of active wakefulness, on the one hand, and the extreme lowering of cognitive control during sleep, on the other hand. Evidence for this extreme lowering of cognitive control during sleep comes from findings of consistent down-regulation of lateral PFC activation during sleep compared with resting wakefulness (Braun et al., 1997; Maquet et al., 1996; Nofzinger, Mintun, Wiseman, Kupfer, & Moore, 1997), as well as aminergic demodulation and cholinergic activation (Mamelak & Hobson, 1989; Sutton, Mamelak, & Hobson, 1992). In addition, cognitive studies show that the frequency of thought decreases as one moves from a state of quiet wakefulness to sleep onset, and continues to decrease during NREM sleep until it reaches its nadir during REM sleep (Fosse et al., 2001). The frequency of hallucinations, on the other hand, follows the opposite trend, with lowest occurrence during quiet wakeful state and peak occurrence during REM sleep (Fosse et al., 2001). While REM and NREM differ along various dimensions, this difference appears to be a matter of degree; the same phenomena occur during both types of sleep states, but tend to be observed more frequently during REM (Fosse et al., 2001; Ji & Wilson, 2007; Sutherland & McNaughton, 2000; Wilson & McNaughton, 1994).

The proximity of resting wakeful states to sleep states on a wake–sleep continuum suggests that spontaneous thought, which is most likely to occur during resting states, may bear important similarity in its functions and mechanisms not only to waking thought processes, but also to sleep-related mentation. Indeed, recent theoretical proposals and experimental evidence is beginning to link the phenomenon of off-line processing during sleep to the off-line mental processing that occurs during wakefulness.

Off-line processing during sleep

The kind of off-line processing that occurs during sleep is known to benefit subsequent thinking, decision making, and memory in crucial ways. Not only is sleep deprivation detrimental to cognitive functioning in general, but there are clear improvements in memory and problem-solving ability following a period of sleep compared with following a period of wakefulness (Ellenbogen et al., 2007; Hu, Stylos-Allan, & Walker, 2006; Wagner, Gais, Haider, Verleger, & Born, 2004).

The memory improvement associated with sleep has been linked to what appears to be a replay of recent experiences in the cortex and hippocampus. Single-cell recordings in the rat show that cells that fire together during a waking experience tend to also fire together during subsequent REM sleep (Wilson & McNaughton, 1994) and NREM sleep (Ji & Wilson, 2007; Sutherland & McNaughton, 2000). This replay is temporally structured and can reflect tens of seconds to minutes of behavioral experience reproduced at an equivalent timescale (Louie & Wilson, 2001), suggesting episodic memory trace reactivation during sleep.

Dreaming in humans may be a manifestation of a similar replay of experiences at the neuronal level. Findings from neuroimaging studies in humans show that brain regions that are activated during learning experiences are re-activated during subsequent REM (Maquet et al., 2000) and NREM sleep (Peigneux, Laureys et al., 2004). Moreover, the amount of activation in the hippocampus and parahippocampus during NREM sleep is positively correlated with performance improvement on the following day (Peigneux, Laureys et al., 2004). Consistent with these findings, dreaming about newly learned material enhances subsequent recall of that material (Nielsen & Stenstrom, 2005) and pre-sleep stories are better recalled in the morning if subjects dreamt frequently about constituents of the stories during the night (Fiss, Kremer, & Litchman, 1977). Thus, the off-line replay of episodic experiences during sleep appears to be associated with subsequent improvements in memory and performance.

The literal replay of episodic memories, however, occurs very rarely during sleep (about 1–2% of dream reports; Fosse, Fosse, Hobson, & Stickgold, 2003). Instead, the reproduction of isolated fragments of episodic memories is much more common (about 28–38%; Cavallero,

Foulkes, Hollifield, & Terry, 1990). Moreover, memory elements that are reproduced during sleep derive their sources not only from relatively recent experiences arising during the day or week before the dream (Nielsen, Kuiken, Alain, Stenstrom, & Powell, 2004) but also from fairly old memories such as those arising from between the ages of 10 and 19 (Grenier et al., 2005). It seems that far from simply being the passive reactivation of recent memories, off-line processing during sleep is a much more active, complex activity.

Recent theories about the functions of sleep are beginning to view it as an active process of memory consolidation and re-consolidation (Maquet, 2001; Stickgold, Hobson, Fosse, & Fosse, 2001), with memories re-activated in order to alter their strengths, structures, and associations (Stickgold, Malia, Maguire, Roddenberry, & O'Connor, 2000) and to link them adaptively to current motivational concerns (Paller & Voss, 2004). The physiological properties of REM sleep (tonic aminergic demodulation and phasic cholinergic activation) are thought to lead to hyperassociative mentation, marked by an increase in unexpected associative sequences (Mamelak & Hobson, 1989; Sutton et al., 1992) and a preferential access to weak, unusual associations between concepts (Stickgold et al., 1999). For instance, when objects in dreams are suddenly and unexpectedly transformed into other objects, they are normally related to each other by unpredictable and weak associations (Rittenhouse, Stickgold, & Hobson, 1994). In this way, the off-line processing during sleep appears to allow for unpredictable but potentially valuable associations to be tested and strengthened, if appropriate (Stickgold et al., 2000)—by strengthening connections among dispersed cortico-cortical and hippocampo-cortical connections (Paller & Voss, 2004).

Importantly, memories appear to be consolidated adaptively, in relation to current problems, goals, and experiences (Paller & Voss, 2004). The contents of dreams are often structured around the individual's dominant, pre-sleep concerns (Hartmann, 1998) and emotions appear to play a key role during this consolidation process (Nielsen & Stenstrom, 2005). The amygdala, which controls the encoding and retrieval of emotional memories and maintains direct reciprocal connections with the hippocampus, is more activated during REM sleep than during wakefulness (Hobson, Pace-Schott, Stickgold, & Kahn, 1998). Together with the hippocampus, it plays a crucial role in the process of transforming emotionally rich episodic memories into semantic memories of lower emotional charge— a crucial aspect of memory consolidation.

The process of "dismantling" episodic memories of their contextual and emotional associations and consolidating them into semantic memory is considered to be tightly linked to medial temporal lobe functioning. However, while the hippocampus serves to provide access to complete episodic memories during wakefulness (Moscovitch, Nadel, Winocur, Gilboa, & Rosenbaum, 2006), its function during sleep appears to be different (Nielsen & Stenstrom, 2005). The replay of episodic memories that occurs during sleep is not dependent on the hippocampus and, if anything, occurs more frequently when the hippocampus is damaged. The dreams of patients with hippocampal damage frequently replay complete episodic memories of actual events in a stereotyped, repetitious way, and without symbolic elaborations (Torda, 1969). Similarly, patients with post-traumatic stress disorder, who suffer diminished hippocampal capacity, experience the frequent replay of nightmares that are highly episodic in nature (Mellman, 1997), suggesting a dysfunction of cortical memory consolidation during sleep.

Overall, the functions of off-line processing during sleep appear to be geared toward the incorporation of new episodic memories into semantic memory (consolidation) and the re-activation of old memories and associations in order to adaptively change their strength and connections (re-consolidation). As cholinergic transmission rises and aminergic transmission decreases, a progressive disinhibition of numerous cortical and subcortical systems occurs, including internal pulse-generation systems such as the anterolateral pons, which leads to progressive excitement of the multimodal sensory areas (Fosse et al., 2001) that may lead to the spontaneous reactivation of memories. At the same time, medial temporal lobe structures, including the hippocampus, contribute to the adaptive consolidation of these memories and to the altering of their association strengths. Indeed, sleep is considered to be an obvious time for such replay and cortical modification to occur, because there is no competition from external sensory inputs that ordinarily have strong influence on multimodal sensory cortices during active wakefulness (Stickgold, 1998). However, conditions during restful wakefulness, when an individual is not engaged in an active task involving the processing of external sensory inputs, resemble closely those during sleep. Indeed, the functions of sleep are beginning to provide clues regarding the possible functions of off-line mental processing during wakefulness.

Off-line processing during wakefulness

Recently emerging evidence has suggested that off-line processing during wakefulness resembles in its functions and effects the off-line processing that occurs during sleep. For instance, a neural replay of recent experiences during periods of quiet wakefulness has been observed in the rat, reminiscent of the replay observed during sleep (Foster & Wilson, 2006; Sutherland & McNaughton, 2000). Similarly, recent neuroimaging studies in humans demonstrate that neural activity related to post-training learning and memory consolidation occurs during the period of wakefulness following training. Thus, learning-dependent changes have been observed in spontaneous brain activity while subjects perform an unrelated task after learning either a spatial or procedural memory task (Peigneux, Schmitz, & Willems, 2007). Similar learning-dependent post-training neural activity for the same tasks is known to occur during both NREM (Peigneux, Melchior et al., 2004) and REM sleep (Maquet et al., 2000).

Recent behavioral findings in humans complement these neural results by demonstrating that there are memory improvements that follow periods of wakefulness, resembling those that occur after equivalent periods of sleep (Ellenbogen et al., 2007). Thus, memory consolidation appears to occur during both wakefulness and sleep, with off-line processing beginning during the wakefulness following given experience, and continuing during subsequent sleep (Peigneux et al., 2006). Spontaneously arising cognitions during wakefulness that are often experienced in the form of mind wandering may then represent, at least in part, the products of the memory consolidation process.

Mind wandering as a manifestation of off-line processing during wakefulness

In the same way that nighttime dreams are considered to be linked to the reactivation of experiences in the process of memory consolidation, mind wandering may be the result of a similar reactivation of experiences and their combination in the process of off-line memory consolidation and re-consolidation. The replay of experiences during wakefulness may be facilitated by relatively low levels of external stimulation (e.g., quiet, restful environment) or by the turning of attention away from external stimuli (i.e., "tuning out")—both of which are known to be associated with a higher incidence of mind wandering (e.g., Singer, 1981; Smallwood & Schooler, 2006). During these states, the involvement of sensory cortices with external stimuli would be lower, which would facilitate the cortico-hippocampal interplay that is considered to be crucial for the process of memory consolidation (McClelland, McNaughton, & O'Reilly, 1995).

Thus, mind wandering may be the subjective experience resulting from ongoing off-line processing, including the reactivation and recombination of recent experiences. When it occurs during a task, mind wandering may be a manifestation of off-line processing that occurs in parallel with task-related thought. It could lead to the experience of a frustrating distraction or a sudden insight. In the absence of a task or under conditions of low attentional demand, off-line processing may be richer and manifest itself in the form of daydreaming. Regardless of the situation in which it occurs, however, off-line processing during wakefulness appears to be just as necessary for successful semantic memory formation as off-line processing during asleep. The effect of this off-line processing on subsequent performance and memory may explain why, despite its reputation for uselessness, mind wandering is in fact associated with a number of benefits for cognition and memory.

COGNITIVE BENEFITS OF SPONTANEOUS THOUGHT

A growing body of research demonstrates that spontaneous mentation can be highly beneficial in a wide range of cognitive domains, from memory and thought, to emotion, motivation, and decision making. In this section, we review findings which suggest that far from being an undesirable and wasteful distraction from task-related activity, spontaneous thought appears to be a highly beneficial, essential part of human cognition.

Memory and thought

One particularly striking example of the benefit of off-line processing for memory comes from a study of relational memory by Ellenbogen and colleagues (2007), who found greater inferential ability on a transitive inference task following an extended period of off-line processing (a 12-hour delay during which subjects remained awake) as compared with a shorter time period (a 20-minute delay). During a transitive inference task, subjects learn premise pairs and then later apply the interrelationships between these pairs to infer the relationship between items not previously presented together. For example, after learning the premise pairs A > B and B > C, when presented with the item A?C, one should infer that A > C. The 12-hour group showed improved relational memory compared with the 20-minute group. The memory improvement on items with one degree of separation was very similar to the improvement observed after 12-hour delay that included sleep (although after sleep, an additional improvement on items with two degrees of separation was observed). Thus, off-line processing during wakefulness appears especially beneficial for the consolidation of associations and relational memory.

Spontaneously occurring cognition also benefits goal-directed and creative thought by enriching the outcome of the thinking process and broadening its scope. Although it has been notoriously difficult to study, the thought phenomenon of insight is considered to occur spontaneously following a period of off-line processing (e.g., Dorfman, Shames, & Kihlstrom, 1996; Gabora, 2010; Schooler & Melcher, 1995; Smith, 1995; Wallas, 1926). Spontaneous cognition has also been closely linked to creative thought. Many creative artists and scientists have linked important insights to their daydreams (Klinger, 1990) and empirical findings show that the frequency of reported daydreaming is correlated with a subject's creativity (Singer & Schonbar, 1961). Experimental findings also show that when a creative task is preceded by a period of distraction, the generated ideas are less obvious and more creative compared with those generated after an equivalent period of deliberate thought (Dijksterhuis & Meurs, 2006). This phenomenon has been ascribed to the unfocused, spontaneous thought processes occurring during a distracting task (Dijksterhuis & Nordgren, 2006). The benefits of spontaneous cognition for creative thought is perhaps best recognized by modern practitioners in the creative fields, who regard spontaneously occurring thought as one of the two key components of the creative process—a crucial part of the interplay between critical and spontaneous cognition known as "flip-flop" thinking (Charles Dobson, personal communication).

Emotion and motivation

Spontaneous thought has also been shown to have a beneficial effect on emotional processing. For example, in one study by Paton et al. (reported by Singer, 1981), subjects were insulted by an experimenter while performing a task. Following the insult, one group of subjects was shown either neutral or aggressive images and instructed to use them to construct fantasies, whereas another group was not given the opportunity to engage in fantasy. Subsequently, the insulted group that did not have an opportunity to mind wander reported higher levels of anger than both mind-wandering groups, suggesting that mind wandering can provide a form of effective emotional regulation and the opportunity to formulate an alternate perspective in assessing one's emotions.

The content of spontaneously occurring mentation, such as mind wandering and daydreaming, is known to be closely related to current concerns and motivations (Singer, 1981). An interesting connection between off-line processing and motivation has been suggested by findings from single-cell recordings in the rat that have revealed a replay of experiences during restful wakefulness (Foster & Wilson, 2006). This replay has a unique, reverse form. For example, if the rat visited locations A, B, and then C, while running on a track in search of a reward, this sequence would be replayed as C, B, and then A while the rat is resting on the track, having reached the reward. Foster and Wilson proposed that this reverse replay serves the process of assigning motivational value to experiences through reward-related dopamine release: Those experiences that are temporally closer to the reward, and hence more predictive of a reward, are replayed first and assigned a higher motivational value through dopamine release; the further away from the reward an experience is, the later it is replayed, thus achieving the assignment of a decreasing gradient of motivational value to experiences depending on the extent to which they predict a reward. This assigning of value provides the advantage of increasing the availability of information regarding a reward, thereby potentially allowing it to guide choice at locations distant from the goal. Thus, the replay of events during periods of rest seems to be of significance for motivational learning, in addition to its role in memory consolidation.

Decision making

Spontaneous, unconscious thought also appears to benefit decision making, especially when it comes to complex decisions. This phenomenon is clearly illustrated in the work of Ap Dijksterhuis and colleagues. For example, in a series of studies, subjects received information about various alternatives (e.g., apartments, roommates) with the goal to decide which alternative is the most attractive (Dijksterhuis, 2004). Subjects chose either immediately, after a period of deliberately thinking about the various alternatives, or after performing a distracting task (n-back or anagram solving) during which their attention was turned away from the alternatives. During this distraction period, participants were assumed to engage in unconscious, spontaneously occurring thought. Out of the presented alternatives, one alternative was classified by the experimenter as the best choice due to it being characterized by more positive and fewer negative attributes as compared with the other alternatives. Subjects who performed a distracting task made a better decision, as indexed by making a stronger distinction between the most attractive alternative and the least attractive alternative, than those who were asked to consciously deliberate before making their decision. Supporting the assumption that participants were engaging in unconscious, spontaneously occurring thought, additional evidence indicated that the mental representations of the various alternatives changed during the distraction period, having become clearer and better organized, eventually having led to better decisions.

This benefit of spontaneous thought may be particularly relevant to complex decisions that require a large amount of information to be considered. This was illustrated in a study in which subjects were asked to select which one of four cars they would buy, given a list of each car's attributes (Dijksterhuis, Maarten et al., 2006). Decisions were classified as either simple (4 attributes) or complex (12 attributes), based on the number of attributes ascribed to each car. The attributes were either positive or negative. The cars were characterized by differing percentages of positive attributes. Subjects were either asked to think about the cars for 4 minutes before making their choice or they were given a distraction task (anagram solving) for 4 minutes and were told that following this task they would be asked to select the best car. The group of subjects that engaged in deliberate thought regarding their decision made a better choice in the simple decision conditions. For the complex decision, however, the group that performed a distracting task made better decisions compared with the deliberate thinking group. This effect could be due to the fact that deliberate, conscious thought has a relatively low capacity (Miller, 1956), leading choosers to take into account only a subset of the relevant information for a given decision (Dijksterhuis, 2004; Wilson & Schooler, 1991). Spontaneously occurring unconscious thought, on the other hand, has a much broader focus, allowing for large amounts of information to be integrated into an evaluative summary judgment (Dijksterhuis, 2004). Also, as mentioned previously, evidence suggests that reorganization of representations occurs during unconscious thought leading to clustering and polarization of information, thus allowing for better decision making (Dijksterhuis, 2004; Dijksterhuis, Maarten et al., 2006).

Spontaneous thought may facilitate decision making through several mechanisms. It may allow for broader connections to be made among concepts in the mind than directed thought. Spontaneous thought may also allow the mind to devote sustained periods of "off-line" thought to a decision. Such off-line thought may be conducive to unconscious processes useful to decision making, such as pattern recognition and weighting multiple factors in a decision. Thus, by engaging in spontaneous thought, the mind may be employing a large arsenal of unconscious decision-making processes.

In summary, empirical findings indicate that far from being wasteful and undesirable, spontaneous thought can be shown to produce strong benefits throughout human cognition and everyday life. While the negative aspects of spontaneous thought are typically emphasized, it is important to keep in mind the existence of these benefits. It is up to future research to develop a greater understanding of the mechanisms by which spontaneous thought occurs and the circumstances that bring about both its beneficial and detrimental interactions with cognitive processes.

CONCLUSIONS

We often rebel against our own propensity to engage in spontaneous thoughts and try to banish them from our minds, treating them as a harmful distraction. Whether we like it or not, however, we spend a third of our waking lives engaged in thoughts unrelated to the present task (Kane et al., 2007; Klinger & Cox, 1987). We now know that the third of our lives we spend on sleep is by no means wasteful but is instead necessary for us to be able to function during the remaining two-thirds of our lives. It may well turn out that spending a portion of our waking lives letting our mind wander is just as important for our successful functioning during the remaining waking time when we may be engaged in more deliberate, focused thought.

The kind of spontaneous thought processes that occur during periods of distraction or rest appear to facilitate memory consolidation—or the integration of isolated episodic experiences into a coherent, meaningful autobiographical structure that gives us a sense of self. Similarly to sleep, the function of spontaneous thought may be to help us make sense of our experiences by building a coherent and meaningful structure out of the isolated, and at first unrelated, events that constitute our everyday lives. In contrast to sleep, however, wakefulness may allow this integration to occur at a more conscious level—by allowing spontaneous thought to interact with deliberate, goal-directed thought.

When we let our minds wander, we shift our mode of thinking to a more spontaneous, less controlled kind of thinking, which can help us reach more creative, less predictable conclusions. This could broaden the amount of information and the number of factors we could take into account while thinking. It seems that in most cases when it produces a cognitive benefit, spontaneous thought either precedes or follows a period of more goal-directed, deliberate thought. This temporal alternation between the two different modes of thought may be what leads to some of the most beneficial outcomes, such as new insights, deeper levels of understanding, and novel, creative ideas. The nature and mechanisms of this alternation, as well as the existence of an optimal proportion of time spent in each thinking mode, remain to be examined in future research.

Perhaps one of the biggest benefits brought about by spontaneous thought appears to be in the area of complex decision making. Spontaneous thought facilitates the process of making sense of our experiences, the drawing of connections between memories and concepts, the broadening of attentional focus to include a larger amount of information into consideration, and the process of assigning motivational value to experiences—all factors that are essential in making a good decision in a complex situation.

The American playwright Lillian Hellman once said "Decisions, particularly important ones, have always made me sleepy, perhaps because I know that I will have to make them by instinct, and thinking things out is only what other people tell me I should do." Her intuition regarding the importance of instinctual, spontaneous thought in making complex decision has been borne out in multiple psychological findings since. The process of deliberately thinking things out may be a part of the decision process, but it is the more spontaneous, defocused thinking mode—which Hellman correctly intuited as vaguely reminiscent of sleep—that may be necessary for important decisions to be successfully made. Although things are beginning to change, to this day, the majority of what we know about spontaneous thought comes from our intuitions and subjective introspections. One thing, however, is fairly clear; further progress in our understanding of human thought and decision making would be impossible without taking into account spontaneous thought. Doing so presents some of the biggest challenges to experimental investigation, and yet holds some of the biggest promises for the advance of our understanding of human thought and decision making.

REFERENCES

Achim, A. M., Bertrand, M.-C., Montoya, A., Malla, A. K., & Lepage, M. (2007). Medial temporal lobe activations during associative memory encoding for arbitrary and semantically related object pairs. *Brain Research*, *1161*, 46–55.

Andreasen, N. C., O'Leary, D. S., Cizadlo, T., Arndt, S., Rezai, K., Watkins, G. L. et al. (1995). Remembering the past: Two facets of episodic memory explored with positron emission tomography. *American Journal of Psychiatry*, *152*, 1576–1585.

Antrobus, J. S. (1968). Information theory and stimulus-independent thought. *British Journal of Psychology*, *59*, 423–430.

Antrobus, J. S., Singer, J. L., & Greenberg, S. (1966). Studies in the stream of consciousness: Experimental enhancement and suppression of spontaneous cognitive processes. *Perceptual and Motor Skills*, *23*, 399–417.

Bargh, J. G. P., Lee-Chai, A., Barndollar, K., & Trotschel, R. (2001). The automated will: Nonconscious activation and pursuit of behavioral goals. *Journal of Personality and Social Psychology*, *81*, 1014–1027.

Bettman, J. R., Luce, M. F., & Payne, J. W. (1998). Constructive consumer choice processes. *Journal of Consumer Research*, *25*, 187–217.

Beversdorf, D. Q., Hughes, J. D., Steinberg, B. A., Lewis, L. D., & Heilman, K. M. (1999). Noradrenergic modulation of cognitive flexibility in problem solving. *Neuroreport*, *10*, 2763–2767.

Binder, J. R., Frost, J. A., Hammeke, T. A., Bellgowan, P. S., Rao, S. M., & Cox, R. W. (1999). Conceptual processing during the conscious resting state: A functional MRI study. *Journal of Cognitive Neuroscience*, *11*, 80–95.

Braun, A. R., Balkin, T. J., Wesenten, N. J., Carson, R. E., Varga, M., Baldwin, P. et al. (1997). Regional cerebral blood flow throughout the sleep–wake cycle. An H2(15)O PET study. *Brain*, *120*, 1173–1197.

Buchsbaum, B. R., Greer, S., Chang, W.-L., & Berman, K. F. (2005). Meta-analysis of neuroimaging studies of the Wisconsin Card-Sorting Task and component processes. *Human Brain Mapping*, *25*, 35–45.

Camfield, D. (2005). Neurobiology of creativity. In C. Stough (Ed.), *Neurobiology of exceptionality* (pp. 53–72). New York: Kluwer Academic/Plenum Publishers.

Carlsson, I., Wendt, P. E., & Risberg, J. (2000). On the neurobiology of creativity. Differences in frontal activity between high and low creative subjects. *Neuropsychologia*, *38*, 873–885.

Cavallero, C., Foulkes, D., Hollifield, M., & Terry, R. (1990). Memory sources of REM and NREM dreams. *Sleep*, *13*, 449–455.

Chamberlain, S. R., Muller, U., Blackwell, A. D., Robbins, T. W., & Sahakian, B. J. (2006). Noradrenergic modulation of working memory and emotional memory in humans. *Psychopharmacology*, *188*, 397–407.

Christoff, K., & Gabrieli, J. D. E. (2000). The frontopolar cortex and human cognition: Evidence for a rostrocaudal hierarchical organization within the human prefrontal cortex. *Psychobiology*, *28*, 168–186.

Christoff, K., Gordon, A. M., Smallwood, J., Smith, R., & Schooler, J. W. (2009). Experience sampling during fMRI reveals default network and executive system contributions to mind wandering. *Proceedings of the National Academy of Sciences*, *106*, 8719–8724.

Christoff, K., Ream, J. M., & Gabrieli, J. D. (2004). Neural basis of spontaneous thought processes. *Cortex*, *40*, 623–630.

Cohen, J. D., & Servan-Schreiber, D. (1992). Context, cortex, and dopamine: A connectionist approach to behavior and biology in schizophrenia. *Psychological Review*, *99*, 45–77.

Crawford, J. R., Bryan, J., Luszcz, M. A., Obonsawin, M. C., & Stewart, L. (2000). The executive decline hypothesis of cognitive aging: Do executive deficits qualify as differential deficits and do they mediate age-related memory decline? *Aging, Neuropsychology, and Cognition*, *7*, 9–31.

Csikszentmihalyi, M. (1990). *Flow*. New York: Harper & Row.

Cunningham, S., Scerbo, M. W., & Freeman, F. G. (2000). The electrocortical correlates of daydreaming during vigilance tasks. *Journal of Mental Imagery*, *24*, 61–72.

de Bono, E. (1970). *Lateral thinking*. New York: Penguin.

Descartes, R. (1637/1998). *Discourse on method* (D. A. Cress, Trans.). Indianapolis, IN: Hackett.

Desimone, R., & Duncan, J. (1995). Neural mechanisms of selective visual attention. *Annual Review of Neuroscience*, *18*, 193–222.

Dietrich, A. (2004). The cognitive neuroscience of creativity. *Psychonomic Bulletin and Review*, *11*, 1011–1026.

Dijksterhuis, A. (2004). Think different: The merits of unconscious thought in preference development and decision making. *Journal of Personality and Social Psychology*, *87*, 586–598.

Dijksterhuis, A., Maarten, B., Nordgren, L., & van Baaren, R. (2006). On making the right choice: The deliberation-without-attention effect. *Science*, *311*, 1005–1007.

Dijksterhuis, A., & Meurs, T. (2006). Where creativity resides: The generative power of unconscious thought. *Consciousness and Cognition*, *15*, 135–146.

Dijksterhuis, A., & Nordgren, L. F. (2006). A theory of unconscious thought. *Perspectives on Psychological Science*, *1*, 95–109.

Dorfman, J., Shames, V. A., & Kihlstrom, J. F. (1996). Intuition, incubation, and insight: Implicit cognition in problem solving. In G. D. M. Underwood (Ed.), *Implicit cognition* (pp. 257–296). New York: Oxford University Press.

Duncan, J., Burgess, P., & Emslie, H. (1995). Fluid intelligence after frontal lobe lesions. *Neuropsychologia*, *33*, 261–268.

Ellenbogen, J. M., Hu, P. T., Payne, J. D., Titone, D., & Walker, M. P. (2007). Human relational memory requires time and sleep. *Proceedings of the National Academy of Sciences of the United States of America, 104*, 7723–7728.

Feist, G. J. (1998). A meta-analysis of personality in scientific and artistic creativity. *Personality and Social Psychology Review, 2*, 290–309.

Fink, A., & Neubauer, A. C. (2006). EEG alpha oscillations during the performance of verbal creativity tasks: Differential effects of sex and verbal intelligence. *International Journal of Psychophysiology, 62*, 46–53.

Fiss, H., Kremer, E., & Litchman, J. (1977). The mnemonic function of dreaming. *Sleep Research, 6*, 122–136.

Fosse, M. J., Fosse, R., Hobson, J. A., & Stickgold, R. J. (2003). Dreaming and episodic memory: A functional dissociation? *Journal of Cognitive Neuroscience, 15*, 1–9.

Fosse, R., Stickgold, R., & Hobson, J. A. (2001). Brain-mind states: Reciprocal variation in thoughts and hallucinations. *Psychological Science, 12*, 30–36.

Fosse, R., Stickgold, R., & Hobson, J. A. (2004). Thinking and hallucinating: Reciprocal changes in sleep. *Psychophysiology, 41*, 298–305.

Foster, D. J., & Wilson, M. A. (2006). Reverse replay of behavioural sequences in hippocampal place cells during the awake state. *Nature, 440*, 680–683.

Gabora, L. (2002). *Cognitive mechanisms underlying the creative process.* Paper presented at the Proceedings of the Fourth International Conference on Creativity and Cognition, Loughborough, UK.

Gabora, L. (2003). *Contextual focus: A cognitive explanation of the cultural transition of the Middle/Upper Paleolithic.* Paper presented at the Proceedings of the 25th Annual Meeting of the Cognitive Science Society, Hillsdale, NJ.

Gabora, L. (2010). Revenge of the "neurds": Characterizing creative thought in terms of the structure and dynamics of human memory. *Creative Research Journal, 22*, 1–13.

Giambra, L. M. (1989). Task-unrelated thought frequency as a function of age: A laboratory study. *Psychology and Aging, 4*, 136–143.

Giambra, L. M. (1995). A laboratory method for investigating influences on switching attention to task-unrelated imagery and thought. *Consciousness and Cognition, 4*, 1–21.

Grenier, J., Cappeliez, P., St-Onge, M., Vachon, J., Vinette, S., Roussy, F. et al. (2005). Temporal references in dreams and autobiographical memory. *Memory and Cognition, 33*, 280–288.

Hartmann, E. (1998). *Dreams and nightmares: The new theory on the origin and meaning of dreams.* New York: Plenum.

Hasher, L., & Zacks, R. T. (1988). Working memory, comprehension, and aging: A review and a new view. In G. H. Bower (Ed.), *The psychology of learning and motivation: Advances in research and theory* (Vol. 22, pp. 193–225). San Diego, CA: Academic Press.

Heilman, K. M., Nadeau, S. E., & Beversdorf, D. O. (2003). Creative innovation: Possible brain mechanisms. *Neurocase, 9*, 369–379.

Hobson, J. A., Pace-Schott, E. F., Stickgold, R., & Kahn, D. (1998). To dream or not to dream? Relevant data from new neuroimaging and electrophysiological studies. *Current Opinion in Neurobiology, 8*, 239–244.

Howard-Jones, P. A., Blakemore, S.-J., Samuel, E. A., Summers, I. R., & Claxton, G. (2005). Semantic divergence and creative story generation: An fMRI investigation. *Cognitive Brain Research, 25*, 240–250.

Howard-Jones, P. A., & Murray, S. (2003). Ideational productivity, focus of attention, and context. *Creativity Research Journal, 15*, 153–166.

Hu, P., Stylos-Allan, M., & Walker, M. P. (2006). Sleep facilitates consolidation of emotional declarative memory. *Psychological Science, 17*, 891–898.

Janis, I. L., & Mann, L. (1977). *Decision making: A psychological analysis of conflict, choice, and commitment.* New York: Free Press.

Ji, D., & Wilson, M. A. (2007). Coordinated memory replay in the visual cortex and hippocampus during sleep. *Nature Neuroscience, 10*, 100–107.

Jung-Beeman, M., Bowden, E. M., Haberman, J., Frymiare, J. L., Arambel-Liu, S., Greenblatt, R. et al. (2004). Neural activity when people solve verbal problems with insight. *PLoS Biology, 2*, 500–510.

Kahneman, D. (2003). A perspective on judgment and choice: Mapping bounded rationality. *American Psychologist, 58*, 697–720.

Kane, M. J., Brown, L. H., McVay, J. C., Silvia, P. J., Myin-Germeys, I., & Kwapil, T. R. (2007). For whom the mind wanders, and when: An experience-sampling study of working memory and executive control in daily life. *Psychological Science, 18*, 614–621.

Kischka, U., Kammer, T., Maier, S., Weisbrod, M., Thimm, M., & Spitzer, M. (1996). Dopaminergic modulation of semantic network activation. *Neuropsychologia, 34*, 1107–1113.

Klinger, E. (1990). *Daydreaming: Using waking fantasy and imagery for self-knowledge and creativity.* New York: St. Martin's Press.

Klinger, E., & Cox, W. M. (1987). Dimensions of thought flow in everyday life. *Imagination, Cognition and Personality, 7*, 105–128.

Kounios, J., Frymiare, J. L., Bowden, E. M., Fleck, J. I., Subramaniam, K., Parrish, T. B. et al. (2006). The prepared mind: Neural activity prior to problem presentation predicts subsequent solution by sudden insight. *Psychological Science, 17*, 882–890.

Lepage, M., Habib, R., Cormier, H., Houle, S., & McIntosh, A. R. (2000). Neural correlates of semantic associative encoding in episodic memory. *Cognitive Brain Research, 9*, 271–280.

Lipnicki, D. M., & Byrne, D. G. (2005). Thinking on your back: Solving anagrams faster when supine than when standing. *Cognitive Brain Research, 24*, 719–722.

Locke, J. (1690/1979). *An essay concerning human understanding.* New York: Oxford University Press.

Louie, K., & Wilson, M. A. (2001). Temporally structured replay of awake hippocampal ensemble activity during rapid eye movement sleep. *Neuron, 29*, 145–156.

Luria, A. R. (1966). *Higher cortical functions in man.* London: Tavistock Publications.

Mamelak, A., & Hobson, J. A. (1989). Nightcap: A home-based sleep monitoring system. *Sleep, 12*, 157–166.

Maquet, P. (2001). The role of sleep in learning and memory. *Science, 294*, 1048–1052.

Maquet, P., Laureys, S., Peigneux, P., Fuchs, S., Petiau, C., Phillips, C. et al. (2000). Experience-dependent changes in cerebral activation during human REM sleep. *Nature Neuroscience, 3*, 831–836.

Maquet, P., Peters, J., Aerts, J., Delfiore, G., Degueldre, C., Luxen, A. et al. (1996). Functional neuroanatomy of human rapid-eye-movement sleep and dreaming. *Nature, 383*, 163–166.

Mason, M. F., Norton, M. I., Van Horn, J. D., Wegner, D. M., Grafton, S. T., & Macrae, C. N. (2007). Wandering minds: The default network and stimulus-independent thought. *Science, 315*, 393–395.

McClelland, J. L., McNaughton, B. L., & O'Reilly, R. C. (1995). Why there are complementary learning systems in the hippocampus and neocortex: Insights from the successes and failures of connectionist models of learning and memory. *Psychological Review, 102*, 419–457.

Mellman, T. A. (1997). Psychobiology of sleep disturbances in posttraumatic stress disorder. *Annals of the New York Academy of Sciences, 821*, 142–149.

Mendelsohn, G. A. (1976). Associative and attentional processes in creative performance. *Journal of Personality, 44*, 341–369.

Miller, E. K., & Cohen, J. D. (2001). An integrative theory of prefrontal cortex function. *Annual Review of Neuroscience, 24*, 167–202.

Miller, G. A. (1956). The magical number seven, plus or minus two: Some limits on our capacity for processing information. *Psychological Review, 63*, 81–97.

Milner, B. (1964). Some effects of frontal lobectomy in man. In J. M. Warren & K. Akert (Eds.), *The frontal granular cortex and behavior* (pp. 313–334). New York: McGraw-Hill.

Molle, M., Marshall, L., Lutzenberger, W., Pietrowsky, R., Fehm, H. L., & Born, J. (1996). Enhanced dynamic complexity in the human EEG during creative thinking. *Neuroscience Letters, 208*, 61–64.

Molle, M., Marshall, L., Wolf, B., Fehm, H. L., & Born, J. (1999). EEG complexity and performance measures of creative thinking. *Psychophysiology, 36*, 95–104.

Moscovitch, M., Nadel, L., Winocur, G., Gilboa, A., & Rosenbaum, R. S. (2006). The cognitive neuroscience of remote episodic, semantic and spatial memory. *Current Opinion in Neurobiology, 16*, 179–190.

Nielsen, T. A., Kuiken, D., Alain, G., Stenstrom, P., & Powell, R. A. (2004). Immediate and delayed incorporations of events into dreams: Further replication and implications for dream function. *Journal of Sleep Research, 13*, 327–336.

Nielsen, T. A., & Stenstrom, P. (2005). What are the memory sources of dreaming? *Nature, 437*, 1286–1289.

Nofzinger, E. A., Mintun, M. A., Wiseman, M., Kupfer, D. J., & Moore, R. Y. (1997). Forebrain activation in REM sleep: An FDG PET study. *Brain Research, 770*, 192–201.

Paller, K. A., & Voss, J. L. (2004). Memory reactivation and consolidation during sleep. *Learning and Memory, 11*, 664–670.

Peigneux, P., Laureys, S., Fuchs, S., Collette, F., Perrin, F., Reggers, J. et al. (2004). Are spatial memories strengthened in the human hippocampus during slow wave sleep? *Neuron, 44*, 535–545.

Peigneux, P., Melchior, G., Schmidt, C., Dang-Vu, T., Boly, M., Laureys, S. et al.

(2004). Memory processing during sleep mechanisms and evidence from neuroimaging studies. *Psychologica Belgica*, *44*, 121–142.

Peigneux, P., Orban, P., Balteau, E., Degueldre, C., Luxen, A., Laureys, S. et al. (2006). Offline persistence of memory-related cerebral activity during active wakefulness. *PLoS Biology*, *4*, e100.

Peigneux, P., Schmitz, R., & Willems, S. (2007). Cerebral asymmetries in sleep-dependent processes of memory consolidation. *Learning and Memory*, *14*, 400–406.

Raichle, M. E. (1998). The neural correlates of consciousness: An analysis of cognitive skill learning. *Philosophical Transactions of the Royal Society of London B*, *353*, 1889–1901.

Raichle, M. E., MacLeod, A. M., Snyder, A. Z., Powers, W. J., Gusnard, D. A., & Shulman, G. L. (2001). A default mode of brain function. *Proceedings of the National Academy of Sciences of the United States of America*, *98*, 676–682.

Rasmussen, K., Morilak, D. A., & Jacobs, B. L. (1986). Single unit activity of locus coeruleus neurons in the freely moving cat. I. During naturalistic behaviors and in response to simple and complex stimuli. *Brain Research*, *371*, 324–334.

Razumnikova, O. M. (2000). Functional organization of different brain areas during convergent and divergent thinking: An EEG investigation. *Cognitive Brain Research*, *10*, 11–18.

Razumnikova, O. M. (2007). Creativity related cortex activity in the remote associates task. *Brain Research Bulletin*, *73*, 96–102.

Rittenhouse, C. D., Stickgold, R., & Hobson, J. A. (1994). Constraint on the transformation of characters, objects, and settings in dream reports. *Consciousness and Cognition*, *3*, 100–113.

Robbins, T. W. (1997). Arousal systems and attentional processes. *Biological Psychology*, *45*, 57–71.

Schneider, W., & Shiffrin, R. M. (1977). Controlled and automatic processing I: Detection, search, and attention. *Psychological Review*, *84*, 1–66.

Schooler, J. W., & Melcher, J. (1995). The ineffability of insight. In S. M. Smith, T. B. Ward, & R. A. Finke (Eds.), *The creative cognition approach* (pp. 97–133). Cambridge, MA: MIT Press.

Shallice, T. (1982). Specific impairments of planning. *Philosophical Transactions of the Royal Society of London. Series B, Biological Sciences*, *298*, 199–209.

Shulman, G. L., Fiez, J. A., Corbetta, M., Buckner, R. L., Miezin, F. M., Raichle, M. E. et al. (1997). Common blood flow changes across visual tasks: II. Decreases in cerebral cortex. *Journal of Cognitive Neuroscience*, *9*, 648–663.

Silver, J. A., Hughes, J. D., Bornstein, R. A., & Beversdorf, D. Q. (2004). Effect of anxiolytics on cognitive flexibility in problem solving. *Cognitive and Behavioral Neurology*, *17*, 93–97.

Simon, H. A. (1955). A behavioral model of rational choice. *Quarterly Journal of Economics*, *69*, 99–118.

Singer, J. L. (1981). *Daydreaming and fantasy*. Oxford: Oxford University Press.

Singer, J. L., & McCraven, V. G. (1961). Some characteristics of adult daydreaming. *Journal of Psychology: Interdisciplinary and Applied*, *51*, 151.

Singer, J. L., & Schonbar, R. A. (1961). Correlates of daydreaming: A dimension of self-awareness. *Journal of Consulting Psychology*, *25*, 1–6.

Smallwood, J., Davies, J. B., Heim, D., Finnigan, F., Sudberry, M., O'Connor, R. et al. (2004). Subjective experience and the attentional lapse: Task engagement and disengagement during sustained attention. *Consciousness and Cognition*, *13*, 657–690.

Smallwood, J., O'Connor, R. C., Sudberry, M. V., Haskell, C., & Ballantyne, C. (2004). The consequences of encoding information on the maintenance of internally generated images and thoughts: The role of meaning complexes. *Consciousness and Cognition*, *13*, 789–820.

Smallwood, J., & Schooler, J. W. (2006). The restless mind. *Psychological Bulletin*, *132*, 946–958.

Smith, S. M. (1995). Fixation, incubation, and insight in memory and creative thinking. In S. M. Smith, T. B. Ward, & R. A. Finke (Eds.), *The creative cognition approach* (pp. 135–156). Cambridge, MA: The MIT Press.

Stark, C. E., & Squire, L. R. (2001). When zero is not zero: The problem of ambiguous baseline conditions in fMRI. *Proceedings of the National Academy of Sciences of the United States of America*, *98*, 12760–12766.

Stickgold, R. (1998). Sleep: Off-line memory reprocessing. *Trends in Cognitive Sciences*, *2*, 484–492.

Stickgold, R., Hobson, J. A., Fosse, R., & Fosse, M. (2001). Sleep, learning, and dreams: Off-line memory reprocessing. *Science*, *294*, 1052–1057.

Stickgold, R., Malia, A., Maguire, D., Roddenberry, D., & O'Connor, M. (2000). Replaying the game: Hypnagogic images in normals and amnesics. *Science*, *290*, 350–353.

Stickgold, R., Scott, L., Rittenhouse, C., & Hobson, J. A. (1999). Sleep-induced changes in associative memory. *Journal of Cognitive Neuroscience*, *11*, 182–193.

Sutherland, G. R., & McNaughton, B. (2000). Memory trace reactivation in hippocampal and neocortical neuronal ensembles. *Current Opinion in Neurobiology*, *10*, 180–186.

Sutton, J. P., Mamelak, A. N., & Hobson, J. A. (1992). Modeling states of waking and sleeping. *Psychiatric Annals*, *22*, 137–143.

Svensson, T. H. (1987). Peripheral, autonomic regulation of locus coeruleus noradrenergic neurons in brain: Putative implications for psychiatry and psychopharmacology. *Psychopharmacology*, *92*, 1–7.

Teasdale, J. D., Dritschel, B. H., Taylor, M. J., Proctor, L., Lloyd, C. A., Nimmo-Smith, I. et al. (1995). Stimulus-independent thought depends on central executive resources. *Memory and Cognition*, *23*, 551–559.

Torda, C. (1969). Dreams of subjects with loss of memory for recent events. *Psychophysiology*, *6*, 358–365.

Unterrainer, J. M., & Owen, A. M. (2006). Planning and problem solving: From neuropsychology to functional neuroimaging. *Journal of Physiology, Paris*, *99*, 308–317.

Wagner, U., Gais, S., Haider, H., Verleger, R., & Born, J. (2004). Sleep inspires insight. *Nature*, *427*, 352–355.

Walker, M. P., Liston, C., Hobson, J. A., & Stickgold, R. (2002). Cognitive flexibility across the sleep-wake cycle: REM-sleep enhancement of anagram problem solving. *Cognitive Brain Research*, *14*, 317–324.

Wallas, G. (1926). *The art of thought*. New York: Harcourt, Brace and Company.

Wilson, M. A., & McNaughton, B. L. (1994). Reactivation of hippocampal ensemble memories during sleep. *Science, 265,* 676–679.

Wilson, T. D., & Schooler, J. W. (1991). Thinking too much: Introspection can reduce the quality of preferences and decisions. *Journal of Personality and Social Psychology, 60,* 181–192.

CHAPTER TWELVE

Well, what do you want to do? A cognitive neuroscience view of plan decision making

Jorge Moll and Jordan Grafman

INTRODUCTION

Humans spend a great deal of time deciding on which plan to execute and even when to develop a new plan. Plans are a routine human activity. A plan can be defined as a structured event series that generally contains one or more goals. Plans range from the short term and motoric (such as planning a sequence of key presses) (Pascual-Leone et al., 1993) to the long-term and cognitive (such as deciding on the steps required for air-traffic controllers to land a specific airplane) (Suchman, 1987). How plans are decided on has been the focus of study in artificial intelligence (AI) (Allen, Kautz, Pelavin, & Tenenberg, 1991; Hammond, 1994), cognitive science (Friedman & Scholnick, 1997; Hoc, 1988), and neuropsychology (Owen, 1997).

In their prescient book on planning, Miller, Galanter, and Pribram (1960) revealed the difficulty that neuropsychology might have with identifying which brain structures would be concerned with planning as defined by contemporary computer science terminology, eventually admitting "The relation between computers and the brain was a battle the authors fought with one another until the exasperation became unbearable" (p. 197). The responsibility for this difficulty may partly lie in the different methods used to investigate planning by each discipline. Besides their differences, each discipline's methods have their own particular weaknesses. For example, Langley and Drummond (1990) decried the

285

nonexperimental basis of much of the AI literature on planning. They argued, instead, for the development of testable questions that can be experimentally addressed such as: "What are the resources required to generate a plan?"; "In reacting to an unexpected event, how much sampling of the environment is done?"; "What is the ratio of deliberation to execution (and what does that ratio depend on)?"; and "How do subjects modify stored plans versus constructing entirely new plans?"

Many AI and cognitive researchers have also noted the similarity between plans and other knowledge structures such as story grammars, themes, action sets, cases, schemas, and scripts (Schank & Abelson, 1977). All of these knowledge structures represent sequential and structured information that must be sustained in some active state over time for processing (Kolodner, 1993). More importantly for this volume, these same knowledge structures often require an explicit decision to be activated.

In this chapter, we are concerned with identifying the decision processes that are involved in plan development and execution. We will mainly draw on results of studies that explicitly tested planning, although we will cite data from a few studies that investigated script and story processing. Our goal in this chapter is not to describe decision making as it relates directly to objects, scenes, lexical knowledge, and motor actions regardless of their role in constructing and executing a plan, but to provide a description of the cognitive components of plan decision making that can be mapped to the brain. We suggest that the crucial components of plan-specific decision making are primarily stored in the prefrontal cortex (PFC) as a component of the plan itself, with plan execution assisted by motor and other processes carried out by the basal ganglia, motor cortex, and other cortical regions, such as the parietal lobes (Grafman, 1989, 1995; Grafman & Hendler, 1991; Spector & Grafman, 1994), a view that has been supported by recent evidence (e.g., Averbeck & Lee, 2007; Dehaene & Changeux, 1997; Krueger, Moll, Zahn, Heinecke, & Grafman, 2007; Mushiake, Saito, Sakamoto, Itoyama, & Tanji, 2006). Before reviewing the cognitive neuroscience investigation of plan decision making, we will introduce the cognitive and computational science perspectives on planning, setting the groundwork for our claims about which plan-specific components of decision making are distinctively stored in the human PFC.

COGNITIVE AND COMPUTATIONAL PERSPECTIVES ON PLANNING

Cognitive scientists generally describe planning as the process of deciding on an abstract sequence of operations intended for achieving some goal (Hayes-Roth & Hayes-Roth, 1979; Scholnick & Friedman, 1987). The *representation* of this sequence is called a plan (Wilensky, 1983). A plan can be represented internally (in the planner's mind) or externally (e.g., a blue-print, travel route). There are still two predominant views of planning within cognitive psychology: *Successive refinement models* and *opportunistic models*. Successive refinement models propose that planning is a top–down hierarchical process, much like a computer program, that controls the order in which a series of operations can be performed (Miller et al., 1960; Newell & Simon, 1972; Sacerdoti, 1975). Opportunistic models propose that planning is a data-driven process that can operate concurrently at several different levels of abstraction, with decisions at any level affecting subsequent decisions at both higher and lower levels (Hayes-Roth & Hayes-Roth, 1979). It seems intuitive that these are not absolute views and that hybrid models have a place in cognitive neuroscience as well.

The view of planning as successive refinement had its beginning in the work of Miller et al. (1960). They proposed that a plan is "any hierarchical process in the organism that can control the order in which a sequence of operations can be performed" (p. 16). These plans usually include hierarchically organized subplans, which can include further subplans, down to the level of motor action (Das, Kar, & Parrila, 1996). At each level or subplan, the planner executes a TOTE (Test-Operate-Test-Exit) unit, where the planner *tests* to see if a goal is satisfied. If it is not, she *operates* to achieve the goal, *tests* the efficacy of the operation, and then if the goal is met, *exits*. On exiting, the planner moves to the next step in the sequence (Scholnick & Friedman, 1987). This hierarchical, top–down view of planning is evident in many cognitive models, including planning as problem solving within the SOAR (State, Operator, and Result) architecture (Rosenbloom, Laird, & Newell, 1993), Schank and Abelson's (1977) view of plans as a general mechanism underlying the formation of scripts, and in views of planning drawn from AI (Fikes & Nilsson, 1971; Sacerdoti, 1975).

An alternative to the hierarchical, successive refinement models of planning is the *opportunistic model*, such as that proposed by Hayes-Roth and Hayes-Roth (1979). They proposed that at each point in the planning process a planner's current decision affects the opportunities available and the decisions that must be made later in the development of a plan. Thus, plans grow incrementally as each new decision is incorporated into, and revises, previous decisions, creating a multidirectional, revisionary, planning process. Thus, decisions can be made at any level of abstraction at any point in the planning process. In some domains and planning situations, this process will begin at a high level of abstraction and the plan will develop in an orderly, top–down expansion of goals and subgoals, much like in planning by successive refinement. In other domains and planning situations, however, this process will begin as a series of concrete local decisions and the planning process will move between highly abstract decisions and concrete local decisions, often without an overall framework for the decision-making process (Pea & Hawkins, 1987). This basic model of opportunistic planning became the inspiration for many cognitive psychologists studying planning in adults and in children (Baker-Sennett, Matusov, & Rogoff, 1993; Dreher & Oerter, 1987; Pea & Hawkins, 1987).

Both successive refinement and opportunistic planning have been supported empirically, and both appear to explain some central aspect of human planning. Successive refinement models capture the top–down, goal-directed characteristics of human planning (Anderson, 1983) but would lead to the conclusion that young children, who consistently find the use of hierarchies and the process of sequencing difficult, cannot plan (Das et al., 1996). This conclusion has been undermined by results of developmental studies showing that children do plan, and are often quite good at it (for an excellent review of the development of planning, see Friedman, Scholnick, & Cocking, 1987). Opportunistic planning, in turn, has been criticized for making "distractibility" a central aspect of human planning, overlooking a great deal of evidence suggesting that human behavior is controlled by organized structures (Anderson, 1983) and that the many opportunities to decide on aspects of a plan are primarily based on previous experiences in planning with similar environmental contingencies. It appears that both views are necessary to accurately describe the process of planning. When factors such as age, cortical damage, knowledge of the planning domain, and constraints placed on planning efficiency by the human cognitive system are examined, it is clear that both successive refinement and opportunistic planning play a role.

Improvements to the analysis and design of total-order planning algorithms (see Figure 12.1) continue to appear in the literature (Blum & Furst, 1997). In the last decade, however, AI research has focused on *integrating* planning and execution operations, with new information becoming known to the agent in the course of action. This work on

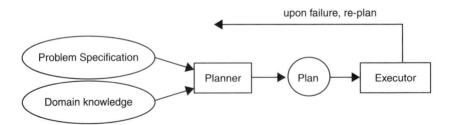

Figure 12.1   The total-planning framework. Unlike opportunistic planning models, the "total-order" planning framework provides the planning agent with all necessary knowledge from which the agent is expected to produce a complete, fully specified plan *before any actions are taken.*

"reactive" or "dynamic-world" planning often uses techniques entirely different from those in the traditional AI planning literature (Chapman, 1991). Reactive planning implies a "least commitment" strategy, which allows plans to be more easily modified as planning progresses (similar to opportunistic planning). For example, knowledge that there are no newspaper stands beyond the security checkpoint can be integrated into the plan in Figure 12.2 by inserting an arrow from "Buy newspaper" to "Go through security checkpoint". In contrast, more reasoning and re-planning will normally be required to correct a sequential plan relative to new information—the system will have to change ordering decisions to which it has already committed, and it will have to reason afresh about the validity of the new plan. The trade-offs for the efficiencies of partial-order representations are that more memory, and in some cases more complex algorithms leading to a decision, are also required.

Based on the discussion of cognitive and computational planning models, it is possible to construct a framework for the cognitive neuroscience investigation of planning. This framework indicates the complexities facing investigators attempting to disambiguate the cause of planning failures in patients or brain activation profiles in normal subjects performing a planning task. Plans have a number of cognitive components (Figure 12.3). Each plan as well as plan event has a characteristic time duration; event order is generally in a left to right direction, although most plans have some level of branching or recursiveness. The number of plan events composing a plan can vary across plans. Plans can be based on well- or ill-structured problems. The key features of plan development are somewhat different from those of plan execution, although some overlap is apparent. The general characteristics of plans have to do with conditions for their retrievability and instantiation. Frequency, imageability, saliency, and motivation are relevant characteristics of any form of knowledge representation including plan-level knowledge. Total-order plans are those that do not allow any deviation from the plan path. Partial-order plans allow for opportunistic deviations and the ability to rejoin the plan path at a juncture close to where you left it.

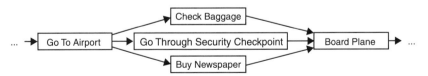

Figure 12.2 A partially-ordered plan. An action at the tail of an arrow must be executed some time before the action of the head of that arrow, but these are the only constraints on execution order. In the shown partial plan, Check baggage, Go through security checkpoint, and Buy newspaper may be executed in any order.

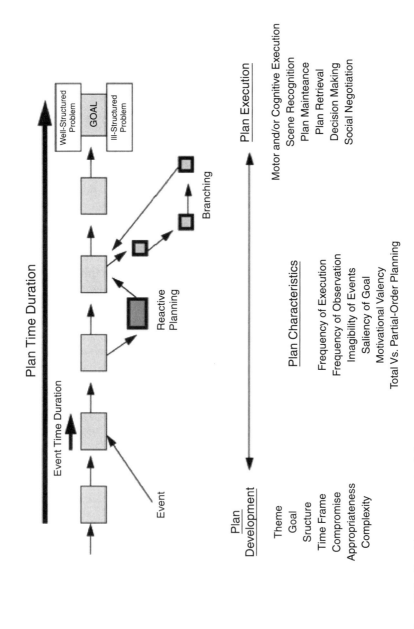

Figure 12.3 Cognitive components of plans.

In order to understand the overall meaning of a plan, conceptual and semantic knowledge must be distilled and integrated across individual plan events, each of which has its own semantic and conceptual value. Reactive planning involves the unexpected introduction of another plan event in the main plan path, whereas branching is the process whereby the main plan path is appended with a subsidiary path which returns to the main plan path at the point you left it. Well-structured problems have an explicit goal that can induce the plan path selection. Ill-structured problems require the formation of goals *and* multiple plan paths.

Note that the sequential structure of plan events depends to some extent on whether the transition from one plan event to another is characterized by physical (e.g., in order to take a shower you must step into the shower stall), social (e.g., in the United States, the population generally showers once per day in the morning before eating breakfast and leaving for work), or individual constraints (e.g., individuals having their own idiosyncratic sequence in carrying out a plan) (Figure 12.4). This latter constraint or, viewed from a different perspective, ability allows for the most flexible and inventive of human behaviors.

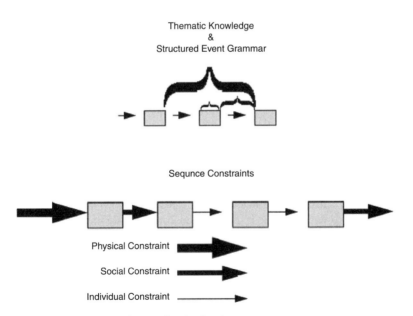

Figure 12.4   Transitional constraints in planning.

COGNITIVE NEUROSCIENCE PERSPECTIVES
ON PLANNING

In general, most cognitive neuroscience (CN) studies have tested subjects in well-structured scenarios where an explicit goal is explained to the subject who then attempts to decide how to achieve the goal before (in some cases) executing the plan (Owen, Downes, Sahakian, Polkey, & Robbins, 1990; Owen, Doyon, Petrides, & Evans, 1996). On occasion, ill-structured problems are presented to the subject, who then has to decide on the goals of the activity as well as the plan to achieve those goals. In addition, ill-structured problems make it more likely that some form of reactive planning (deciding to change the structure of the plan on-line) will be required during execution of the plan (Spector & Grafman, 1994). A limitation of many CN planning studies is the time domain within which the plan may be developed and executed. In most cases, the time is constrained due to the limits of the neuropsychological evaluation procedures and the problem itself is often artificial. In rare instances, the planning and execution of real-life activities are observed where the timescale can be as long as several hours. Although planning problems may also be reflected in the performance of simple everyday tasks, like brushing your teeth or making coffee (Schwartz, Reed, Montgomery, Palmer, & Mayer, 1991), our emphasis in this review is on higher-level cognitive plans.

The main paradigms used in CN planning studies are those evaluating subject route finding, Tower Task performance, and performance in simulated or real-life scenarios. In each of these paradigms, subjects are first usually asked to assemble in their mind the required actions they need to make in order to achieve the instructed goal (planning time), which is followed by the execution of the task (planning execution). Most often, subject response times and accuracy scores are used to derive inferences about planning failures. In general, patients with frontal lobe lesions and those with subcortical disorders (such as Parkinson's disease) affecting the basal ganglia or cerebellum are the most impaired on a variety of planning paradigms. There are many other CN studies using tasks that require processing similar to what a subject might do in constructing and executing a plan, including script-event generation and verification studies whose results we believe are relevant for understanding which brain regions subserve plan decision making.

Route finding and learning tasks concerned with documenting planning failure require that subjects clearly perceive the geometric properties of the route and that they possess the basic visuo-spatial, motoric, and attentional skills to perform the task. In order to decide how to navigate through a complex maze, the subject must identify perceptual landmarks, generate sequences of proper turns, encode the overall path as a plan, and commit the plan to memory. The plan execution phase begins as soon as the path is encoded. Patients with PFC lesions are able to navigate routes but they are particularly impaired in learning new routes or in utilizing old routes in order to adapt to a new route (Karnath & Wallesch, 1992; Karnath, Wallesch, & Zimmermann, 1991). Flitman and his colleagues have used O^{15} Positron Emission Tomography (PET) to demonstrate that the right PFC is particularly active during the retrieval of an encoded route compared with when a subject is simply traversing a seen maze (Flitman, Cooper, & Grafman, 1997). The anterior cingulate cortex was also active during task performance, a finding that is compatible with current views on the role of this brain region in active monitoring of outcomes and errors, in this case the path chosen by participants (Botvinick, Cohen, & Carter, 2004). These findings suggest that subjects tend to navigate mazes using an opportunistic (rather than a "look-ahead") strategy, which depends more on the immediate maze environment and perceptual/spatial processing decisions, whereas the retrieval of a complete cognitive plan for traversing the maze requires PFC mediation.

Tower-type tasks are composed of three or more pegs with a number of disks sitting on the pegs (see Figure 12.5). There is usually a beginning

Tower of Hanoi

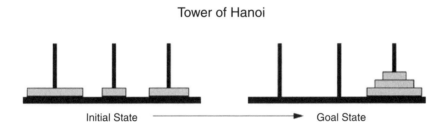

Tower of London

Figure 12.5 The Towers of Hanoi and London are illustrated here. While each has three pegs, the number, size, and color of the disks may vary. Both tasks require that subjects move the disks across the pegs to achieve a goal state. Each task only allows for one disk to be moved at a time. The Tower of Hanoi task does not allow for a larger disk to be put on top of a smaller disk. The Tower of London task must be solved in the minimum number of moves or the subject must begin to execute the plan anew.

state and a goal state. In order to achieve the goal state, subjects have to move the disks and place them on the other pegs according to the rules of the particular Tower task adapted (the most commonly used tasks in the CN literature are the Tower of Hanoi (ToH; Goel & Grafman, 1995), Tower of London (ToL; Shallice, 1988), and Tower of Toronto (Saint-Cyr, Taylor, & Lang, 1988). In general, on Tower tasks, the larger the number of moves required to achieve a goal state, the more difficult the problem appears to the subject. Using five-disk ToL problems, Ward and Allport (1997) found that planning actions on-line were limited by the difficulty in evaluating and deciding on one course of action or one subgoal chunk from the set of competing actions at each step in the course of plan execution, with increased pre-move preparation time related to the number of competing alternative choices. Dehaene and Changeux (1997) used a connectionist model to simulate performance on the ToL task. They postulated that planning requires working memory units, plan units that cause novel activation patterns among lower level operation units generating a plan, and reward units that evaluate the correct or incorrect status of a plan and help bias decision making. Remarkably, they found that each additional indirect move added about 110 simulation cycles to the solution time, whereas each additional direct move required only 45 additional cycles. As the authors pointed out, these findings are supported by empirical findings (Ward & Allport, 1997), with the difference that human subjects are typically able to represent whole series of moves as a single chunk, a feature that could not be simulated by their model. An additional finding was that when plan units were "damaged", the operation network became effectively disconnected from the reward network, making it difficult for the model to judge the relevance of individual ToL moves to achieving the overall plan, although the decision to move could still be made. The model predicted that a patient might find it difficult to select a move, although they would be able to verify whether a move shown to them would be correct.

PET functional neuroimaging studies identify a large set of brain areas that are activated during performance of the ToL by normal subjects. However, when performance on the easy ToL problems was subtracted from the harder ToL problem brain activation profile, only right Brodmann's area 10 and left Brodmann's area 9 along with premotor cortex remain significantly activated (Baker et al., 1996). Morris, Ahmed, Syed, and Toone (1993), using single photon emission computed tomography (SPECT), found left PFC activation related to ToL performance, such that the more difficult the problem (as indicated by greater subject planning time and number of moves), the greater the left frontal activation. If normal subjects are given feedback on their ToL performance during PET functional neuroimaging, additional activation can be seen in the orbitofrontal and medial caudate brain regions (Elliott, Frith, & Dolan,

1997). In a more recent study, Fincham, Carter, Van Veen, Stenger, and Anderson (2002) have employed functional magnetic resonance imaging (fMRI) and an adaptation of the ToH task in normal volunteers to study the neural correlates of manipulation and planning of goals. They identified two distinct profiles: One in which activation time courses varied parametrically with goal-processing operations (including the right dorsolateral PFC [BA9], bilateral parietal cortex [BA40/7], and bilateral premotor cortex [BA6]), and the other in which activation became pronounced only during goal-processing intensive trials (the left inferior frontal gyrus [BA44]). Depressed patients performing the ToL during PET scanning fail to show activation in the ventromedial cortex or striatum and show no augmentation in activation from easy to difficult problems (Elliott et al., 1997).

These findings indicate that impaired planning in depression is associated with PFC and striatal dysfunction, thereby providing further support that successful planning is linked to frontostriatal integrity.

Goel and Grafman (1995) confirmed that patients with PFC lesions are impaired on the ToH task. They noted, however, that the deficit was apparent when patients had to overcome a prepotent strategy and make a counter-intuitive move (regardless of problem difficulty). This finding suggested that frontal lobe lesion patients could initiate a plan similar to controls but had difficulty branching out from the main plan path (see also Morris, Miotto, Feigenbaum, Bullock, & Polkey, 1997). Carlin, Bonerba, Phipps, Alexander, Shapiro, and Grafman (2000) found that patients with PFC lesions due to penetrating head injury and dementia had similar difficulties on the ToL task, but noted that lesion patients had a primary execution deficit, whereas the dementia patients were impaired in both plan development and execution. Colvin, Dunbar, and Grafman (2001) used an analogue of the Tower task called the Water Jug task and found that patients with PFC lesions had difficulty making a decision requiring the conceptual comparison of nonverbal stimuli and had particular difficulty making counter-intuitive moves if the "wrong" move looked perceptually similar to the goal state. A recent study by Carder, Handley, and Perfect (2008) reinforced this interpretation. Task-switching capability is important for developing and executing plans when opportunistic shifting between subgoals is necessary. Rogers, Sahakian, Hodges, Polkey, Kennard, and Robbins (1998) found that patients with left frontal lobe lesions showed increased time costs associated with predictable switches between tasks when there was interference between the tasks and when available task cues were relatively weak and arbitrary. On the other hand, we have obtained evidence that patients with right frontal lobe lesions are particularly impaired when they have to decide which advice they are receiving is best for forecasting an outcome (Gomez-Beldarrain et al., 2004).

Shallice and Burgess (1991, 1996) have studied patients with frontal lobe lesions as they execute real-life plans. These patients performed normally on many standard cognitive tasks evaluating perception, language, and episodic memory, and most of these tasks required decision making, indicating that deficits in plan development and implementation involve plan-specific failures in deciding. The real-life tasks involved shopping and similar activities that needed to be performed within a time limit. Their patients were able to remember each task and its different rules of engagement. Impaired plan execution and goal attainment was observed when the patients failed to appropriately divide their time on each of a set of tasks. Some patients appeared unable to reactivate, after a delay, a previously generated intention to perform a task when they were not directly signaled by a stimulus in the environment. Shallice and Burgess speculated that an internal marker may be set for stored plans, whereas for new plans or plan development the marker(s) may be more fragile and subject to interference when patients have frontal lobe brain damage. They term this deficit a "strategy application disorder". Goldstein, Bernard, Fenwick, Burgess, and McNeil (1993) evaluated a patient with a unilateral left frontal lesion who performed normally on standard neuro-psychological tests and who learned the rules to a multiple errands task designed by Shallice and Burgess. The patient's errors were characteristic of a planning failure and included deficits in executing multiple errands, inefficiency (e.g., he could have bought all the goods he needed from one store at one time—instead he returned to the store more than once), rule breaking (he left the neighborhood to purchase some goods), disinhibition, and post-hoc rationalizations for his inappropriate behaviors.

Bechara, Damasio, Damasio, and Anderson (1994) found that patients with ventromedial frontal lobe lesions performing a gambling task tended to choose from the high risk, quick payoff cards rather than the low paying but better long-term risk cards (see also Bechara, this volume). They hypothesized that these patients had a dissociation between knowledge of the ramifications of their plan and somatic input that would have alerted them to the negative consequences of their chosen plan. Goel, Grafman, Tajik, Gana, and Danto (1997) examined patients with frontal lobe lesions on a realistic financial planning task and found that patients with frontal lobe lesions were impaired at the global level of planning but had normal local-level performance. That is, patients with frontal lobe lesions had difficulty in organizing and structuring their plan development space. They were able to begin planning but were unable to adequately divide their cognitive efforts among each planning phase. They spent too much time planning for events that would occur in closer chronological proximity to the planning development time. Patients expressed consternation that there were no right or wrong answers and no obvious termination points in their planning task, and often decided to terminate the testing session before they specified all their plan details or satisfied the task goals. Interestingly, the patients did not attempt (as did controls) to negotiate some apparent constraints imposed by the investigators. The patients' planning failures were attributed to difficulty in generalizing from particular events, failure to shift between mental sets, poor judgment regarding the adequacy and completeness of the plan, and inadequate access to structured event complexes (i.e., memory for plan-level attributes such as thematic knowledge, plan grammars, etc.). Neuropsychological studies in community samples have also confirmed that various real-life measures related to financial abilities, including income and credit card use, are tied to PFC function (Spinella, Yang, & Lester, 2007).

Scripts are knowledge structures that resemble plans and contain information pertinent to carrying out an action sequence, including characterizations of the events, the temporal order of events, and thematic information. Script tasks typically ask participants to sort events, to make decisions about a set of events they are shown (e.g., are they in the correct order or do they belong to the same script?), or to carry out a typical script in real time. CN research on script processing (Sirigu et al., 1998; Sirigu, Zalla, Pillon, Grafman, Agid, & Dubois, 1995; Sirigu, Zalla, Pillon, Grafman, Dubois, & Agid, 1995; Sirigu, Zalla, Pillon, Grafman, Dubois, & Agid, 1996) indicates that patients with PFC lesions have selective difficulty generating (or sorting) an appropriate script-event sequence, particularly when the events came from scripts that subjects were less familiar with. Functional neuroimaging findings indicate significant right PFC activation when subjects make script-event sequence decisions, whereas the left PFC is more active when subjects judge whether a single event was a member of a particular script (Partiot, Grafman, Sadato, Flitman, & Wild, 1996). Nichelli, Grafman, Pietrini, Clark, Lee, and Miletich (1995) demonstrated that normal subjects also activated the right PFC when determining the moral of a story. In addition, when normal subjects mentally generate nonemotional script events, they activate the lateral PFC and posterior temporal cortices, but when they mentally generate emotional scripts, they activate the ventromedial PFC and anterior temporal cortices (Partiot, Grafman, Sadato, Wachs, & Hallett, 1995). Furthermore, ventromedial and frontopolar sectors of the PFC are reliably engaged both by making explicit judgments (Greene, Nystrom, Engell, Darley, & Cohen, 2004; Heekeren, Wartenburger, Schmidt, Schwintowski, & Villringer, 2003; Moll, de Oliveira-Souza, Bramati, & Grafman, 2002; Moll, Eslinger, & de Oliveira-Souza, 2001) and by passive exposure to morally salient social events (Moll, de Oliveira-Souza, Eslinger et al., 2002, 2007), irrespective of stimulus modality, as reviewed by Moll, Zahn, de Oliveira-Souza, Krueger, and Grafman (2005). Electrophysiological experiments showing that activity measured in single neurons within the monkey PFC code for specific behavioral sequences in a long-term fashion lend strong support to the view that sequential knowledge is indeed represented within PFC networks. PFC neurons are thus involved in storing event sequences and in planning multiple future events during dynamic behaviors (Grafman, 1995; Mushiake et al., 2006). Recent fMRI studies in humans strongly support this notion. The pole of the medial prefrontal cortex was recruited when normal volunteers thought about future actions (Okuda et al., 2003); in addition, topographically distinct subregions of the medial PFC seem to be differentially engaged in the processing of event sequences, depending on how often such activities were performed in daily life (Krueger et al., 2007).

In summary, patients with frontal lobe lesions unambiguously demonstrate difficulty in developing and/or executing a plan. Patients with subcortical lesions to structures that receive frontal lobe projections (e.g., those with Parkinson's disease or cerebellar atrophy) may have a similar, but milder, planning problem (Berns & Sejnowski, 1998; Grafman, Litvan, Massaquoi, Stewart, Sirigu, & Hallett, 1992; Morris, Downes, Sahakian, Evenden, Heald, & Robbins, 1988; Pascual-Leone et al., 1993; Wallesch, Karnath, Papagno, Zimmermann, Deuschl, & Lucking, 1990). Patients with lesions outside the area of the frontal lobe–basal ganglia–cerebellum axis may fail on planning tasks but not because of an essential deficit to plan-level processes but because of, for example, cognitive deficits in spatial perception or language comprehension. Category-specific plan impairment may also be observed with ventromedial frontal lobe lesions affecting social-cognitive or emotionally arousing plans more than nonsocial, unemotional cognitive plans, partially due to damage to the ventromedial cortex, or its dissociation from the autonomic nervous system (Bechara et al., 1994). Planning processes requiring the structural analysis of plans may be more compromised by left PFC lesions, whereas the temporal and dynamic aspects of plans may be more compromised by right prefrontal lesions. All of these impairments in patients may lead to faulty decision making. If all of the above processes are intact (as they may be in some patients and most normal volunteers), then decision making about plans tends to proceed normally.

PLANNING AND PFC: EMERGING THEMES

Plan decision making is a cognitively complicated affair. Functional neuroimaging studies in normal subjects point to the importance of the PFC in plan decision making. In patients, one or more processes dependent on the PFC may be impaired leading to insufficient or inaccurate information on which to base a decision. Rarely is the information completely intact yet the decision alone impaired. Despite the complexity of plan development, execution, and decision making, sufficient knowledge has been gained from recent CN planning research studies in order to provide some promising leads for future research. Clearly the major representation of plan-level knowledge in the human brain appears to be in the PFC. The failures in planning associated with PFC lesions include problems in required plan processes, such as both top–down and bottom–up plan development, in the development and execution of novel plans, in the analogical mapping of plans, in parallel processing, in opportunistic/partial-order planning, in time management, in both development and execution of a complete plan event sequence, in discriminating between relevant and irrelevant events, in both well- and ill-structured planning, accessing category-specific plans, and in the adequate successive refinement of plans. The next time you ask somebody "Well, what do you want to do?", give them some deserved time to sift through all this processing before they decide.

The obvious cognitive-processing deficits that appear responsible for these planning failures include representational degradation (e.g., making low frequency plans more difficult to retrieve), difficulty in inhibiting prepotent plans and other action units (disinhibition), deficits in thematic induction (which can hinder plan retrieval), plan grammar deficits (leading to failures in following a sequential path), and modality-specific failure in plan development and retrieval (distinguishing between verbal/propositional, visual, and real-time representation of plan behavior), and impaired opportunistic, partial-order processing. Patients with frontal lobe lesions may exhibit one or more of these deficits and they can all lead to decision-making deficits.

Recent animal and human research suggests that neural networks in the PFC are specialized for sustaining information processing over long periods of time even in the absence of stimulus-specific input (Cohen et al., 1997; Courtney, Ungerleider, Keil, & Haxby, 1997; Fuster, 1995; Goldman-Rakic, 1996; Miller, Erickson, & Desimone, 1996). These observations indicate that the neural mechanisms required to support plan-level processing (which by definition would need to occur over long periods of time and need to be sustained in the absence of stimulus-specific behavior) are available in the PFC (Moll et al., 2005; Ruchkin, Grafman, Cameron, & Berndt, 2003; Wood & Grafman, 2003). The PFC, however, is a large structure and in addition to possessing the general processing capability to handle many aspects of plan-level behavior, including processing multiple plans simultaneously (Lingard & Richards, 1998), the findings we have reviewed also suggest some specificity in the topographical representation of several of the cognitive processes responsible for plans (see Figure 12.6).

In this chapter, we have argued that the PFC is crucial for mediating

Mapping Planning Processes to Brain

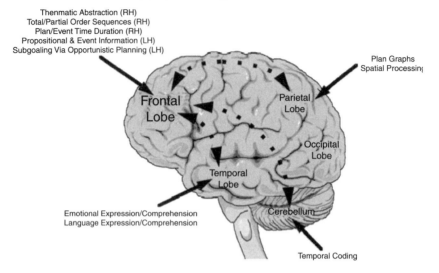

Thenmatic Abstraction (RH)
Total/Partial Order Sequences (RH)
Plan/Event Time Duration (RH)
Propositional & Event Information (LH)
Subgoaling Via Opportunistic Planning (LH)

Plan Graphs
Spatial Processing

Frontal Lobe

Parietal Lobe

Occipital Lobe

Temporal Lobe

Emotional Expression/Comprehension
Language Expression/Comprehension

Cerebellum

Temporal Coding

Figure 12.6   Mapping planning processes to brain. This cartoon figure of the brain indicates that many plan-level processes are most likely stored and subserved by the prefrontal cortex. There is some evidence that indicates which hemisphere (RH = right; LH = left hemisphere) is predominant in mediating a particular planning process (see text). Plan-level knowledge in the prefrontal cortex must be linked or bound to information-processing components stored in other brain areas (as shown in the figure) in order for a complete characterization of the plan to be formed. Presumably, the hippocampus and other memory structures contribute to this linkage.

planning functions that are extended in time and composed of a set of sequential events. It is currently possible to make some claims about the role of several PFC regions in planning functions. For this purpose, we can crudely divide the PFC into left and right sectors, medial and lateral sectors, dorsal and ventral sectors, and anterior and posterior sectors. Wood and Grafman (2003) have proposed assigning different representational forms of the structured event complex to each of these areas and we can use that same schema for describing planning functions, since we believe that plans are just one form of a structured event complex. There is evidence that the left PFC focuses on the specific features of individual events (including features and meanings) that make up a plan, whereas the right PFC mediates the integration of information across events (including the acquisition of meaning and features at the macro-plan level, such as thematic knowledge). We hypothesize that the medial PFC stores key features of predictable over-learned cognitive plans that have a contingent relationship with sensorimotor processes and are less often modified, or strongly linked to socially reinforcing associations (Moll et al., 2005). The lateral

PFC would store key features of plans that are frequently modified to adapt to special circumstances, especially those requiring bridging short event sequences and those cued by visuo-motor and spatial information (Heekeren, Marrett, Ruff, Bandettini, & Ungerleider, 2006). The ventral PFC is concerned with social-category-specific plans that often have an emotional component, especially those involving behavioral shifts (Kringelbach & Rolls, 2003). The dorsal PFC is concerned more with aspects of plans representing mechanistic activities without a social component (e.g., repairing a food processor). Finally, the anterior PFC tends to represent plans of long duration composed of many events, whereas the posterior PFC tends to represent plans and actions of short duration and fewer events (e.g., such as a simple association) (Krueger et al., 2007). Since no single PFC region would represent all features or components of a plan, specific plans would tend to evoke selected patterns of PFC activation. Any region could participate in plan processing, depending on the type of plan, with the different plan (and cortical) subcomponents being differentially weighted in importance (and activation) depending on the kind of plan, the moment-by-moment demands of the plan, and previous experience with the plan. For example, the left anterior ventromedial PFC would be expected to represent a long, multi-event sequence of social interactions (i.e., a social plan) with specialized processing of the meaning and features of single events within the event sequence making up the plan, including the computation of their temporal and sequential dependencies and primary meaning. This view differs from that of Newman and colleagues (Newman, Carpenter, Varma, & Just, 2003), who assign different processes to each hemisphere. For example, they hypothesize that the right PFC is more involved in the generation of a plan and the left PFC is more involved in the execution of a plan based on functional neuroimaging and computational modeling of Tower of London performance. Our view is that either hemisphere can initiate and guide plan execution, but only specific features of the plans would be encoded and stored in subregions within each hemisphere.

The PFC is connected to many other brain regions and, in particular, the basal ganglia may play an important role in learning and executing over-learned cognitive plans. We suspect that the execution of a routine plan would rely more and more over time on the simpler sensorimotor components of the activity rather than the associated complex cognitive knowledge contained in the plan. This would result in the recruitment of selected basal ganglia structures to help mediate the sensorimotor activity. In turn this would result in decreased activation in the PFC, since the cognitive components of the plan would cease to be essential for the execution of the action. This reduction of PFC resources as a plan is routinely repeated allows for the same resources in the PFC to be reallocated to novel plans or to further improvements of plan strategy for the same class of goals, leading to the possibility of multitasking behavior. Many of the subregions within the PFC are monosynaptically connected to subcortical structures such as the amygdala and nucleus accumbens that mediate the retrieval of affective input and its binding to cognitive processes, so we anticipate that social plans and other plans of personal relevance to the agent would be infused with reinforcement cues that bias the development and execution of the plan (Moll, Krueger, Zahn, Pardini, de Oliveira-Souza, & Grafman, 2006; Tanaka, Doya, Okada, Ueda, Okamoto, & Yamawaki, 2004). Decision making about plans can reflect these simpler processes or in a slower fashion reflect the more cognitively taxing deliberations when a new plan is required. In either case, to fully understand the decision requires a thorough task analysis of plan development and execution.

PLANS AND DECISIONS

Planning was defined as the process of deciding on an abstract sequence of operations intended for achieving a goal. This definition of planning makes the critical role of decision making within planning salient. Our aim in this chapter was to provide a description of the cognitive components of planning that can be mapped to the brain, with an eye toward highlighting the role of decision making in the planning process. We presented converging evidence to demonstrate that the most important components of plan-specific decision making (i.e., decisions that are made in the context of a plan) are primarily stored in the PFC as components of the plan itself, with plan execution assisted by motor and other processes carried out by the basal ganglia, motor cortex, and cortical regions such as the parietal lobes. In other words, the decision-making components of planning are encoded within the neural circuitry of the relevant plan, and engaged when the plan is activated in the PFC.

We also distinguished between two predominant views of planning. Successive refinement models emphasize the top–down control of operations in the course of planning. Such models advocate the execution of TOTE units along various levels of the plan. In contrast, opportunistic models emphasize bottom–up influences on planning, whereby decisions made at any point in the course of plan execution influence the opportunities available later in the development of a plan. According to opportunistic models, each new decision incorporated into the plan revises previous decisions, and decisions can be made at any level of abstraction at any point in the planning process. Given that both models have been supported empirically, there is good reason to believe that each reflects an aspect of planning behavior. Recent work on reactive or dynamic-world planning has focused on integrating planning and execution operations to account for the ways in which new information becoming available to the agent can alter decisions about courses of actions. Differences between successive refinement and opportunistic models are relevant here again. Specifically, whereas revising a sequential plan relative to new information will require more reasoning for altering prior ordering decisions, partial-order representations may in turn require more memory and complex algorithms for decisions in the face of new information. We presented evidence to demonstrate that PFC neurons (in concert with their subcortical connections) are involved in these dynamic aspects of planning behaviors, with contributions of different PFC regions varying as a function of the specific features of the plan.

FUTURE DIRECTIONS

Future CN planning research should focus on further advances on: (1) how event sequences are formed; (2) whether there is unique information that can be abstracted *across* a sequence of events; (3) whether plans are organized by category and frequency; (4) more explicit depiction of the plan-level cognitive processes referred to in this review (e.g., plan grammars); (5) what evidence is required to induce a decision (exclusive of environmental time constraints); and (6) more precise mapping of plan components to sectors within the human PFC and basal ganglia using more sophisticated neuropsychological tasks, lesion mapping, and functional neuroimaging methods.

It is our view that human CN research is in a position to deliver crucial evidence regarding both the cognitive architecture and the neural topography of plan decision making. By being able to represent and execute plans, we are able to integrate events from the past, present, and future into a single plan-level memory unit (Grafman, 1995; Haith, Benson, Roberts Jr., & Pennington, 1994). Planning enables us to outwit other animals and to cope with a changing environment while achieving myriad goals (Nichelli, Grafman, Pietrini, Alway, Carton, & Miletich, 1994). Planning is a crowning achievement of human cognition and represents a prominent feature in any portrait of the brain's cognitive functions whose understanding will, hopefully, be attained over the next few decades.

REFERENCES

Allen, J. F., Kautz, H. A., Pelavin, R. N., & Tenenberg, J. D. (Eds.). (1991). *Reasoning about plans*. San Mateo, CA: Morgan Kaufmann.

Anderson, J. (1983). *The architecture of cognition*. Cambridge, MA: Harvard University Press.

Averbeck, B. B., & Lee, D. (2007). Prefrontal neural correlates of memory for sequences. *Journal of Neuroscience*, *27*, 2204–2211.

Baker, S. C., Rogers, R. D., Owen, A. M., Frith, C. D., Dolan, R. J., Frackowiak, R. S. J. et al. (1996). Neural systems engaged by planning: A PET study of the Tower of London task. *Neuropsychologia*, *34*, 515–526.

Baker-Sennett, J., Matusov, E., & Rogoff, B. (1993). Planning as a developmental process. In H. W. Reese (Ed.), *Advances in child development and behavior* (Vol. 24, pp. 253–281). New York: Academic Press

Bechara, A., Damasio, A. R., Damasio, H., & Anderson, S. W. (1994). Insensitivity to future consequences following damage to human prefrontal cortex. *Cognition*, *50*, 7–15.

Berns, G. S., & Sejnowski, T. J. (1998). A computational model of how the basal ganglia produces sequences. *Journal of Cognitive Neuroscience*, *10*, 108–121.

Blum, A., & Furst, M. (1997). Fast planning through planning graph analysis. *Artificial Intelligence*, *90*, 281–300.

Botvinick, M. M., Cohen, J. D., & Carter, C. S. (2004). Conflict monitoring and anterior cingulate cortex: An update. *Trends in Cognitive Sciences*, *8*, 539–546.

Carder, H. P., Handley, S. J., & Perfect, T. J. (2008). Counterintuitive and alternative moves choice in the Water Jug task. *Brain and Cognition*, *66*, 11–20.

Carlin, D., Bonerba, J., Phipps, M., Alexander, G., Shapiro, M., & Grafman, J. (2000). Planning impairments in frontal lobe dementia and frontal lobe lesion patients. *Neuropsychologia*, *38*, 655–665.

Chapman, D. (1991). *Vision, instruction, and action*. Cambridge, MA: MIT Press.

Cohen, J. D., Perlstein, W. M., Braver, T. S., Nystrom, L. E., Noll, D. C., Jonides, J. et al. (1997). Temporal dynamics of brain activation during a working memory task. *Nature*, *386*, 604–608.

Colvin, M. K., Dunbar, K., & Grafman, J. (2001). The effects of frontal lobe lesions on goal achievement in the Water Jug Task. *Journal of Cognitive Neuroscience*, *13*, 1129–1147.

Courtney, S. M., Ungerleider, L. G., Keil, K., & Haxby, J. V. (1997). Transient and sustained activity in a distributed neural system for human working memory. *Nature*, *386*, 608–611.

Das, J. P., Kar, B. C., & Parrila, R. K. (1996). *Cognitive planning: The psychological basis of intelligent behavior*. New Delhi: Sage.

Dehaene, S., & Changeux, J.-P. (1997). A hierarchical neuronal network for planning behavior. *Proceedings of the National Academy of Sciences USA*, *94*, 13293–13298.

Dreher, M., & Oerter, R. (1987). Action planning competencies during adolescence and early adulthood. In S. L. Friedman, E. K. Scholnick, & R. R. Cocking (Eds.), *Blueprints for thinking: The role of planning in cognitive development* (pp. 321–355). Cambridge: Cambridge University Press.

Elliott, R., Baker, S. C., Rogers, R. D., O'Leary, D. A., Paykel, E. S., Frith, C. D. et al. (1997). Prefrontal dysfunction in depressed patients performing a complex planning task: A study using positron emission tomography. *Psychological Medicine*, *27*, 931–942.

Elliott, R., Frith, C. D., & Dolan, R. J. (1997). Differential neural response to positive and negative feedback in planning and guessing tasks. *Neuropsychologia*, *35*, 1395–1404.

Fikes, R., & Nilsson, N. J. (1971). STRIPS: A new approach to the application of theorem proving to problem solving. *Artificial Intelligence*, *2*, 189–208.

Fincham, J. M., Carter, C. S., Van Veen, V., Stenger, V. A., & Anderson, J. R. (2002). Neural mechanisms of planning: A computational analysis using event-related fMRI. *Proceedings of the National Academy of Sciences USA*, *99*, 3346–3351.

Flitman, S., Cooper, V., & Grafman, J. (1997). PET imaging of maze processing. *Neuropsychologia*, *35*, 409–420.

Friedman, S. L., & Scholnick, E. K. (Eds.). (1997). *The developmental psychology of planning*. Mahwah, NJ: Lawrence Erlbaum.

Friedman, S. L., Scholnick, E. K., & Cocking, R. R. (Eds.). (1987). *Blueprints for thinking: The role of planning in cognitive development*. Cambridge: Cambridge University Press.

Fuster, J. M. (1995). Memory and planning: Two temporal perspectives of frontal lobe function. *Advances in Neurology*, *66*, 9–20.

Goel, V., & Grafman, J. (1995). Are the frontal lobes implicated in planning functions: Re-interpreting data from the Tower of Hanoi. *Neuropsychologia*, *33*, 623–642.

Goel, V., Grafman, J., Tajik, J., Gana, S., & Danto, D. (1997). A study of the performance of frontal patients in a financial planning task. *Brain*, *120*, 1805–1822.

Goldman-Rakic, P. (1996). The prefrontal landscape: Implications of functional architecture for understanding human mentation and the central executive. *Philosophical Transactions of the Royal Society of London: B (Biological Sciences)*, *351*, 1445–1453.

Goldstein, L. H., Bernard, S., Fenwick, P. B. C., Burgess, P. W., & McNeil, J. (1993). Unilateral frontal lobectomy can produce strategy application disorder. *Journal of Neurology, Neurosurgery, and Psychiatry*, *56*, 274–276.

Gomez-Beldarrain, M., Harries, C., Garcia-Monco, J. C., Ballus, E., & Grafman, J. (2004). Patients with right frontal lesions are unable to assess and use advice to make predictive judgments. *Journal of Cognitive Neuroscience*, *16*, 74–89.

Grafman, J. (1989). Plans, actions, and mental sets: The role of the frontal lobes. In E. Perecman (Ed.), *Integrating theory and practice in clinical neuropsychology* (pp. 93–138). Hillsdale, NJ: Lawrence Erlbaum.

Grafman, J. (1995). Similarities and distinctions among models of prefrontal cortical functions. In J. Grafman, K. J. Holyoak, & F. Boller (Eds.), *Structure and function of the human prefrontal cortex* (Vol. 769, pp. 337–368). New York: New York Academy of Sciences.

Grafman, J., & Hendler, J. (1991). Planning and the brain. *Behavioral and Brain Sciences*, *14*, 563–564.

Grafman, J., Litvan, I., Massaquoi, S., Stewart, M., Sirigu, A., & Hallett, M. (1992). Cognitive planning deficit in patients with cerebellar atrophy. *Neurology*, *42*, 1493–1496.

Greene, J. D., Nystrom, L. E., Engell, A. D., Darley, J. M., & Cohen, J. D. (2004). The neural bases of cognitive conflict and control in moral judgment. *Neuron*, *44*, 389–400.

Haith, M. M., Benson, J. B., Roberts Jr., R. J., & Pennington, B. F. (Eds.). (1994). *The development of future-oriented processes*. Chicago: University of Chicago Press.

Hammond, K. (Ed.). (1994). *Proceedings of the second international conference on artificial intelligence planning systems*. Menlo Park, CA: AAAI Press.

Hayes-Roth, B., & Hayes-Roth, F. (1979). A cognitive model of planning. *Cognitive Science, 3*, 275–310.

Heekeren, H. R., Marrett, S., Ruff, D. A., Bandettini, P. A., & Ungerleider, L. G. (2006). Involvement of human left dorsolateral prefrontal cortex in perceptual decision making is independent of response modality. *Proceedings of the National Academy of Sciences USA, 103*, 10023–10028.

Heekeren, H. R., Wartenburger, I., Schmidt, H., Schwintowski, H. P., & Villringer, A. (2003). An fMRI study of simple ethical decision-making. *Neuroreport, 14*, 1215–1219.

Hoc, J.-M. (1988). *Cognitive psychology of planning*. London: Academic Press.

Karnath, H. O., & Wallesch, C. W. (1992). Inflexibility of mental planning: A characteristic disorder with prefrontal lobe lesions? *Neuropsychologia, 30*, 1011–1016.

Karnath, H. O., Wallesch, C. W., & Zimmermann, P. (1991). Mental planning and anticipatory processes with acute and chronic frontal lobe lesions: A comparison of maze performance in routine and non-routine situations. *Neuropsychologia, 29*, 271–290.

Kolodner, J. (1993). *Case-based reasoning*. San Mateo, CA: Morgan Kaufmann.

Kringelbach, M. L., & Rolls, E. T. (2003). Neural correlates of rapid reversal learning in a simple model of human social interaction. *Neuroimage, 20*, 1371–1383.

Krueger, F., Moll, J., Zahn, R., Heinecke, A., & Grafman, J. (2007). Event frequency modulates the processing of daily life activities in human medial prefrontal cortex. *Cerebral Cortex, 17*, 2346–2353.

Langley, P., & Drummond, M. (1990). Toward an experimental science of planning. In DARPA (Ed.), *Proceedings of the workshop on innovative approaches to planning, scheduling and control* (pp. 109–114). San Mateo, CA: Morgan Kaufmann.

Lingard, A. R., & Richards, E. B. (1998). Planning parallel actions. *Artificial Intelligence, 99*, 261–324.

Miller, E. K., Erickson, C. A., & Desimone, R. (1996). Neural mechanisms of visual working memory in prefrontal cortex of the macaque. *Journal of Neuroscience, 16*, 5154–5167.

Miller, G. A., Galanter, E., & Pribram, K. (1960). *Plans and the structure of behavior*. New York: Holt, Rinehart & Winston.

Moll, J., de Oliveira-Souza, R., Bramati, I. E., & Grafman, J. (2002). Functional networks in emotional moral and nonmoral social judgments. *Neuroimage, 16*, 696–703.

Moll, J., de Oliveira-Souza, R., Eslinger, P. J., Bramati, I. E., Mourao-Miranda, J., Andreiuolo, P. A. et al. (2002). The neural correlates of moral sensitivity: A functional magnetic resonance imaging investigation of basic and moral emotions. *Journal of Neuroscience, 22*, 2730–2736.

Moll, J., de Oliveira-Souza, R., Garrido, G. J., Bramati, I. E., Caparelli-Daquer, E. M. A., Paiva, M. M. F. et al. (2007). The self as a moral agent: Linking the neural bases of social agency and moral sensitivity. *Social Neuroscience, 2*, 336–352.

Moll, J., Eslinger, P. J., & de Oliveira-Souza, R. (2001). Frontopolar and anterior temporal cortex activation in a moral judgment task: Preliminary functional MRI results in normal subjects. *Arquivos de neuro-psiquiatria, 59*, 657–664.

Moll, J., Krueger, F., Zahn, R., Pardini, M., de Oliveira-Souza, R., & Grafman, J. (2006). Human fronto-mesolimbic networks guide decisions about charitable donation. *Proceedings of the National Academy of Sciences USA, 103*, 15623–15628.

Moll, J., Zahn, R., de Oliveira-Souza, R., Krueger, F., & Grafman, J. (2005). Opinion: The neural basis of human moral cognition. *Nature Reviews Neuroscience, 6*, 799–809.

Morris, R. G., Ahmed, S., Syed, G. M., & Toone, R. K. (1993). Neural correlates of planning ability: Frontal lobe activation during the Tower of London test. *Neuropsychologia, 31*, 1367–1378.

Morris, R. G., Downes, J. J., Sahakian, B. J., Evenden, J. L., Heald, A., & Robbins, T. W. (1988). Planning and spatial working memory in Parkinson's Disease. *Journal of Neurology, Neurosurgery, and Psychiatry, 51*, 757–766.

Morris, R. G., Miotto, E. C., Feigenbaum, J. D., Bullock, P., & Polkey, C. E. (1997). The effect of goal–subgoal conflict on planning ability after frontal- and temporal-lobe lesions in humans. *Neuropsychologia, 35*, 1147–1157.

Mushiake, H., Saito, N., Sakamoto, K., Itoyama, Y., & Tanji, J. (2006). Activity in the lateral prefrontal cortex reflects multiple steps of future events in action plans. *Neuron, 50*, 631–641.

Newell, A., & Simon, H. A. (1972). *Human problem solving.* Englewood Cliffs, NJ: Prentice-Hall.

Newman, S. D., Carpenter, P. A., Varma, S., & Just, M. A. (2003). Frontal and parietal participation in problem solving in the Tower of London: fMRI and computational modeling of planning and high-level perception. *Neuropsychologia, 41*, 1668–1682.

Nichelli, P., Grafman, J., Pietrini, P., Alway, D., Carton, J. C., & Miletich, R. (1994). Brain activation during chess deliberation. *Nature, 369*, 191.

Nichelli, P., Grafman, J., Pietrini, P., Clark, K., Lee, K. Y., & Miletich, R. (1995). Where the brain appreciates the moral of a story. *Neuroreport, 6*, 2309–2313.

Okuda, J., Fujii, T., Ohtake, H., Tsukiura, T., Tanji, K., Suzuki, K. et al. (2003). Thinking of the future and past: The roles of the frontal pole and the medial temporal lobes. *Neuroimage, 19*, 1369–1380.

Owen, A. M. (1997). Cognitive planning in humans: Neuropsychological, neuroanatomical and neuropharmacological perspectives. *Progress in Neurobiology, 53*, 431–450.

Owen, A. M., Downes, J. J., Sahakian, B. J., Polkey, C. E., & Robbins, T. W. (1990). Planning and spatial working memory following frontal lobe lesions in man. *Neuropsychologia, 28*, 1021–1034.

Owen, A. M., Doyon, J., Petrides, M., & Evans, A. C. (1996). Planning and spatial working memory: A positron emission tomography study in humans. *European Journal of Neuroscience, 8*, 353–364.

Partiot, A., Grafman, J., Sadato, N., Flitman, S., & Wild, K. (1996). Brain activation during script event processing. *Neuroreport, 7*, 761–766.

Partiot, A., Grafman, J., Sadato, N., Wachs, J., & Hallett, M. (1995). Brain activation during the generation of non-emotional and emotional plans. *Neuroreport, 6*, 1269–1272.

Pascual-Leone, A., Grafman, J., Clark, K., Stewart, M., Massaquoi, S., Lou, J.-L. et al. (1993). Procedural learning in Parkinson's disease and cerebellar degeneration. *Annals of Neurology, 34*, 594–602.

Pea, R. D., & Hawkins, J. (1987). Planning in a chore-scheduling task. In S. L. Friedman, E. K. Scholnick, & R. R. Cocking (Eds.), *Blueprints for thinking: The role of planning in cognitive development* (pp. 273–302). Cambridge: Cambridge University Press.

Rogers, R. D., Sahakian, B. J., Hodges, J. R., Polkey, C. E., Kennard, C., & Robbins, T. W. (1998). Dissociating executive mechanisms of task control following frontal lobe damage and Parkinson's disease. *Brain, 121*, 815–842.

Rosenbloom, P. S., Laird, J. E., & Newell, A. (Eds.). (1993). *The SOAR papers: Research on integrated intelligence.* Cambridge, MA: MIT Press.

Ruchkin, D. S., Grafman, J., Cameron, K., & Berndt, R. S. (2003). Working memory retention systems: A state of activated long-term memory. *Behavioral Brain Sciences, 26*, 709–728; discussion 728–777.

Sacerdoti, E. D. (1975). *The nonlinear nature of plans.* Proceedings of the Fourth International Joint Conference on Artificial Intelligence (pp. 206–214). San Mateo, CA: Kaufmann.

Saint-Cyr, J. A., Taylor, A. E., & Lang, A. E. (1988). Procedural learning and neostriatal dysfunction in man. *Brain, 111*, 941–959.

Schank, R. C., & Abelson, R. P. (1977). *Scripts, plans, goals, and understanding.* Hillsdale, NJ: Lawrence Erlbaum.

Scholnick, E. K., & Friedman, S. L. (1987). The planning construct in the psychological literature. In S. L. Friedman, E. K. Scholnick, & R. R. Cocking (Eds.), *Blueprints for thinking: The role of planning in cognitive development* (pp. 3–38). Cambridge: Cambridge University Press.

Schwartz, M. F., Reed, E. S., Montgomery, M., Palmer, C., & Mayer, N. H. (1991). The quantitative description of action disorganization after brain damage: A case study. *Cognitive Neuropsychology, 8*, 381–414.

Shallice, T. (1988). *From neuropsychology to mental structure.* Cambridge: Cambridge University Press.

Shallice, T., & Burgess, P. W. (1991). Deficits in strategy application following frontal lobe damage in man. *Brain, 114*, 727–741.

Shallice, T., & Burgess, P. W. (1996). The domain of supervisory processes and temporal organization of behaviour. *Philosophical Transactions of the Royal Society of London B, 351*, 1405–1412.

Sirigu, A., Cohen, L., Zalla, T., Pradat-Diehl, P., Van Eeckhout, P., Grafman, J. et al. (1998). Distinct prefrontal regions for processing sentence syntax and story grammar. *Cortex, 34*, 771–778.

Sirigu, A., Zalla, T., Pillon, B., Grafman, J., Agid, Y., & Dubois, B. (1995).

Selective impairments in managerial knowledge following prefrontal cortex damage. *Cortex*, *31*, 301–316.

Sirigu, A., Zalla, T., Pillon, B., Grafman, J., Dubois, B., & Agid, Y. (1995). Planning and script analysis following pre-frontal lobe lesions. In J. Grafman, K. J. Holyoak, & F. Boller (Eds.), *Structure and function of the human prefrontal cortex* (Vol. 769, pp. 277–288). New York: New York Academy of Sciences.

Sirigu, A., Zalla, T., Pillon, B., Grafman, J., Dubois, B., & Agid, Y. (1996). Encoding of sequence and boundaries of scripts following prefrontal lesions. *Cortex*, *32*, 297–310.

Spector, L., & Grafman, J. (1994). Planning, neuropsychology, and artificial intelligence: Cross fertilization. In F. Boller & J. Grafman (Eds.), *Handbook of neuropsychology* (Vol. 9, pp. 377–392). Amsterdam: Elsevier Science.

Spinella, M., Yang, B., & Lester, D. (2007). Prefrontal systems in financial processing. *Journal of Socio-Economics*, *36*, 480–489.

Suchman, L. A. (1987). *Plans and situated actions*. Cambridge: Cambridge University Press.

Tanaka, S. C., Doya, K., Okada, G., Ueda, K., Okamoto, Y., & Yamawaki, S. (2004). Prediction of immediate and future rewards differentially recruits cortico-basal ganglia loops. *Nature Neuroscience*, *7*, 887–893.

Wallesch, C.-W., Karnath, H. O., Papagno, C., Zimmermann, P., Deuschl, G., & Lucking, C. H. (1990). Parkinson's disease patient's behavior in a covered maze learning task. *Neuropsychologia*, *28*, 839–849.

Ward, G., & Allport, A. (1997). Planning and problem-solving using the five-disk Tower of London Task. *The Quarterly Journal of Experimental Psychology*, *50A*, 49–78.

Wilensky, R. (1983). *Planning and understanding: A computational approach to human reasoning*. Reading, MA: Addison-Wesley.

Wood, J. N., & Grafman, J. (2003). Human prefrontal cortex: Processing and representational perspectives. *Nature Reviews Neuroscience*, *4*, 139–147.

CHAPTER THIRTEEN

Decision junctures in the creative process

Oshin Vartanian

INTRODUCTION

Traditionally, researchers investigating the problem of creativity have neglected to study the role of decision making in the creative process (see Sternberg, 1999). This is a curious state of affairs, given that our own experience suggests that creative solutions to seemingly intractable problems indeed require decision making at crucial junctures. This oversight may be attributable to a tendency to view creativity as a distinct type of cognition (Weisberg, 1986), thereby motivating researchers to study only those processes that appear to be uniquely linked to creativity (e.g., insight). However, when creative thinking is viewed as one of many avenues for solving everyday problems, the role of decision making in the path to creative solutions becomes readily apparent.

My aim in this chapter is to demonstrate that the creative process can be represented as a sequence of generation-and-verification cycles where decision making can be shown to play an important role in both generation and verification parts of the cycle, but to varying degrees and in different ways. Specifically, I will demonstrate that decision making plays a key role in idea generation by delimiting the problem space to a manageable size, and in solution verification by selection the most viable of generated solutions for further consideration. I will start by reviewing the basic cognitive architecture of the creative process, and then discuss relevant research from experimental psychology and cognitive neuroscience that offers support for various components of this model. Having demonstrated that the neural architecture of creativity is hierarchical and componential (Simon, 1962, 2005), I will end by placing creativity more firmly within a family of higher-cognitive activities (e.g., planning, reasoning, etc.) that are built on largely shared component neural systems (see also Christoff, Gordon, & Smith, this volume).

DEFINING THE CREATIVE PROCESS

While creativity in the arts and sciences is affected by situational, emotional, and motivational factors, I will limit my discussion of creativity to *cognitive* factors that influence creative *problem solving* in the scientific domain (see Vartanian & Goel, 2007). Most researchers now agree that a solution to a given problem is creative if it is considered both novel and useful within a given context. The strength of this definition is that while it easily applies to groundbreaking solutions to grand scientific problems, it can also satisfy novel and useful solutions to more mundane, everyday problems. This extension is purposeful in that it allows us to study creativity as a process undertaken by most people, rather than by the elite few. For example, suppose that you follow a well-rehearsed route to your workplace and back everyday. This route consists of a stretch of a few miles on the highway. Then one evening while you are getting ready for an important meeting at work you find out from the local news broadcast that this particular stretch of highway will be closed the next day for construction, and that your normal route will not satisfy the condition of getting you to your workplace for this important meeting on time. You must therefore generate an alternative plan of action. In response to this challenge you acquire a relevant map, plan a novel route that will get you to work using public transportation, and devise a timetable that will get you there on time. You follow this new plan of action and get to work on time for the meeting. According to our working definition, you have acted creatively by devising a novel and useful solution to the problem of getting to work on time.

Now, let us consider the steps in this example more carefully. Specifically, how did you arrive at this creative solution to the problem? Most researchers agree that you completed at least one generation-and-verification cycle, alternatively also labeled a generation-and-exploration cycle (Campbell, 1960; Eysenck, 1993; Simonton, 1989). Briefly, what this implies is that at the outset you must have generated a few hypothetical plans of action or hypotheses, which you then subjected to a selection process. The hypothetical plans may not necessarily be full-fledged plans of action, and may consist of unrefined ideas and thoughts. The quality of your ultimate plan of action is a function of the effectiveness of your generation as well as subsequent verification processes. Furthermore, while simple problems may be solved by the execution of a single generation-and-verification cycle, most real-world problems will require multiple successive cycles where the output of one cycle will be fed into the next cycle.

Traditionally, creativity researchers have been disproportionately concerned with studying factors that affect the generative process, based on the underlying assumption that a person will think or act more creatively as a function of the quantity of hypotheses or plans of action that are generated at the outset. For example, Vartanian, Martindale, and Kwiatkowski (2003) have shown that the quantity of generated solutions in a divergent thinking task predicts success in an inductive reasoning task. Furthermore, in divergent thinking tasks, wherein subjects are instructed to generate solutions to open-ended problems or prompts, quantity (i.e., number of generated solutions) accounts for the majority of variance in performance (Plucker & Renzulli, 1999), more so than originality (i.e., uniqueness of responses) or flexibility (i.e., categorical diversity of responses). In contrast, the verification process that is used to select a plan of action has received far less attention, because of the underlying assumption by creativity researchers that the verification process is more characteristic of noncreative than creative thinking. This assumption is inaccurate. Simply put, merely observing that a product is creative does not enable one to determine the relative contributions of the generation and verification steps in the creative process. In order to achieve that aim, one must study the underlying cognitive processes that lead to the creative product, and by doing so we take the first steps toward highlighting the role of decision making in novel idea generation.

NOVEL IDEA GENERATION

How does one generate an idea? An idea rarely emerges fully formed. Rather, it has various components that must be generated or activated separately and combined to form it. A generally accepted model is that this process involves the novel and useful *combination* of concepts previously thought to be unrelated (Poincaré, 1913). There is much experimental support for this idea. When previously unrelated concepts are brought into the focus of attention and combined, the resultant concepts can contain novel emergent properties that none of the constituent concepts contained beforehand (e.g., Hampton, 1987). To the extent that creative concepts are characterized by novelty, this suggests that the process of combining concepts can function as an engine for creativity.

However, how are those initial constituent ideas activated in working memory, and made available for combination to begin with? Campbell (1960) argued that this process is not goal-oriented, but rather "blind". In other words, the person does a *random* search through the contents of consciousness to initiate the process. Many scholars have questioned this assumption (e.g., Eysenck, 1993; Martindale, 2007). Given the vast amount of content in consciousness, it is unlikely that a person would stumble on the *relevant* portions thereof through random search. Although at the outset one does not possess the solution to the problem, one is nevertheless aware of the problem for which one intends to find a solution. Given this awareness, it is quite likely that the problem itself would act as a prime for activating relevant content in consciousness through spreading activation. However, even as a prime it is likely that this process will activate far too much content in consciousness. Consider a hypothetical situation where a scientist must find a drug to help stop the spread of a new strain of virus. It is unlikely that in searching for a cure our scientist will consider all information linked to that virus and ways of stopping its spread. More likely, his or her experience and expertise will inform a decision as to which ideas are worth pursuing and which ideas should be discarded (Eysenck, 1995; Weisberg, 1999). The decision regarding the scope of ideas to consider will have a direct impact on the number of potentially useful combinations that can be considered per unit of time, thus affecting the likelihood of arriving at creative solutions.

Experimentally, the combinatorial process of idea generation can be investigated at two different stages. The first stage involves judging whether two concepts are related or unrelated. The second stage involves combining the two concepts into a novel concept. Because for the most part combining concepts that are already related will not result in the generation of creative products, researchers interested in this problem have focused almost exclusively on the second stage, which involves the conceptual combination of seemingly unrelated concepts. Specifically, they have investigated the representational properties of concepts (e.g., flexibility) that enable people to combine them into novel concepts more efficiently (Baughman & Mumford, 1995).

In contrast, Vartanian, Martindale, and Matthews (2009) focused on the first stage, which they argued was more fundamental to the creative process. Specifically, they hypothesized that creative people—operationalized as those scoring high on tests of divergent thinking—may be faster at judging relatedness between ideas before any attempt is made to combine them into novel concepts. Because it is only the combination of seemingly unrelated concepts that results in the generation of creative ideas, the ability to judge relatedness faster could function as a means for faster rejection of concept pairs that hold little promise as building blocks for creative ideas. Over time, this ability would lead to a substantial advantage in the number of potentially useful relationships that could be assessed per unit of time. In turn, this would result in a higher frequency of creative ideas assessed in one's lifetime, as is typical of eminent people (Eysenck, 1995; Martindale, 2001). They tested the hypothesis that people with higher divergent thinking ability are faster at judging whether two concepts are related or unrelated by presenting subjects with successive word pairs, picture pairs, or word–picture pairs, and instructing them to determine whether the two were related or unrelated. They also systematically varied the degree of semantic relationship between the items in each pair based on word association norms. The results showed that subjects with higher creative potential were significantly faster at making the relatedness judgment regardless of semantic relatedness, or whether the pairs were words, pictures, or word–picture pairs. Equally important, there was no link between IQ and speed of judging relatedness. These results demonstrate that there may be individual differences (unrelated to IQ) that confer to creative people the advantage of judging whether concepts are related or unrelated.

Thus far I have argued that decision making may play a role in the generation as well as the verification aspects of the creative process. Specifically, creative people may be faster at judging relatedness between concepts, which may in turn confer an advantage in deciding which concepts to subject to the combinatorial process at the beginning of concept generation. The underlying idea is that at the outset of the creative process, the selection of the contents of consciousness is not random, but at least partly intentional.

In the next section, I review neuroimaging and neuropsychological studies that shed light on the neural systems underlying creativity. In so doing, I shall highlight those cognitive components unique to the creative process, as well as those components (e.g., decision making) that are shared by other types of mental activities, in particular reasoning and planning.

CREATIVITY AND THE BRAIN

The human brain has evolved to generate cognitive and behavioral outputs in the face of incomplete information (Montague, 2006). Although lack of complete information can have its disadvantages, it can also force the organism to generate or mentally simulate novel courses of action or hypotheses, which it can then enact. In this respect a classic and important distinction in the problem-solving literature involves the difference between well-defined and ill-defined problems (Reitman, 1964). Well-defined problems involve completely defined start states, end states, and transformation functions (Goel, 1995). Most laboratory tasks of planning and problem solving fall under this category, such as the well-known Tower of Hanoi and Tower of London tasks (see Moll & Grafman, this volume; Shallice, 1988). In contrast, most real-world problems are of the ill-defined variety. For example, consider the problem described earlier in this chapter of devising an alternative route to work. Although the start and end states are known, the transformation functions are not obvious (i.e., how, given the start state, one arrives at the goal state). The critical feature of such ill-defined problems is that they require the problem solver to generate or mentally simulate courses of action that can subsequently be selected for best fit.

Much evidence from the neurosciences suggests that there is some degree of functional specialization between the two hemispheres for generating responses to well- and ill-defined problems. Specifically, the left hemisphere appears to be functionally specialized for handling well-defined problems. Based on his seminal work involving split-brain patients, Gazzaniga has proposed the notion of the "left hemisphere interpreter" (Gazzaniga, 2000; Wolford, Miller, & Gazzaniga, 2000). As the term implies, the left hemisphere appears to be specialized for locking on to patterns in the environment for the purpose of validity confirmation. In other words, the left hemisphere detects regularities in the environment that the organism can act upon. Well-defined problems are ideal for this pattern-matching activity because they provide the organism with sufficient information to detect regularities in the problem space. Consistent with this notion, there is a wealth of evidence from neuropsychological and neuroimaging studies implicating the left dorsal lateral prefrontal cortex (DLPFC) in deductive reasoning paradigms where subjects are asked to judge whether a conclusion follows logically from given information (Goel, 2007; Knauff, Fangmeier, Ruff, & Johnson-Laird, 2003; Reverberi, Lavaroni, Gigli, Skrap, & Shallice, 2005). Deductive reasoning paradigms are ideal for such pattern-driven confirmatory activity because the structure of the arguments contains all the necessary information for making validity judgments.

In contrast, recent evidence has linked the right PFC to the generation of courses of action under ill-defined, indeterminate, and ambiguous conditions. For example, Goel and Vartanian (2005) presented subjects with the classic Match Problems task from the creativity literature (Guilford, 1967). Match Problems involve an arrangement of matches that must be reorganized to make other patterns by removing matches. The critical requirement is that the final pattern must not contain any incomplete squares. Like all problems, it can be characterized by an initial state, a goal state, and a transformation function that maps the initial state onto the goal state. The start state in Match Problems is completely and unambiguously characterized by the given pattern of matches. The goal state is specified in terms of an abstract rule that can map onto an unknown number of specific patterns. The transformation function is also specified and on the surface seems trivial: Remove a specified number of matches. The task is to apply this transformation function using a generate-and-evaluate strategy to make patterns that satisfy a given rule.

Goel and Vartanian's experiment involved two conditions. In the Match Problems condition, subjects were presented with an identical 22-match configuration on each trial, and instructed to remove a specific number of matches from this configuration to generate a specific number of fully formed squares. The number of to-be-removed matches and fully formed squares varied across trials. Their task was to indicate the number of ways in which any given problem could be solved (i.e., 0–4). This required the generation of possible solutions and the subsequent selection of the correct number of viable solutions as the final response. In contrast, in the baseline condition subjects were presented with the same 22-match configuration in which a certain number of matches had already been removed by the experimenters to satisfy a specific instruction. Again, instructions and provided solutions varied across baseline trials. Their task was to indicate whether the presented configuration qualified as a solution to the problem. This required judging whether the presented solution was accurate or not, but no requirement to actually generate any solution. Based on the logic of cognitive subtraction, we reasoned that the comparison of Match Problems and the baseline condition would reveal the neural correlates of solution generation in Match Problems.

The direct contrast of the Match Problems and baseline trials revealed activation in the left DLPFC and right ventral lateral PFC. To further explore the role of the left DLPFC and right ventral lateral PFC in hypothesis generation, we divided problems in the Match Problems condition between those that required "set shifts" versus those that did not. To illustrate the notion of a set shift, consider the problem depicted in Figure 13.1. The subject is instructed to remove nine matches to make three squares. Nothing in the task instructions requires that the size of the squares be the same. However, maintaining size constancy is implicitly reinforced by the mental set created by the explicit concrete representation of the start state pattern (maintaining the contiguity of the squares is another implicitly enforced constraint). Although the problem depicted in Figure 13.1 can be solved in two ways, most subjects declare that this rule cannot be satisfied (i.e., number of solutions is zero). It has been long recognized that successful solutions to such Match Problems require what Guilford (1967) referred to as "set shifts" to overcome perceptual or conceptual fixation. The concept of "lateral transformation" in the problem-solving literature encompasses the same idea as the concept of a set shift (Goel, 1995). A lateral transformation is a movement from one state in a problem space to a horizontally displaced state rather than a more detailed version of the same state. Goel (1995) has proposed that

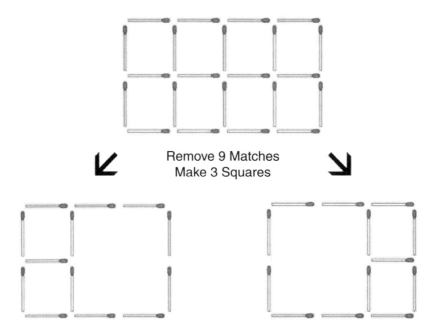

Figure 13.1   A sample trial from Match Problems that requires a set shift for solution (see text).

lateral transformations are facilitated (or hindered) by the structure of mental representations. Representations that are imprecise, ambiguous, fluid, indeterminate, or vague facilitate lateral transformations. Mental representations that are precise and concrete can hinder lateral transformations. For example, the concrete representation of the initial state of Match Problems creates an implicit perceptual representation that hinders lateral transformations or set shifts. Lateral transformations are necessary for overcoming set effects and facilitate *widening* of the problem space. It has further been suggested that processing these vague, indeterminate, or ill-structured representations may involve the right PFC (see Goel, 2002; Jung-Beeman, 2005; Jung-Beeman et al., 2004).

When Goel and Vartanian contrasted those set-shift trials that had been solved successfully with those that had not, there was exclusive activation in the right ventral lateral PFC. They therefore concluded that while the left DLPFC and right ventral lateral PFC form the neural system engaged in hypothesis generation, it is only the latter that is involved when set shifting has occurred for breaking a perceptual set. Strong support for this interpretation comes from a study of the problem-solving ability of patients with focal brain lesions and normal controls on Match Problems

(Miller & Tippett, 1996). Miller and Tippett administered Match Problems to 53 patients with focal brain lesions, and 20 normal controls. The patients were categorized based on lesion location and included left frontal, left temporal-occipital, left central-parietal, right frontal, right temporal-occipital, and right central-parietal cases. The researchers administered two types of problems. One type required set shifting to arrive at correct solutions, whereas the other type consisted of problems that required straightforward match removal for solution (i.e., generate–evaluate strategy). Miller and Tippett reported that patients with left frontal, left temporal-occipital, and right temporal-occipital lesions exhibited no overall difficulty in the task. In contrast, patients with focal right frontal lobe lesions were impaired specifically on those problems that required set shifts. This selective impairment in performance was especially apparent in patients with lesions to right *ventral* (as opposed to dorsal) PFC. Miller and Tippett concluded that "the right frontal region was found to play a predominant role in permitting a subject to shift approach in the present context, with the orbital and ventro-lateral region of this lobe particularly necessary for permitting major strategy changes" (p. 396). For Miller and Tippett, set shifts were instances of strategy shifting.

The convergence between Miller and Tippett's neuropsychological results and Goel and Vartanian's neuroimaging results suggests that the ventral region of right PFC may be necessary and sufficient for set shifting in the context of Match Problems. More generally, the results of the two studies are consistent with earlier findings linking right PFC to problem solving under ill-defined, indeterminate, and ambiguous conditions where the perceptual or cognitive constraints on the task must be reduced for problem solution. For example, in a related study, Vartanian and Goel (2005) demonstrated that the same region of the right PFC is sensitive to the level of external constraints placed on the task, being activated more when task constraints are reduced (see also Goel, Tierney, Sheesley, Bartolo, Vartanian, & Grafman, 2007; Vartanian & Goel, 2007). This is consistent with findings from Match Problems where the right PFC is involved in the generation of hypotheses or courses of action under ill-defined conditions.

However, it is also known that problem solving in the real world unfolds against a background of changing rather than static conditions. As such, it is likely that successful problem solving is a function of flexible navigation between states of cognition that facilitate problem solving under unconstrained *and* constrained conditions, depending on varying task demands. A critical mechanism for modulating such flexible cognitive navigation is attention, and I shall next turn to a discussion of its role in creative problem solving.

ATTENTION AND FLEXIBILITY IN PROBLEM SOLVING

The literature linking creative thinking to "defocused attention" is an old one (see Eysenck, 1995; Mendelsohn, 1976). The basic idea underlying this linkage is that spreading the "spotlight" of attention facilitates the simultaneous consideration of more concepts, thus increasing the likelihood that unrelated concepts would be merged to create novel concepts. However, despite the intuitive appeal of this idea, there is little biographical evidence from the studies of eminent creative people to suggest that their cognition is characterized by a stable state of defocused attention. On the contrary, in his cognitive disinhibition hypothesis (CDH), Martindale (1999) has hypothesized that rather than having a stable disposition toward defocused attention, creative people are better at adjusting their focus of attention depending on task demands (see also Ansburg & Hill, 2003; Rawlings, 1985). In essence, creative people exhibit differential rather than reduced focusing of attention. Under conditions where the problem is relatively ill defined and ambiguity is high, creative people are more likely to defocus attention. This tendency makes the central task more susceptible to interference by seemingly irrelevant information, some of which may provide the building blocks for creative solutions. In contrast, under conditions where the problem is well defined and ambiguity is low, creative people are more likely to focus attention. This inhibition of irrelevant stimuli will make focusing on promising candidate ideas easier.

Evidence from early electroencephalography (EEG) studies offered indirect support for CDH. Martindale and Hines (1975) measured EEG alpha-wave activity while subjects completed creativity and intelligence tests. EEG alpha-wave activity is an *inverse* measure of cortical arousal: Higher EEG alpha-wave activity indicates lower cortical arousal. Furthermore, higher cortical arousal indicates more focused attention (Martindale, 1999). Martindale and Hines reported that in creative people there was a lower level of cortical arousal while they were engaged in the creativity test, but higher arousal during the intelligence test. In contrast, people lower in creativity exhibited equally high levels of arousal across creativity and intelligence tests. These results suggest that in creative people focus of attention and level of cortical arousal varies as a function of task demands. Specifically, their attention is more defocused only when they are engaged in creative tasks, but not otherwise.

In a follow-up EEG study, Martindale and Hasenfus (1978) further investigated the link between flexibility in attention and cortical activity in two experiments. Again, alpha-wave activity was used as an inverse measure of cortical activity. Martindale and Hasenfus reasoned that creative story generation consists of two phases: A phase in which the subject thinks about the story to be written (inspiration phase), and a phase in which the subject writes the story (elaboration phase). Furthermore, they reasoned that unlike uncreative subjects, creative subjects would defocus attention only during the inspiration phase of story generation, and that this would be reflected by lower cortical activity. The results from the first experiment confirmed their predictions. Then, in the second experiment half of the subjects were instructed to be as creative as possible, whereas the others were not given any instruction to that effect. The results showed that creative subjects exhibited lower cortical activity in the inspiration phase only when they were told to be as creative as possible. The results of Martindale and Hasenfus were in line with those of Martindale and Hines by indicating that creativity is associated with mental flexibility.

In a more recent test of CDH, Vartanian, Martindale, and Kwiatkowski (2007) conducted a study to determine whether creative people are in fact more variable in their focus of attention. Vartanian et al. administered two types of reaction time (RT) tasks to subjects of varying creative potential. One task type involved elementary RT tasks that invoke responses in relation to unambiguous stimuli (Hick Task, Concept Verification Task). The second task type consisted of complex RT tasks that invoke responses in relation to ambiguous, interference-inducing stimuli (Negative Priming, Global-local). Given the unambiguous nature of the stimuli in the former task type, Vartanian et al. hypothesized that there would be a narrowing of the focus of attention in creative people, leading to faster RT than in less creative subjects. In contrast, given the ambiguous nature of the stimuli in the latter task type, there would be a widening of the focus of attention in creative people, leading to slower RT than non-creative subjects. This is precisely the pattern found in a sample of university students in the United States, which has since been replicated in a sample of secondary school students in Russia (Dorfman, Martindale, Gassimova, & Vartanian, 2008). Confirming predictions derived from CDH, the results indicated that in creative people defocused attention is a variable state rather than a stable trait (see also Vartanian, 2009).

However, CDH is also relevant in terms of predicting states of cognition as a function of *stages* of problem solving. Given that in earlier phases of problem solving the problem space is relatively ill defined (Goel, 1995), defocusing attention should be more advantageous by increasing the likelihood that more information is brought to bear on the problem. In contrast, in later stages of problem solving when people are verifying developed ideas, performance will benefit through the inhibition of irrelevant stimuli and added focus on the central task. For example, it is known that real-world planning tends to unfold along different levels of granularity (see also Jung-Beeman, 2005). In the earlier phases of planning when the problem space is relatively ill defined, concepts generated by normal controls tend to be more abstract in nature (Goel, 1995). As the problem space itself becomes relatively better defined in the course of planning, concepts generated by normal controls tend to become progressively more concrete. Failures in planning can arise if the subject is unable to navigate flexibly between abstract and concrete levels of cognition in the course of planning as a function of task demands. Specifically, whereas stagnation at a concrete level of conceptualization will be disadvantageous in the earlier stages of planning, stagnation at an abstract level of conceptualization will be disadvantageous in later stages of planning.

There is recent neuropsychological evidence to support the idea that the inability to adjust levels of abstraction can hamper planning under ill-structured conditions. Vartanian, Goel et al. (2009) administered an ill-structured travel planning task to normal controls and patients with focal brain lesions to the frontal lobes. As expected, normal controls generated plans of higher quality than patients with lesions to the right frontal lobe. Furthermore, by conducting a verbal protocol analysis (Ericsson & Simon, 1993) Vartanian et al. were able to demonstrate that the difficulties exhibited in planning by patients with right frontal lobe lesions were linked to stagnation in concretization during the planning process. Specifically, whereas normal controls were able to vary the level of abstraction in their thinking in the course of plan generation, patients with right frontal lobe lesions could not. Regression analyses showed that the ratio of abstract-to-concrete thinking predicted quality of plan: When this ratio was disproportionately small—as was the case in patients with lesions to the right frontal lobe—the quality of plan was low.

Although there is now evidence from both the creative problem-solving and planning literatures to suggest that performance benefits from flexible cognition, the mechanism whereby the focus of attention is regulated in relation to task demands has yet to be pinned down. Martindale has argued that in creative people the mechanism that facilitates this differential focusing of attention is inhibition, and that its regulation is automatic or reactive rather than one requiring self control. There are several sources of support for this idea but the most important evidence involves the poor performance of highly creative people on biofeedback tasks, unlike less creative people who improve across trials at increasing or decreasing alpha-wave amplitude (Martindale, 1989, 1999, 2007; Martindale & Armstrong, 1974). These findings suggest that creative people lack the self control necessary to regulate their focus of attention. According to Martindale this regulatory process is bottom–up, driven by the structure of the problem space: Ill-defined, ambiguous problem spaces widen the focus of attention, whereas well-defined, unambiguous problem spaces narrow it.

This view is not universally accepted. For example, results from a number of recent studies indicate that some components of creative cognition may be strongly influenced by top–down processes (Gilhooly, Fiortou, Anthony, & Wynn, 2007; Haider, Frensch, & Joram, 2005). On the whole, the available data point to a bidirectional model of creativity according to which focus of attention is modulated by top–down and bottom–up processes, but that reliance on top–down and bottom–up processes may vary as a function of the *stage* of problem solving: Whereas bottom–up processes dominate in the earlier phases of problem solving, top–down processes gain dominance in later stages (Gilhooly et al., 2007). Top–down processes in later stages of problem solving may also draw more heavily from executive resources.

CREATIVITY: A HIERARCHICAL MENTAL ACTIVITY

In this chapter, I have followed the lead of other researchers and argued that the creative process is best viewed as a sequence of generation-and-verification cycles leading to novel and useful solutions (Campbell, 1960; Eysenck, 1993; Simonton, 1989). In addition, I have argued that decision making plays an important role in the generation and verification parts of this cycle, but to different extents and in different ways. Specifically, I have argued that the selection of concepts that form the building blocks of creative ideas in the generation phase of the cycle is not "blind" as suggested earlier (Campbell, 1960). Rather, at least to a certain extent, the person decides which elements to focus on for the combinatorial process. This decision may be based on experience and expertise in the relevant topical area (Eysenck, 1995; Weisberg, 1999).

In support of this idea, recent evidence has shown that creative people are faster at judging whether two concepts are related or unrelated (Vartanian, Martindale et al., 2009). Given the combinatorial nature of novel idea generation, the ability to judge relatedness faster can lead to a substantial advantage in the number of potentially useful relationships that can be assessed per unit of time, in turn resulting in a higher frequency of creative ideas assessed in one's lifetime, as is typical of eminent people (Eysenck, 1995; Martindale, 2001). This suggests that even at early stages of problem solving, deciding which concepts to pursue can influence problem-solving efficiency. In addition, decision making also plays a critical role in the verification stage for selecting generated concepts for further scrutiny, potentially as inputs into subsequent generation-and-verification cycles.

Successful problem solving—whether it is creative or otherwise—requires flexible navigation between focused and defocused states of cognition (Goel, 1995; Martindale, 1999). Indeed, there are recent experimental data to indicate that creative subjects are better able to adjust their focus of attention as a function of task demands (Dorfman et al., 2008; Vartanian,

Martindale et al., 2009; Vartanian et al., 2007). To the extent that creativity benefits from flexible strategy shifting, there is now converging evidence from lesion studies, EEG, and fMRI that the right PFC—in particular its ventral lateral aspects—may be mediating flexibility in problem solving. Of course, recent reviews have shown that the ventral lateral aspects of the PFC play a critical role in regulating inhibition—cognitive as well as motor (Aron, Robbins, & Poldrack, 2004). Clearly, regulating cognitive flexibility requires inhibition (Martindale, 1999), and it is likely that the role of the ventral lateral PFC in flexibility may be a function of its more basic role in regulating inhibition—an assertion that would be consistent with CDH.

Critically, as is the case for other higher-order mental activities (e.g., reasoning, planning, etc.), there appears to be no unitary brain "module" for creativity. At the brain level, complex higher-order mental activities appear to be based on distributed networks, built upon component neural systems that are reconfigured dynamically in relation to task demands (e.g., Goel, 2007). In this sense the neural architecture of creativity is hierarchical (Simon, 1962). A hierarchical functional organization for complex systems makes evolutionary sense because it is more efficient for the brain to reconstitute component systems to serve multiple complex activities than it would be to create separate systems for each complex activity.

An important feature of complex hierarchical systems is that they tend to be "nearly decomposable" into component processes (Simon, 2005). The neuroscientific approach to studying higher cognitive abilities has relied heavily on this characteristic, decomposing complex activities into component processes that can be studied in relative isolation. For example, for creativity, the component processes of interest discussed in this chapter included cognitive flexibility and decision making, although many others are involved as well (e.g., memory, attention, etc.). This componential approach has demonstrated that higher-order mental activities that appear different at the "macro" (i.e., behavioral) level (e.g., creativity and planning) are frequently built on largely shared cortical infrastructures at the "micro" (i.e., neural) level. In this chapter I have argued that decision making is one of many component processes in creativity, just as it is in reasoning, planning, and problem solving. By focusing on component processes, the neurosciences of higher cognition are contributing to the emergence of a science of *thinking* that encompasses commonalities among mental activities, while remaining responsive to evolutionary considerations for cortical organization.

REFERENCES

Ansburg, P. I., & Hill, K. (2003). Creative and analytic thinkers differ in their use of attentional resources. *Personality and Individual Differences, 34*, 1141–1152.

Aron, A. R., Robbins, T. W., & Poldrack, R. A. (2004). Inhibition and the right inferior frontal cortex. *Trends in Cognitive Sciences, 8*, 170–177.

Baughman, W. A., & Mumford, M. D. (1995). Process-analytic models of creative capacities: Operations influencing the combination-and-reorganization process. *Creativity Research Journal, 8*, 37–62.

Campbell, D. T. (1960). Blind variation and selective retention in creative thought as in other knowledge processes. *Psychological Review, 67*, 380–400.

Dorfman, L., Martindale, C., Gassimova, V., & Vartanian, O. (2008). Creativity and speed of information processing: A double dissociation involving elementary versus inhibitory cognitive tasks. *Personality and Individual Differences, 44*, 1382–1390.

Ericsson, K. A., & Simon, H. A. (1993). *Protocol analysis: Verbal reports as data* (rev. ed.). Cambridge, MA: MIT Press.

Eysenck, H. J. (1993). Creativity and personality: Suggestions for a theory. *Psychological Inquiry, 4*, 147–178.

Eysenck, H. J. (1995). *Genius: The natural history of creativity.* Cambridge: Cambridge University Press.

Gazzaniga, M. S. (2000). Cerebral specialization and interhemispheric communication: Does the corpus callosum enable the human condition? *Brain, 123*, 1293–1326.

Gilhooly, K. J., Fiortou, E., Anthony, S. H., & Wynn, V. (2007). Divergent thinking: Strategies and executive involvement in generating novel uses for familiar objects. *British Journal of Psychology, 98*, 611–625.

Goel, V. (1995). *Sketches of thought.* Cambridge, MA: MIT Press.

Goel, V. (2002). Cognitive and neural basis of planning. In L. Nadel (Ed.), *Encyclopedia of cognitive science* (Vol. 3, pp. 697–703). New York: Macmillan.

Goel, V. (2007). Anatomy of deductive reasoning. *Trends in Cognitive Sciences, 11*, 435–441.

Goel, V., Tierney, M., Sheesley, L., Bartolo, A., Vartanian, O., & Grafman, J. (2007). Hemispheric specialization in human prefrontal cortex for resolving certain and uncertain inferences. *Cerebral Cortex, 17*, 2245–2250.

Goel, V., & Vartanian, O. (2005). Dissociating the roles of right ventral lateral and dorsal lateral prefrontal cortex in generation and maintenance of hypotheses in set-shift problems. *Cerebral Cortex, 15*, 1170–1177.

Guilford, J. P. (1967). *The nature of human intelligence.* New York: McGraw-Hill.

Haider, H., Frensch, P. A., & Joram, D. (2005). Are strategy shifts caused by data-driven processes or by voluntary processes? *Consciousness and Cognition, 14*, 495–519.

Hampton, J. A. (1987). Inheritance of attributes in natural concept conjunctions. *Memory and Cognition, 15*, 55–71.

Jung-Beeman, M. (2005). Bilateral brain processes for comprehending natural language. *Trends in Cognitive Sciences, 9*, 512–518.

Jung-Beeman, M., Bowden, E. M., Haberman, J., Frymiare, J. L., Arambel-Liu, S.,

Greenblatt, R. et al. (2004). Neural activity when people solve verbal problems with insight. *PLoS Biol*, *4*, 500–510.

Knauff, M., Fangmeier, T., Ruff, C. C., & Johnson-Laird, P. N. (2003). Reasoning, models, and images: Behavioural measures and cortical activity. *Journal of Cognitive Neuroscience*, *15*, 559–573.

Martindale, C. (1989). Personality, situation, and creativity. In J. A. Glover, R. R. Ronning, & C. R. Reynolds (Eds.), *Handbook of creativity* (pp. 211–232). New York: Plenum.

Martindale, C. (1999). Biological bases of creativity. In R. J. Sternberg (Ed.), *Handbook of creativity* (pp. 137–152). New York: Cambridge University Press.

Martindale, C. (2001). Oscillations and analogies. Thomas Young, MD, FRS, Genius. *American Psychologist*, *56*, 342–345.

Martindale, C. (2007). Creativity, primordial cognition, and personality. *Personality and Individual Differences*, *43*, 1777–1785.

Martindale, C., & Armstrong, J. (1974). The relationship of creativity to cortical activation and its operant control. *Journal of Genetic Psychology*, *124*, 311–320.

Martindale, C., & Hasenfus, N. (1978). EEG differences as a function of creativity, stage of the creative process, and effort to be original. *Biological Psychology*, *6*, 157–167.

Martindale, C., & Hines, D. (1975). Creativity and cortical activation during creative, intellectual and EEG feedback tasks. *Biological Psychology*, *3*, 91–100.

Mendelsohn, G. A. (1976). Associative and attentional processes in creative performance. *Journal of Personality*, *44*, 341–369.

Miller, L. A., & Tippett, L. J. (1996). Effects of focal brain lesions on visual problem-solving. *Neuropsychologia*, *34*, 387–398.

Montague, R. (2006). *How we make decisions*. New York: Plume.

Plucker, J. A., & Renzulli, J. S. (1999). Psychometric approaches to the study of human creativity. In R. J. Sternberg (Ed.), *Handbook of creativity* (pp. 35–61). New York: Cambridge University Press.

Poincaré, H. (1913). *The foundations of science*. Lancaster, PA: Science Press.

Rawlings, D. (1985). Psychoticism, creativity and dichotic shadowing. *Personality and Individual Differences*, *6*, 737–742.

Reitman, W. R. (1964). Heuristic decision processes, open constraints, and the structure of ill-defined problems. In M. W. Shelley & G. L. Bryan (Eds.), *Human judgment and optimality* (pp. 282–315). New York: John Wiley.

Reverberi, C., Lavaroni, A., Gigli, G. L., Skrap, M., & Shallice, T. (2005). Specific impairments of rule induction in different frontal lobe subgroups. *Neuropsychologia*, *43*, 460–472.

Shallice, T. (1988). *From neuropsychology to mental structure*. Cambridge: Cambridge University Press.

Simon, H. A. (1962). The architecture of complexity. *Proceedings of the American Philosophical Society*, *106*, 467–482.

Simon, H. A. (2005). The structure of complexity in an evolving world: The role of near decomposability. In W. Callebaut & D. Rasskin-Gutman (Eds.), *Modularity* (pp. ix–xiii). Cambridge, MA: MIT Press.

Simonton, D. K. (1989). Chance-configuration theory of scientific creativity. In B.

Gholson, W. R. Shadish, R. A. Neimeyer, & A. C. Houts (Eds.), *Psychology of science* (pp. 170–213). New York: Cambridge University Press.

Sternberg, R. J. (1999). *Handbook of creativity*. New York: Cambridge University Press.

Vartanian, O. (2009). Variable attention facilitates creative problem solving. *Psychology of Aesthetics, Creativity, and the Arts, 3*, 57–59.

Vartanian, O., & Goel, V. (2005). Task constraints modulate activation in right ventral lateral prefrontal cortex. *NeuroImage, 27*, 927–933.

Vartanian, O., & Goel, V. (2007). Neural correlates of creative cognition. In C. Martindale, P. Locher, & V. M. Petrov (Eds.), *Evolutionary and neurocognitive approaches to aesthetics, creativity and the arts* (pp. 195–207). Amityville, NY: Baywood.

Vartanian, O., Goel, V., Bartolo, A., Hakim, L., Ferraro, A.-M., Budriesi, C. et al. (2009, March). *The role of right prefrontal cortex in real-world planning.* Slides presented at the annual meeting of the Society for Cognitive Neuroscience, San Francisco, CA.

Vartanian, O., Martindale, C., & Kwiatkowski, J. (2003). Creativity and inductive reasoning: The relationship between divergent thinking and performance on Wason's 2-4-6 task. *Quarterly Journal of Experimental Psychology: A, 56*, 641–655.

Vartanian, O., Martindale, C., & Kwiatkowski, J. (2007). Creative potential, attention, and speed of information processing. *Personality & Individual Differences, 34*, 1370–1380.

Vartanian, O., Martindale, C., & Matthews, J. (2009). Divergent thinking is related to faster relatedness judgments. *Psychology of Aesthetics, Creativity, and the Arts, 3*, 99–103.

Weisberg, R. W. (1986). *Creativity, genius and other myths*. New York: W. H. Freeman.

Weisberg, R. W. (1999). Creativity and knowledge: A challenge to theories. In R. J. Sternberg (Ed.), *Handbook of creativity* (pp. 226–250). New York: Cambridge University Press.

Wolford, G., Miller, M. B., & Gazzaniga, M. (2000). The left hemisphere's role in hypothesis formation. *Journal of Neuroscience, 20*, RC64.

Author index

Abbott, L., 184
Abelson, R. P., 286, 287
Achim, A. M., 265
Adams, C. M., 151, 152*f*, 153–154, 162, 200, 201
Adolphs, R., 139
Aerts, J., 267
Agid, Y., 297
Aharon, I., 151, 153, 162, 200
Ahmed, S., 294
Aigner, T. G., 175
Aitken, M. R. F., 60
Akitsuki, Y., 204
Alain, G., 269
Aleman, A., 231, 234
Alexander, G., 295
Alexander, G. E., 147
Alexopoulos, G. S., 210
Allen, J. F., 285
Allen, P. A., 34
Allport, A., 294
Allport, D., 31
Alonso, A., 99
Alonso, J. M., 12
Alting von Geusau, N. J., 155, 159, 162
Alvarez, R. P., 62, 64
Alway, D., 303

American Psychiatric Association, 204–205
Amitai, Y., 101
Anand, A., 209
Anderson, A. K., 203
Anderson, C. H., 13, 114, 118
Anderson, J., 288
Anderson, J. R., 295
Anderson, S. W., 75, 86, 296, 298
Andersson, J., 60
Andreasen, N. C., 260, 264
Andreiuolo, P. A., 297
Andrew, C., 206, 207
Andrews, C., 149, 174, 201
Anen, C., 163, 236
Anisman, H., 212
Ansburg, P. I., 320
Anthony, S. H., 323
Antrobus, J. S., 263
Aosaki, T., 147
Apicella, P., 154
Apple, C., 103
Arambel-Liu, S., 265, 318
Ariely, D., 200
Armstrong, J., 322
Arndt, S., 260, 264
Arnell, K. M., 22

329

Subject index